Robert Thomson was born at Croft Spa in the North Riding of Yorkshire and has strong connexions with the North-East of England. He was educated at the Royal Grammar School, Newcastle-upon-Tyne, and at University College, Oxford. After five years of war service he joined the staff of Durham University in 1949. At first he lectured in philosophy but since 1955 he has taught psychology both at Durham and at what was then King's College, Newcastle. Since 1964 he has been Senior Lecturer in psychology at Leicester University.

His main fields of interest are the history of psychology, learning theory and systematic psychology. In collaboration with his colleague Professor Sluckin he has written on cybernetics. His *Psychology of Thinking* was published by Penguin Books in 1959.

He is married to Winifred Smith, a former teacher of English at Sheffield University. They have a daughter and a son.

The Pelican
History of Psychology

*

ROBERT THOMSON

PENGUIN BOOKS

Penguin Books Ltd, Harmondsworth, Middlesex, England
Penguin Books Inc., 3300 Clipper Mill Road, Baltimore, Md 21211, U.S.A.
Penguin Books Australia Ltd, Ringwood, Victoria, Australia

—

First published 1968
Copyright © Robert Thomson, 1968

—

Made and printed in Great Britain
by Hazell Watson & Viney Ltd
Aylesbury, Bucks
Set in Linotype Baskerville

To

WINIFRED, JENNIFER
AND DAVID

Contents

CONTENTS

Part Three: Psychology Today

Editorial Foreword

LEGEND has it that Psyche eventually became mortal. Psychology too has undergone a metamorphosis from a world of spirit and mind to one of body and behaviour. For some psychologists she still trails clouds of glory, having links with philosophy, phenomenology and theology; for others she is altogether more mundane, and the important links are with physiology, zoology and engineering. These diversities are stimulating to psychologists, but, for laymen, the contemporary scene is bewildering, all the more so because psychological dissensions often make news. It is only by using a historical perspective that sense can be made of modern psychology, made up as it is of a mixture of subjects, each with its own language, methods and subject matter – Behaviourism, psycho-analysis, theories of decision making, clinical psychology, personality and ability testing, the study of working conditions, the perception of space, developmental psychology, and so on. Perhaps the one thing they have in common is a concern with behaviour, using that word in a broad sense.

The diversity comes partly from historic roots in other disciplines and partly from demands which are made on professional psychologists by education, medicine, industry and society in general. In this book, Robert Thomson investigates all these influences; but much of what he has to say is concerned with individuals, many of them not psychologists, who have influenced the course of events in the subject. They include philosophers, physicists, physiologists, medical practitioners, zoologists, geneticists, theologians, engineers, educationalists and psychiatrists.

It takes something of a polymath to make sense of such

a mixture, and it is fortunate that Mr Thomson is a philosopher as well as a psychologist, and has a wide knowledge of many disciplines. In this history he concentrates on the last hundred years, and especially the last few decades, which have seen many psychological revolutions. In reviewing the post-war scene, he notes that the days of the grand all-embracing theory appear to be over; that many psychologists are now prepared to investigate thoroughly a small segment of life, with no hope or intention that their findings will solve any problems other than the one they are working on. This is a result not so much of disenchantment as of scientific rigour. The various arts, sciences and technologies which make up the family of subjects called Psychology are not fundamentally incompatible, but they do have different aims and answer different questions. However, there are psychologists who can begin, in a modest way, to see a 'meta-psychology' spanning the several psychological subjects. They may be wrong, as previous generations have been; but it must be remembered that in psychology, as in other things, history never quite repeats itself.

B. M. FOSS

Preface

IN writing a general political, economic or social history the author has at his disposal considerable resources: original documents, scholarly articles in journals, learned books dealing with special topics within the period and critical biographies of the leading historical figures. The historian of psychology has none of these aids. The original books and papers in which psychologists of the past published their results are available, but there are few papers or notebooks showing how they worked towards their conclusions. Until 1965 there was no journal specializing in the publication of papers on the history of psychology. Few books exist on special topics within this field of study. Apart from Ernest Jones's life of Freud there are hardly any major biographical works on great psychologists. Hence there are few researches into the history of psychology to consult. The basic work has still to be done.

The historian of psychology should ideally do more than concern himself simply with results and theories. He should examine the activities of the men who produced this work and seek to trace the ways in which they were influenced by their social and intellectual environment. However, until the patient and scholarly work of delving into the background of each psychologist or group of psychologists has been done we can only present a surface picture along the lines laid down, albeit skilfully, by Boring, Gardner Murphy, J. C. Flugel and other general historians of psychology.

It might be as well, at this stage, to warn the general reader that the theories of Freud, Jung and other 'psycho-analytically' oriented psychologists have never dominated psychology – however much they may have attracted the

PREFACE

interest of the layman. Even at their zenith they had to
contend with rival schools and techniques. The reader
should therefore not be surprised if they occupy a less
prominent position in this book than he had expected.

*

I would like to thank my colleagues Professor Sluckin and
Dr Roy Davies, whom I consulted on specific points, Mrs
Margaret Frape for typing the greater part of the manu-
script at short notice and my wife for reading it through
and helping to make it more explicit.

Introduction

FOR thousands of years men have been asking and trying to answer questions about human and animal nature which can properly be categorized as psychological questions. Within our own civilization alone, many writers of distinction have contributed to the discussion, which centres on explaining characteristic human experiences and behaviour patterns.

Aristotle's work known as *De anima* remains one of the great psychological treatises in spite of its antiquity. There are interesting points of correspondence between the psychological writings of Thomas Hobbes (1588–1679) and those of psychologists who have published in the twentieth century. Contemporary psychologists acknowledge the thinking of British philosophers of the seventeenth and eighteenth centuries as their ancestors, especially John Locke (1632–1704), David Hume (1711–76) and the erudite Scots who lived at the end of the eighteenth and beginning of the nineteenth century – Reid, Stewart and Thomas Brown. Many non-systematic and more purely literary figures, such as Montaigne, had given astute descriptions of human reactions.

However, psychology, as we now know this diverse and many-sided discipline, is not simply a set of theoretical questions and problems. It involves also the methods and techniques whereby such problems are analysed and interpreted, and in terms of which solutions are attempted. Psychology is now regarded as a group of disciplines which are empirical and scientific in their methods. From this point of view, it is a science of comparatively recent origin and growth. The first psychologists, distinct from other species of inquirer, emerged round about the year 1880. Before that, especially in the early decades of the nineteenth century, there had been some psychological work by physicists or physiologists, but no psychologists were recognized as such. Psychological questions before the early years of the nineteenth century had either merged with epistemological questions concerning the scope and limits of human knowledge, or had been tackled by rationalistic methods – *a priori* principles and non-empirical assumptions governing the answers.

It would seem that a history of psychology should begin with the work and thought of men who were the first to be differentiated, as psychologists, from philosophers, physicists, physiologists (or literary figures with a speculative bent, like Coleridge). But this proposal would not be altogether practicable. Psychology did not have a simple and definable start. The influences which shaped its beginnings must be traced back for some distance. The problem is to decide how far back to go. As most histories of psychology start at the seventeenth century, or even at the Greco-Roman period, the decision is not easy. However, it would seem not unreasonable to start at the beginning of the nineteenth century. Most of the influences from remoter periods were absorbed and integrated in the philosophical and scientific writings and in the thinking of men who were the immediate predecessors of the first generation of psychologists. Since psychology appears only in the last two decades of the nineteenth century as an independent and clearly defined discipline, to begin at around the year 1800 is to leave some space to examine the roots out of which the new science grew.

Whatever the complexity of the ancestry of psychology, it would seem that modern psychology had two parents – the dominant philosophy of the early nineteenth century and the contemporary physiology. After its birth the influence of a near relative, medicine, was considerable, and the family of one of the parents, biology, appears to have moulded some of the outstanding features of the new arrival. However, once launched into active life, other outside influences have modified its development – the social and 'cultural' sciences in particular, but also the demands of a complex technological society that the new subject should be capable of practical application and not remain secluded in an academic ivory tower.

This book will begin by showing how philosophy, and certain aspects of science at the beginning of the nineteenth century, gave rise to a new discipline and how psychology has developed since then in its main outlines. The development will be described, selectively and briefly of necessity, down to 1940. A concluding chapter sketches (in merest outline) what has happened in the years 1940–55, and to compensate for its sketchiness there is a more than usually ample reading-list to help the curious reader to get up to date.

PART ONE

From the Beginning to the
First World War

CHAPTER ONE

The Beginnings of Psychology within Philosophy

EVER since the seventeenth century, Britain had been prominent in philosophy. Since Locke, philosophers had attempted a new definition of the scope, nature and limits of human knowledge more in accord with new scientific ideas, and had tried to examine the logical criteria for different types of true proposition. The British philosophers tended to make their theories depend upon a kind of psychology for its ultimate premises.

It was this psychological foundation for philosophical discussions which grew into the dominant psychology of the first half of the nineteenth century. This psychology was not based on any systematic observation other than the writer's introspections of his own states of mind, and was purely rationalistic in method – a matter of drawing inferences from statements accepted as sound, and systematizing the results of such deductive reasoning. The psychologists of the nineteenth century exploited this traditional 'mental philosophy', as it was called, and attempted to make it more empirical.

The data of psychology were limited, within this tradition, to the contents of the individual's consciousness – what goes on 'in the mind' when a person sees something, or remembers a past event, or puzzles over a problem, or experiences a distinct emotion. These complex states of consciousness were often discussed in terms of a dualistic theory. Many regarded mental states as being distinct from physical changes in the brain and nervous system, in so much as they had properties which could not be re-

19

duced to physics and chemistry. Even those materialists who wished to reduce mental states to brain functions agreed that the two aspects should be separately described, and so psychology had the special task of describing sensations and ideas as they appear to conscious or sentient human beings.

Most thinkers also accepted 'sensationism', the concept that states of consciousness could be analysed into sensations derived from the reactions of the sensory nervous processes, and imagery derived from sensory origins. This implied an atomistic, analytical approach to the description of consciousness. To analyse the conscious mind into its basic elements ('sensations' and 'ideas' of different types) was the primary job of the psychologist. How these basic elements were related to produce complex states of mind was often explained in terms of an associationist theory. Discoverable laws determined under what conditions elements came together and remained relatively secure in their combination. Some psychologists regarded laws of association as sufficient explanation of the compounding or blending of the elements; while others thought that the mind executes acts of judgement, or operates in terms of further innate principles of organization which order sensations and ideas. However, 'associationism', the appeal to associative principles as the chief operation of the mind, was common to several leading writers. Associationists often implied that the mind is a complex mechanical system which operates according to principles similar to those accepted in physical science, and thus the concept of a 'soul' or 'self' is unnecessary. Others, usually the Scots philosophers associated with the Kirk, defended an organizing, synthesizing, higher functionary against the mechanistic associationists.

Finally there was a common tendency towards 'intellectualism', in the sense that psychologists believed that we know our mental life, by introspection, for what it is. All our basic modes of awareness and the basic operations of intellect, senses and will are open to scrutiny and description. Thus, the individual consciousness and its contents and operations was open to scrutiny by any normal human being. Psychology was principally a descriptive science, and the main objective was to provide philosophers with an account of the workings of the mind which they could take into consideration when dealing with the theory of knowledge and ethics. There was no need for any elaborate techniques of analysis, since the subject matter was there for any man to observe in his own states of consciousness.

However, a shift towards a more empirical introspectionist psychology is noticeable in several of the leading writers in psychology in the early decades of the nineteenth century.

Prominent among these was Thomas Brown (1778–1820), a Scotsman who graduated in medicine at Edinburgh. He was invited to assist the ageing and eminent Professor of Moral Philosophy at Edinburgh University, Dugald Stewart, from 1810 to 1820. In fact, Brown shared Stewart's title to the chair. He was an able man and a brilliant lecturer. When he died in 1820 at the age of 42 his lectures were published as *Lectures on the Philosophy of the Human Mind*. This book is important for three reasons: its popularity in the subsequent decades; its originality; and the fact that it is an ingenious compromise between two rival theories – the strictly analytic (atomistic) mechanistic associationism of Hume and Hartley on the one hand, and on the other the Scottish school of Thomas Reid, which insisted on the unity of the soul and on the active powers of the human mind.

Brown skilfully replaced the concept of 'association' with that of 'suggestion'. All connexions between the elements of consciousness, discrete sensations and ideas, he reduced to the principle of 'co-existence'. One mental event suggests another, either in virtue of resemblance or contrast; or simply through proximity in time and place. However, Brown introduced Locke's hypothesis that, in addition to ideas derived from sensory stimulation, we have ideas derived from 'reflection' upon data supplied through the senses. Awareness of relationships between objects and events is not a sensory element, or an association of sensory elements, but rather something imposed upon sensory data by a 'higher centre'. Capacities exist to intuit relations and make judgements and comparisons. Associationism is thus both included and modified in Brown's theories.

His originality follows from his refusal to be contented with only general laws of association. He wanted to be able to explain how particular and specific connexions are formed between three or four concrete images – how specific sequences come to be what they are. His self-observation led him to form 'Secondary Laws of Association'. It was not until the latter half of the century, when experimental psychology was a going concern, that the importance of Brown's hypotheses were appreciated. H. C. Warren, in his *History of Association Psychology* (1921) summarizes Brown's laws:

(1) 'The longer we dwell on objects, the more fully do we rely on our future remembrance of them.' The duration of the original experience is relevant.
(2) 'The parts of any train of ideas appear to be more closely and readily suggested in proportion as they have been more frequently renewed.' The relative frequency of a connexion is a factor.
(3) The relative liveliness of an association strengthens the connexions between its elements.
(4) Recency of occurrence affects likelihood of recall.
(5) The fewer the alternative associations, the more likely will two specific elements be connected.
(6) There are constitutional differences between individuals which strengthen one set of tendencies rather than another.
(7) Varying emotions, interests and needs will affect what associations are formed or strengthened.

PSYCHOLOGY WITHIN PHILOSOPHY

(8) Acute disturbances such as ill-health, intoxication, etc., influence associations.

(9) Prior habits and dispositions will determine how an individual reacts in a given situation, what is noticed or ignored.

Here the emphasis on emotional and constitutional factors and on individual differences are both original. For the first time there is the recognition that general laws require modification in terms of special conditions. Many of these hypotheses are testable and relevant and have become incorporated in experimental studies of, for example, learning syllables in rote learning.

Another of Brown's innovations was his modification of sensory data by emphasizing the importance of 'muscle sense', giving rise to ideas of resistance and solidity. He incorporated kinaesthetic sensations (that is, sensations derived from the activity of muscles and glands) in his theory of space perception. It may be that our primary information about, for instance, a rose comes from visual impressions and sensations of smell. It is only when we handle the object, picking it up and moving it, that we both confirm and extend our knowledge of its properties. As we shall see later, this view became incorporated in the writings of Wundt and Titchener and led to early experiments on muscular sensations.

Brown's interests were on the whole much more empirical and practical than those of his predecessors, such as Hume and Reid. He wanted to explain actual, concrete experiences rather than reach broad general truths. Although Brown remains within the old tradition – he relies on self-observation, quotes from classical texts, and occasionally makes a point with a Latin verse – nevertheless, his speculations have often bridged the gap between rationalist and empirical psychology.

Brown's progressive tendencies are apparent in contrast with the arch-priest of associationism, James Mill (1775–1836), in whose theory the mechanical compounding of sensory and ideational elements, on the basis of association alone, reached an extreme.

Mill was a poor Scot who received help from a wealthy patron to get an education at Edinburgh University. In 1802 he went to London and worked as a journalist. He wrote chiefly on politics and government for radical periodicals. His fortunes changed in 1817 through the success of his *History of India*, coming as it did at the beginning of Britain's imperial rule. Soon afterwards he was appointed an official of the East India Company, earning £2,000 a year, a very large income in those days. In 1829, simply out of intellectual interest, he published a psychological treatise, *The Analysis of the Phenomena of the Human Mind*.

In this work he followed Hume and Hartley in reducing all the contents of human consciousness to two types of element: sensations (the products of stimuli impinging on peripheral sense organs) and ideas (the reproductions of such impressions, or compounds of such). All our perceptions, memories and thoughts are the result of the processing of sensory and ideational data. The mechanism on which such processing depends is the power of associating ideas. Mill believed that there was no need to postulate any power or force or causal agency to account for association. Objects of sensation are such that certain sensory processes recur together, simultaneously or successively. Out of such natural concurrences and the way we react, the associative process arises in our minds. 'Our ideas spring up . . . in the order in which the sensations existed, of which they are copies. This is "the association of ideas" by which term, let it be remembered, nothing is meant to be expressed, but the order of occurrence.' The only principle involved in association is 'contiguity': the fact that A and B come together in space and time is the only basis for association.

Our perception of physical objects is always the result of synchronous associations. The shape, size, weight, colour and hardness of a stone combine to form our 'percept' and then 'idea' of a stone. How we learn words and speech is a matter of successive associations, words going together in sequences according to rules descriptive of their usual presentation.

Mill dealt with the strength of associations in terms of the frequency and vividness of the items related. He put forward a strictly mechanistic view of the mind in which sensations are the basis for all the variety of experience. The human being is as much under stimulus-control and 'reinforcement schedules' as Skinner's rats (pp. 230–34).

Mill's system had a weakness that proved fatal. In order to explain such complex experiences as thinking and planning, he had to make use of the concept of synchronous association – the association of synchronous stimuli combining or blending into a compound. Thus the idea of weight involves both the idea of resistance and that of direction (extension, place, motion). Ideas of objects involve the synchronous associations of simpler ideas – a tree is a combination of the simpler ideas of trunk, branches, leaves, bark. Mill extended this simple principle until he reached a *reductio ad absurdum*. Thus whenever we use abstract ideas such as 'house' or 'furniture', he had to assume these to be products of fusion combining every simple idea relevant to the abstract entity. A 'house' was thus compounded of ideas of slates, bricks, planks, pipes, etc., etc., into one complex idea. The 'Universe' was the combination of ideas of everything that exists. How could the individual consciousness, as a matter of fact, achieve this Herculean feat and hold, in a single instant, an unlimited number of fused, blended, telescoped ideas in one conceptual hold-all? How could it be shown, by analysis, that so many separate elements exist and are related in such compound ideas? The principle of association had been pressed beyond the limits of credibility as an empirical construct. However, something might be salvaged from this wreck of the associationist theory. It was his son, John Stuart Mill, who assisted in this operation.

J. S. Mill (1806–73) was one of the most brilliant and eminent men of his generation. At the age of 17, after a most rigorous and extraordinary private education at the hands of his father, he entered the East India Company. He remained there until 1858, doing work which today would be that of a high-ranking civil servant in the foreign or colonial office of a great power. After earning his living as a writer on political and social affairs and becoming one of the leading 'intellectuals' of mid-Victorian England, he entered parliament as a Liberal. Throughout his career as journalist and writer he produced a number of academic books which have become philosophical classics. His *Logic* (1836) and his works on economics are still studied as among the major early works of their respective disciplines. His contributions to psychology are contained in two main sources. In 1865 he published *An Examination of Sir William Hamilton's Philosophy*, and in 1869 he edited, with copious notes and comments, his father's *Analysis*. Book VI of his *Logic* contains three short chapters on psychology as a science. Although distinctly subsidiary to his philosophy, politics and economics, Mill's psychology was widely studied as the product of one of the most brilliant minds of the age.

J. S. Mill regarded the mind as active, and thus capable of synthesizing sensory and ideational data into new forms. He accepted much of his father's associationism – sensations and ideas were the elements of experience; similarity, contiguity, frequency and inseparability were the basis for associations between elements. However, association was conceived on a new analogy. Mill talked of 'mental chemistry'. Ideas may coalesce by forming rapid associations in which some ideas become so peripheral as to drop out. Total perceptions may be telescoped and economized. Hence the associated whole may not be the mere sum of its parts. It may result in something new with emergent properties, just as two chemicals combine to produce a new substance with properties of its own. The laws of the whole may not be predictable from a knowledge of its elements. Compounds must be studied independently of their elements. We must always go to experience and find out how each complex came into being and what are its peculiar laws. The rationalist approach of simply deducing possible properties from a knowledge of elements will not work.

In his theory of perception J. S. Mill differed considerably from his father. Accepting that we are capable of expectations, J. S. Mill argued that, once having had sensations, 'we are capable of forming the conception of possible sensations'. While sensations are brief and transitory, our conceptions of physical objects are of permanent and fixed entities. This is in virtue of the fact that our capacity to expect sensations is a permanent disposition. When we are perceiving, we are 'expecting' or 'believing' in the permanent possibility of sensations not actually present. Attitudes bridge the gaps in our sensory intake. When we glance in a room and see a fire we know it will burn if touched, that it will die out if unattended. Indeed most of our behaviour depends on such attitudes embedded in perceptual response. All such 'possibilities of sensation' are associated to form our knowledge of the perceivable world. This is a form of 'context theory' of meaning which attracted many nineteenth-century psychologists. We find it in Ach's 'determining tendencies' (p. 86), and in Titchener's context theory (p. 144).

There may have been less that was original in J. S. Mill's psychology than there was in his other writings. He rationalized and tidied up associationism as left by his father; but his prestige gave his vision considerable authority. He was widely read and admired by German intellectuals and did much to popularize the British empiricist psychology on the continent in the 1870s.

The greatest of the British psychologists of this period was Alexander Bain (1818–1903). Bain was an Aberdonian, the son of a poor weaver. He left school at the age of 11 and worked first as an errand boy and then as a weaver. He educated himself at evening classes at the local Mechanics Institute and eventually won a scholarship to Marischal College, now part of Aberdeen University. In 1840 he graduated as an M.A. in Greek, Latin, Mathematics, Science and Philosophy. For the next twenty years Bain lived by writing, coaching pupils and examining for various boards. As an agnostic and a radical he found it difficult to get academic posts. On moving to London he was befriended by J. S. Mill and met many of the leading intellectuals of the times. His first entry into the academic world was a lecturing appointment at the new Bedford College for Women (1851–4). In 1860 the two colleges at Aberdeen (Marischal and King's) were combined to form a new university and Bain was elected to the Logic chair. In 1876 he founded the journal *Mind*, which, although philosophical, published psychological papers by Francis Galton, Wundt, William James and himself. Until 1895 when his health began to fail he was a leading figure in British psychology. However, his main contribution was made during his free-lancing days before academic preferment came. In 1855 he published *The Senses and the Intellect* and in 1859 *The Emotions and the Will*. These two massive volumes were the culmination of the British philosophical psychology, but they also contained much forward-looking material.

Bain is often classified as an associationist. However, he was not a rigorous one. He allowed for innate forms of organization, and asserted that not all mental states are the product of sensory stimulation. His method was derived more from natural history than from the philosophical tradition of introspection. He carefully observed other people in ordinary everyday situations. Indeed, he preferred observation of other subjects to self-scrutiny. Animal behaviour also interested him (he gives a detailed description of the movements of twin lambs during their first twenty-four hours of life). He was not unsympathetic towards the use of laboratory experiments, although he doubted if experiments could isolate and measure crucial variables, and never took the step of becoming an experimentalist. However, he did move towards a new conception of psychology.

In the first place Bain's were the earliest psychological publications in which a scientific account of the brain and nervous system was presented as a necessary foundation. The sense organs, the sensory and motor nerves, the brain, the musculature, reflexes and instincts are all dealt with. 'The mind is completely at the mercy of the bodily conditions; there being no trace of a separate, independent, self-supporting spiritual agent.' This interest in the physiological mechanisms underlying behaviour stimulated his interest in movement and activity. 'Movement precedes sensation, and is at the outset independent of any stimulus from without.' The organism is basically active and dynamic. It is not an inert system dependent on stimuli impinging on the peripheral sensory receptors before it acts. Stimuli merely determine the direction of activity. Moreover there are inner 'drives' which determine the organization of behaviour which must be considered along with habits, emotions and attitudes. 'Action' is an important concept in Bain's writings. He is the first psychologist to make learning and habit central topics. He held that learning begins with random movements. Those actions which tend to bring pleasant results are repeated; those resulting in pain or frustration are not. Repetition of specific patterns produces 'habits'. William James quoted Bain with approval, and James's pupil, Thorndike, is probably Bain's immediate successor in studying 'trial-and-error' learning – the phrase was used by Bain and later exploited by Lloyd Morgan. We have moved a considerable distance from the reduction of the subject matter of psychology to 'sensations and ideas' and a good distance towards the behaviouristic psychology of the twentieth century.

In *The Emotions and the Will*, Bain discussed a means

of diagnosing character (based on the compilation of case histories) and also the possibilities of devising tests for assessing ability and aptitudes for jobs. He expressed the hope that psychology might be applied to problems of training in industry, sport and the armed forces. Thus most of Bain's discussions fall within the scope of empirical psychology as we know it today. J. C. Flugel's description of Bain as 'the first psychologist' is not inappropriate. His method, subject matter and style are different from those of his predecessors. Yet he stopped short of making the full transition. In the revisions of his books, he ignored the psychophysics of Fechner, the physiology of Helmholtz and the psychological studies of Darwin (see Chapters 3 and 5). While in certain respects he looked boldly ahead to a new kind of psychology, he also remained rooted in the tradition of Locke and Brown.

Bain's achievements were considerable and he stands as an important transitional figure between the old and the new. It was the 'English' psychology – owing so much to the Scottish thinkers of the eighteenth century – which provided the theoretical foundations for the first generation of psychologists, who, although they were Germans, looked more to British ideas than to those of their own eminent philosophers.

GERMAN PHILOSOPHICAL PSYCHOLOGY IN THE EARLY NINETEENTH CENTURY

Under the influence of Kant and Fichte, German philosophy was involved with issues too metaphysical to have much direct influence on the growth of empirical psychology. There were influences at work, however, in the writings of a few prominent Germans which stimulated the emergence of psychology as an independent discipline. J. F. Herbart (1776–1841) was perhaps the greatest of these. He had studied under Fichte at Jena. Later, as a private tutor to the children of the Governor of Interlaken, he became interested in educational problems, visiting Pestalozzi, the educational reformer. He returned to private study at Göttingen from 1802 to 1809 and obtained a junior teaching post there. In 1809 he succeeded Kant as Professor of Philosophy at Königsberg, where he remained for twenty-four years. His work there was primarily concerned with working out a scientific system of education based on psychology. In 1838 he returned to Göttingen and held the chair of philosophy there until his death. During his lifetime his reputation was considerable and his educational theories continued to be discussed throughout the nineteenth century. His *Lehrbuch zur Psychologie* (1816) and his *Psychologie als Wissenschaft* (1825) were widely studied as coming from an authority on educational reform. Herbart's view of psychology is simply stated. Psychology is a science which is based on experience, metaphysics and mathematics – an unusual view for this period. However, Herbart did not think that psychology could ever be an experimental science. Nor did he think that physiology was a necessary foundation study. What he did assert was that psychology should be an independent *Wissenschaft* – distinct from both philosophy and physiology. This was a new viewpoint.

Herbart regarded psychology as an empirical science, with observation of what goes on in the individual's field of consciousness as its aim. The description of the contents and acts of the mind was its subject matter. For this, experimental methods were not suitable. Also, he believed psychology to be metaphysical in so far as it was not a natural science. It aimed at answering questions about human nature which originated in philosophical discussion on the nature of knowledge and the basis for ethical conduct. Philosophers, in Herbart's view, had attempted to answer these questions by employing the wrong methods. Psychology must also use mathematics. The attributes of mental states must be measured and their relationships must be statistically treated. It must be possible to measure the strength of ideas in relation to each other, and some mathematical treatment of mental dynamics (the way ideas combine, conflict, modify each other) may be possible.

Herbart compared psychology with mechanics, in so far as it deals with the statics and dynamics of the soul – the unity which is the mind. The basic contents of the mind are 'ideas' and these interact with each other so that each idea varies in strength. A may inhibit B, so that A and B may be related in an equation. At least two attributes of ideas – time and intensity – can be measured, while ideas also differ in quality from each other. The aim of the study of consciousness is the production of mathematical laws, relating to measurable properties of ideas and exhibiting their dynamic interaction. Herbart thus presented a view which moved towards the conception of psychology as a science, while rejecting the use of experimental methods or the application of physiological knowledge. He regarded ideas as active and operative forces. Thus, two ideas which oppose each other diminish each other. If two ideas are compatible they retain their intensity. However, there are so many ideas that conflict is inevitable. Inhibited ideas are not destroyed. They remain active below the threshold of consciousness. Unconscious ideas are just as important for the composition of consciousness as any other material. Ideas rise above the threshold only if they fit in with the temporary configuration. Once an idea rises above the threshold it is 'apperceived' – it both becomes conscious and is assimilated into a complex of on-going experiences.

Many of these concepts were seminal. Fechner (pp. 54 ff.) seized upon the concept of the threshold of awareness and the idea that the contents of consciousness could be measured. Wundt (pp. 67 ff.) explained perceptual organization in terms of 'unconscious inference'. The notion that unconscious ideas are dynamically striving for expression was later to be developed by Freud.

Herbart presented a mixture of progressive and reactionary ideas. However, his immediate impact in Germany in the 1820s was to suggest: (1) that psychology could become an independent empirical science, studying what actually occurs in conscious experience; (2) that mathematics might be applied to mental events.

Herbart's influence was reinforced by that of Hermann Lotze (1817–81), whose reputation as a philosopher was considerable during the middle years of the century. Lotze studied medicine at Leipzig but was more interested in philosophy and psychophysics. After qualifying, he practised for a year only, and in 1839 returned to Leipzig, teaching in the faculties of both medicine and philosophy. The publication of his *Metaphysik* in 1841, and his *Logik* in 1843 established his reputation as a philosopher of distinction. On the death of Herbart in 1841 he accepted the chair of philosophy at Göttingen, and remained there as a considerable intellectual power for nearly forty years. It was in his *Medizinische Psychologie* (1851) that his views on psychology were defined. Through this book, and through three distinguished pupils and friends – Brentano, Stumpf and G. E. Müller – Lotze came to have his place in the development of psychology in Germany.

Lotze had thoroughly mastered the physiology of his time, and he sought to unify physiology and psychology in a systematic form. His basic teaching was simple and may seem pedestrian today. He argued that mental processes must be defined in terms of underlying physical processes in the brain and nervous system. At the same time, he maintained that physiology may not explain every aspect of human experience. The understanding of our hopes and strivings may have to be in 'molar' terms. Thus psychology remains a distinct discipline.

Apart from presenting a considerable amount of data on the physiology of the senses, Lotze illustrated the relevance of physiology to psychology by formulating a theory to explain our perception of space. Philosophers had raised the question whether our perception of a world of objects in space is innate and unanalysable, or whether non-spatial elements somehow generate our sense of a

33

spatial order. Lotze put forward the theory that our perception of space is built up by association from sensory data – a combination of associationist theory and physiology. He postulated that each stimulus impinging on the retina produces a sensation related to the point of the retina affected. In each case the sensation differs qualitatively from sensations aroused by the same stimulus on other points of the retina. Each specific point has its 'local sign'. How are these local signs related so as to give rise to our perception of visual space? Lotze argued that when the eye turns to fixate an object as clearly as possible, certain muscular sensations are produced. Since the direction and magnitude of the arc through which the eye moves are different for each point on the retina, for each point there is a distinctive 'feeling of position'. All these fall into an orderly and graded series. After many repetitions, each specific stimulus can stimulate, through association, replicas of the muscular sensations previously excited as the eye moved towards its point of fixation. In this way, stimuli which are non-spatial generate space-perception. Thus each stimulus arouses a number of quite distinct sensations, each with a location. Through associative processes, these come to form a graded series, and this order is the basis for our world of visual space. Lotze modified this theory by suggesting that a 'tendency' to movement, without movement actually occurring, could create a local sign – thus accounting for the fact that we can locate an object without moving our eyes.

Lotze's importance, however, was simply that he corrected Herbart's cautious attitude, and insisted that both the methods and the data of physiology are relevant to the solution of many basic psychological questions originally formulated by philosophers. His presentation of the physiological researches of Weber and Johannes Müller (Chapter 2), and his multiple examples, convinced many that a new approach to psychology was needed.

German philosophy was not lacking in advocates for an

independent and scientific psychology. However, it was the British mental philosophy which was the dominant force during the early decades of the nineteenth century and which influenced the course of psychology most immediately. Both Helmholtz and Wundt, who did as much as any others to establish experimental psychology as a new discipline, accepted much of the British outlook as a theoretical basis for their new science. In France, Ribot's *Psychologie anglaise contemporaine* of 1870 (see p. 190) was a clear and persuasive exposition of the Mills, Bain and Spencer tradition and advocated it as a great intellectual achievement. It was widely read in Germany.

In the United States the leading universities, such as Harvard and Princeton, made the works of such writers as Reid, Stewart and Brown the basis of courses in mental philosophy down to the 1870s, and Bain was an accepted modern authority in most early psychology courses. The British writers, although coming at the end of a long tradition, were also the starting-point for the first generation of the 'new psychology'.

The study of individual consciousness and the objective description of perceptual contents was still a major topic. That psychology should become more objective, quantitative and strictly empirical, and that physiology was relevant to our understanding of perception, were propositions generally accepted in mental philosophy by the mid-century. The question 'Could the methods and techniques of experimental science (in particular, those of physiology) be applied to the study of psychological data?' was formulated. Could psychology be transformed from an armchair activity, an adjunct to philosophy, and made a branch of experimental science? It was Wundt, as we shall see, who asked this question most explicitly and who attempted to provide a practical answer by establishing such a science. However, before his work began in the 1870s, physiologists without such a specific objective had actually demonstrated the practicality of such a science. If philosophers had formulated some basic problems for psychology to tackle, it was left to adventurous physiologists to show that researches could be carried out within the physiology laboratory that might be exploited by scientists interested in establishing a new psychology as a scientific discipline in its own right.

CHAPTER TWO

The Beginnings of Psychology within Physiology

D URING the first half of the nineteenth century, the possibility of experimental psychology developing within the established science of experimental physiology became increasingly greater. Physiology had made rapid advances since the middle of the eighteenth century, and by the time that psychology was emerging in the 1880s as a new discipline, a considerable background of physiological knowledge about the workings of the brain and nervous system, as well as of the human sensory processes, was available. Moreover, methods of experimental investigation and apparatus for studying the senses could be easily adapted by the new science. The philosophers had made the senses, seen as channels of information concerning reality, and the resulting field of consciousness the central topics in psychology. It remained for physiologists to suggest rigorously empirical and experimental ways and means for studying psychological data. What were the main developments within the physiology of the early nineteenth century from which the new experimental discipline, psychology, emerged?

SENSORY AND MOTOR NERVES AND THE DOCTRINE OF SPECIFIC ENERGIES

Some of the chief discoveries in the first decades of the nineteenth century were the work of Charles Bell (1774–1842), a Scottish physiologist and surgeon. Many of his researches were originally published privately, either in lectures or in privately printed papers, and it was not until his book *The Nervous System of the Human Body* appeared in 1830 that he obtained credit for his work – indeed his discoveries are linked with the names of others,

Magendie and Johannes Müller, whom he clearly preceded. It was Bell who discovered that there are both sensory and motor nerves, anatomically and functionally discrete, the one set communicating signals from both external and internal environment, and the other initiating responses. Moreover, nervous reaction occurs in one direction only. Bell traced in detail the pathways of the nerves throughout the human body.

His findings led him to look for other functional properties of the nerves, and in 1811 he formulated the doctrine of the specific energies of nerves. This doctrine came to play an important part in the development of psychology. Bell argued that since the nerves intervene between events in our external environment and human consciousness, they must influence the character of our experiences in perception. It must be that each nerve, once activated, imposes its own particular characteristics or energies on the quality of what is experienced. Bell argued from anatomical data that specific nerves react only to certain limited types of stimuli and not to any others. Unless an 'appropriate' stimulus sets it off, a nerve will remain inert.

From this it follows: (1) The same stimulus may produce different sensations according to the particular nerves it activates. Thus a blow to the head produces such diverse sensations as pain, flashes of light and ringing noises – the one stimulus producing sensations peculiar to the nerves activated in skin, eyes and ears. (2) Again, different stimuli acting on the same nerve will always produce the same kind of sensation. Visual sensations occur when light waves impinge on the eye, if the eyeball is pressed with a finger, if a blow is struck near the eye socket, if chemicals or electricity is applied to optical nerves. If a metal point is placed on the tongue certain nerves give rise only to a sensation of touch, others only to a sensation of taste. Every nerve produces its characteristic qualities of sensation in consciousness, and these qualities depend primarily on the structure and functioning of the nerve and its central connexions. Bell's doctrine received a precise and detailed formulation in Johannes Müller's monumental textbook of physiology published in 1833-40 (see p. 48).

It was Müller who drew certain conclusions from this hypothesis. 'The immediate objects of the perceptions of our senses are merely particular states induced in the nerves, and felt as sensations, either by the nerves themselves, or by the sensorium.' The nerves do not simply communicate the existence or properties of objects and events: they provide the mind with its data in terms of their own functions and properties. This conclusion seemed to confirm the philosophers' conclusion that what we know in immediate experience are our own states of mind and that these are sensations, or complexes of sensations. The description and analysis of consciousness into basic elements, and the derivation of each element from a specific nervous reaction, seemed to be the obvious programme for psychology. There must be only a few specific qualities or energies which belong to each sensory mode, and physiology might assist psychology in suggesting what these basic properties of perceptions are. The methods of physiology might even be extended to psychology in place of armchair descriptions of the contents of consciousness. The two disciplines were becoming complementary.

The doctrine of the specific energies of nerves provided support for what was still a relatively new idea (although ancient in origin), namely that the brain is the seat of the mind. Bell insisted that 'all ideas originate in the brain: the operation of producing them is the remote effect of an agitation or impression on the extremities of the nerves.' The doctrine raised problems. What was the exact locus of specificity – the peripheral sense organ, the peripheral nerves, the spinal cord or the central brain?

THE PHYSIOLOGY OF THE BRAIN 1800–70

The doctrine that the mind is located in the brain was established by the end of the eighteenth century. Luigi Rolando (1770–1831) attempted a comprehensive anatomy of the brain and carried out elementary and crude experiments (1809). He held that the cerebral hemispheres are the seat of 'higher' mental functions, and he provided pathological data and postmortem examples in support of his somewhat vague generalizations.

Pierre Flourens (1794–1867), however, was a physiologist of genius. He was master of a precise surgical technique, ingenious in devising original and stimulating experiments, and accurate in his deductions from the data available to him. Working in Paris as a professor of physiology, he published his results before the Académie des Sciences in 1824–5, and presented a collected edition of his papers in 1842.

Flourens' main interest was in the functions of specific parts of the brain. His method was original. He performed delicate surgical operations on the brains of living animals, removing certain parts and observing the effect on behaviour. His anatomical studies enabled him to isolate distinctive regions for investigation – the cerebral hemispheres, cerebellum, corpora quadrigemina, medulla oblongata, spinal cord, and nerves. By removing a part, cleanly and without damage to adjacent areas, he was able to carry out experiments on the localization of function. His results were impressive. The removal of the cerebral lobes led to total loss of voluntary action and of all perceptual reactions. Animals thus treated remained motionless and did not respond to visual or auditory stimuli, although the pupils of the eye still contracted to light – sensory reactions without vision. The removal of the cerebellum did not affect sensation or prevent movement. It did, however, prevent efficient or controlled movements. In attempting to walk or fly, the animal without a cerebellum fell over. Thus coordination and control of movement was located in this sphere. The medulla proved to be the centre of the nervous system, ordering sensations before the total perceptual field emerged. The corpora quadrigemina was related to seeing, blindness resulting from its removal, even with the cerebrum intact. The nerves were responsible for the excitation of central processes and muscles, and the spinal cord was a conduction agent.

Besides plotting the specific functions of parts of the brain, Flourens generalized thus: 'All these diverse parts of the nervous system have all specific properties, proper functions, distinct effects; and, in spite of this marvellous diversity of properties, functions and effects, they nevertheless constitute of it a unique system.' In spite of localization of function, the nervous system operates as a unified whole. There is overall integration. This generalization resulted from Flourens' discovery that a function can be acquired again after the removal of that part of the brain responsible for it. This view that localization occurs within the organization of the whole anticipated those of Franz and Lashley in the twentieth century. The recovery of function after its abolition by loss of a part of the brain has remained a problem for neurophysiology ever since. The prevailing emphasis has switched from localization to 'field' theory and back again, yet Flourens 'unity and diversification' has remained a sane attitude.

Flourens thus established the notion of the brain as the seat of the mind on a firmly empirical basis, and physiology as an essential foundation for psychology. The experimental method was also demonstrated as the only valid means of investigating problems in physiological psychology. Armchair speculation of the kind conducted intelligently by Hartley and less happily by Franz Gall and the popular 'phrenology' movement of the time was now revealed as inadequate.

After Flourens, brain physiology made steady but slow

progress. In 1842 Stilling devised a way of cutting a continuous series of sections of brain tissue which greatly advanced anatomical studies. In 1833 J. J. Lister, using an improved microscope of his own invention, discovered the existence of a cell-structure in the blood and in animal tissue. Three years later, Robert Remak found that the grey matter of the human brain is cellular in structure. The same years C. G. Ehrenberg traced in detail the fibres of the white matter of the brain, and showed that this substance consists only of conduction fibres. Nerve cells now appeared as fundamental units in living tissue – including the brain.

By the 1850s. it was known that millions of such cells connected by minute fibres constitute the stuff of the brain. It was not until Camillo Golgi developed a method of staining tissue with silver nitrate in 1878 that he put forward the picture of the anatomy of the brain as a network, or system of interrelated networks, of cells. The neurone theory did not emerge until the 1890s, and the details of the system are still far from being described even today. However, by the 1850s the simple sketch map of the brain as consisting of tiny cells connected by fibres was established.

Flourens had thought of the brain as relatively simple. Soon it was revealed as intricately complex in anatomy, and therefore in mode of functioning. This general picture seemed, down to the end of the century, to be not incompatible with the associationist theories of the empiricist philosophers. The many 'ideas' of the mind, connected in an infinitely large number of combinations by the laws of association to form complex states of consciousness, might have a physical substratum in this infinite number of brain cells and their inter-connexions. Obviously, associationist systematic psychology was over-simplified. but physiological knowledge might help to sophisticate the theory.

The theory of localization of function received further reinforcement through Paul Broca's assertion that the centre for speech is at the base of the frontal convolution of the left cerebral hemisphere. This precise localization has since been questioned. Broca had conducted an autopsy on a former patient and had discovered a lesion at precisely this point. Before his death, the patient had suffered a peculiar disability. He had been unable to talk, although he communicated intelligently and successfully through signs and there was nothing wrong with the larynx or other organs of articulation. This began a movement supporting the theory of the exact localization of every function, and Flourens' idea of a 'field' or 'general' action of the brain as a whole fell into temporary neglect.

Broca's outlook appeared to receive support from other researches. In 1870 Fritsch and Hitzig discovered the localization of motor-functions in the cerebral cortex. Hitzig had noticed that the electrical stimulation of the cortex of a man led to a movement of his eyes. With Fritsch, he systematically investigated the effect of stimulating electrically the exposed cortex of a dog. In a specific region of the cortex they found that a strong current provoked convulsive movements; but weak currents, applied more specifically, isolated centres for five different groups of muscles from neck to foreleg. Sir David Ferrier (1843–1928), of King's College Hospital, London, performed similar experiments on monkeys, dogs, cats, rabbits and rats, greatly improving the techniques of electrical stimulation.

A detailed map of the 'motor' centres thus emerged in the 1870s. Soon afterwards, the sensory centres were located – vision in the occipital lobe, hearing in the temporal lobe and somesthetic sensation in the post-central region. In Ferrier's *The Functions of the Brain* (1876) this knowledge was systematized, and some sections of the book were directly addressed to psychologists. Thus the brain, although still beyond the reach of a complete scientific understanding, was given its modern role in the early part of the nineteenth century before psychology emerged as an independent discipline.

THE PHYSIOLOGY OF SENSATION 1800–70

The first half of the nineteenth century provided scientists with considerable knowledge of the sensory processes. This knowledge was of immediate interest to systematic psychologists, who attached primary importance to sensation and perception in the mind.

Vision was a thoroughly investigated subject. Sir Isaac Newton's *Opticks* (1704) had initiated a continuous tradition of research by physicists and physiologists on sound lines. Both Bell (*The Anatomy of the Human Body*, 1803) and Johannes Müller (*Handbuch der Physiologie*, 1834–40) were able to treat the subject in detail. Both these celebrated textbooks have as central topics the physics of the stimulus, the anatomy of the eye and the eye as a complex mechanism. Apart from the variability of the curvature of the lens, more or less everything about the mechanics of the eye was known. However, both Bell and Müller, influenced by their doctrine of specific energies of nerves, were concerned with the 'problem of perception'. How does the nervous system carry information about the properties of stimulus-objects and events to the mind? Size, shape, colour and position in space must be communicated through the image on the retina and by the nerves leading from thence to the occipital lobe.

Many specific problems issued from this line of thinking. Several theories were forthcoming as to how the image was focused on the retina. The view which predominated, put forward by Thomas Young in 1807 and evidenced by Helmholtz in his great publication of 1856–66 (p. 63), was that there must be alteration in the curvature of the lens. Evidence was provided by Sanson's experiments and those of Helmholtz. Helmholtz's explanation of the means by which the lens might change shape was that the lens is elastic and subject to tension.

The problem of binocular vision was also well on the

way towards solution. How do the retinal images from two separate eyes become a single perception? By the time that Müller wrote of this subject in his textbook, a plausible answer was available. Half the fibres from each retina cross at the point known as the optic chiasma, but the other half do not. The projections of the two retinas on the brain may thus be superimposed, and with a point-for-point coincidence produce a single image-pattern in the brain.

As early as 1613, the horopter had been defined. The two retinas consist of points which correspond. The locus of all points the imagery of which falls on corresponding points of the two retinas is the horopter. It was Müller who demonstrated that the horopter may be conceived as a circle, which passes through the fixation point and the optical centres of the two eyes – in the horizontal plane, anyway. It was known that vision is not single for parts of a field of vision which do not lie on the horopter, and this set an interesting problem for physiologists. Increasingly, physiologists came to believe that central processes, in the light of experience, correct the information presented by the visual apparatus so that double images are 'reduced' to one.

There were many problems related to vision being investigated by physiologists – how we come to perceive colours, how depth and solidity are essential dimensions in what is perceived through the retinal image, how distant objects are compared for actual size, etc. (The detailed history of these thorough and minute researches are given in Chapters 1 to 8 of E. G. Boring's scholarly book *Sensation and Perception in the History of Experimental Psychology*, 1942.) Thus the mechanisms of the peripheral sense-organs for vision, and something of the operation of the sensory nerves, were charted well before psychology became an experimental science.

In the field of hearing both Bell and Müller presented a comparative anatomy of the ear in different types of animals. The details of structure were known, but theories con-

cerning how the instrument worked were speculative, and
some of Müller's speculations were wide of the mark. The
working of the ear in relation to pitch, tone and successive
noise, together with the problems of the localization of
sounds and the limits of hearing, were given empirically
grounded theories in the massive and monumental researches of Helmholtz published in 1863 (p. 63).

It was the comparatively neglected sense of touch, however, which stimulated psychology as much as any other
branch of sensory physiology. Neither Bell nor Müller had
a great deal to offer in this field. It was Ernst Heinrich
Weber (1795–1878), the Professor of Physiology at Leipzig
from 1818 until 1860, who conducted research on touch.
He published his first treatise in 1834 (*De tactu*) and his
second in 1846 (*Der Tastinn und das Gemeingefühl*).
He held that the sense of touch yields three distinct
types of sensations: those of pressure, temperature and
locality. His many and varied experiments provided the
starting point for all subsequent research into tactual
sensation. Some of these directly helped the growth of
psychology.

Weber was interested in discovering what distance apart
two points of a pair of compasses must be before a blind-
folded subject can detect two distinct sensations when he
is touched with them. He found that this varied for different parts of the body, the distance being smallest at the
fingertips and greatest on the shoulder. He concluded that
nerve fibres must be differently distributed, so that spatial
discrimination through touch is most accurate where
fibres are most dense. The concept of 'limen' or 'threshold'
was invented by Weber in discussing the variation in distance between points before a single impression of touch
became double.

However, it was his experiments on muscle-sensation
which aroused most interest. To what extent do muscular
sensations contribute towards our discriminations between objects of differing weight? Weber initiated the
familiar experiment in which subjects lift pairs of weights,

either simultaneously or successively, and judge which of the two is heavier. Weber discovered that if subjects *lifted* weights discriminations tended to be much more accurate than if the weights were placed on their outstretched palms. Muscular sensation assisted discrimination of weight differences. By varying the magnitude of weights, he discovered that discrimination depended not only on the absolute magnitudes, but also on the relative difference between the two (the ratio of a magnitude to a standard). The difference between two weights was accurately perceived when their magnitudes were in the ratio of 29 : 30.

He next investigated visual stimuli by presenting subjects with straight lines in order to judge which of each pair was the longer. He found that most subjects could discriminate between two horizontal lines, of different length and placed at varying distances, only if one was at least 1/100th to 1/50th longer than the other. Otherwise no difference could be detected. He came to the conclusion that the ability to discriminate between two stimuli, of any sensory modality, depended not on the absolute magnitude of the difference but upon the relative difference expressed in terms of the ratio of one to the other. Within each stimulus-magnitude (e.g. intensity of light, length of lines) there was a 'just noticeable difference' (j.n.d.) which was constant. A constant fraction for j.n.d.s in the increase or decrease of a stimulus dimension could therefore be determined by experiment.

This generalization has not been confirmed. However, the concept of measuring j.n.d.s in relation to differences in increase or decrease of a stimulus-magnitude was one which could be exploited in experiments in physiological psychology. Individual differences in sensory discrimination might be studied, and techniques for investigating psychological reactions experimentally devised. Weber thus began the development of psychophysical methods of research on which early experimental psychology relied to a considerable extent. The measurement of two-point thresholds for touch-sensations, the study of visual acuity, the measurement of just noticeable differences between discriminatory acts – all these were the extension of experimental methods to the study of *behaviour* rather than to the study of physiological mechanisms. That Weber worked at Leipzig all his life and that experimental psychology was first regarded there as an independent discipline was no accident. Before experimental psychology was recognized as something new and different, it was being practised by experimental physiologists, of whom Weber was one of the first.

THE INFLUENCE OF JOHANNES MÜLLER

Müller (1801–58) has already appeared as a joint-author of the doctrine of specific energies of nerves. His influence on the new science was considerable. As Professor of Physiology at Berlin in 1833–58 he was the great authority on his subject, and both Helmholtz and Wundt were among his pupils – together with most of the leading physiologists in Germany during the nineteenth century (du Bois-Reymond, for example). Müller described the basic functions of the sensory-motor system in detail for the first time, discovered the reflex as the basis of the spinal cord's activity, and demonstrated how the vocal cords function in relation to vocal pitch. He excelled as a teacher, possessing encyclopedic knowledge and great skill at systematizing the established facts. His reputation attracted young scientists to Berlin from all over Europe, and he extended this influence in his great *Handbuch der Physiologie* (1834–40). This was one of the most influential textbooks of the day.

The book not only presented and systematized the physiological knowledge of his time, but explored the possibility of using physiology as a means of studying human consciousness through the operation of the nervous system. The topics covered in detail were: (a) the circulation of the blood and lymph; (b) the chemistry of respiration, nutrition, growth, reproduction, digestion and excretion; (c) the physiology of the nerves; (d) muscular movement and reflex action; (e) the five senses; (f) mental processes – association, memory, thinking, etc.; (g) embryology and infant development. At least five parts of the book contained data of interest to psychologists, and certain parts tackled psychological questions directly from the physiological point of view. Together with its presentation of the doctrine of specific energies, these features made it a basic study for all those interested in the mind.

REFLEX ACTION AND REACTION TIME

The concept of reflex action was defined more clearly in the early nineteenth century. Müller did basic research and incorporated it in his textbook, although he acknowledged the work of predecessors. Marshall Hall (1790–1859), a Scottish physician working in London, was an eager physiological researcher, and presented papers to the Royal Society regularly. In studying respiratory processes, he noted that a decapitated newt reacted to stimulation of the skin. He thereupon experimented on a snake by severing its spinal cord between the second and third vertebrae. He observed that the animal remained motionless apart from gasping and slight head twitches, and continued indefinitely in this condition. However, stimulation to parts of the body produced vigorous movements. This demonstrated that action can be mediated by the spinal cord disconnected from the brain. It was argued that this had been demonstrated before by other researchers. Nevertheless, Hall's experiment was a convincing one. He defined the mechanisms (reflexes) which thus operated independently of the brain, and focused attention on the reflex arc. Hall regarded reflexes as the basis for fixed, involuntary movement beyond the control of the brain and consciousness. Later, Pavlov demonstrated that reflexes could be 'conditioned' and might be the physical basis for simple learning operations (p. 161). This, however, was a long way ahead. Reflexes remained something of a mystery in physiological psychology after Hall's papers of 1833 and 1837, and were left to physiologists to investigate. It is interesting that their existence was known so early and linked with involuntary unconscious reactions.

The main interest on the 'response' side of early experimental psychology was centred on 'reaction times'. The study of reaction times started long before the Dutch scientist Donders began in 1865 to study the factors intermediate between stimulus and response, which methods Wundt exploited in the 1880s (pp. 70 ff.).

In 1796, the Astronomer Royal at Greenwich sacked his assistant observer because he found the latter's observations of star movements differed widely from his own. Later, in 1813, Bessel, a German astronomer, postulated that the difference between the two observers might be due to innate personal differences in ability to discriminate. Reaction time to visual stimuli might differ. He tested his hypothesis by comparing the times taken by various trained observers to react to the coincidence of a star with a mark on a telescope lens. There were considerable individual differences. These differences, between say A and B, he called the 'personal equation'. This discovery set astronomers a problem, since it meant that observations were bound to be influenced by these personal differences. Making observations of the transit of stars involved the coordination of ear and eye – the observer had both to watch the movement of the star in relation to wires across the lens and to count seconds from the ticks of a clock. The immediate problem of either calculating the personal equation or eliminating it led to the 'complication experiment' – in which individual reaction-times were involved in an awkward synchronization of a series of auditory impressions with a visual impression (hence the 'complication' of more than one kind of response in the observer).

The practical difficulty was eventually solved by the

invention of a chronograph, a satisfactory model being evolved in 1850 in the U.S.A. This instrument consisted of a revolving drum with a paper fitted to the curved surface. Two ink-pens drew two parallel lines on the surface of the paper. An electro-magnet connected to one pen caused it to jerk every second and so produce a regular wave-like line measured off in seconds. The second ink-pen was connected so that when an observer noticed the star crossing a line and pressed a key, the second pen made a jag in the line. The time of transit could be read off the drum graph. It was this device that made easy the measuring of the absolute personal equation. With the invention of electrical devices which were practically instantaneous in operation it was possible to make a point of light move across a telescopic field, so that the chronoscope could record automatically the moment of its 'bisection' on a crucial wire or 'line'. Each individual astronomer could now be tested for his 'personal equation' against this apparatus. What was being measured was the individual 'reaction' times of astronomers to visual stimuli. Of course many investigations into these phenomena were conducted in some puzzlement, until Helmholtz demonstrated, in 1850, that the nervous impulse takes time to travel, and succeeded in measuring the speed of transmission in animals and man.

Since this is so, a man's body does not immediately obey his mind. Given a stimulus, it takes time for it to register within the nervous system; given an impulse, it takes time for ideas to form or movement to occur. What delays occur in different parts of the nervous system between sense-organ and peripheral nerve, between brain reaction and motor nerve, between nerve and muscle? And what time does it take to recognize, recall, decide, choose, judge, or execute other mental processes? The reaction-time experiment, although starting within astronomy, became part of the equipment of physiological psychologists. Helmholtz again, as we shall see, performed the first reaction-time psychological experiments, although the exploitation of these did not come until the 1880s, when Wundt's laboratory was in full swing at Leipzig.

This sketch of some of the features of physiology in the period from 1800 to 1870 serves to show that experimental psychology was growing up spontaneously within physiology. Many of the problems, methods and techniques of the new psychology were formulated and tested within the development of experimental physiology. However, there were steps to be taken before the new discipline emerged definitely and unambiguously.

The philosophers had evolved systematic psychology to the point at which it seemed to converge towards the physiology of the times. Psychology was the description and analysis of the contents of consciousness. Consciousness depended on sensations and images derived from the senses for its basic materials.

There was clearly an intimate relationship between mental states and mental acts as revealed to introspection, and the sensory processes and brain functions studied by experimental physiology. Apart from being complementary, or even two different aspects of the same thing, what the two sciences described must be related specifically to each other. It might even be the case that the psychologist's interest in describing 'sensations' as the basic elements or contents of the mind might be made more exact and controlled if the methods of experimental physiology could be extended to psychology. Hitherto, the psychologist had relied on his own 'armchair' introspection to provide him with descriptions of the contents and operations of the conscious mind. Could experimental physiology be extended to include such descriptions within the scope of its techniques? This had already happened by the 1850s in the work of Weber and Helmholtz. It only remained for somebody to formalize methods whereby psychological variables such as 'sensations' could be isolated and certain of their dimensions subjected to measurement. Could this be achieved? If so, psychology could become a branch of experimental science, and the speculations of philosophers would no longer be the only method of conducting psychological investigations. Between 1840 and 1870 steps were taken to convince scientists that an experimental science of psychology was possible and practicable.

CHAPTER THREE

The Emergence of Experimental Psychology

THE steps by which psychology was removed from being a branch of philosophy – and also a fringe interest of physiologists of a speculative frame of mind – to becoming an experimental science in its own right were principally, indeed almost exclusively, the work of three German scientists, each a man of considerable genius: Gustav Fechner, Hermann von Helmholtz and Wilhelm Wundt.

FECHNER AND PSYCHOPHYSICAL METHODS

Gustav Fechner (1801–87) was the son of a Lutheran pastor who died when Fechner was only five. In spite of poverty he went to Leipzig University in 1817 to study medicine. After he had qualified in 1822 he ceased to be interested in the unscientific medical knowledge of the time and turned to physics and mathematics. He lived by translating French scientific handbooks into German. This work won him a teaching appointment in physics, and down to 1839 he pursued a highly successful career as a physicist. In 1826 Ohm had formulated his law stating the relationship between current, resistance and electromotive force in an electric circuit. Fechner went on to demonstrate how quantitative measurements of direct currents were possible, and his reputation as a leading scientist was established. He enjoyed during the 1830s a period of great intellectual activity. He published many articles and had a circle of able associates, including E. H. Weber, A. W. Volkmann, and the young Lotze, who came as a student in 1834. This happy period however tempted Fechner to overwork and in 1839 he had a severe breakdown. He had injured his eyes as a result of gazing at the sun through coloured glasses while researching on after-sensations. This eye trouble seems to have coincided with a psychological disorder. For three years Fechner lived as a hermit in a darkened room. He could not concentrate or control attention or thinking. At the end of that time he began to recover, but he remained an invalid until 1851.

During this protracted illness and withdrawal from academic activity Fechner became deeply religious. He turned to metaphysical philosophy, became interested in spiritualism and was obsessed with the idea that all forms of materialism were evil. In his youth he had contributed articles to literary periodicals under the name of 'Von Mises', and he now wrote again, attacking the materialist 'night view' of existence, and arguing that the soul and its future beyond the material world was the only reality. To discover a way to refute materialism – the explanation of all phenomena in terms of physics and chemistry – became his mission in life. His method was to prove that physical aspects of the world are 'fictions' and that mental events (the attributes of immortal and immaterial spirit) are the sole reality. From this ancient metaphysical problem nobody would have predicted anything in the least relevant to the creation of an experimental science. However, Fechner was a scientist of outstanding ability and in his personal spiritual crisis he hit on a method for refuting materialism which produced surprising results. One morning in October 1850, while lying in bed and thinking about his problem, he had an inspiration. He would meet the enemy and beat it with its own weapons. He argued, illogically, that since conscious events (mental states) are correlated with events in the brain and nervous system, then if only one could establish a relationship between the two in the form of an equation (making 'a relative increase in bodily energy the measure of the increase of the corresponding mental intensity') this would abolish dualism. Since mental states are known directly and certainly for what they are and since neurological events are postulated only on the basis of experiences, it is the mental event which 'remains' when dualism is abolished.

He postulated, probably helped by Weber's Law, enunciated in 1846 (see p. 47), that an arithmetic series of 'mental' intensities might correspond to a geometric series of physical increases, and that a ratio might emerge which would give him a means of measuring changes in mental states. If sensations are a basic content of consciousness and are directly related to physical events as the effects of 'stimuli', the problem was this: how can sensations as such be measured? We can measure attributes of a stimulus (a beam of light, a tone, a weight placed in the hand), but how can the resulting sensation, in consciousness, of light, sound or pressure be measured?

How to make such measurements, as part of a metaphysical attack on materialism, was considered in a programme of experimental research which Fechner called 'psychophysics'. During the 1850s, aided by Volkmann (by then Professor of Physiology at Leipzig), he carried out a massive project of experimental research. In 1860 the results of the work of nine intensively active years appeared as the celebrated *Elemente der Psychophysik*. The main upshot was the development of statistical and experimental techniques which were sufficiently rigorous and sophisticated to substantiate the claim that psychological variables could not merely be investigated through the experimental methods of the physical sciences, but could also be *measured*. The essential conditions for the foundation of an experimental science of human nature had been achieved. For this achievement Fechner cared nothing. He was simply seeking empirical data to use in the context of an overall metaphysical argument.

It is one of the paradoxes in the history of science that the development of one of the most quantitatively sound techniques in experimental psychology was devised by a mystic obsessed by religious ideals and living in an otherworldly atmosphere, for the purpose of refuting a doctrine widely held by men of science. However, Fechner's life, before his breakdown in 1839 and subsequent 'conversion', proved him to be a man of considerable scientific genius, and it is only surprising that the greatest fruits of this ability came to maturity in such circumstances.

What did Fechner do for psychology? His aim was to measure 'subjective' sensations. He started from the work of his Leipzig colleague Weber. As we have seen (p. 47), the latter had carried out experiments on the human capacity to make accurate discriminations. He had noticed that if we try to compare, for example, two lines which are almost equal, we often fail to notice any difference and judge them 'equal' in length. The smallest noticeable difference is about 1/50th of the length of one of the two lines, whatever the actual values involved. Weber investigated weight discriminations, discriminations of pitch and visual discriminations of different types of stimuli. From his experiments he formulated a law – that the smallest perceptible difference between two excitations, of the same sensory mode, is always due to an actual, measurable, difference, which increases proportionately to the excitations. Thus, equal relative increments in stimuli are proportional to equal increments of sensation.

This law does not provide the basis for a sensory scale, which was what Fechner required in order to demonstrate a precise parallel between physical and mental events (stimuli-sensations). However, Weber gave him his basic concept, that of 'just noticeable differences' (j.n.d.s) between two sensations in the same modality. Fechner wanted to measure by how many degrees one sensation is greater than another. Even at a commonsense level, it was obvious that three similar candles are not necessarily three times as bright as one, or two trumpets twice as loud as one. It might be possible, Fechner thought, that the intensity of a sensation (of brightness, loudness, etc.) increases, not proportionately to the intensity of the source of stimulation, but more slowly. In order to measure differences between sensations, Fechner devised three experimental methods or techniques. He was also indebted to Weber for the idea on which they are based – that of 'limen' or 'threshold'. The term can mean either (a) the measurable intensity of a stimulus needed for a sensation to occur at all – the initial or minimal amount of intensity needed to produce a response in a person, or (b) the differential threshold – the amount by which a stimulus must be increased or decreased in intensity in order that a person perceives a change. Fechner's basic strategy was to try to measure the degree by which an *increase* in sensation is *less* than an increase in its stimulus. His 'psychophysical' methods were devised and applied in order to exemplify this.

The first is called either the Method of Limits or the Method of Smallest Perceptible Differences. In this, Fechner changed his stimulus by discrete, measured steps until his experimental subject reported a change in the intensity of his sensation (of brightness, loudness, etc.). First he began by presenting so weak a stimulus that the subject did not react. Then he gradually increased it until a sensation was reported. Next he provided an adequate stimulus intensity and diminished it bit by bit until the subject reported cessation of sensation. Arranging the results over a number of trials gave an absolute threshold. By taking *two* stimuli, a standard and a comparison, and by then varying the comparison until the subject's reports of difference changed to 'no difference', he established the 'differential threshold'.

Conversely, it is possible to start from a situation in which the subject reports no difference, until a difference is noted once the comparison stimulus has been changed by a specific degree. In using the method to determine 'differential limen', Fechner counted up the number of j.n.d.s in order to construct a sensory scale for measuring each sensation in relation to changes in intensity in the stimulus. Taking all j.n.d.s to be equal, Fechner thus constructed his sensory scale (counting up j.n.d.s from absolute limen).

In his second method (Constant Method, or Right and Wrong Cases), Fechner presented stimuli or stimulus differences in a random order, and treating each S (or S-difference) as constant, he calculated the relative frequency with which a specific judgement had been made for each stimulus presented. He derived a curve of 'percentages' plotted against stimulus values, and deduced 'absolute threshold' as the point at which sensation is reported as frequently as it is not reported. For differential threshold there were three functions – one for each of the three possible responses in comparing stimuli (greater, equal, less).

The third method (Average Error) derived from a situation in which Fechner gave his subject a standard stimulus and also the chance to manipulate apparatus so that the comparison stimulus could be changed by the subject. The subject does this until he can perceive no difference between the comparison stimulus and the standard. The average constant error and the average variable error were calculated from the data of each experiment.

Exploiting these techniques in an extensive programme of experiments, Fechner produced from the results a law applicable to all modes of sensation – sight, hearing, touch, etc. This was achieved as the result of analysing his data and making an elaborate mathematical deduction. His law was simply '$S = K \log I$', where I is a scale of stimulus intensity and S a scale of sensation. The sensation increases as a logarithm of the stimulus value. On the assumption that all j.n.d.s are equal, he simply had to count the number of j.n.d.s to discover the magnitude of any sensation – its distance above absolute threshold for that sensory mode.

Fechner's technical achievements were not without their flaws and limitations. However, with refinements and modifications, his methods have proved sound and are still embodied in much psychological investigation – perhaps more in the field of mental testing (which did not develop until long after Fechner's death) than in experimental psychology. His achievement was to devise *methods* which were both experimental procedures and statistical tools for empirical research in relation to human behaviour. (In subsequent developments the j.n.d.s can be dispensed with in relation to supraliminal sensations.) Even if the methods had not stood the test of time, this contribution to the foundation of the new science of psychology cannot be underestimated.

'Sensations' had hitherto been items in the stream of consciousness open to vague introspections and describable only in terms of words borrowed from everyday speech. Now they were reactions capable of objective investigation and indirect measurement. Fechner demonstrated the possibility, indeed the practicability, of psychology becoming an experimental and quantitative science. The first step towards a scientific psychology had been taken, and a pattern set for psychological inquiry. An environmental variable related to behaviour was isolated and manipulated by the experimenter and attributes subjected to exact measurement. Measurable changes in this stimulus were then correlated with determinable (and in this case measurable) changes in some response dimension. Statistical analysis of a large number of such discoverable correlations could then yield an empirical law or generalization which might be useful in giving a more exact account of behaviour and its predisposing conditions than was otherwise obtainable.

In the years subsequent to the publication of the *Elemente der Psychophysik*, Fechner concerned himself with the possibility of an experimental investigation of aesthetic judgements (he published his *Vorschule der Aesthetik* in 1876), involved himself in controversies with critics of specific points in his work over the application of psychophysics and published a final attack on 'scientific materialism' in a large book, *Die Tagensansich* (1879). His final formulation of his psychophysical techniques came in a book, *Revision der Psychophysik,* in 1882 – five years before his death at the age of 86. As much as any other he merits the title of 'founder' of experimental psychology.

HERMANN VON HELMHOLTZ

Helmholtz (1821–94) was one of the greatest of the nineteenth-century scientists. He was a thorough-going empiricist with none of Fechner's metaphysical tendencies, yet he was also a man of many interests. His primary field was physics, where his technical skill as an experimenter enabled him to make fundamental advances in optics and acoustics. These interests led him to drift into physiology, and it was as a physiologist that he did research which today would be classified as experimental psychology. It was the quality of his research work in this new field and his prestige as a scientist which helped experimental psychology to become quickly established in Germany.

Helmholtz, the son of a schoolmaster, was born at Potsdam. He was a precocious child who disliked school but learnt much on his own. In 1838, at the age of 17, he knew that he wanted to be a physicist specializing in optics, but pure science offered few possibilities for a career at that time and so Helmholtz chose medicine. On qualifying, he served in the Prussian army as a surgeon (1842–9). Stationed during this time in Berlin, he seized the opportunity to study part-time at the university. Magnus, the physics professor, and Johannes Müller befriended him and helped him to get the formal training he wanted. Several of his fellow students during these years not only remained life-long friends but themselves became famous scientists. They included Brucke (Vienna – physiology), Virchow (Berlin – pathology) and du Bois-Reymond (Berlin – physiology).

In 1847, while still an army surgeon, he read a paper in which he gave a mathematical formulation of the Law of the Conservation of Energy, the first rigorous statement of the principle, well supported by empirical evidence from his own work and his wide reading. His reputation grew rapidly, and in 1849 he was appointed Professor of Physiology at Königsberg. During this period he emerged from obscurity into the centre of the contemporary scientific world. From 1856 to 1871 he was Professor of Physiology at Heidelberg – with a brief interlude at Bonn – and finally, in 1871, he settled in Berlin as Professor of Physics. His death in 1894 was partly the result of injuries sustained from a fall while returning to Germany from Chicago.

Helmholtz established his reputation in physiology in 1850, when he measured the speed of the nervous impulse. Previously estimates had differed, but most physiologists thought it was high – 9,000 feet per minute (150 feet per second) to 57,600 million feet per second. Helmholtz had invented the myograph, a revolving drum for recording muscular contractions, and he proceeded to take a muscle with its motor nerve attached and to measure the delay in contraction for different lengths of the nerve. He used a frog's 'nerve-muscle preparation', and found that the speed of transmission along the nerve was only 90 feet per second. He also studied a human sensory nerve by asking a subject to signal with the hand as soon as he felt different parts of the body stimulated. He found the speed varied between 50 and 100 feet per second. This discovery showed that movement was not an instantaneous expression of 'will' but a temporal series of events. Sensation, thought and movement follow each other and do not occur spontaneously.

This immediately raised a host of problems for students of behaviour. What is the range of individual differences with regard to different kinds of response? What temporal delay occurs in the functioning of the different parts of the system (peripheral receptor organs, sensory nerves, central brain process, motor discharge, muscle contraction), and what is involved in the timing of behaviour? Does a stimulus S_1 with a greater 'intensity' than stimulus S_2 (of the same sensory modality) make for difference in reaction? What is the essential character of a nervous impulse?

How does the brain connect the sensory with the motor side? The reaction experiment was thus also introduced into psychology – the subject reacting to a specific stimulus by a sign or movement, making possible the indirect investigation of intervening processes. This was exploited on a wide scale in the 1880s by Wundt's students.

In 1851 Helmholtz invented the ophthalmoscope so that he could look directly into a subject's eye – the beginning of his many researches into physiological optics. It was in this year that he developed a theory of colour vision, originally put forward by Thomas Young (1773–1829). Helmholtz maintained that there are three receptor mechanisms in the eye which, when stimulated, give rise to sensations of red, green and blue. Each receptor is subjected to maximum stimulation by a particular wave length and to a lesser extent by wave lengths immediately next on the spectrum. However, such adjacent wave lengths also stimulate the other two receptors and so 'mixed' colours result. This theory implied that there must be areas in the brain which specialize in producing sensations received from the three basic retinal mechanisms – both for the pure colours and their mixtures – a form of specific energies of nerves theory. The theory has survived and Helmholtz's discovery – that three elementary colours can be mixed to provide all possible shades and hues – is a basic fact of experience.

Helmholtz's work on visual mechanisms and visual perception now began. His *Handbuch der physiologischen Optik* appeared in three parts in 1856, 1860 and 1866. It was a giant work, combining original research, the systematic presentation of all crucial research by others, and the construction of basic theories to answer fundamental questions. The work was revised and published again after his death in 1896. Editors revised it with additions in 1911 and the work was again reprinted in 1925. An English translation has recently (1960) been reissued, and it remains a fundamental text. It is impossible to indicate the richness of this work. The three volumes deal with the physiology of vision, the sensory system and perceptual organization, while the discussion of physiological and psychological questions concerning vision is based on physics throughout. In the last volume Helmholtz had a section giving his views on psychology.

In 1863 he published a similar, but briefer work, on hearing, *Die Lehre von den Tonempfindungen*, which contained some of his most original researches. From a detailed anatomy of the ear, a resonance theory of hearing and examinations of the combination of tones, it goes on to discuss problems about the nature of music.

These two books on vision and hearing were of great importance for psychology. Fechner had shown that psychology could use experiments in which psychological variables could be measured. Helmholtz showed how research techniques in physics and physiology could be applied to answer questions of a psychological character in relation to visual and auditory perception. Helmholtz's main contribution was to demonstrate what could be done by way of designing and executing scientific laboratory experiments. True, many of his problems were strictly within the fields of physics or physiology, but he did include in his great research programme specifically psychological problems. For Helmholtz, psychology did not necessarily require independence of status – it emerged as a group of problems within the experimental investigations of the senses; that it was a branch of experimental physiological science he had no doubt. He demonstrated the existence of a group of psychological problems amenable to investigation by experiment and capable of employing the exact measurement of certain variables. Thus a second and large step was taken towards the establishment of experimental psychology within the sciences.

Apart from his strictly physiological investigations of the mechanisms involved in seeing and hearing – the essential sensory processes on which we depend for our perceptual experiences – Helmholtz had several contributions to make to the psychology of perception, which had become the central topic in systematic psychology in the 1850s.

At Königsberg, he had met with Kant's philosophical ideas which stressed the primacy of 'intuition' in the mind. Basic judgements about what exists and what are the fundamental attributes of things and their relations to each other are made in terms of inborn, innate, native categories. This was in opposition to the view of the British empiricist school of philosophers, who tended to follow Locke's dictum that the mind at birth is a *tabula rasa*. It is only as a result of our experiences, our interactions with the environment through our perceptions, that we come to build up the concepts in terms of which the world is interpreted and understood. Helmholtz scornfully rejected Kantian ideas and vigorously embraced empiricism as the basis for a scientific philosophy. His studies in physics and physiology seemed to confirm the basic assumptions of the empiricists. Hence the British empiricist philosophy of mind was incorporated into Helmholtz's perceptual theories – and bequeathed to Wundt and the Leipzig psychologists.

Helmholtz's doctrine of 'unconscious inference' followed from his empiricism. When we perceive, our conscious experience contains much that is not represented either in the stimulus situation or in the contribution of the receptor mechanisms. Past experience contributes something, but this contribution is unconsciously added to the total reaction. The objects we perceive, together with their changing attributes and relationships, are not simply the effect of external stimuli and the reactions of the sensory-receptor systems. Central processes 'interpret' or 'process' the information to provide a finished perception. Boring's example (*History of Experimental Psychology*, p. 308) of stereoscopic vision illustrates this doctrine: a geometer, with the data of retinal disparity and binocular parallax, could estimate the depth of distant objects in his visual field. Yet, in perceptual experience, he can make valid estimates of distances instantly. Thus 'pure perceptions' are rare. 'Objects' known in perceptual experience are aggregates of sensations. These aggregates are the product of associative and trial-and-error learning where stimuli come regularly together. We 'construct' objects and events on this basis. Helmholtz thus confirmed the general approach of empiricist philosophies and handed on this theoretical orientation to the rising school at Leipzig.

Before leaving Helmholtz, something must be said about his research. His method of tackling three auditory perception problems illustrates his originality as a scientist.

In considering the perception of individual tones, Helmholtz postulated a mechanism in the ear which can receive all the variations of pitch which a person can discriminate. He determined experimentally the highest and lowest pitch and the number of tones in between. Later the basilar membrane, in the inner ear, was found to supply such a postulated mechanism. (The development of the study of this mechanism is traced by S. S. Stevens and H. Davis in *Hearing: Its Psychology and Physiology*, 1938, which shows how clearly the problem was defined by Helmholtz.)

Discrimination of pitch greatly interested Helmholtz. In the course of his investigations, he discovered what underlies differences in tone, quality, and timbre, or why the same note sounds different for different instruments, as middle C on a flute sounds different from middle C on a piano, or middle C sung by a vocalist. Helmholtz discovered that each note is associated with overtones which vibrate more rapidly than the fundamental tone. Using resonators and varying the intensity of the overtones he produced artificially in the laboratory the characteristic 'quality' of different musical instruments – an empirical confirmation of his hypothesis.

He also studied the phenomena of 'discord' and 'harmony' in music, although his theories were less successful in this field. However, his work laid the foundations for nearly all future physiological and psychological research into the sensory processes and perceptual organization. The authority of this great scientist, amply supported by the quality of his research, drew attention to the new development within experimental science – the application of scientific methods to problems in psychology.

WILHELM WUNDT AND THE LEIPZIG SCHOOL

Wundt (1832–1920) is regarded as the first experimental psychologist and the man who established this discipline as a scientific pursuit in its own right. Yet he held a chair of philosophy and wrote several purely philosophical works on logic and ethics. He was not as original a scientist as Helmholtz nor had he Fechner's technical genius. Yet he was a great administrator and a man with a remarkable capacity for work. He left over 500 works – some admittedly short articles, but others being bulky volumes. Of Wundt, however, it may be said that he was first and foremost a psychologist. He deliberately set out to make experimental psychology an independent and self-sufficient discipline within the academic syllabus. He established the first laboratory specially designed and equipped to study psychological problems, and he trained the first generation of students by supervising for the Leipzig Ph.D. degree in psychology. His claim to be the essential founder of experimental psychology – the man to take this third and decisive step – is a firm one.

Wundt was born in 1832, the son of a Lutheran pastor. He was an only child and led a quiet, studious life as a boy. His serious and lonely upbringing was an appropriate beginning for the life of the dedicated, industrious and earnest scientist. 'Humourless, indefatigable, aggressive', Boring calls him. Wundt was well equipped for the prodigious effort of taking psychology out of physiology and systematic philosophy and creating a new discipline.

In 1851 he went to Tübingen to study medicine but transferred to Heidelberg after a year. He qualified in medicine but was drawn to physiology. In 1856 he went to Berlin to study with Johannes Müller. At Berlin he received the stimulus of a broader education, attending Magnus in physics, du Bois-Reymond in physiology. Later in 1856 he returned to Heidelberg as *Dozent* in physiology. Two years later Helmholtz came to Heidelberg and Wundt was appointed his assistant. They worked together for thirteen years until Helmholtz left for Berlin in 1871. The two men respected each other, although they never appear to have become close friends. However, it was during this period of association with Helmholtz that Wundt turned from physiology to the new psychology. The shift was emphasized when he accepted the chair of inductive philosophy at Zurich in 1874.

In 1875 he went to Leipzig as Professor of Philosophy; the philosophy department was also responsible for psychology. It was thus that Wundt founded the German tradition of experimental laboratories within philosophy schools. Wundt had already published his 'system' for a new philosophy in *Grundzüge der physiologischen Psychologie* (1873-4). He soon turned to more active experimental research. In 1879 the first psychological laboratory was established. He soon collected research pupils and assistants. In 1881 he established a journal, *Philosophische Studien*, which published experimental reports as well as theoretical papers in psychology. Leipzig rapidly became the centre of experimental psychology. Kraepelin, Lehmann, Külpe, Meumann, Mentz, Möbius, Wirth, Düre, Klemm, Salow – many of whom were to become the founders of psychology schools in German universities – all studied under Wundt in the 1880s. American pupils, led by Cattell, also flocked to Leipzig; G. S. Hall, Angell, Scripture, Witmer, Warren, Judd are a few who were to become, as we shall see later, founders of psychology in the U.S.A. Titchener and Spearman were Wundt's most distinguished British pupils. Although the new psychology spread rapidly to other centres in Germany and America, Leipzig remained a flourishing and dominant centre until 1914, when everything was disrupted by war.

Wundt argued explicitly for a separate science of psychology. He constructed a system laying down principles and methods and basic technical concepts; he initiated experimental research on major psychological problems and supervised the first generation of research scientists. He wrote massive books systematizing the results of early research and edited the first journal in which papers could be published. All this demanded a rare combination of talents.

Wundt's work falls into two main categories: systematic thinking about scope and methods, and experimental research. His system was developed and modified between 1858 and 1920, while his research proceeded steadily throughout his long and industrious life. His *Beitrage*, published in parts between 1858 and 1862, was a formal argument for an independent science of psychology, together with an account of early experimental research. The *Physiologische Psychologie* (first published in 1873-4 and revised, expanded and rewritten in 1880, 1887 and 1911) expounded his system – the methods and principles of experimental psychology – and presented all his experimental results to date. The *Grundzüge der Physiologischen Psychologie* (1874) was a systematic handbook which expounded some of his basic principles. In the 1880s Wundt fulfilled his obligations as a philosophy professor (nominally) by writing purely philosophical works (*Logik*, 1883; *Ethik*, 1886; *System der Philosophie*, 1889) – the latter being 2,500 pages of scholarly argument. In the 1890s, he turned to problems in psychology which could not be studied in the laboratory – thinking, language use, social customs, etc. These he called '*Volkerpsychologie*' (folk psychology), and anthropological research provided the basic data for psychological discussion in this large and diverse field. Between 1900 and 1920 Wundt published ten volumes of 'folk psychology'. His interests were by no means confined to laboratory studies and he did not regard experiment as the only valid instrument for investigating psychological problems.

Wundt's systematic psychology and his empirical work both deserve separate mention.

Psychology required some definition concerning its scope, methods, basic principles and assumptions. Wundt worked these out in detail. The methods were simply those of experimental physiology as developed by such scientists as Helmholtz. A controllable and measurable stimulus is presented to a subject under conditions known to the experimenter and a response is observed or reported. The introspection of intervening processes between stimulus and response is essential, since the immediate contents of consciousness are the subject matter of psychology. The use of scientific instruments may make both the reporting of mental states and the observation of response more accurate. Wundt's conception of experimental psychology was original – no one had previously laid down the principles to be followed for a general science of the mind. Yet he borrowed many fundamental ideas from the British empiricist tradition, following J. S. Mill's systematic psychology closely. The subject matter of psychology is the individual consciousness. Sensations (the product of sense-organs being stimulated and nervous impulses reaching the cortex) are the ultimate elements out of which our experience is built. Physiology explains how we come to have particular sensations, but the description and analysis of immediate experience is the task of psychology. Sensations must be classified into separate 'modes' (visual, auditory, olfactory, kinaesthetic, etc.) and their attributes determined along specific dimensions (intensity, duration, extension, etc.). Images are derived from sensations and are the result of similar cortical activity. Experience exhibits certain attributes which are not derived from the sensory-receptor system. Wundt used the term 'feeling' to indicate these. In 1893 he devised a theory of feelings. They could be classified along these dimensions: pleasant – unpleasant; tense – relaxed; excited – depressed.

Elements combine to form complex states of consciousness, and complexes of sensory elements have each a characteristic feeling-tone. In sequences, such feelings exhibit regularities of development of the kind we recognize as 'emotions'. Acts of will are simply a sequence of feelings with identical contents which are related to reflex acts in such a way as to produce action of an 'adaptive' character. Evolutionary processes have shaped our basic emotional-drive sequences and the acts associated with them. Reflex acts, sensations, images, feelings, emotions, voluntary acts – all these are fundamental processes in terms of which conscious experience can be analysed. What integrates these elements and gives the mind its unity? Wundt used the term 'apperception' to describe the process whereby certain elements are focused and made dominant in consciousness. The organization which follows an act of apperception was a complex act of 'creative synthesis'. Thus any reaction could be analysed in terms of the scheme: Stimulation – Perception (mere presentation of sensa in consciousness) – Apperception (identification, appropriation, synthesis) – Will (feelings summate to emotive-drive issuing in action).

The analogy with J. S. Mill's psychology is close. Both men adopt an atomistic approach to the field of consciousness, modified by an emphasis on the unity of the subject, the activity of the whole being towards purposeful action. Wundt made considerable use also of 'association' as an important process. Elements do not simply become associated successively and continuously in that whenever A appears, B immediately follows. Elements can become fused into complexes so that one simultaneously arouses several others. 'Assimilation' and 'complication' processes also involve associations (for example between elements of different modalities).

Wundt's system was simply the application of well-tried methods in physiology and psychophysics to problems which had already been defined by philosophical thinking and physiological research. Physiological psychology was simply the use of physiological techniques to study sensory processes and perception.

The empirical work of the Leipzig laboratory, although simply developing and systematizing the experimental work already done by Fechner, Helmholtz and Weber, was nevertheless important. It demonstrated that experimental psychology had work to do and could produce results. Between 1881 and 1903 *Philosophische Studien* reported about one hundred researches. About a third of these dealt with 'sensation', and just under 60 per cent with 'sensation and perception' topics. Indeed, Wundt's research could be classified under four headings: vision and hearing experiments; reaction experiments; psychophysical experiments; and association experiments.

For the first time a number of psychologists were working together as psychologists and publishing results. Although the experiments might have fitted many systematic psychological presentations other than Wundt's, his views did supply a theoretical justification for the new enterprise. What work was done in this early phase of experimenting? At first, perhaps under the influence of Helmholtz, sensation and perception were the dominant fields, with a greater interest in visual perception than in other sensory modes. Experiments on colour discrimination, visual contrast, after-images, binocular vision, the perception of 'form' and optical illusions were popular. Psychophysical studies of the relation between controlled light stimuli and the reactions of the retina were made. Kirschmann carried out studies of colour blindness; Titchener's celebrated work on binocular vision and Thiéry's studies of optical illusions all began along a tradition of experimental investigations which continues today.

The group developed psychophysical studies of touch and of hearing (tonal fusion, analysis of intervals). Most characteristic, however, were the reaction experiments. Wundt regarded these as important, since he hoped to use the basic experimental design to investigate the three postulated stages between stimulus and response (perception – apperception – will). The reaction experiment was derived partly from the 'personal equation' problem in astronomical observation and partly from Helmholtz's measurement of the speed of nervous impulse in the sensory nerves. In a simple reaction a subject reacts as quickly as possible to a single stimulus by pressing a key. In discrimination reaction he reacts to one stimulus (for example a red light) by pressing a key but not to a second (a green light). In choice reaction he reacts with the right hand to one stimulus (red) but with the left hand to another (green).

Reaction times were measured in different conditions – for example the subject would first attend primarily to the signal and the results would be compared to those of another experiment in which he attends primarily to his finger movements. In the latter experiment, it was found that reaction times were noticeably longer if the subject attended to the stimulus than if he concentrated on his movement. Wundt hypothesized that this was due to the process of 'apperception', and he hoped to be able to use the experimental set-up to measure the time taken for apperception to occur, and perhaps also to study certain features of the complex part played by reaction in perception. However, this programme received a blow from one of Wundt's pupils, Külpe (pp. 84 ff.), who showed in 1891 that the procedure was suspect. When conditions of reaction are made complex it is not the case that one process is added while others remain unchanged. The whole task is changed from start to finish. In spite of this, the reaction experiment yielded many simple findings. For example, much was discovered about individual differences in the ability to compare intervals – to reproduce intervals of varying length on request, or to estimate an interval when the beginning and end are signalled by different types of stimuli. Again, Wundt's development of the word-association experiment devised by Galton (p. 103–16) in the 1870s was highly successful.

In many ways Wundt's experiments were unadventurous, pedestrian and over-indebted to traditional methods. Yet their thoroughness, and the fact that they concentrated on a narrow field that could be well and truly explored gave a valuable impetus to this first major attempt to establish experimental psychology. It may be that Wundt was not so gifted an experimental scientist as he was a philosopher of science. However, his experiments successfully demonstrated the validity of his psychological system and of his arguments for a science of psychology. His achievement in establishing the Leipzig laboratory and initiating the new discipline with such thoroughness, competence and energy cannot be underestimated.

CHAPTER FOUR

Psychology in Germany 1880–1914

ALTHOUGH academics specializing in the new psychology
soon appeared in the German and Austrian universities,
psychology still continued to be influenced by other scientists. Ewald Hering (1834–1918), a man of great eminence
who was professor of physiology at Prague (1870–95) and
Leipzig (1895–1918), had studied under Fechner in his
student days at Leipzig. He disputed several of Helmholtz's theories. Helmholtz had argued that space forms
are built up in experience and that we learn the location
of the local signs. Hering argued that each retinal point
has three local signs (for height, right–left position, and
depth). Helmholtz was an empiricist in his theory of space
perception; Hering a nativist, believing that given functions of the nervous system determine how we perceive – a
point of view that continued into Gestalt psychology in
the twentieth century. Hering was a gifted experimenter
and his invention of apparatus greatly benefited experimental psychology (the Hering window for contrast effects,
the colour-mixer, and the Hering stereoscope, to mention
only three familiar pieces). His influence during the two
decades before 1914 as a leading German scientist in the
physiology of vision was considerable, especially as a critic
of Helmhotz and Wundt.

HERMANN EBBINGHAUS

The period was dominated by Leipzig, but there were
other men of eminence in German psychology. The most
original was Hermann Ebbinghaus (1850–1909). He studied
at Bonn, Berlin and Halle between 1867 and 1870, specializing in history and philosophy. He graduated in 1873
after serving in the army during the Franco-Prussian War.

For seven years he lived as a private scholar, visiting France and England. In France he came across a copy of Fechner's *Elemente*, which greatly excited him. In England he studied the works of associationist psychologists.

It occurred to him that exact experimental methods might be applied to such higher mental functions as memory, as well as to sensation, and he proceeded to devise experiments, with himself as subject and experimenter, to test out the possibility. The result of this self-taught psychologist's efforts was a new type of experiment, which still remains a stock-in-trade of the experimental psychologist. In 1880 Ebbinghaus went to Berlin as a *Dozent* and in 1885, after intensive work involving incredible self-organization as subject-experimenter, he published his treatise on memory (*Über das Gedächtnis*), a work whose contents are still quoted in contemporary textbooks. A professorship came to him (most justifiably) the following year, and he remained at Berlin until 1894, when he accepted the chair of philosophy at Breslau. He died at the age of 59, in 1909, after spending his last few years at Halle.

From 1886 onwards he left 'memory' alone and confined himself to three contributions to experimental psychology: psychophysical researches into colour contrast; the founding of a new journal (*Zeitschrift für Psychologie*), which gave opportunities for psychologists outside the Leipzig school to publish their work; and the writing of a brilliant, lucid, yet rigorous textbook, *Grundzüge der Psychologie*, which he did not live to complete. Volume 1 appeared in 1902, but the second volume was not finished by Ebbinghaus – although Dürr wrote it up from his notes. His reputation rests partly on this remarkable original textbook together with his treatise on memory.

It is not possible, in the limited space of a general history, to do justice to Ebbinghaus's work on remembering and forgetting – not only the first, but one of the most successful, attempts to study a 'higher mental process' experimentally. However, some mention must be made of its contents. Ebbinghaus made two useful technical innovations. He adapted statistical methods from physics, whereby the accuracy of an observation could be estimated through the variability of several observations about a mean. He was able to disregard variable errors through repeating observations to an extent that errors in one direction were roughly cancelled by those in the opposite direction. Secondly, he eliminated qualitative variable error by getting rid of all meaning in the data to be learnt in his experiments. Words have associations from past experience which might make it easier for a certain person to learn them. Ebbinghaus therefore invented over 2,000 'nonsense' syllables – artificial words like 'dak', 'var' and 'zub'. When such syllables are combined in groups, differences in difficulty between them can be treated as variable errors. Nonsense syllables presented in series were the basic material to be learnt by rote and tested in terms of how many could be reproduced. Since any set of syllables were of equal difficulty, an experiment could be repeated several times and an average result obtained with reference to basic measurements.

By averaging the number of repetitions of lists of varying length, before one errorless reproduction, Ebbinghaus estimated 'memory span'. He found that he could recall up to 7 syllables at one attempt. However, he needed fifteen repetitions to learn 12 syllables and fifty repetitions to learn 30. (This is the 'learning method'.) This design proved capable of refinement in the hands of succeeding experimentalists, especially J. M. Cattell (pp. 137 ff).

In another set of experiments, Ebbinghaus investigated what happens when a series is practised beyond the point at which learning is complete (overlearning). He introduced the 'saving method', whereby the amount of effort needed to recall old learning is estimated. A subject is given two lists of nonsense syllables with 40 items in each and learns both until they can be recalled without error or prompting; he is then tested twenty-four hours afterwards. It may be that the same number of items can be recalled in each list the following day (say 14). However, the first list may now require only twenty practice run-throughs to enable the subject to regain the whole of it, while the second list may need thirty. This simple approach gave a better estimate of retention than measuring the number of items recalled or forgotten. It was also possible to compare how much work is required, after a lapse of time, to relearn material, distinguishing between material that has been learnt (and no more) and material which has been overlearnt (it may take twenty repetitions to learn a list to a fixed criterion of accuracy, but thirty-two to enable the subject to recall it without error twenty-four hours later). Overlearning may save time, since a list learned, but only just learned, may require thirty or more repetitions next day if it is to be recalled. Ebbinghaus worked out the ratio of overlearning to saving of effort, and showed that the number of repetitions saved was about one third of the number of repetitions required for overlearning – additional amounts of overlearning produced uniform amounts of saving. This enabled 'forgetting' to be studied quantitatively – decrements resulting from varying intervals between learning and recall could be plotted on 'curves' of forgetting. This proved a fruitful experimental pattern and is still employed, with refinements and improvements, in contemporary work.

Ebbinghaus also studied the efficiency of different strategies of practice. Is it better to learn a series in one session or to split practice up into shorter periods with rest intervals between each shorter session? Is 'massed' or 'spaced' practice more efficient? Ebbinghaus demonstrated in a series of experiments that in the rote learning of nonsense syllables 'spaced' repetition was more efficient than 'continuous' repetition.

These were a few of the many experimental schemes which he invented and exploited in his celebrated monograph. As much as any experimental study, they revealed the ability of psychologists to adapt the methods of experimental science and statistics to the study of human behaviour. Although his output was slight compared with

78

that of Wundt, Ebbinghaus revealed what the Leipzig psychologists failed to reveal – that imaginative, original and fruitful experiments could be contrived in psychology and that the new science was not merely an application of safe and sure techniques already worked out by physiologists and physicists.

G. E. MÜLLER

G. E. Müller was born in the same year as Ebbinghaus, but lived until 1934. For forty years (1881–1921) he exercised a considerable influence on German psychology, and was reported in 1892 by an American visitor as having one of the finest research laboratories for psychology in Germany. He was purely an experimental psychologist, with no tendencies towards philosophical theories or systematizing of results. His chief fields of research were psychophysics, visual perception and, following the publication of Ebbinghaus, memory. He had a flourishing school and trained many men in psychology who were later to become distinguished in the subject. Indeed he may be said to share with Wundt the credit for training the first generation of experimental psychologists in Europe. F. Schumann (later professor at Frankfurt), Külpe (of Würzburg fame – see pp. 84 ff.), Alfons Pilzecker (a distinguished researcher into kinaesthetic sensations), David Katz and Edgar Rubin (two of the founders of Gestalt psychology – see pp. 243 ff.) were all assistants to Müller. Jaensch and Spearman (p. 186), two distinguished figures in the 1920s, also studied as Müller's research students.

Müller was born in Saxony and studied philosophy and history at Leipzig. In 1869 he went to Berlin to continue his humanistic studies, which were interrupted by service in the Prussian army during the Franco-Prussian war. Like many men since, Müller found that military service shook him out of his previous interests. He became interested in a scientific approach to philosophy and wrote a degree thesis.

During a long and severe illness, which forced him to convalesce with his parents, he studied psychophysics and corresponded with Fechner. He wrote a thesis on the methods of psychophysics which in 1876 won him a job at Göttingen. Apart from a short period as Professor at Czernowitz (1880–81), he remained at Göttingen for the rest of his life. Lotze (p. 33) went to Berlin in 1881 and Müller succeeded him as Professor of Philosophy. In the next forty years he made Göttingen a centre for experimental psychology which rivalled Leipzig.

What made Müller, who had no scientific training, so central a figure? Part of the answer is that he was a dedicated and highly competent experimentalist.

In the first part of his career, he carried out a programme of research along fairly orthodox lines, studying the variables influencing judgements of weight and also problems in the field of tactual space perception. Then, in 1896–7, he published articles on colour vision. He attempted to overcome the deficiencies in Hering's theory (p. 75) by arguing that the three basic dimensions (black-white, yellow-blue, red-green) depend on reversible photochemical substances. He also argued that the molecular action of the cortex arouses a constant grey, as a sort of 'base'. Hering had postulated a complicated compound of sensations, the elements of which were exactly weighted to neutralize each other, except that a slight mixing of factors results in grey. Müller's theory was not only simpler; he was able to produce some empirical evidence to support it. It was Müller's theory which came to overshadow Hering's, although it embodies many of Hering's assumptions.

Müller's greatest work was on memory. He took the research up at the point at which Ebbinghaus left it. Müller used the revolving drum, which enabled data to be presented to subjects in a uniform manner and at a rate of exposure which could be exactly controlled and varied by the experimenter. A slot in the drum enables the observer to receive one syllable or word in one unit of time. He also devised a method for constructing lists of nonsense syllables of equal difficulty – thus improving the basic experiments.

Müller and his assistants devised the 'method of hits' in which a syllable is presented and the subject has to recall the one which followed it in a list he had already learned. This technique allowed for the measuring of speed of recall, which Müller demonstrated to be an index of the strength of an association. He also developed the 'method of paired associates'. Mary Calkins, an American pupil, had invented this method of presenting pairs of items (having no relation) such as a word and a number. Pairs early and late in a series were contrasted with pairs in the middle; those pairs which were frequently presented were contrasted with those less frequently presented; thus the influence of recency, frequency, etc., were investigated in the forming of associations. Müller adopted this technique and used it to investigate many new variables in rote-learning. He demonstrated how 'attitude' was important. Mere repetition was less efficient than fewer repetitions with an intention to learn quickly. He found that the middle terms in a series are more difficult to learn than those at the beginning or the end, and that when two associations are of equal strength a repetition strengthens the older established of the two.

Again, Müller demonstrated that it is often more efficient to learn 'wholes' (going through material from start to finish without interruptions) than to learn 'parts' (dividing the material into bits and learning each small part separately). The role of 'whole', as contrasted with 'part' learning in different contexts, became a topic in the study of retention and recall. Thus the old 'laws of association' became investigated quantitatively by the application of the methods of the laboratory, a distinct achievement for a young science. Müller's authority as a psychologist drew able pupils from all over Europe and from America. This authority is measured by the fact that Titchener's second volume of *Experimental Psychology* was postponed by two years because Müller published a handbook of psychophysics in 1903. So much new and important material was assembled in Müller's book that Titchener had to include most of it in his comprehensive textbook.

CARL STUMPF

Another figure, independent of Leipzig and important as the founder of psychology at Prague and Munich as well as in Berlin (where he was professor from 1894–1922), was Carl Stumpf (1848–1936). Stumpf was essentially a philosopher who was also a very fine musician. He could play six musical instruments competently and had a thorough mastery of theory. He studied philosophy at Würzburg (1865–7) and Göttingen. At Würzburg he was captivated by the philosopher Franz Brentano (1838–1917), and was converted to his view that the methods of the physical sciences are the only true philosophical methods. Lotze at Göttingen encouraged his interest in science, and he took courses in physics and physiology. He succeeded Brentano at Würzburg as professor in 1873, and after six years began his academic wanderings to Prague, Halle, Munich and finally Berlin (1894).

He cultivated scientific psychology simply in the interests of his philosophical pursuits. However, he is important for a variety of reasons. In the first place he pursued empirical work of a highly original character. His love of music led him to study psychological problems of tone. His researches were published in two volumes, the celebrated *Tonpsychologie*, in 1883 and 1890. This was the most important work on the psychology of the sense of hearing since Helmholtz, and it has since shared an honoured place with the *Tonempfindungen* as a classic in our knowledge of sounds. He isolated and studied the psychological phenomenon of 'tonal fusion' – the fact that tones an octave apart seem to 'fuse' and that this involves musical consonance; while if a tone is sounded with another a semi-tone above it, then the two are heard as musically discordant. He studied the phenomenon both acoustically and from the point of view of musical theory. He derived several laws from his researches to explain fusion, for example: (1) degree of fusion is a function of the vibration ratio of the component; (2) degree of fusion is the same for any octave interval (i.e. for 3rd and 10th, 5th and 12th); (3) degree of fusion is not affected by timbre – by qualities of the instrument producing the tones. He also studied the attributes of tones – pitch, loudness, brightness. volume.

This work demonstrated that experimental psychology could do more than study psychophysical or visual illusion problems – it gave insight into the nature of musical appreciation hitherto unknown. In the first volume of the work, Stumpf also revised many of the basic concepts of psychophysics, and the many things he had to say on attention, fatigue, analysis and comparison stimulated discussion in systematic psychology. Also, his view that the interpenetration of separate tones to produce a total perception different from the sum of its parts was an anticipation of a basic Gestalt conception (Chapter 13).

Stumpf's second claim to importance is his theoretical orientation. Brentano, whose influence was a dominant factor in Stumpf's thinking, had published *Psychologie vom empirischen Standpunkte* in 1874. In this work, Brentano attacked the view of the British empiricists – and of Helmholtz and Wundt – that consciousness may be analysed into contents (sensations, images and feelings) as the basic elements of experience. Mental 'acts' are the fundamental category. We experience sensations, but what is basic is the activity of seeing colours, shapes and objects, hearing sounds, feeling ourselves move. The activity of the mind in judging, sensing, imagining, hating, etc., is the true object of psychological studies. The mind is creative and interpretive in that any act is intentional – it implies and 'demands' an object. We cannot see without seeing *something* or other – even if we are wrong about what we believe it to be. Stumpf followed Brentano in his systematic writings. Psychology must study 'functions', such as perceiving, desiring, willing, conceiving; and also

'relations' among the objects and events which we in-
tuitively recognize in experience.

This divergence from the orthodox 'empiricism' of
Wundt's system, with its analysis of consciousness into con-
tents, formed more than a half-way stage between the early
German psychology and the Gestalt school of the 1920s.
It is not insignificant that both Koffka and Köhler, two
leaders of Gestalt theory (Chapter 13), were pupils of
Stumpf at Berlin and that Wertheimer was also a pupil
and a close associate of Stumpf's chief associate, Schumann.
The Berlin school was never as influential as those of
Leipzig or Göttingen, but it was large and well equipped
by 1900, and trained several independent-minded experi-
mentalists.

KÜLPE AND THE WÜRZBURG SCHOOL

The most original and divergent group of psychologists in
Germany at the time worked at the University of Würzburg between 1900 and 1914. The leader was Oswald
Külpe (1862–1913). Born in Latvia, Külpe went to study
at Leipzig in 1881 and specialized in history. He fell under
the spell of Wundt's philosophy and became interested in
experimental psychology. In 1883, he went to Göttingen
as a pupil of G. E. Müller and wrote his doctoral disserta-
tion in experimental psychology after three years' research.
After a last flirtation with historical studies, he finally
chose psychology, working as Wundt's assistant at Leipzig
from 1886 until 1894. He did a considerable amount of
experimental work in the Leipzig laboratory and published two books. His *Grundriss der Psychologie* (1893)
was an exposition of Wundt's system, and was translated
into English by Titchener (*Outlines of Psychology*, 1895),
remaining an authoritative book for many years. His second book was a manual of experimental psychology reporting the Leipzig work in detail. In 1894, he was appointed
professor at Würzburg and became interested for the next
six years in purely philosophical problems. Two important

philosophical texts and a treatise on Kant were the fruits of these years.

However, Külpe did not neglect his major interest. He directed the work at the Würzburg laboratory with vigour and encouraged new approaches to the possibilities of experimental psychology. He felt that Ebbinghaus had pointed to limitations in the work of the Leipzig school, with its psychophysical techniques and its emphasis on sensation and perception. Thinking as well as learning and memorizing should be investigated. Külpe's thinking as director stimulated an able group of assistants and research students, and it was their experiments which emerged in the first decade of the twentieth century to stir up controversy within Germany.

K. Marbe, who was to succeed Külpe in the Würzburg chair, published his study of the judgement of weights in 1901. Marbe found that in judging which of two weights was the heavier, no sensory or imaginal contents occurred as basis for an act of judgement. Various vague 'attitudes' (*Bewusstseinslagen*) passed through consciousness – hesitation, doubt, waiting for an answer. The intelligent response did not result from comparing images of the two reactions in 'weighing'.

H. J. Watt, a Scot who later taught psychology at Glasgow but who at the time was working under Külpe, then attacked thought-processes directly. His method was to present a stimulus word and require the subject to produce a response word under varying 'constraints' which formulated a specific 'task' (given a species word, name a coordinate species; given a word naming a 'whole', respond by naming a part, etc.). Watt devised the procedure of breaking down the experimental situation into phases: (*a*) the preparatory phase in which the task is defined, (*b*) the appearance of the stimulus word, (*c*) the searching for the reaction word, (*d*) the occurrence of the reaction. He concentrated in each experiment on one phase only, so that the subject could explore his reactions thoroughly.

Watt discovered that it was the first phase only which

was of any importance in determining the reaction. Once the '*Aufgabe*' or task is conceived, the subject is ready to respond. 'Thought' occurs spontaneously on the presentation of the stimulus. Sensations, images or 'acts' do not occur during stages *b–d*. It is a 'set' or 'readiness' established at phase *a* which controls the behaviour. This was a shock for those who had implicitly accepted the assumptions of British empiricism, associationism, and Wundt's systematic theory. Psychology existed to observe, describe and analyse the contents of consciousness, but in intelligent judging, choosing and deciding there were no contents.

This finding was confirmed independently by papers published in the same year by Binet in France (pp. 191 ff.) and Woodworth in America (pp. 273 ff.) – in cognitive tasks subjects reported that important aspects of the experience yielded no sensory or imaginal contents.

In 1905 at Würzburg Ach wrote a monograph reporting further Würzburg researches, in which he introduced the concept of 'determining tendency' to describe a factor which links associations, habits and skills into an orderly purposeful sequence, from the '*Aufgabe*' established at the beginning to the conclusion of a task requiring thinking. Ach performed experiments in which conflicts between strongly established associations and determining tendencies were established, and the associations broken or overcome by the unconscious working of the 'determining tendency'. This work established a new kind of investigation – the study of the factors involved in a task in which positive choice or decision is the response.

Other Würzburgers, Messer and Karl Bühler, published further experiments. Bühler introduced a clinical interview technique to elicit information from his subjects which shocked pure experimentalists. Bühler's theoretical writing emphasized the non-sensory character of many items in consciousness during cognitive tasks, and he argued that there were 'thought elements' which did not belong to the same category as sensations or images. Imageless thought depended on processes which Wundt and Helmholtz had failed to discriminate.

In 1909 Külpe left Würzburg for Bonn. In 1912 he published an article summarizing the results of the Würzburg school, and a year later, at the age of 53, he died, leaving a large programme unfinished. He regarded the work done at Würzburg under his direction as preliminary to new developments which would effect a major shift in psychology. He did not either live to see this development or leave any sufficient projects to begin it. With his death, the Würzburg school ceased to function and its members went their various ways, soon to be diverted by the catastrophic upheavals of the First World War and the subsequent changes in the course of psychology.

What was the achievement of this short-lived organization of psychologists in a small German university? In some respects they were negative – providing a shock and making psychologists re-think the principles on which experimental psychology in Germany had been established.

They convinced many that the conditions which influence our behaviour in thinking and choice are not present in consciousness. Consciousness, as the field for investigation, description, analysis and measurement, provides no data for important aspects of behaviour. This was a negative but shattering hypothesis, since it exposed the limits of the experimental research so far accomplished in Germany. Introspection – the essential instrument of psychological research – although used by the Würzburgers, was revealed as less useful than had been uncritically assumed for centuries. Moreover, introspection came under critical review as the result of the bitter and public dispute over 'imageless thought' which Wundt started. Wundt attacked the Würzburg research in scathing terms. He argued that their experiments disregarded fundamental principles of scientific observation and that their conclusions were invalid. Titchener, a pupil and to a considerable extent a disciple of the Leipzig school, attacked 'imageless thought' in his book *The Experimental Psychology of the Thought*

Processes (1909). He accepted Watt's 'determining tendencies' as a valid empirical concept, but argued that the vague 'attitudes' and 'sets' were reducible to sensory contents which had their origin in kinaesthetic and organic sensations involved in thinking.

This attitude of opposition led the Würzburg psychologists to increase their efforts to prove their theses in experiment. J. R. Angell at Chicago (a pupil of Külpe's – see Chapter 6), R. S. Woodworth (who had produced similar data – see Chapter 15), together with Marbe and Messer and Bühler, produced new experimental results. Titchener's pupils tried to repeat the Würzburg experiments – finding sensory contents of the kind which fitted their theory. This dispute, where introspection under laboratory conditions failed to produce agreement among experimental psychologists about the data observed, led many to come to regard introspection as a weak instrument. It provided Watson, Thorndike and others, who were formulating new conceptions about the proper scope and methods of psychology, with a powerful argument for their new programme of 'Behaviourism'.

In emphasizing that little occurred between the stimulus and the reaction in their experiments, the Würzburgers shifted the emphasis from content of consciousness to conduct or response. Their theory that much organization goes on below the threshold of consciousness reinforced the view of the rising psycho-analytic schools, that many unconscious processes play a crucial part in human nature. Thus the small group of researchers made a contribution from within experimental psychology to the revolutionary movements which were to disrupt psychology during and after the First World War.

However, the Würzburg group were a minority and came late in the pre-war period. Leipzig and Wundt dominated German psychology from 1880 onwards and it was Wundt's pupils who were identified as the leaders of the 'new psychology'. Ernst Meumann (1862–1915), who taught at Zürich, Münster and Hamburg; Alfred Lehmann (1858–1921) of Copenhagen; Lunge, Kieschmann, Kiesow, Mentz, Mosch, Möbius, Wirth, Duff, Kreiger, Klemm – all these men carried on Wundt's work in German universities, while Titchener took the Leipzig type of experimental psychology to the U.S.A. at Cornell in 1892.

Experimental psychology aimed at the description and analysis of the contents of consciousness in terms of sensations, images and feelings, attempting to isolate and measure the basic attributes of the elements out of which complex states of mind were built up. Psychophysical methods, elaborate 'brass' instrumentation apparatus derived from experimental physiology and statistical formulae, were applied to make the old associationist-empiricist philosophy of mind into an empirical and experimental science. This systematic viewpoint had already been challenged in America in the late 1890s, but it was soon to meet further criticisms. Down to 1914, the 'new psychology' had presented a coherent consistent theory, and a group of experimental results which fitted neatly into a pattern. It looked as if experimental psychology was established on firm foundations and was going to make slow but certain progress along these lines, finally settling down, along with physics and physiology, as another branch of experimental science. Physics and physiology simply studied the same phenomena from different angles. Psychology studied what appears in human consciousness; physiology studies how the brain and nervous system function in order to produce the final result – conscious experience; while physics studies the objects and events known only to consciousness but independently of the properties attributed to the external world by the human knower. This appearance of scientific psychology was soon to alter out of all recognition.

Many of the assumptions of Wundt and the other German experimentalists were to be challenged as invalid – as borrowings from epistemological theories which could no longer be defended. By the 1920s psychology – even experimental and physiological departments of psychology – became an affair of rival 'schools', each with its own view about the proper scope, methods and principles which psychology should adopt as a science of behaviour and experience. In spite of their minor disagreements, the Germans in Wundt's time were fundamentally in agreement about their new science. Soon their two basic assumptions – 'psychology as the science of consciousness' and 'introspection as the essentially psychological method' – were to be discarded by many psychologists. The new psychology was soon to become the old psychology. Indeed when one looks back on the work of the Germans up to 1914, much of it seems remote and archaic – to be dismissed as introspectionist, mentalistic, elementarist, and pursued with instruments that measured comparatively trivial attributes.

The work of this generation of experimental scientists must not be dismissed so cavalierly. Much of it was sound and has become incorporated within the results of more sophisticated research. In cases where measurement was done for measurement's sake, or trivial experiments were conducted on peripheral data, at least techniques and skill in psychological laboratory experiments were being practised. The transition from the philosophy of mind to empirical psychology was made, and not without its successes – as in the work of Fechner and Ebbinghaus. The work of these liberal Germans, who were often gifted musicians and learned humanists as well as original scientists, cannot be underestimated in the shaping of psychology as an independent discipline. Even if some of their discourse is as remote as the life they led, in an imperial Germany that is far removed from the Germany of a century later, it is still worth studying for its dedication, industry and, sometimes, its imagination.

If the British laid the foundations for modern psychology in their philosophy and through their physiologists, the Germans took over much of the physiological research and turned one branch of it into experimental psychology. It was left to the Americans to advance the new discipline towards the status of being much more than an offshoot of physiology. There were other factors at work as early as the 1850s and 1860s which were to take psychologists off in other directions than those defined clearly by Wundt. To these other influences we must now turn.

CHAPTER FIVE

The Evolutionary Doctrine

CHARLES DARWIN:
BIOLOGIST AND PSYCHOLOGIST

THE year 1859, when Charles Darwin (1809–82) published *The Origin of Species by Natural Selection*, is an important date in the history of psychology. The concept of evolution had a long history before Darwin, but the Darwinian theory brought the evolutionary thesis to the notice of all intelligent readers and produced impressive empirical evidence in its support. Darwin was influenced in formulating his theory by reading two works, neither of them biological: Lyell's *Principles of Geology* (1830–33) and Malthus's *Essay on the Principles of Population* (1798).

Lyell suggested that evolution is a *fact*. He argued that the rock strata found in the Earth's crust have been formed through a series of major crises in the history of the planet. Different strata have evolved at different times, the product of specific and datable major changes. This thesis suggested to Darwin that organic matter might also have evolved from simple to complex forms through a succession of historical changes over long periods of time.

During his voyage on the *Beagle* with a scientific expedition to the South Seas (1831–6), Darwin had been able to observe a wide variety of species existing in this isolated set of islands. He asked himself: 'Why is each particular species of plant and animal so perfectly adapted to the conditions of its environment?' He noticed the obvious fact that out of every generation of a particular species some individuals survive and reproduce while others die before they can reproduce. What principle, if any, governs this 'selection' of survivors? What governs the size of population for any given species at any given period, and why do certain specific 'types' within a species survive while others fail to do so?

In 1838, after returning to England from his scientific exploration, Darwin happened to read Malthus's *Essay*. The subject of this treatise is the relation of birth-rate to death-rate. Rightly or otherwise, Malthus believed that all improvements in output of food would follow an arithmetical progression (an increase by a constant quantity such as 1–3–5 ...), while increase in human population would conform to a geometrical progression (an increase by a constant ratio such as 1–3–9 ...). Hence, there would be an excess of population in relation to the available amount of food per head. Granted this grim situation, if humanity is to survive as a whole some individuals must be eliminated. All will die of starvation unless a sufficient minority of unfortunates dies off and leaves sufficient food for the survivors. Malthus thought that disease, infant mortality and starvation, supported by war, suffice to keep the balance of food against empty stomachs. The basic hypothesis is, therefore, that the number of offspring in any one generation is invariably greater than the number able to subsist on the available resources necessary for life. There is a struggle for existence among human beings (or rather a struggle for the control of the means of subsistence) in which the stronger survive at the expense of the weak.

The theory remains controversial. However, its present significance is that it supplied Darwin with the hypothesis for which he was struggling. Darwin had noticed that in most of the species he had studied in the field, the number tends to remain stationary, although there are always in each generation more offspring than parents. Having read Malthus, Darwin was, in his own words, 'well prepared to appreciate the struggle for existence ... it at once struck me that ... favourable variations would tend to be preserved and unfavourable ones destroyed. The result would be the formation of a new species.'

Darwin's theory of evolution may be briefly characterized by reference to three concepts:

(1) Variation. Members of a single species vary among
themselves. Variations survive only if they are well
adapted to their surroundings.

Thus environment can influence variations – acting
either on the whole organism or only on some part of
it – and thus produce radical changes. The slight
variations which offspring exhibit from their parents
are the raw material out of which major variations
develop. 'Owing to this struggle for existence, any
variations, however slight, and from whatever cause,
if it be in any degree profitable to an individual ... in
its infinitely complex relations to other organic beings
and to its physical conditions of life, will be inherited.'

(2) The struggle for existence. The 'struggle' is a consequence of the fact that plants and animals produce
more offspring than can possibly survive. Either individual struggles with individual within the species, or
species contest against each other for means of subsistence; or else the living thing merely struggles
against the physical conditions of its environment
(plants on the edge of a desert with superior water-
storage mechanisms have a better chance of survival
than others).

(3) Natural selection. 'As many more individuals of each
species are born than can possibly survive: and as,
consequently, there is a frequently recurring struggle
for existence, it follows that any being, if it vary however slightly in any manner profitable to itself ... will
have a better chance of surviving, and thus be naturally
selected.' Darwin had little empirical data to support
this hypothesis except an analogy with the facts of
artificial selection operated by humans in breeding
domestic animals with special characteristics (game
dogs, for example). He argued there must be analogous
influences at work in nature, selecting those varieties
of a species best fitted to survive in a specific environ-

ment. In support of this analogy, Darwin argued that human animal breeders do not originate the variations on which they work – they simply strengthen desirable variations which exist. The breeder provides an artificial control for a natural process: nature provides her own controls for the same natural process. The theory, of course, left speculative the mechanisms which are involved in developing an 'ability' to adapt and survive.

Darwin was not content to rest on his laurels. In 1871 he published *The Descent of Man*, in which he argued that man was descended from an ape-like ancestor. That man has evolved through a long series of developments from simpler animal forms was an obvious hypothesis suggested by the original theory of evolution. In discussing this relationship to lower animals, Darwin suggested that man's intellectual powers were different only in degree and not in kind from certain vertebrates.

This extension of the theory provoked a violent reaction from the public. Theologians were shocked at the open contradiction of the doctrine that man had been specially created by God, and many feared the consequences for society of this 'lowering' of the human status.

The controversy reinforced Darwin's keen interest in the psychological consequences of his general biological theories. He turned to psychological researches in defence of his thesis that human and animal behaviour are in many ways similar, since man is as much a product of evolution as any other living thing. In so doing, he became one of the first empirical psychologists in an entirely new tradition. His major work is still one of the classics of psychology: *The Expression of the Emotions in Man and Animals* (1872).

Darwin's approach to his subject is empirical and descriptive without being experimental – the application of the methods of field studies in natural history to psychology. In the Victorian manner, he collects observations and classifies under appropriate categories. For example, he takes examples of the sounds emitted by various animals, in situations where such general reactions as fear or sexual excitement appear to be dominant. He compares his results with observations of human vocalizations during emotional reaction, and notes how characteristic variations in loudness, resonance, pitch and timbre are associated with specific expressions of particular emotions. He then considers the bodily movements associated with such general emotional reactions as terror, anger, affection. Again, he takes example after example from observations of animals. He demonstrates: (a) that physical symptoms are specific to certain general types of 'emotive' reaction; (b) that, among the variations, there are common features among different species; (c) that there is often a direct comparison with human emotional signs.

In dealing with human emotion, Darwin collected data from psychiatrists reporting on emotive behaviour of mental patients, and also from explorers who supplied him with anthropological observations of the expression of emotions in various primitive peoples. In addition, he carried out two sets of observations: (1) on his own children in typical infant reactions – screaming when hungry and frustrated, crying when admonished; (2) on a variety of subjects whom he photographed when actually reacting emotionally or (in the case of a number of actors) when simulating specific emotions. From these he gave minute descriptions of facial expression, bodily tension, posture and characteristic movements during an emotional reaction.

An example of Darwin's study of human emotion will serve to illustrate his method. When studying euphoria (joy, happiness, high spirits), Darwin investigated the physiology of laughter. He took innumerable photographs of people laughing and analysed the universal characteristics of their facial expression. He photographed a subject whose mouth and lips had been stimulated by the galvanizing of the zygomatic muscles, thus producing an artificial smile. This photograph was shown to twenty-four people, along with a set of subjects giving normal smiles. Every one of the subjects remarked that this particular photograph was different, unnatural, and Darwin discovered the reason – the orbicular muscles of the lower eyelid were not sufficiently contracted to produce the total effect of a natural smile! Darwin investigated the different sorts of stimulus-situations which provoke laughter and smiles (surprise and release from tension or strain, jokes, good news etc.), and he instanced the case of a girl born blind and deaf who could not have learned to smile and laugh through imitation, who laughed and clapped her hands when pleased. The physical reactions must be innate and inherited – but why just these responses should be associated with certain stimulus situations Darwin could not explain from his observations. They are, Darwin thought, probably of pre-human origin, since monkeys, when pleased with a gift of food, made sounds similar to human laughter, exhibiting vibrations of jaws and lips, the mouth drawn backwards and upwards, the cheeks wrinkled and eyes bright.

From his survey of the facts available, Darwin concluded that the expression of emotion could be understood in terms of three principles:

(1) Given a complex emotional state (anxiety or anger) tension may be reduced by the performance of an action which serves either to remove the stimulus situation or reduce the tension evoked by it. In time, this specific action may cease to be of any use in doing either of these things. Nevertheless, it may continue as a habit associated with the emotional reaction. For example, in describing a terrifying scene, the narrator often closes his eyes as if to shut off the painful sight.

(2) When a specific action or movement is associated with a particular emotion, the arousal of a contrary emotion is likely to evoke a movement of a directly opposite kind. If a dog approaches a distant human figure, it may exhibit 'hostile-suspicious' reactions (head raised, tail erect, hairs bristling). If it recognizes the figure as a

friend, at once the physical reactions are reversed – the body sinks low, the tail falls limp, the hair lies smoothly, etc. None of these latter 'friendly' symptoms serves any useful purpose – they are simply the opposite of the hostile movements.

(3) Many actions which express emotions are the direct result of neurological changes which either prepare the subject to react appropriately (e.g. by fight or flight in dangerous situations), or serve to reduce tensions. Perspiration in fear and anxiety and the trembling of muscles in anger are two familiar such reactions. However, some of these reactions may have ceased to have any practical value, and become simply signs of a particular emotive state.

All these overt aspects of an emotional response – like the complicated inner processes – are innate. Learning and imitation may modify them, but they are not the product of learning. However, we learn to react to the emotions of others, and emotional expressions are a primitive basis for more complicated forms of communication. In *Mind* (1887), Darwin published the results of day-to-day observations on one of his children from birth to the age of about 3 years, including a brief account of the origin and development of speech and of expressive cries of discomfort, pleasure, etc., which described in detail the expression of infantile emotions.

Darwin thus appears as one of the first writers to treat psychological topics empirically. His importance in the development of psychology reaches far beyond the limits of his particular findings. The expanding group of investigations which was to become psychology was given a completely new lead through his work.

It is true that long after Darwin was published, indeed almost down to the end of the century, some influential academic psychologists continued to follow the traditional model for psychological investigation. The essential data of psychology was the field of consciousness. Whether introspection was carried out in the laboratory under experimental control, or in the armchair, this self-observation was the basic method of investigation. Once obtained, the contents or processes of conscious experience were analysed into basic elements (sensations or imagery or mental acts), and the operations in terms of which these units were combined into complexes investigated or speculated upon. (This view was favoured at Cornell University under Titchener between 1892 and 1925.)

Darwin presented an entirely new approach to the subject matter of psychology. He makes observable factors the primary data; what he singles out for description is overt behaviour, and its overt characteristics. If responses can be correlated with introspected feelings or moods, this is permissible. But his main interest is in observing and describing overt behaviour, and the environmental factors to which it is related. The approach of the zoologist observing a species in the field is extended to human and animal psychology.

Darwin's approach to his data is genetic or developmental. He likes to explain any characteristic behaviour by showing how it originated in the individual or in the species, and to trace how it developed under the influence of its environment until it reached its present form. This attempt to treat a type of reaction historically is now well established in clinical and abnormal psychology, and in child psychology. However, no one before Darwin made this approach to the subject matter of psychology an obvious one. In time, psychologists came to see that it was part of their job, not merely to account for the origin and development of specific skills (for example, the capacity to calculate), but also to be able to treat the total personality as the product of complex developmental processes beginning at birth and going on throughout life.

Locke, the authority from whom many basic maxims in the old associationist psychology had derived, had regarded the mind at birth as a *tabula rasa*, a clean slate on which information and skills were printed through 'experience' (that is, through knowledge derived through reflection on the data supplied by means of perceptual processes). Darwin emphasized the importance of heredity. He believed that much of importance in human nature is passed on from parent to offspring.

He thereby initiated the Nature v. Nurture controversy in modern psychology. In present-day terms, we are still asking how much of our behaviour is organized by genetic and constitutional factors, and how much is the result of learning, training and other environmental influences. Darwin believed that both influences are important, but that psychology tends to neglect hereditary factors.

Darwin was far from neglecting the importance of environmental factors on behaviour. He presented the image of organisms placed in a physical and organic environment which presents many obstacles to survival. The human race, in primitive conditions, still has to struggle against threats. Even in civilized settings, the individual must both find means of adapting the environment so as to meet his basic needs, and also to adjust his needs to the limitations which his environment imposes. Darwin gave psychology the broad concepts of 'adjustment' and 'adaptation', presenting human beings as active, striving, outward-oriented beings whose behaviour is largely a means of meeting the problems presented by the physical and social environment. This dynamic conception of behaviour, together with the idea of 'success' or 'failure' in making adequate adjustments, was something completely new. The older psychology emphasized that man is a self-conscious, introspective being who interprets his experience in terms of reason and sentiment. The mind or field of consciousness was regarded as something removed from the outer world, of which it only had indirect and imperfect knowledge.

Darwin's approach introduced the conception of man as a being striving through his actions towards specific goals determined by his interaction with his environment. The questions and problems involved in psychology changed entirely in the course of the century following his

Origin of Species. How do humans learn their many habits and skills? What factors are involved in motivated behaviour? In what ways are human beings different from each other, and for what reasons, in their capacity to adjust and adapt?

Darwin's general theory made the study of animal behaviour an important part of psychology. In what respects do animals have similar behavioural capacities to human beings? Can some animals recognize human beings as familiar? Can any animal be said to possess even rudimentary intelligence and to execute simple reasoning tasks? Or do animals achieve their adaptations by other means than those available to human beings? In which case, what constitutes the basis for man's superior intellectual skills? Comparative psychology is thus defined as a field for investigation. Man could no longer be studied as an isolated phenomenon, a superior 'mind' cut off from the rest of nature. Human beings were to be compared – function for function – with the more adaptable animals and especially with the ape family.

All this implied a methodological revolution. Psychology must be closely related to the biological sciences, even though not all its problems could be treated in terms of their methods, techniques and concepts. However, it was obvious that psychology might adopt and refine some of the basic methods of biology in tackling its new questions, and use information from these sciences to do much more than explain how the senses work. Not merely have words like 'stimulus', 'response', 'instinct', 'drive', 'reflex', 'threshold', 'fatigue', 'filter', 'inhibition', 'set', 'tension' become commonplace in the literature of contemporary psychology; many theories in psychology are self-consciously biological. This revolutionary placing of psychology in the family of the sciences close to biology was initiated by Darwin's work.

Finally, Darwin emphasized the variations occurring within each species which are crucial for survival. He drew attention to the possibility that individual humans vary along specific dimensions – general ability, specific aptitudes, character, 'stability' of temperament and so on. The psychologist must discover which factors are the ones that vary, and which variations make for crucial differences between one human being and another. It might even be possible to measure certain dimensions accurately and make exact comparisons between individuals. Once the range of individual differences is mapped it may be possible to discover whether or not differences in, for example, intelligence are inherited, or acquired through favourable environment and training, or whether a combination of factors is involved.

The older psychology has been mostly concerned with making generalizations which applied to all or most human beings – with remembering, reasoning or experiencing pleasure or pain. Darwin's interest in the variability of individuals within a species and the reasons for such variations opened up another new set of questions for psychologists to tackle.

While the Germans had shown that the methods of the scientific laboratory could be applied to psychology, they had confined their studies to the sensory processes and perception, and had adhered to introspection of consciousness as defining their data. Darwin applied the whole of the methods of the biological sciences to psychology, and defined a far wider field of problems and topics than had hitherto seemed possible. In many ways, he deserves as much as any other man the credit for launching the modern science of psychology.

In one respect only, Darwin's example and influence as a psychologist has tended to be ignored. His practice in his psychological studies was strictly empirical. He observed, described, classified, collected information, performed a few simple researches, only extracting such generalizations as his limited studies warranted. No elaborate theory was constructed, either as a preliminary or as a consequence of his empirical work. The major sin of many more contemporary psychologists has been the extent to which

THE EVOLUTIONARY DOCTRINE

theory construction, well beyond the implications of established empirical generalizations, has been carried out
somewhat recklessly. As a psychologist, Darwin was always
a sound and sober scientist.

HERBERT SPENCER:
SYSTEMATIC PSYCHOLOGIST

Darwin was anticipated by Herbert Spencer (1820–1903),
both in his accepting evolution as a principle accounting
for the diversity of living forms, and in his applying that
principle to psychology. In an article published in 1852,
Spencer put forward an evolutionary theory in opposition
to the 'special creation' theory, and in his *Principles of
Psychology* (1855) he argued that, 'mind can be understood
by showing how mind is evolved', though it was the revised
edition of this book (1870–2), where the evolutionary emphasis was far more basic, which proved most influential.
Spencer's psychology is essentially philosophical: the definition of fundamental concepts and theories and their
systematic interrelating into a logically coherent system.

He made no observations nor did he make use of any
specific empirical data. Since the turn of the century his
somewhat pretentious, long-winded and verbose psychological works have ceased to be read. Many of his original
ideas have been absorbed and transformed in the general
thinking of psychologists. However, he was a great intellectual power in his day – especially as a writer on social and
political matters – and he deserves to be remembered as an
early influence reinforcing and supporting the impact of
Darwin's genius on the new developmental approach to
psychology.

FRANCIS GALTON: PSYCHOLOGIST OF GENIUS

Far more significant was the work of one of psychology's
real geniuses – the half-cousin of Charles Darwin and a
scientist of eminence in his own right. Like Darwin,

Francis Galton (1822–1911) had sufficient private means to live without the necessity of having a job. He began his scientific life as a geographer and explorer, penetrating hitherto unknown parts of Africa. His interest in meteorology led him, on his return to England, to construct the first weather maps of the British Isles. Galton's weather maps appeared daily in *The Times* from April 1875 onwards, and he discovered and named the phenomenon of the 'anticyclone'. However, his travels turned his restless and inquiring mind away from geographical and meteorological interests towards anthropology. He observed the enormous differences between people both as cultural groups and as individuals within each group, and this became the root of his interest in human nature.

Galton wished to evaluate the basic individual differences between human beings, and to subject the crucial factors involved to precise measurement. He singled out 'ability' as a dimension for possible study, and in doing so laid the foundations for that branch of psychology known as psychometrics (broadly, the application of statistics to the measurement of individual differences with references to behavioural variables, and the use of psychometric techniques in the construction and validation of psychological tests).

The faculty-psychology of his time recognized the existence of special abilities or talents – for music, mathematics, athletic skills, etc. Galton, however, insisted that there was a general (intellectual) ability which was primary. Some individuals were gifted in a wide variety of cognitive skills, however much special interests and training might bias them towards the exploitation of some specialized ability (in scientific research, for example). Galton wanted to be able to measure the level of general ability of one individual in relation to a representative sample of other individuals in his culture, to discover how high levels of ability were distributed throughout a given population, and to determine whether or not such high ability is inherited. The result of his research appeared in *Hereditary*

Genius (1869), one of the great scientific works of the Victorian age.

'I propose to show in this book that man's natural abilities are derived from inheritance, under exactly the same limitations as are the form and physical features of the whole organic world.' 'I claim to be the first to treat the subject in a statistical manner, to arrive at numerical results and to introduce the "law of deviation from average" into discussions on heredity.' These two statements make clear what was evolutionary in Galton's approach. Both claims were a big step forward: to suggest that be-

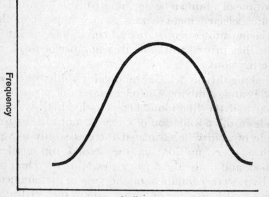

haviloural and mental traits might be inherited, and to suggest that differences between minds could be measured.

A Belgian mathematician, Quételet, had recently shown that certain bodily measurements, such as the height and chest-girth of army recruits, were distributed among the total population in a frequency roughly approximate to Gauss's 'normal law', which is expressed graphically in the well-known bell-shaped 'probability' curve (see figure). If the base line represents units in terms of which some human attribute is measured (e.g. height in feet and inches, to the nearest inch), and the vertical axis represents the number of individuals in a given population corresponding to each value set out along the base line, then the curve represents the 'frequency distribution' of the attribute in the population. The crown of the 'bell' shows that the vast majority of individuals do not vary much from the strict statistical average measurement, while individuals with exceptionally large or exceptionally small heights are the minority groups at either end of the curve – the distribution falling off regularly in either direction towards extremes. Galton took a big leap – purely intuitive – when he ventured the hypothesis that: (a) This form of distribution would apply to every measurable physical attribute of a human being; and (b) it would equally apply to any selected mental trait. As a working hypothesis – requiring subsequent statistical corrections against errors – this has proved workable in a number of psychometric investigations.

Taking this model, Galton divided ability into 16 equal grades and, applying Quételet's tables of probability, he calculated the likely number of individuals within each grade in the population of Great Britain. In the topmost grade of ability he estimated there was only one person within every million; in the second top grade 1 in 79,000; and in the third 1 in 4,300. More than half in each million were contained in the two grades immediately above and below (or on either side of the vertical in the bell curve), and four-fifths of the total population were in the four grades covering the mid-point on the ability scale.

Galton then asked what the frequency was of the highest grades of ability among the kinsmen of men who may be judged to be of outstanding ability? He selected individuals rated as eminent (on the basis of 'recognized eminence') in various professions – law, literature, art, science, classical scholarship, the church – and traced the pedigree of each individual. From his tables of figures, he found that of all the members of the High Court between 1660 and 1865 80 per cent of those holding office as Lord Chancellor and 36 per cent of other judges had eminent relatives. Combining all groups he showed that in 31 per cent of the cases in his sample, illustrious men had eminent fathers and 48 per cent of these men also had eminent sons. Galton concluded that his results suggest that outstanding ability is inherited.

Apart from its statistical techniques, this early investigation reveals certain weaknesses. The crux of the study is the selection of a sample of the population for scrutiny and statistical description and analysis. Galton selects individuals who are of 'recognized' eminence – they have succeeded in reaching high office in church or state or professions. He then examines the pedigree, and counts the number of relations who also succeed in reaching such positions of eminence in English society. The result appears to show that most outstanding places in the learned professions are occupied by people from a limited number of 'able' families: there is a natural aristocracy of talent which seemed, in the Victorian England of 1869, to be the property of the professional upper-middle classes. The criterion of selection of the sample is suspect. In Victorian England people were selected for the professions largely on the basis of family connexion. Only upper-middle-class boys got the education and the privileged entry to key jobs in law, universities, etc. Fathers used wealth and social status to place their sons in good professions, and working-class or lower-middle-class youths had few opportunities for competing, until the reforms of the twentieth century widened the ladder of educational opportunity. It is significant that Galton does not include successful business men from industry and commerce who, throughout the nineteenth century, were increasing Britain's wealth by their enterprise and astute marketing. It did not seem to occur to him that a wealthy manufacturer who had risen from humble origins might require a high degree of intelligence, as well as a capacity for hard work and hard bargaining. Galton's criterion of 'ability' derived from this pedigree was therefore suspect.

Further, since biological science at the time had no

clear conception of the mechanisms of heredity (Mendel's papers were published in obscure journals in the late 1860s, but were not known to the scientific world until 1900), Galton assumed a neurological mechanism for the transmission of outstanding ability. The effect of this was to over-emphasize the hereditary factors, and undervalue possible environmental factors in the development of ability.

By coming down so overwhelmingly in favour of hereditary intelligence, Galton ignored the possibility of research into environmental influences – home environment and early training, effects of education and life 'experiences' – on the growth of both general and special abilities. To allow for environmental influences is to open the possibility of unexploited sources of ability in a community, which may be thwarted by unfavourable social circumstances and lack of proper training facilities. Subsequent experience suggests that such sources must have existed in the under-privileged lower-middle and working classes of Victorian England. Why did Galton fail to realize this possibility and to carry out investigations to see whether or not 'ability' of a high order existed in other sections of the population than that of eminent men and their families?

Part of the answer is that he was over-committed to the hereditary emphasis in Darwinism. The concept of the transmission of basic characteristics was new and exciting, and Galton wanted to show that the evolutionary theory applied to human nature as well as to butterflies and sweetpeas. Possibly also he was unconsciously influenced by social and political prejudices. His book can be regarded as a defence of the 'Establishment' as it existed in 1870: as demonstrating the intellectual superiority of the upper-middle classes, who thereby were best fitted to continue to occupy the key jobs in society. Since high ability is not as likely in working-class people, training and education for each ability is not likely to make much difference to their minds – so run the implications of *Hereditary Genius*.

If there is an occasional 'sport' who develops high ability, this is likely to drive him upwards towards a position of greater eminence. For the mass of the lower classes, more mundane work and therefore less intellectual education is the inevitable fate. It was in 1870 that the Liberal administration under Gladstone passed Forster's Education Act, which vastly increased the scope of elementary education (although this was not finally made compulsory until 1880). High Tories may have been alarmed at this attempt to educate the masses, especially as the left wing of the Liberal party led by the able John Dilke was very radical (even republicanism was advocated).

To press such a point is probably unfair to Galton, who would probably have supported popular education had he believed in its efficacy. It may be that at least something of a belief in the intellectual (and moral) superiority of his own social class prejudiced him in selecting his criterion of 'ability'. Whatever influences were at work, they marred *Hereditary Genius* as a scientific treatise, and stand as a warning that rigorously 'objective' psychology is an ideal to be achieved only occasionally and with difficulty. Because his involvement with his subject matter is so intimate and complex, the psychologist is vulnerable to hidden prejudices which may contaminate his supposedly scientific investigations with a politico-ethical bias.

Galton's contributions to psychology were diverse and his later work was on the whole of more lasting quality than *Hereditary Genius*. In 1884 at the International Health Exhibition in London, he established an 'Anthropometric Laboratory' with equipment of his own invention. It has been described as the birthplace of the mental-testing movement. Subjects were invited to take part in a variety of tests designed to collect data on individual differences in basic human attributes. Many of the measurements, such as body measurement (height, weight), or measurements of muscular strength, were physical. But psychological variables – sensory capacities (the ability to discriminate accurately between different intervals of pitch, etc.); reaction times; the associative processes involved in recall, imagery and the formation of habits – were also investigated.

It was in the course of these investigations that Galton devised a method of ranking. If the members of a group being tested are ranked in order of their scores, a statistical scale can be derived such that any individual is placed in relation to the percentage of the group which is above him. The scale was divided at the 25 per cent, 50 per cent and 75 per cent points into four parts called 'quartiles'. The 50 per cent point was called the 'median'. If absolute measures of a basic trait or attribute cannot be devised, then such a scale can at least show that an individual is in one quartile or another. Newer techniques have improved this device in descriptive statistics, but it is the root idea in, for example, attempts to measure differences in 'intelligence', which cannot be measured absolutely as can weight, height or muscular strength.

It was during this period that Galton had the assistance of a young American, J. M. Cattell, who had previously studied under Wundt. When Cattell left England in 1888 to take up a professorship in the U.S.A., he took with him the stimulus of Galton's work. In the 1890s Cattell carried out extensive pioneer work on mental tests, and one of his pupils, E. L. Thorndike, became one of the psychologists who worked out our present-day intelligence tests (see Chapter 6). Thus, Galton was the source of both the American and British testing movements – a contribution to psychology as important as, or perhaps even more important than, the application of experimental methods in psychology.

Galton made a second great contribution to statistical psychology in his invention of 'correlation', originating both the basic concept and the first attempt to establish a workable means of measuring it.

Correlation is the positive tendency for two magnitudes of two different attributes to be related in a mathematically determinable ratio (or, strictly, for any two factors to be related, even if they cannot be measured). Thus it has been found that scores on tests which measure basic abilities in 'verbal facility' correlate precisely with scores on tests which measure mechanical skills. People who score high, middling or low marks on the one set of tests tend to get a very similar high, middling or low score on the other type.

It was Galton who hit upon the possibility of discovering such correlations. His interest was aroused by the attempts of Bertillon, a Belgian criminologist, to describe and identify criminals largely on the basis of physical characteristics of a measurable kind: twelve basic body measurements were used (height, head measurements, etc.). Galton thought Bertillon's scheme could be simplified if only one could discover a degree of concomitant variation between, for example, height and arm length. He wanted to find out whether there was a correlation between measures of different bodily characteristics (total height, arm length, finger lengths, weight, etc.), and to work out a way of expressing this numerically. Galton discovered from taking a large number of measurements that the separate measurements of an individual are related to each other, and he worked out a means of expressing the relationships involved. This was a measure of what is now called covariance. Galton discovered the average measure for each item, and then looked to see if the two measurements he was interested in were *both* well above or below average. If they both vary by a similar amount from average, there is high correlation between the two. If the amount of variation from average differs considerably between the two, the correlation is lower. Galton worked out a way of getting round differences in units of measurement so that a correlation could be calculated, and he used the numeral '1' to indicate exact correlation, and plus ($+$) and minus ($-$) zero (o) to indicate positive and negative amounts of correlation.

In thus devising the basic concept of correlation and the earliest elementary means of measuring it, Galton provided psychometrics with its most potentially powerful tool. He also changed the conception of what sort of empirical problems are basic to the science of psychology. Many psychologists would argue today that correlation provides a model for what much fundamental research in psychology should be. Given certain traits or skills, what other behavioural characteristics may be predicted on a basis of established correlations? 'What goes with what?' It may be that physiologists and geneticists and others have to be called in to explain why these correlations are what they are, but it is the psychologist's job to discover significant correlations. Does a high score in cognitive tests A, B and C correlate closely with potential high ability in scientific research? Does a particular set of results on 'personality tests' X, Y and Z correlate with a tendency towards a specific form of psychopathological disorder? What are the measurable traits of a person liable to break down easily when exposed to the stress of battle?

Psychologists spend a great deal of time tracking down high correlations between different measurable factors in behaviour and this is highly characteristic of many basic research problems. Behind the multifarious projects in behavioural research being carried out in laboratories, clinics and elsewhere stands the father figure of Francis Galton.

The immediate practical consequences of Galton's work were useful for criminology. He found that for nearly all physical measurements of the human body, correlations were positive and high (e.g. 0.7 for height and length of middle finger). Hence, if only part of a body is found, one can reconstruct basic bodily dimensions with considerable accuracy. However, Galton discovered that one factor was a foolproof means of identification – 'fingerprints'. His papers on this topic led Scotland Yard to adopt fingerprinting as a means of criminal investigation, and to establish a library of fingerprints of known criminals. This discovery is typical of Galton's amazing versatility.

Galton's psychological research was by no means confined to psychometric projects, although his great dictum was that measurements in psychology should be accurate wherever possible. In his most famous publication, *Inquiries into Human Faculty and Its Development* (1883), he describes an interesting hotch-potch of investigations. They include the celebrated questionnaire into the extent and quality of the use of mental imagery which was sent to different groups of people and revealed a considerable range of individual differences, from those who experience no visual imagery at all to very vivid 'visualizers', who are able to form an image of an earlier perception with great detail and with clarity of colour, etc. Incidentally, this appears to be one of the first attempts to use the questionnaire as a means of collecting psychological data.

In studying associative processes, Galton developed a procedure similar to the 'free association' method of the psycho-analytic school. He prepared a list of 75 words and having written each on a separate slip set them aside for a week. He then selected the slips at random and timed himself until a word had produced two ideas (either words or images). He immediately tried to recall the origin of these ideas and the connexion each had with the stimulus word. He worked through the list four times at intervals of a month and then reviewed his results. He had elicited 505 ideas of which 29 appeared in all four trials, 36 in three, 57 in two, and 107 in one only. The ones which recurred most frequently dated from boyhood and youth; those which came up only once were mostly from recent experiences; 32 per cent were visual images, 22 per cent were representations of actions, 45 per cent were purely verbal associations and 1 per cent were obscure. Galton thought the experiment might have value if a large number of subjects were used. He postulated that one might find various levels of the mind at work in the selection of association words and imagery. 'There seems to be a presence-chamber where full consciousness holds court, and an ante-chamber just outside, crowded with ideas lying beyond the ken of consciousness; out of this ante-chamber the ideas most nearly allied to the problem at issue appear to be summoned in a mechanical or a logical way, and so have their turn of audience.' Below this is a deeper level where older and remoter ideas are stored, which can only be evoked with difficulty. In this outline there is a sketch of psycho-analytic conceptions of unconscious mental processes. Furthermore, Galton believed that original or creative thinkers depend upon a subtle interplay between conscious and unconscious processes for the fusion of original material. This capacity he called 'fluency', a factor which later psychometricians have attempted to measure in both standardized and in unstructured tests.

In his later years Galton's influence was directed mainly in one or other of two directions. He realized that, as civilization became increasingly complex as a result of technological advances, a great strain would be exerted on the limited number of able people in society. It was therefore necessary for 'the well-being of future generations that the average standard of ability ... should be raised'. He defined a new field of study to which he gave the name Eugenics: 'the study of agencies under social control which may improve or impair the racial qualities of future generations either physically or mentally'. A eugenics laboratory and a Chair endowed by Galton at London University have contributed towards this ideal. The main work of this school has been the development of statistical techniques, especially in relation to the biological sciences.

Galton's other main work was the organization of psychological research in Britain. He had advocated an anthropometric survey of the population of Britain, and in 1903 set about a project to develop and standardize tests of intelligence and of specific abilities in schools. William McDougall (pp. 177 ff.) was in charge, and Cyril Burt (pp. 328 ff.), Charles Spearman (pp. 186 ff.), J. C. Flugel and William Brown were all in the research group. For ten years much useful research work was done, and Burt was appointed first school psychologist to the London County Council. Burt's work on gifted, backward, defective and delinquent groups of children, and also on identical twins reared apart, yielded the basic data from which later child and educational studies grew. Thus Galton made a contribution to applied as well as to academic psychology, for it was his agitation which resulted in Burt's appointment as the first full-time educational psychologist.

However, it was with heredity that Galton remained chiefly concerned. He had been impressed with the way in which one race had supplanted others in Africa, and by the historical decline of families, communities and nations. The British and European nations were involved in inbreeding their influential classes to an extent that a future decline in the race might occur. The planning of a physically and mentally vigorous race was essential for survival. It may be that Galton's hope for a science of eugenics was premature, although his concern with improving human stock was a sensible one.

In his *History of Experimental Psychology*, Boring suggests that Galton was a genius who never quite attained greatness. His diversity of interests, both within psychology and in such other fields as geography, meteorology, anthropology, criminology, statistics and biology, prevented him from completing any major project. It is suggested that he started interesting projects, often on the basis of completely original ideas, but then dropped them after a 'pilot' study in order to turn to something new. He was an explorer who sketched maps and expeditions for others to finish in detail. There is something in this, although it might be argued that Galton's diversity and breadth were positive virtues compared with the staid and narrow path followed by contemporary German experimentalists.

There is no doubt of his genius, nor of the importance of the stimulus he gave to the study of the individual personality. The techniques he developed for this purpose have all been exploited as basic instruments of research: the normal curve, rating scales, coefficients of correlation, mental tests, questionnaires. As Burt, one of his last associates, has said: 'When he took it up, individual psychology was just a speculative topic for the fancies of the poet, the novelist, the biographer, and the quack and charlatan on the seaside pier. By the time he left it and handed it on to others, it had been transformed into a reputable branch of natural science – perhaps for mankind the most important branch there is.' Few of the founders of psychology can claim a finer assessment than this.

THE BEGINNINGS OF COMPARATIVE PSYCHOLOGY: SPALDING, ROMANES, MORGAN AND HOBHOUSE

Darwin's work directed the attention of scientists to the problem of explaining animal behaviour. How do animals adjust to their environment? Are they simply complicated automatons as Descartes had suggested, or do they have primitive capacities for learning new habits and skills and even for remembering useful information? Are the more advanced animals such as horses, dogs and apes capable of any form of intelligent behaviour? If so, what is it that accounts for man's superior intellect? Is his intellect so very much superior to that of a chimpanzee? It was realized that much work was needed before any of these questions could be answered. For one thing, few systematic and accurate observations of the sort of behaviour animals exhibit had been carried out before Darwin. Observations were needed prior to explanations and comparisons with man.

The British were first in the field. It is sad to record that two of the very gifted pioneers in animal behaviour, Douglas Spalding (1840–77) and G. J. Romanes (1848–99), died at the early ages of 37 and 41 respectively, leaving uncompleted many promising projects.

Spalding was a poor man who had been a quarry worker in Aberdeen, where he attended Bain's lectures. He questioned Bain's attempts to explain away instinct as a form of imitative learning, and proceeded to carry out experiments with young chicks. He hooded the chicks when they emerged from the egg at birth and kept them from receiving visual stimulation for three days. When unhooded, Spalding argued, 'in from 2 to 15 minutes they peeked at some speck or insect, showing not merely an instinctive perception of distance, but an organized ability to judge, to measure distance, with something like infallible accuracy.' He carried out experiments in which young chicks reacted defensively by flying away, hiding, etc., on being shown a hawk for the first time – an innate response independent of learning or imitation. Spalding also noted that very soon after emerging from the egg, chicks exhibit a 'following response' – usually to the mother hen. This response, however, can become connected with other objects – for example a human being – if this becomes familiar to the chicks in the earliest period after hatching. Spalding had identified a form of learning which is now separately categorized as 'imprinting' and which has been the subject of much research in the 1960s.

G. J. Romanes is sometimes dismissed as an anecdotal psychologist who collected stories about people's clever pets and wrote them up in popular lectures. This is extremely unfair to Romanes, who carried out many important experimental and field studies of a strictly scientific character. He did have a tendency towards slightly anthropomorphic explanations of animal behaviour, using terms borrowed from everyday descriptions of human activity to characterize animal performances. However, this fault is readily correctable in his writings and does not mar the excellence of his observations.

He was, like Darwin and Galton, a man of private means who made research his main interest. He studied at Cambridge (1867–72) and learnt physiology there. He established a marine laboratory on the coast of Ross-shire in north-west Scotland, and did much of his research there in the summer months, returning to write and lecture in Oxford and London during the winters. At his death he had plans for many experimental projects and for a major book on human psychology.

Romanes combined experimental method with systematic theory. His important book *Jelly-Fish, Star-Fish and Sea Urchins* (1885) reports how he measured the timing of responses in these creatures, discovering facts about the 'latency and summation' of stimuli.

He found that if an Aurelia is stimulated electrically, the response (muscular contraction) is feeble and takes $\frac{5}{8}$ second to occur. If a second shock of the same intensity is given as soon as the muscle relaxes, there is a stronger contraction with shorter latency. This process is repeated for eight to ten successive stimulations until a maximum contraction occurs. Romanes thought this 'summation of stimuli' might apply over a wide range of behaviour. Hence, the temporal properties of responses are important for coordinated reactions: the interval between successive stimuli is a significant factor in the strength of the ultimate response in a series of responses, quite apart from the strength of each stimulus.

Romanes carried out further experiments on 'homing' responses in bees and pigeons; the effects of isolation from other members of the species on the acquisition of characteristic bird calls; the sense of smell in crabs; and the associative powers of a chimpanzee.

In his theoretical framework for a comparative psychology, Romanes worked on Darwinian lines. He regarded adjustment as dependent on the ability to discriminate and classify stimuli from the senses. Most living things have some capacity for reacting differently to familiar (as contrasted with new) types of stimulus. At which point does 'intelligence' emerge? Romanes introduced the concept of 'recept' which he defined as 'a spontaneous association formed unintentionally as what may be termed an unperceived abstraction'. Thus recepts can be acquired by infants and animals, and are rather similar to Harlow's 'learning sets', which his chimpanzee subjects acquire in discrimination learning tasks. (See H. F. Harlow, 'The Formation of Learning Sets', *Psychological Review*, 1949.) Human beings have the capacity to use symbols, and 'named recepts' are the most primitive type of 'concept' or 'category word'. Language is the essential instrument for thought and hence animals have no intelligence. *Mental Evolution in Man* (1888), in which the evolution of thought and language is discussed, is Romanes' main theoretical work.

Were it not for his *Animal Intelligence* (1882), in which he attempts an over-comprehensive account of animal behaviour, and falls back on anecdotal material to fill in gaps, Romanes might have escaped the tag of being 'speculative'. His main work is on strictly empirical and soundly discursive lines.

The most influential of the earlier students of animal behaviour was C. Lloyd Morgan (1852–1936). Lloyd Morgan was not particularly active in research,* and would probably have been overshadowed by both Spalding and Romanes had they lived. He did most of his experimental work in the period 1885–1900.

At the root of Lloyd Morgan's work was his celebrated canon for research in animal behaviour: 'In no case may we interpret an action as the outcome of a higher faculty, if it can be interpreted as the outcome of the exercise of one which stands lower in the psychological scale.' Careful observations, either under experimental conditions or in the field, were the only data, and interpretations must avoid all traces of anthropomorphism.

Lloyd Morgan was primarily interested in distinguishing between innate and acquired behaviour. He collected a mass of data, both from strictly scientific papers and from his own observations, on young birds and mammals, and this material opened up a new field for future research when it appeared in *Habit and Instinct* (1896) and *Comparative Psychology* (2nd edition 1903).

He used the word 'instinct' to classify behaviour or acts which (a) are common to all members of the species, (b)

* The fact that he became Principal of the University College of Bristol in 1887 (a post he retained until 1910, when the college attained full university status) may have diverted him away from research.

are fairly uniform and repetitive in form, (c) are made in response to a specific stimulus, (d) have a clear connexion with the anatomical structure and physiological functioning of the animal. He had no time for a usage which implied any mysterious 'inner power' or unknown neural mechanism. He pointed out that many 'instincts' are largely a type of compound reflex action; a number of reflex acts are coordinated in a serial response. Thus, the water-beetle weaves with her spinnerets a delicate silken cocoon in which she deposits her eggs, and this behaviour involves reflexes connected with the emission of fluid, reflexes to mould the cocoon and supply it with air, and others making for the laying of eggs in a regular pattern. The reflexes are local responses to specific cues, so there must be some central mechanisms organizing the separate reflexes into a complex means-end sequence. It may be that the overall structure and total physiology, rather than any specific central process, determine the organization of reflexes into instinctive acts.

However, inherited responses are not rigid. Most animals have innate abilities (a) to form some kind of association – stimulus S_1 produces response R_1, (b) to react to pain with withdrawal–escape reactions, and to pleasure with retention–approach reactions. These pleasure–pain reactions help the organism to confirm or 'reinforce' those innate or accidental reactions which are pleasant and make them habitual through repetition, and to inhibit painful congenital or accidental reactions. Acquired acts arise from the modification or confirmation of innate responses.

Lloyd Morgan's studies laid the foundations for later work on animal learning. He carried out experiments with young chicks on the development of their capacity to discriminate between suitable food and, for example, sour-tasting caterpillars or neutral specks of dirt. He used the term 'trial and error' to describe the method whereby responses which do not achieve the end required are dropped from the sequence, and also the phrase 'reinforcement of successful modes of response' through the pleasure–pain mechanism – both concepts which became common to many discussions about learning in the twentieth century. He also studied the part played by imitation in animal learning. Noticing that a hen shows chicks how to pick up grain by pecking the ground in front of them and then dropping bits of food, Lloyd Morgan proceeded to train newly hatched chicks by using a pair of forceps to pick up grains dropped in front of them. He observed how three young linnets placed separately with three different foster parents (a skylark, woodlark and meadow pipit) each acquired the song of its foster parent. When later placed among songsters of their own species they did not abandon their acquired song.

His general conclusion was that animals do not exhibit any intelligence in learning. 'Animals deal with difficulties by the method of trial and error ... the perception of relations as such is not necessary to the performance, and is therefore by our canon of interpretation excluded.'

However, if he excluded anything analogous to 'reasoning' in animals, he was prepared to allow that many animals have something analogous to human consciousness. They may act as complex automatons but they have 'sentience', which modifies their reflexes and complicates the organization of their behaviour. If a chick, seeing a cinnabar caterpillar for the first time, pecks and seizes it, it usually ejects it on tasting. On a second presentation, it often approaches the caterpillar, hesitates and then leaves it alone. It may wipe its bill on the ground as it does on ejecting food with a sour taste. Lloyd Morgan argued that some revival of bitter taste (for example from secretions associated with 'ejection responses') may be the physical substitute for memory. There is an association between the stimulus object (caterpillar) and its sour taste – a fragment of the total ejection response must be elicited by the stimulus object to serve as the warning signal. There is a feeble flicker of sentience, or simple consciousness, involved in this type of learning. This model is similar in its basic plan to the more sophisticated 'representational mediating responses' in C. E. Osgood's 'mediation hypothesis' version of Hull's learning theory, expounded in his *Method and Theory in Experimental Psychology* (1953). Lloyd Morgan once again anticipates Behaviouristic interpretations of animal learning, despite his dallying with the concept of 'consciousness' in animals.

In his later years, Lloyd Morgan moved away from the observation of animal behaviour and devoted himself – apart from running a new university – to philosophical writing. His book *Emergent Evolution* (1923) was intended as a philosophical theory based strictly on biological evidence. The book argues that in the course of evolution new features emerge wholly within the natural order and without the aid of mysterious entities like Bergson's 'vital energy'. Thus, consciousness is something new in the evolutionary process – coming late and only in the more complexly developed animals. Also in the course of human evolution, conscious reactions evolve to 'higher forms' which make complex memory and reasoning capacities possible for the first time. Thus, although all living beings are part of one natural order, there emerge different levels of organization, especially when behaviour is considered. Lloyd Morgan, although he contributed many of the basic ideas for Behaviourism (he uses the word 'behaviour' to indicate the main data of psychological research), would not have accepted the radical reductionism of its most rigorous forms.

The last of these British comparative psychologists was L. T. Hobhouse (1864–1928). Hobhouse began his career teaching philosophy at Oxford, then worked as a journalist on the *Manchester Guardian* and finally became Professor of Sociology at the London School of Economics. Having studied physiology and biochemistry at Oxford, Hobhouse spent part of his time in Manchester doing experimental work with animals at the zoo.

This interesting work and the theories derived from it were published in his *Mind in Evolution* (1901). Hobhouse had a conception of adaptability in the lower forms of life as being controlled by mechanisms operating on what would today be called 'homeostatic' principles: thus, when stimulated, organisms are apt to react as if there was a tendency to return to some kind of equilibrium. Thus adaptation is a sort of 'correlation' – the organization of parts in the interest of specific goals or needs. Reflex and instinct are simple hereditary forms of correlation. As living things evolve, correlations become more complex and more directly related to the experiences of the individual. Hobhouse believed that whereas man was infinitely more complicated than any other animal, some animals display perceptual learning and 'practical judgement'. Not only can cats and dogs learn in very few trials, but they also learn by observing demonstrations of a skill.

Hobhouse performed experiments in which animals were placed in situations where they had to obtain a food reward by doing something outside their normal repertory. In one experiment, meat was placed on a card, the card was placed on a shelf and a string attached to the card was left hanging. After a dog had pawed in vain Hobhouse would pull the string and bring down the meat. In some cases the animal seemed to grasp the point immediately and solved the problem on its next trial. The move from 'trial and error' to success was not gradual.

Moreover, the animal could often adapt the newly learned trick in solving another problem – there was 'generalization' of the response. It was Hobhouse who demonstrated that a chimpanzee could use a short stick to reach a longer stick and so draw a banana into its cage – an experiment included later in Köhler's more celebrated work. Hobhouse, however, did not credit chimpanzees with any understanding of their actions. They could learn to 'apply one object to another' and obtain some degree of freedom from the immediate demands of perceptual stimulation. However, conceptional thinking was far beyond their scope. Man exists on a higher plane of evolution in which clearly defined concepts of self-identity, causal relationships, functional relationships, social organization, etc., give rise to new forms of behaviour and experience. Hobhouse's general theory is not unlike that of Lloyd Morgan. Thus some interesting early experiments on animals were performed by Hobhouse during his period as a Manchester journalist, many of which anticipate the work of the Gestalt school published in the 1920s. Hobhouse was the last British worker in the field of comparative psychology for almost fifty years. The initiative moved across the Atlantic, where Thorndike and Yerkes, together with such early Behaviourists as Hunter and Watson, performed laboratory experiments which have become familiar to all who have ever read a textbook of experimental psychology (Chapter 6).

By 1900, those British thinkers within the group responsible for developing Darwin's theory had already made a considerable impact on psychology. Moving cautiously within the strict implications of this theory, they initiated much original work which provided foundations for the new scientific study of human animal behaviour. Darwin's ideas were influential elsewhere, particularly in the U.S.A., where psychology flourished more vigorously than in any other country. A consideration of the development of psychology in the U.S.A. is partly the continuation of the influences released by the impact of Darwin.

CHAPTER SIX

Psychology in the U.S.A. 1880–1914

IN no part of the world has psychology received greater encouragement than in the U.S.A. The beginnings of psychology there are difficult to date. In the first half of the nineteenth century, it was taught by professors of philosophy who followed the Scottish school, Thomas Brown and Thomas Reid being popular texts.

Unquestionably two of the father figures were William James and G. Stanley Hall. There is a dispute as to which of these two introduced experimental psychology into the syllabus, a dispute which turns on what is meant by 'an early course in experimental psychology', and the extent to which official recognition is an important criterion. There can be no doubt of the importance of these two men: James an intellectual force, demonstrating that there is a science of psychology and illustrating its scope and methods; Hall an administrator and teacher, founding effective teaching departments and research schools, and editing the first scientific journals in the subject. Not only did these two men establish academic psychology in the U.S.A., they also laid the foundations of a distinctively American tradition which broke free both from British empiricism in theory and German experimentalism in method.

WILLIAM JAMES

William James (1842–1910) was a fascinating and enig-matic figure. Everyone acknowledged his greatness, yet it is difficult to point to specific achievements in psychology as the basis of his reputation. He came from a wealthy and gifted family, Henry James the novelist being his brother. He began as an art student, switched over to a technological training, and finally qualified as a physician, though never actually practising medicine. He was appointed instructor in anatomy and physiology at Harvard. It was during this period that he became interested in experimental psychology, and in 1875–6 he set up a tiny laboratory, presenting a course entitled 'The Relations between Physiology and Psychology'. This course could claim to have been the first formal instruction in experimental psychology ever given in a university.

During the 1880s, while still nominally a teacher of physiology, James wrote a series of articles in *Mind*, the British journal devoted more to philosophy than to psychology. In 1890 he published *The Principles of Psychology*, his main contribution to the literature of the subject. Soon afterwards, James's interests turned to philosophical problems and his greatest period of productivity began, resulting in at least six major books on philosophy, which put forward a new theory of knowledge. In 1897, he became Professor of Philosophy at Harvard and his connexion with psychology was effectively severed. He had been the first Professor of Psychology at Harvard (1889–97) and had founded a sound school there which has been a centre of psychological knowledge ever since.

Looking at James's published work we may well ask what he achieved. It is admitted that he made the transition from mental philosophy to empirical psychology in America in a smooth but definite manner: that he put psychology firmly and squarely on the academic map as an empirical science. But what else? He did not invent or develop new and fruitful methods or techniques, as did Fechner or Helmholtz; he did not systematize the results of experimental work and formulate a theory about the methodology of the new science, as did Wundt; he did not define a new area for investigation, as Galton did when he demonstrated that it is possible to measure individual differences in intelligence and other basic traits; nor did he expound any theory which stimulated thought about psychological questions, as did Darwin, Dewey, Freud and

Watson. He was not an experimentalist, except in his earliest phase, and left few original experimental results. What then is there in his writings which earns James his place as one of the distinguished founders of psychology?

Boring suggests that James made two contributions. (1) He opposed the rigidity and narrowness of Wundt's German experimentalism. (2) In working out an alternative approach, he avoided a rigid system or school, sketching out instead a large number of fruitful lines of development. These pointed clearly ahead to the two American 'movements' of Functionalism and Behaviourism which revolutionized our conception of the scope and methods of psychology. Also, he laid the foundations for individual psychology of the kind typical of personality studies and clinical psychology (as distinct from psychometrics, which is a methodology exploitable within these broader disciplines), and he made the biological sciences the main foundation studies and model for psychology. Without working out details, James provided a well-drawn grand-plan showing others in what directions to move and how to take the first steps. All this is true of James. Yet he has a stronger claim to greatness. His originality and strength as a psychologist derive from his method of processing the data of psychology, and this is a personal style of thinking rather than a formal method or theory.

The data available to James is now old-fashioned and has been superseded; but *The Principles of Psychology* is still worth studying as a model of how psychological data ought to be dealt with. It is unfortunate that James has had few followers in this respect. He always approaches his material free from the strait-jacket of sophisticated theories or question-begging technical jargon. He deliberately avoids 'structuring' the raw data in terms of hidden assumptions. Many subsequent psychologists have been over-anxious to reach established empirical laws which explain a variety of particular statements of observed fact. In consequence, they have pressed their limited number of observations into an elaborate framework carefully constructed to conform to abstract and fashionable canons of 'scientific method'; Wundt was an early example of this tendency, while C. L. Hull and B. F. Skinner (Chapter 10) within the Behaviourist canon are modern examples of it. James wanted to view data as raw and unprocessed as possible. He had the biological scientist's insight that a natural-history phase often precedes a more sophisticated laboratory-experimental phase in the development of life sciences. Psychology was just beginning, and James wanted simple description and classification of basic facts, together with definition of crucial problems as the first phase. Hence the wide variety of data presented in his book and hence his freedom from the philosophical theories behind British empiricism, German experimentalism and French psychiatry.

James was primarily interested in the problems posed by the facts of psychology. He did not view psychology, as Wundt did, as a set of techniques which provide the answer to specific questions according to the canons of experimental science. Psychology was a group of problems requiring solution along several different lines of attack. Thus James no sooner laid down a principle of classification, a hypothesis, or a theory than he began to question it. If an alternative hypothesis could be found to one which had been suggested, he worried it out; if there was evidence to contradict a generalization, he brought it up; if something was stated as a common fact of observation, James would question the accuracy of the observation. His psychology was critical and problematical. Moreover he showed the problems involved to be of different *kinds*: some could be tackled by designing and carrying out experiments; others by collating different bits of physiological knowledge; some by measuring individual differences and carrying out statistical analysis of various test results; others by speculating between two unconnected statements of fact; others by semantic or logical thinking, producing new categories or definitions.

Given any problem raised by the empirical data, James

liked to analyse, worry and manipulate until all its implications and loose ends had been exposed and a further set of problems defined.

This theoretical and analytical orientation has led some to call James an armchair psychologist. Yet he is different from the armchair theorists of earlier times. He collects strictly empirical data – experimental results, anthropological and clinical reports, physiological and zoological knowledge. His thinking is directed towards (a) defining problems arising directly from such interrelated data, (b) showing what are the gaps in empirical evidence, in relation to specific problems, and suggesting what sort of data is relevant to filling them in. If this is armchair psychology, it is an inevitable part of psychology, as of any other science.

It may be that James would have benefited from doing more experimental research; yet the skill involved in this aspect of psychology – analytical or systematic psychology – may not be related to the skill needed to make good experiments. In any case, James's speculations are always plausible extensions along lines suggested by existing empirical knowledge. James avoids postulating unobservable operations or processes, which cannot be even indirectly tested, and in terms of which overt performances are explained. He sticks closely to his facts, and extrapolates or interpolates with his feet firmly on the ground, his whole outlook being rigorously empirical and scientific. Many active experimental psychologists who indulge in 'theory construction' could learn much from James's care and self-discipline in this respect. Of course, it must be said that much of the data available to him – the product of introspection and early experiments – was weak, but this does not alter the fact that James's *technique* in handling material was extremely sound.

James's *Principles* seems at first sight to be an unsystematic book. Yet it has a plan. Its main concern is the individual personality. The first six chapters are introductory. James introduces biological and physiological information that he is to use later. He shows how 'habit' is of fundamental importance in nervous activity, and therefore in behaviour. He disposes of all the fashionable theories about the nature of 'mind' as irrelevant to psychology, and argues that, 'there is an unmediated correspondence between the succession of states in consciousness with the succession of total brain processes'. Whatever theory one uses, brain processes and states of consciousness are two aspects of the same type of natural phenomena. The biological foundations of psychology are clearly and firmly indicated in these introductory chapters.

After discussing the methods and snares which beset psychological observation, James deals, in a brilliant piece of writing, with his central topic, 'The Stream of Consciousness'. He argues, against the British empiricist psychology and Wundt's German school, that consciousness is not composed of discrete elements joined together. It is a continuous, dynamic complex – a current. It is essentially 'personal' and yet deals with objects and events other than itself. Its main concern is adaptation to the changing stimulation of the environment. The rest of Volume I is an elaboration of this chapter. The chapter on 'Self' expands the conception that experience is highly personal. The processes of selecting and categorizing the 'input' of information from the external world are dealt with in three chapters ('Attention'; 'Conception'; 'Discrimination and Comparison'); and the rest of the volume deals with the theme of 'continuity and change' in the stream of consciousness.

Volume II appears more conventional, the opening chapters being 'Sensation', 'Perception', 'Belief', 'Reasoning', 'Instinct' and 'Volition'. However, James is now exploiting his earlier presentation of physiological data. He is following the working of the nervous system as the basis of behaviour, starting with the peripheral sensory system, going on to the perceptual organization of sensory stimulation, and arguing that cognitive functions are a refinement and elaboration of the afferent perceptual organization. Movement – the efferent system – is the basis for his treatment of instinct, emotion and voluntary action.

The book is revolutionary and forward-looking. In spite of its adherence to 'consciousness' as the main data and 'introspection' as a valid method, James's work is essentially modern in tone and outlook.

The chapter on the 'self' is in many ways typical. The 'self' does not refer to an entity. Everyone has a complex image or concept of himself as a person. The body, its clothing, the house one lives in, one's property, are all part of this conception. But the 'self' also has a behavioural aspect – the role or part one acts out in specific contexts. These roles change: a man is one sort of 'person' in his family, another in his club, another while at work. The conception is influenced by all sorts of environmental factors, and especially by success or failure in striving for goals. At the centre of this conception is physical activity: the operation of the senses, contraction and tension of muscles, movements – all contribute to the feeling of a centre of outgoing activity. This background of feelings, the product of the merging of many neural processes, is the basis for the sense or image of the 'self' which persists through a variety of activities. Images and concepts build up round this physical core to give us a sense of a continuing entity or organization. However, there simply is no homogeneous force or integration of forces behind this image. There is no entity, or substance, or part of a human being which is 'the self'. The transitive states of consciousness we experience and the series of responses we make generate a feeling of connexion between each other and provide a 'feeling' of continuity which serves to confirm our self-identity.

James has no use for an 'ego' or for a number of 'factors' which coordinate to form a personality. The self is simply an idea or concept on a par with other concepts we form. The system of reactions which generate such self-images is unstable – conflict and tension can lead to sudden changes in the role played, or the image in terms of which we think about ourself or our person. In extreme cases, 'dissociation' occurs, and a human being may exhibit two different persons or selves, often contradictory to each other.

In this characteristic chapter, James sketches many conceptions which have been utilized in personality theory and clinical psychology. Future psychologists were to exploit his conceptions more systematically and rigorously, but the original insights and shrewd observations come from William James. An examination of many parts of the *Principles* will reveal similar forward-looking tendencies, along with a scholarly knowledge of all the relevant data available in the 1880s.

It is not difficult, then, to appreciate the importance of James as a founder of modern psychology. He treats psychology as a natural science concerned with the living organism as it strives to adjust to its environment. Psychological functions are treated as refinements of basic biological functions – experience and behaviour serve a variety of ends in the total life of the organism. He regarded mental life as a biological function evolved to enable the human being to adjust to the environment.

James thus came to psychology while it was still a branch of metaphysics and, drawing more on the Darwinian tradition than on German models, transformed the subject into an empirical science. This was no mean achievement, considering that most of his thinking was done in the late 1870s and early 1880s – at the same time as Wundt's earliest work.

What is permanent in James is his general outlook on psychology: he had a saner and more shrewd conception of what psychology is about (or rather how any psychologist should *think* about it at whatever period in its history) than most of his successors. In his thinking, scientific vigour, commonsense and philosophical clarity were nicely balanced. Above all he emphasized the need to study the personality.

HUGO MÜNSTERBERG

In 1892 James brought Hugo Münsterberg (1863–1916) to Harvard to take charge of the work in the experimental psychology laboratory. Münsterberg had been a pupil of Wundt, but had rebelled against the master and had suffered for his effrontery. He strongly emphasized the importance of motor activity as against sensory processes, thus acting as a forerunner of Behaviourism. 'According to the popular view a world of impressions and ideas exists in us entirely independently of our actions and when they are complete and perfect they send their message to some motor apparatus which carries out the order. Such a fancy must be reversed. In every moment the motor situation decides the possibilities in the sensory sphere. Our ideas are the product of our readiness to act. ... We perceive the world just so far as we are prepared to react to certain stimuli.' This was a major shift.

Münsterberg was an active experimenter. Each of his studies was in the form of a monograph rather than a conventional 'paper'. He performed experiments of a highly original kind in such fields as the subjective estimation of time or size, and the influence of drugs on problem-solving. He made a distinction between scientific and humanistic psychology. In the former, physiological experiments are the main interest; in the latter, problems in which value-judgements are unavoidable are discussed (for example, evaluations of 'mental health', which imply judgements about how people ought to behave in a given society). Münsterberg was active in each of these two types of psychology. However, his chief claim to fame was his pioneer work in applied psychology. Here, too, he made a distinction between (a) the experimental or statistical study of basic problems arising from practical affairs and (b) the application to practical activities of methods and techniques evolved in psychology (selection of personnel, vocational guidance, psychotherapy, etc.). He undertook one of the first researches into the effects of advertising on purchasing habits; he devised tests to select people likely to become sufficiently skilful engineers to operate a new type of machine; he was interested in the psychological investigation of factors influencing efficiency in various types of industrial work; and he was interested in criminology (he was the first to try out possible 'lie-detecting' drugs). Much pioneer work in industrial psychology was done under his supervision – a considerable achievement in the period 1900–14.

Apart from his pure, applied and theoretical psychology, Münsterberg was a great writer of popular articles on psychology in weeklies and magazines. This work had a considerable influence in the U.S.A. It put psychology clearly on the academic map and educated the public in its achievements and limitations. Much support for the new science was forthcoming, and psychology soon came to be regarded as a leading subject in America.

Münsterberg's later years were unhappy. When the First World War broke out in 1914 he actively supported Germany. He corresponded with German politicians, and his efforts to prevent the U.S.A. from entering the war on the Western Allied side led to his being regarded as a traitor. He died suddenly in December 1916 while lecturing to Harvard students, and since his death he has been a neglected figure. His work was original and enterprising, greatly extending the scope of psychology as an academic study during its earliest two decades. Together with James, Münsterberg founded an active and vigorous school at Harvard, helping to train Thorndike and Yerkes as Ph.D. students in the 1890s, the first of a series of distinguished pupils.

G. S. HALL

The other 'grand old man' of American psychology, Granville Stanley Hall (1844–1924), has not held such an enduring reputation as William James. He came from a farming family, and after studying at Williams College and encountering Darwin's work, he went on to the Union Theological Seminary, New York, to study for the ministry. He realized that this was not his vocation and, borrowing money, went off to Germany to study philosophy at Bonn and Berlin. A temporary tutorship at Harvard (1876–9) enabled him to study under William James and to obtain a Ph.D. on 'muscular perception of space'. After Harvard, Hall returned to Germany (1879–80), where he studied with Wundt at Leipzig in the first year the psychological laboratory operated there; he was the first American student. In 1882 he was given a lectureship, and in 1884 the chair of psychology at the new Johns Hopkins University. In 1883, he opened the first laboratory in the U.S.A. to be constructed especially for psychological work, and in 1887 founded the *American Journal of Psychology*. No sooner had he begun work, with a new laboratory and a new journal as the main features of psychological work in the U.S.A., than he was asked to become first president of the new Clark University. Here Hall combined the presidency with the chair of psychology, and founded an active graduate school, the object of which was research rather than the teaching of undergraduates. The laboratory was under E. C. Sanford, and a school of educational psychology was established under W. H. Burnham.

In the early 1890s, Hall founded the American Psychological Association, which met regularly to discuss papers by members and generally promote psychological research throughout the U.S.A. Yet Hall was not merely a successful administrator and organizer. He produced and supervised directly a good deal of original work. His early work was clearly influenced by Wundt: at Hopkins he carried out experiments on motor sensations, bilateral asymmetry and movement as the basis of space perception. However, his early affection for Darwin led him away from the analysis of sensory and motor processes, towards the genetic study of human and animal adaptations. He turned to child psychology as his main field of investigation. He used the questionnaire, originated by Galton, as an instrument of research. Over 102 questionnaires were used, inquiring into children's displays of anger, childhood fears, games played with dolls, ideas about the self, the causes of crying, etc., etc. Observations on schoolchildren were carried out systematically in the Worcester State Schools, and over 35,000 records accumulated. A new journal, the *Pedagogical Seminary*, was founded in 1891 to report the result of research in educational and child psychology. Hall published the result of his analyses of many Clark University researches in his two-volumed *Adolescence: Its Psychology* in 1904. It presented a mass of new information and greatly stimulated the psychological study of children and the problems of training and teaching.

Nor was Hall's mind closed to new ideas. Before any other academic psychologist, he grasped the importance of the earliest writings of Freud and Jung. It was he who invited Freud and Jung to America in 1909 and arranged a great conference of American psychologists to hear them expound their theories. His own discoveries about the sexual interests of children made him sympathetic towards Freud's views, and he welcomed an approach which emphasized growth and development while dispensing with both introspection and arid experimentation.

Thus, without developing a systematic theory, Hall shifted the interests of psychologists away from the German model. He trained many of the men who were to found new psychology departments in American universities, and pioneered psychological research in the educational field. As an organizer of scientific psychology his work was efficiently and energetically done; while his own writing and teaching emphasized the developmental and genetic approach to human psychology which Darwin, Galton and James had introduced into psychological science. In the year of his death, 1924, he was president of the American Psychological Association for the second time. Thus, for forty years – the first forty years of psychology in the

U.S.A. – he had a pervasive influence on the discipline, constituting a link between the earliest days and the modern period.

Hall had been the first American to study at Leipzig under Wundt. He was followed by many others. Yet the most influential of these all shared one characteristic of Hall's: they proceeded, on returning to the U.S.A., to deviate widely from the canons and practice of the Leipzig approach. This independence of the pioneers of American psychology was a crucial factor in promoting the rapid changes which, in the first half of the twentieth century, resulted in the development of psychology in so many diverse directions. Not all of these men made brilliant discoveries or introduced new techniques or theories. Nevertheless they continued to develop new ways of psychological thinking which gave American psychology an impetus which the Germans never quite attained.

J. M. CATTELL

J. M. Cattell (1860–1944) had three years at Leipzig as a pupil-assistant to Wundt, and then two years in England as assistant to Francis Galton, whom he described as 'the greatest man I have ever known'. This remark indicates Cattell's orientation in psychology. He had learned from Wundt all the technical skills available to the experimental psychologist; but he had also suffered frustration at the rigid limitations placed by the master on the type of research regarded as scientifically respectable. Galton's developmental approach, and his emphasis on the use of statistics to measure and compare all kinds of individual differences, made a stronger appeal to the young American. Cattell occupied the first chair of psychology to be established at Pennsylvania, but in 1891 he moved to Columbia University, where he remained for twenty-six years.

At first Cattell's work – which was concerned with reaction times and psychophysical experiments, albeit with a distinctive 'functional' and un-Wundtian bias – reflected his German training. However, by 1891 Cattell had turned to investigating the possibility of 'mental tests'. Every year at Columbia fifty freshmen were given tests to measure individual differences – sensory functions, quickness of movement, perception of time-intervals, memory span. Once a large sampling was available, correlational analysis was undertaken. When Binet's tests (pp. 190 ff.) appeared in 1905, Cattell's somewhat disappointing results were eclipsed. Nevertheless this early work was useful in several ways.

For one thing, Cattell devised the 'order of merit ranking method' which has come to be used in many subsequent studies. At first he selected two hundred shades of grey. Subjects were required to order these according to degree of brightness. Errors could be determined by reference to an objective scale for measuring difference in colour-stimuli. From this study, Cattell generalized the method to the field of 'value judgements'. He prepared a list of all people who could be classified as first-class scientific researchers in a particular discipline. Ten distinguished scientists in the field of study then acted as judges, and quite independently of each other ranked the scientists on the list in order of scientific merit. The rankings were combined, and Cattell computed the average position assigned to each individual, and also the variation from judge to judge. Accepting the average rank as an approximation to 'actual order of merit', he used these results in two ways. First, to estimate the accuracy of each judge's estimation, by comparing each ranking with the average rank order. Secondly from the average rankings, together with other data, he made a study of the scientists in relation to place of birth, social status of parents, education, etc. Repeating this study every seven years, he noted changes and trends in the background and training of scientists. This method of ranking constitutes a useful early achievement, and has been adapted widely in psychometric and personality studies.

Another consequence of Cattell's early work on 'mental

tests' was that it interested E. L. Thorndike (pp. 156 ff.), then a pupil of Cattell's and later to become the leading researcher in the field of intelligence testing in the U.S.A. Thus Cattell was a direct link between Galton and the psychometric and testing movement in America.

Although his publications were not many, Cattell's work was of some significance. Boring points out in his *History of Experimental Psychology* that much of Cattell's original work in psychophysics was directed against basic assumptions in Fechner, Müller and Wundt. The important feature of Cattell's psychology was its Galtonian approach: Cattell had no time for theory or 'systems'; he simply wanted a 'description of human nature in respect of its range and variability'. He was interested in the basic skills and capacities in terms of which human beings adjust themselves to their environment, and he sought to discover how exactly individuals differ with regard to specific measurable behaviour. This was empirical and 'individual' psychology without implied controversial or methodological problems. It was typical of the whole trend of American thinking from William James onwards, and gave Cattell the role of man of the moment.

Cattell's main contribution was probably as executive and administrator. He made American psychology a well-organized and integrated discipline. He was editor of six journals, and, with Baldwin, founded the *Psychological Review* in 1894 and also *Psychological Monographs*. These were the vehicles for many original and stimulating papers and they still figure today among the world's leading journals. Cattell was also a founder and an active official of the American Psychological Association, and also of the American Association for the Advancement of Science, which kept psychologists in close touch with leading scientists in other fields through conferences and meetings for the discussion of papers.

In 1917, Cattell was dismissed from Columbia University on account of his vocal and aggressive pacifist stand against America's entry into the First World War. He sued the university and was awarded $40,000 as compensation. He was never reinstated.

In 1921 he founded the Psychological Corporation (organized as a joint-stock company) as an institute for research in applied psychology and as an advisory body for industry, education, etc., on practical psychological problems. This proved highly successful both financially and in terms of scientific achievements.

Cattell was a man of remarkable drive and enthusiasm. Boring says of him, 'In the 1880s and 1890s psychology was new. It needed young aggressive leaders and Cattell was just such a man.' During his time at Columbia he supervised 344 successful candidates for the Ph.D. degree, among whom were many men later to become distinguished psychologists (Woodworth, Strong, Dashiell, to mention only the senior). Through them, he exercised a widespread stimulus to psychology throughout his long and active life. It was his Galtonian approach which made this influence a fortunate one for American psychology at this stage. Anyone committed to a dogmatic and rigorous 'system' would have restricted interest to a narrow range of problems. Cattell kept things going along a broad front and at the same time made sure the problems investigated were sound empirical ones. It was this blend of commonsense and liberalism that made Cattell an important figure.

J. M. BALDWIN

James Mark Baldwin (1861–1934) was a contemporary and collaborator of Cattell's. He belongs to the group which in the 1890s carried out the work begun by James and Hall in the U.S.A. Like so many of the others, he had studied under Wundt at Leipzig, but he had also been stirred by Darwin's writings. He founded the psychology schools at Toronto and Princeton, and re-established the Johns Hopkins laboratory, which had decayed after the departure of Hall to Clark University. Baldwin was a philosopher as much as a psychologist, and his contribution was theoretical. He did original experimental work on kinaesthetics but found it arid and soon re-directed his research interests.

He had four main fields of interest:

(1) Developmental psychology. In 1895 he published *Mental Development in the Child and the Race*. This was an ambitious study of problems in child psychology. *Social and Ethical Interpretation* (1897) continued this study, and presented experimental and observational data on such topics as suggestion and imitation, right- and left-handedness, and the origin and development of speech. The theme is the development of the personality, as viewed from the need to accommodate to society. Individual development is seen as being as much a part of social psychology as of individual psychology.

(2) The psychology of emotion and the study of 'sentiments', 'interests', etc. He argued, against the British empiricists and Wundt, that emotions can be reinstated directly without the aid of cognitive reactions (imagery or perceptual stimulation). Citing clinical data in support of this, he went on to suggest that interests and values have an organization of their own relatively independent of cognitive processes. Affective states are not simply secondary features of a person which are dependent on knowledge about the environment and our relations with it. Baldwin's theory prepared the way for the psycho-analytic emphasis on the primary function of emotion and other affective states in controlling behaviour.

(3) The scope and methods of the new psychology. He argued, against Wundt, that the study of individual differences (rather than the establishment of empirical laws) should be the objective of psychology, and in *Darwin and the Humanities* (1900) he presented the genetic-developmental approach as basic not merely for psychology but for sociology and ethics as well.

(4) The work of French psychologists, an influence which increased as he grew older. He greatly admired Charcot, Janet and Ribot (see Chapters 8 and 9). He

translated their writings and made free use of their approach. In 1913 he left America and lived in France until his death in Paris in 1934. His later writings (for example *French and American Ideals*, 1914) were mainly in the interests of Franco-American understanding.

Baldwin's contribution, like that of Cattell, did not rest solely on his writings and teachings at Princeton and Johns Hopkins. In addition to helping Cattell to found and edit the *Psychological Review*, he founded and edited the *Psychological Bulletin* in 1904. In 1901–6 he published his huge *Dictionary of Philosophy and Psychology*, writing many of the articles in this encyclopedia himself, editing others, and organizing the work of over sixty contributors. His little *History of Psychology* (1913) is one of the first histories.

Baldwin thus contributed to the development of American psychology by modifying the influence of Germany, adapting the ideas of Darwin and Galton, and beginning new fields of investigation (child study for example).

YALE

The University of Yale, celebrated in recent times as a centre of psychological research, made its contribution in the pioneering days.

G. T. Ladd (1842–1921) had initiated experimental psychology at Yale in the late 1880s. His textbook *The Elements of Physiological Psychology* (1887), although presenting the usual fragments of German experimentalism, diverged in a new direction by giving detailed treatment to the physiology of the nervous system. However, Ladd, who was a theologian and philosopher by training, decided to hand over experimental psychology to an assistant.

In 1892, E. W. Scripture (1864–1945) took charge of the laboratory at Yale. He had taken the customary Ph.D. at Leipzig under Wundt, and from 1892 to 1903 spent a useful decade at Yale. He was closer to Wundt than most of the Americans, being dedicated to the conception of psychology as an experimental science which must approach the model of physics as closely as possible. His *New Psychology* (1898) is as typical of his times as any textbook could be. There are nine chapters on the psychophysical study of the perception of time, six on spatial discrimination experiments and eleven on 'energy' (lifting weights, fatigue in voluntary action, resistance to heaviness, etc.). The book is strictly factual, with no theory or discussion of 'problems'; there are 124 illustrations of apparatus and graphs, and almost every page has its tables of psychophysical measurements. Scripture's researches were extremely competent. His field was sensations of tone, on which he published a series of papers in the form of monographs. His pupil, C. E. Seashore (1866–1949), continued this work with success in the 1920s.

Scripture left America in 1903 and studied medicine at Munich, qualifying in 1906 at the age of 42. After studying speech defects at a Columbia University clinic for several years, he went to London in 1912, where he founded a laboratory for the study of speech neurology at the West End Hospital for Nervous Diseases. The rest of his life was devoted partly to this work – investigation into the neurological illnesses responsible for speech disorders – and partly to basic research in phonetics. Thus, even Scripture followed the American tradition of straying from the strict orthodoxy of Wundt's psychology. Indeed, he became interested in Freud's writings and had plans for investigating unconscious processes experimentally. Although his influence after 1903 was only indirect, he forms part of the advance party of American psychologists, since he continued to contribute to American psychological journals. Certainly in the 1890s he laid the foundations of a sound tradition at Yale. 'Experimental Psychology can never rise above a rather amateurish level till the leaders can handle vectors, Hamiltonians, potentials, as well as the representatives of the physical sciences.' It is not too fanciful to see in this dictum the beginnings of a Yale theory of psychology which comes down to our own times.

E. B. TITCHENER AND CORNELL

The year 1892 was an important one in the history of American psychology. Two of the great psychology schools – at Cornell and Chicago – were established in that year, and their rivalry was a stimulating and energizing factor for a quarter of a century. The Cornell department was the work of Edward Bradford Titchener (1867–1927). Titchener was an Englishman who had read philosophy and physiology at Oxford. From 1890 until coming to America, he studied at Leipzig under Wundt. Leipzig influenced him deeply. While exhibiting great independence of interests and bringing much of the British associationist tradition with him, he developed his researches and his thinking along Wundtian lines. He is sometimes regarded simply as an expositor and disciple of Wundt, especially since the organization of teaching at Cornell was modelled closely on that of Leipzig. Titchener was sympathetic to the work of the Würzburg group as well as to that of the Leipzig laboratory, and he did sufficient work at Cornell to constitute a school on his own. Nevertheless, he was in many ways a follower of traditional lines and was opposed to many characteristically American developments.

Although, unlike Wundt, he avoided philosophical theories, he systematically formulated a methodology: the principles in terms of which a strictly experimental and scientific psychology should proceed to achieve its aims. This systematic formulation, together with a massive research programme, constituted a force in American psychology from 1892 until about 1925–30. The Cornell laboratory was for some time the dominating influence in American psychology. It was Titchener as much as anyone else who made experimental psychology an accepted and flourishing academic discipline. It was not simply as an editor of the *American Journal of Psychology*, or as the English translator of Wundt's *Vorlesungen* and

Külpe's *Grundriss,* or as the author of the *Primer of Psychology* (1898) and the monumental textbook *Experimental Psychology* (1901–5) that Titchener exercised influence. He was unquestionably a powerful and magnetic personality. His scholarship, scientific vigour and dedication, combined with his great charm, made him a father figure and leader of a devoted group of pupils. For educated people in America in the years immediately before the First World War, 'experimental psychology' was synonymous with the work done at Cornell and with the Titchener canon. All other psychology – abnormal, child, animal, applied – was 'different'. This is all the more remarkable because of the increasing isolation of Titchener within American psychology. He was unsympathetic to the work published by Cattell and Baldwin in the *Psychological Review*; he found the approach of most members of the American Psychological Association uncongenial to his beliefs about psychology, and he ceased to attend its meetings. And he rarely came to leave Ithaca, the seat of Cornell University, being content to work with his own team along his own lines.

What was Titchener's approach? It must be admitted that it was traditionalist and conservative compared with the new tendencies in America. His psychology has been labelled 'Structuralism' and, in many ways, it is a formulation of the 'new psychology' from Europe. Just as sensory processes and perceptual organization had been made the subject of laboratory investigations by experimental physiologists, Titchener simply wanted to extend the methods of experimental science to mental processes.

The general laws governing mental processes – sensations, imagery, percepts, judgements, acts of recall, etc. – could be discovered by the application of scientific method. Psychology is thus modelled carefully on physics and physiology, but with the contents of human consciousness as its data. Titchener defended the study of consciousness as the main objective of experimental psychology. All science has its beginnings in experience. Physics simply studies experience without reference to human beings, while psychology studies the same data with reference to the person who is subject to the experience. Space, time and mass are thus constant dimensions for the physicist; but in psychology, subjective time is long or short, space large or small, weights light or heavy, according to various factors affecting the person who experiences perceptions of space, time, and weight. For the physicists there is no colour, sound or smell or taste – these qualities depend on the reaction of a given nervous system to stimulation from wave-activity. However, in psychology there are red patches, high vibrating noises and pungent, sickly smells. Thus, the psychologist views experience as a series of contents of consciousness which can be noted, described, and possibly measured. Indeed, these contents are the basis of, for instance, the light waves which the physicist postulates or constructs as the result of reasoning from known sensory reactions (such as seeing red objects). The psychologist's approach to the data – common to psychology and physics – is as fundamental and reasonable as one could wish: scientific observation is all that is required to make psychology a branch of natural science.

Titchener differentiated between the psychological approach to his data and the respective approaches of metaphysics, of commonsense and of practical interests. Metaphysicians do not attempt exact observations of the contents of consciousness: they speculate about the relationship of our experiences to 'reality', with a view of determining the scope and limits of human knowledge (for example, do we know the real properties of physical objects from our sensory experiences?). This is a different sort of inquiry from a psychological one. Psychology is also marked off from our commonsense beliefs and attitudes about mind and consciousness. Titchener regarded commonsense beliefs about human nature as an enemy of genuine psychology – especially did he detest the 'theological' concept of a soul or ego, controlling and organizing our reactions from some inner centre. He believed that scientific psychology does not develop out of our commonsense beliefs and insights: it starts from strictly controlled observations of its data.

Finally, he held that psychology is a pure and general science. It has no practical aims. It does not exist to discover means for improving human performances, to correct human infirmities. It is not a technology or applied science, aimed at helping to cure 'mental illness', improve educational methods or assist in solving human problems in industry. It is impersonal, detached, abstract, yet strictly empirical in its methods, aiming at laws which explain what happens in *any* mind. There may be studies which do aid education, psychiatry or industry, by means of empirical investigations into the factors which influence human behaviour, but these are not part of experimental psychology.

Introspection is the principal method, but this is a skill requiring special training and practice before it can be used. One of the aims of such training is the elimination of habits which interfere with exact observation of the changing contents of consciousness. We tend to read into introspective situations assumptions derived from previous experience or common belief: thus when we try to describe what is perceived when we look at a table, we usually go beyond the sensory contents and attribute all sorts of properties to the object. What the trained observer has to isolate are colours, shapes, degrees of brightness, spatial patterns, central and peripheral items, etc. Thus, introspection must be a technical accomplishment fitted to the requirements of laboratory experiments and never an armchair pastime.

Titchener was strict in making psychology an experimental science, whatever the difficulties involved in disciplining 'introspective' reports. His approach to the data was defined in three stages:

(1) Analysis. The complex content of conscious experience must be reduced to basic elements or units. This is the traditional programme. Titchener wanted more pre-

cise answers to the questions 'what are these elements?', 'what are their attributes?', 'how can we measure these attributes?'

(2) Synthesis. How are these elements combined and arranged into complex structures? What laws govern the combination and sequence of elements?

(3) Explanation. Why are the mental structures what they are observed to be? Psychology provides exact descriptions of conscious experience. Ultimately Titchener maintained it was necessary to explain psychological descriptions by reference to the physiology of the brain and nervous system. Titchener's choice of elements was unoriginal and orthodox. Sensations were the elements of perceptual experience; images were the elements in thinking and imagination; affections were the elements in emotional reactions. Sensations and images have attributes in terms of which they may be defined. They have specific qualities (they are cold, blue, salty, etc.); they vary in intensity (any quality can be placed on a scale running from zero to the highest discriminable limit – thus X is brighter, louder, stronger to a measurable degree than Y); they vary in duration (each quality has existence in time – it appears, is fixated, fades); and they vary in clearness (a quality is central or peripheral in its context). Affections do not have the attributes of clearness but possess the other three. Thus elements (sensations, images, emotions) and their discriminable attributes are the concepts in terms of which conscious states are analysed. Everything that occurs in consciousness is reducible to these elements and their combinations.

As the basis of a psychological programme in the period 1890–1914 this may seem archaic and uninspiring. Yet in his own work, in that of his research students and in his monumental textbooks, Titchener presented some good experimental studies in this context of his times. His erudite knowledge of the literature of experimental psychology enabled him to do some sound psychophysical experiments, and also some interesting work on 'focusing' under the title of 'attention', and this type of work justly earned him a reputation as an experimentalist. However, much of Titchener's research revealed the limitations of his structuralist methodology. Introspection of the contents of consciousness is a dubious technique, and Titchener's involvement in the 'imageless thought' controversy led many to doubt the adequacy of his methods, as also those of Wundt's school. There simply *had* to be some contents of an imagal kind in thinking, even when careful introspection failed to reveal anything between the presentation of a problem and the utterance or execution of the 'correct' solution! Titchener's adherence to the controlled observation of 'internal' conscious states under laboratory conditions was too backward-looking to survive. Yet, throughout the first two decades of the century, Cornell was a point of reference in American thinking about psychology – if only as a stimulus to revolt and disagreement.

FUNCTIONALISM

The most systematic and organized movement against Titchener's approach came from the new university of Chicago, founded in the year in which Titchener arrived in the U.S.A. – 1892.

J. R. Angell (1869–1949) had been a pupil of William James and had studied, inevitably, with Wundt. He was a lifelong friend of Titchener's, whom he had met in Germany, but he could not accept the Englishman's view of psychology. Angell became Professor of Psychology at Chicago in 1894. He did some sound experimental work, trained a whole generation of young psychologists and built up one of the largest psychology schools in the U.S.A.

There arrived at Chicago in the same year, as Professor of Philosophy, a young man named John Dewey (1859–1952) who was destined to become one of America's leading philosophical thinkers. In the 1890s he was interested in the new science of psychology, but was dissatisfied with its methodology and theoretical implications. Angell and Dewey found they had much in common. Together with G. H. Mead and A. W. Moore (both Assistant Professors of Philosophy), they formed a group who earnestly discussed questions about the fundamentals of psychology. Out of these discussions emerged an approach to psychology sufficiently comprehensive and systematic to constitute a 'school', to which the name 'Functionalism' became fixed. Neither Angell nor Dewey had any intention of founding a systematic school, but in fact it became the first in a series of 'schools' or 'systems' which in the first half of the twentieth century divided psychologists, at the same time stimulating new projects and interests.

Functionalism was partly a reaction against the teaching of Titchener and the persisting influence of Wundt in America; partly an attempt to clarify the tendencies which James, Hall, Cattell, Baldwin and others had initiated in their various and diverse psychological writings. Once again, both Dewey and Angell acknowledged their debt to Charles Darwin and the developing biological sciences; the positive side of Functionalism was the development and refinement of ideas within this movement. The other aspect was critical: getting rid of, or at least modifying, conceptions in structuralist psychology which seemed outmoded or mistaken.

The new approach began with the publication of an article by Dewey in the *Psychological Review* (1897), 'The Reflex Arc Concept in Psychology'. The reflex arc was emerging as a working concept. Dewey regarded this as a continuation of a redundant dualism. Sensory and motor functions were treated as two distinct types of existent. He argued against breaking down activity into parts or elements which have then to be related. Activity is continuous: stimulus and response; sensation and movement; sensory, central, and motor portions of an 'arc' split what is continuous and integrated into discrete and artificial units. If these distinctions have any meaning, they point to the fact that different phases in a continuous process serve different functions, although the process, taken as a whole, can only be described and identified in terms of the final result (or function) which the activity achieves. Why distinguish between 'sensation' and 'movement', since one has visual sensations only as a result of 'looking at' or 'discriminating' part of the environment, which in itself involves motor activity of head and eyes when an object is fixated? When one sees food, for example, one may reach out to grasp it, and perceptual and motor activities are coordinated within the goal-directed activity involved in reaching–grasping–bringing to the mouth–biting. Cognitive-affective factors are involved in 'seeing the food, wanting to eat, taking it . . .'.

The distinctions we make in describing the total activity are somewhat artificial and arbitrary in any case. However, the analytic and structuralist psychologists employ concepts which give a misleading description of behaviour. Actions cannot be adequately represented in these terms. Moreover, the context of any action must be considered. The firing of a gun will act as one sort of stimulus for the subject if he is reading, but as quite a different one if he is on sentry duty. Again, in the middle of battle, with its artillery fire, exploding shells, etc., a single shot from a rifle might not be discriminated at all. In other words, how a stimulus impinges on present activity or 'set', how the various systems are integrated, determines the function for the subject on any given occasion.

The only way to allow for these facts, Dewey concluded, is to think of experience and behaviour in terms of the function which a response (or series of responses) serves. What are the consequences for the organism? Does the behaviour enable the organism to change in relation to environmental impositions, or to adjust the environment to satisfy its basic needs? The ends which reactions bring about and the means they constitute in doing so can be expressed in terms of a 'functional' approach. What does a specific action bring off? What difference does it make in the subject's adjustment? Mental processes cannot be separated from the conditions, internal and environmental, which give rise to their occurrence, nor from their effects – of which the human agent frequently has foresight.

Angell took a similar line in his writings. Functionalism deals with operations rather than abstracted 'contents' of consciousness. Instead of analysing states of mind into basic elements, it asks: what does a mental operation accomplish and under what conditions? Functions are 'dispositions'. An identical function may be mediated by different physiological mechanisms and different organizations of responses. It is the 'function' that persists, and recurs, while the contents of consciousness, and the specific response pattern, occur only once. To describe and classify the basic dispositions which humans have is the first task of psychology: the second is to exhibit the biological utility of basic psychological capacities and skills – what they do for the organism in promoting efficient adaptation. The whole setting of an action should be taken into account – including the goal towards which the action can be seen to be directed.

This theoretical statement concerning the scope and aims of psychology had two main effects. In the first place, the Functionalist emphasis on studying the utility of actions in their total context led naturally to attempts to study practical problems. Dewey's interest in education encouraged the systematic study of problems in educational psychology. C. H. Judd (1867–1946) came to Chicago in 1909 as dean of the school of education in which much original work was done, largely under the stimulus of Dewey's theories of education. Judd's textbook *Psychology* (1907), more than Angell's (1904), gave a clear exposition of the Functionalist point of view. Applied psychology received a considerable stimulus from the Functionalists, and most of the first steps in applied psychology in the U.S.A. were taken in the period during which this view was widespread. In 1910 Münsterberg began research into practical problems concerning the psychological causes of industrial accidents, problems of the psychological factors involved in advertising, selection of people likely to have specific motor skills, etc. F. Parsons, in *Choosing a Vocation* (1909), reported the first studies in vocational guidance. Away from Chicago, Columbia University took over the New York Teachers College in 1899 which, with E. L. Thorndike in charge of educational psychology, produced the researches which led to extremely useful intelligence tests for selecting children for higher education.

Secondly, Functionalist theories encouraged flexibility in the design of laboratory experiments in psychology. Thorndike's experiments with animal subjects, reported in his *Animal Intelligence*, used a simple design which was soon extended to human subjects. Given a problem (for example, to find the simplest path through a maze, or to find how to open a door by pulling a loop of cord downwards), the experimenter simply observes (a) whether or not the behaviour of the subject succeeds or fails in reaching the goal, (b) what variables introduced facilitate or inhibit success.

Early examples of this type of experiment were Ruger's problem-solving experiments of 1910. Human subjects were asked to speak their thoughts while trying to disentangle metal mechanical puzzles, while the experimenter described the methods and stages through which they worked towards the solution of the puzzles. More typical of Wundt and Titchener's research were physiological experiments directed towards an analysis of sensory processes or perceptual organization; or the measurement of reaction times; or the establishment of 'thresholds' for the discrimination of different values of a stimulus. The Americans developed less rigorous but often more interesting experiments on learning and thought processes. All this came out of the new interests and attitudes towards the data and methods of psychology stimulated by the Functionalist movement. If Functionalism was chiefly the formulation in abstract terms of new policies, it did at least confirm and strengthen the explorations which Americans were carrying out in these years.

The controversies between Titchener and his associates and the Functionalists merely stimulated the divergent tendencies among American psychologists. Titchener published two articles in the *Philosophical Review* for 1898 ('The Postulates of Structural Psychology') and 1899 ('Structural and Functional Psychology') in which he attacked Functionalist precepts and defended his own approach. J. R. Angell's replies (especially 'The Province of Functional Psychology', *Psychological Review*, 1907) started controversies which continued until as late as 1930. For the first time, the new scientific psychology, which had emerged during the latter decades of the nineteenth century, was divided into rival schools – a feature which was to be even more evident after 1920.

To some this was distressing – natural sciences do not normally divide into rival theories concerning the scope, methods and objectives of the science, generating fundamentally different 'models' of scientific procedure. Many had hoped that theoretical wranglings would have been left behind once psychology escaped from its confinement within the discourse of the philosophy of mind. Hence the anger displayed at the Functionalist revolt by those who had accepted Wundt's teaching or the modified development by Titchener of the 'new psychology'. Others, however, regarded it as a healthy sign that psychologists were exploring new conceptions concerning the scope and methods of their new discipline. The German experimentalists, while doing good service in demonstrating the possibilites of psychology as an experimental science (at least with regard to some questions), had developed their techniques in such a way as to limit the scope of the new science. The sensory processes, perception, reaction times, judgements (usually of size, shape, distance, weight and other sensory modalities), constituted a narrow field of topics. Moreover, the Germans operated within a conceptual framework defined by the philosophical theory common within the British empiricist–associationist school. This prescribed – as Titchener had argued – that consciousness is the data, and the analysis of conscious states into elements (derived from the sensory and perceptual processes) was the main task of descriptive psychology. That this theory is open to serious objections – philosophical as well as methodological – did not occur to Wundt, Helmholtz, Titchener and other leaders within the German 'new psychology'. A revolt was inevitable and the Functionalists were the first to make this explicit.

The Functionalists were accused of introducing ambiguity into psychology by using woolly terms. The concept of 'function' has many different meanings. It is sometimes synonymous with such activity-categories as 'perceiving' or 'recalling'; but it also refers to the utility of an activity, as when perceiving a predator may enable an animal to take defensive action and so survive. We could therefore speak of the 'function of a function …' Harvey Carr, Angell's successor at Chicago, argued that the use of the term 'function' in psychology is similar to its use in biological literature. A function may mean activity such as 'breathing' or 'digesting'; and it may also mean the utility of an activity – the function of breathing being the oxidation of the blood. These two uses may be related by using a third meaning of 'function', familiar in mathematics, where a 'function' denotes a relation of contingency between two items without specifying that relation. To say oxidation is a function of breathing is to refer to one kind of relation (that of 'usefulness'); to say breathing is a function of the lungs is to refer to another type of relation. Psychology may legitimately and fruitfully apply these uses of 'function'. The 'function' of thinking may refer to the job which certain behaviour patterns perform in relation to the total needs of an organism; or the 'function' of reasoning may imply that thinking is the operation of some underlying (for example, cortical) structure.

Carr pointed out that the Functionalist concepts can be used in strictly empirical and descriptive ways, so avoiding the charge that 'utility' implies some teleological form of explanation in terms of mystical 'purposes'. To talk of the utility of an activity is simply to say that, as a matter of fact, it invariably produces effects or results which are definable in terms of 'outcome' for the agent – seeking, seizing and eating food reduces hunger, nourishes, etc.

All this may seem theoretical and remote. Yet the shift in emphasis was considerable – away from the introspective analysis of perceptual data and towards the study of actions and their effects on the subject's relationships to environment. The Functionalists achieved as much as the succeeding Behaviourist school in moving away from the 'establishment' theory of psychology, and their importance cannot be over-estimated. They made articulate a new programme for psychology and began the business of discarding old concepts and assumptions once they had begun to restrict, rather than stimulate, inquiry.

E. L. THORNDIKE, J. B. WATSON AND BEHAVIOURISM

One of the most typically American of the psychologists who emerged in this period, E. L. Thorndike (1874–1949), was clearly influenced by Functionalist principles and is often classified as a Functionalist, although he called himself a 'Connexionist' (p. 163). Thorndike is an important figure. He succeeded Lloyd Morgan as the leading worker in the field of animal behaviour, preferring experiments to field studies; he devised some of the most widely used intelligence tests, and his theories of mental testing were widely accepted in the U.S.A.; he laid the foundations of the most active centre for research in educational psychology in the U.S.A. in the 1920s; and he presented a conceptual framework for psychology – a development of his early studies of learning – which is one of the main sources of the Behaviourist theory of psychology.

Thorndike, unlike so many of his predecessors, received all his training in the U.S.A. After graduating from Wesleyan College he went to Harvard and studied English Literature and Philosophy. He worked under William James and took his Ph.D. on the thesis 'Animal Intelligence: An Experimental Study of the Associative Processes in Animals' (1898). The research was conducted under primitive conditions, as there was no laboratory space available at Harvard. Thorndike's landlady objected to his keeping his chickens in the bedroom, and so William James gave Thorndike his cellar to work in at his home in Irving Terrace – a research project of which James's children approved. In the next year Thorndike left for a post at Columbia University. He finished off his researches into animal intelligence and published the original thesis (Psychological Monograph No. 8, 1898) together with further papers in *Animal Intelligence* (1911).

This work will be discussed in connexion with his formulation of a fundamental principle of learning – the Law of Effect. Cattell had asked Thorndike to generalize his interests from animal learning to the problems of human learning. From 1902 onwards, educational psychology became his major interest. *Educational Psychology* (1903) and the Introduction to the *Theory of Mental and Social Measurements* (1904) were his earliest publications. Most of his work on intelligence tests, however, came later and owed much to the original work of Binet and its refinements by Terman.

Thorndike's work with animals is well known. He was disturbed by the tendency of researchers into animal behaviour to fall back on anthropomorphic explanations, involving the hypothesis that animals can 'think' or recall previous situations. He wanted to explore the possibility of a more purely mechanical explanation of animal adaptability – if only as a corrective to the anthropomorphizing which had been prevalent amongst Darwinians anxious to 'upgrade' the lower animals in the interests of their theory. As a result of his experiments, Thorndike postulated that animals learn responses the consequences of which are 'rewarding', and drop responses the consequences of which are 'punishing' in some sense or other. The 'effect' of making a response, in terms of its 'feedback' to the animal, is the crucial factor determining what it will or will not tend to learn.

To illustrate Thorndike's Law of Effect and make clear its implications, consider a typical experiment of the kind instituted by Thorndike and employed by so many succeeding experimental psychologists. If a rat is placed in a T-shaped maze (with the starting point at the bottom of the vertical line and the 'choice point' at the junction of the vertical with the horizontal), it will be found that most rats over a large number of runs will turn right or left at the choice point with equal frequency. If the rat is deprived of food, and a food reward is placed at the end of the right-hand horizontal, it will be found that a rat will quickly learn always to turn right at the choice point. The presence of the food reward controls the rat's behaviour in turning right instead of left. A number of experiments show that rats will turn right for other 'rewards' than food – water, when thirsty; a mate, when deprived of one for a period of time; escape from a noxious stimulus such as an electric shock – all these act as 'reinforcers' or 'rewards' in controlling a specific response.

It is found that many different kinds of response can be controlled in this way. A rat will learn to run a given sequence in a maze, press a lever downwards twice in rapid succession, turn a wheel in a given direction, pull a chain downwards – indeed, it will perform any learnable response within the limitations of its repertory, under the control of any suitable reinforcing stimulus. This generalization from a large number of experiments is simply the Law of Effect, an inductively established, empirical law. Any reinforcing agent (food, drink, escape from noxious stimulus, etc.) has the property of strengthening any learnable response in an animal's repertory (going right rather than left at a choice point in a maze, pulling a lever downwards, etc.). Thorndike's law describes one set of circumstances in which certain animals learn – a form of learning which need not imply intelligence or memory on the animal's part, since its behaviour is controlled by the presence or absence of an environmental reinforcing stimulus, such as food, consequent upon a specific response for a hungry animal.

However, Thorndike sometimes wrote as if he were prepared to take a step beyond the statement of this simple empirical law. He implied that the only way to increase the strength of a response is through the operation of a reinforcing agent. The necessary condition for any animal-learning is that the response (or series of responses) to be learned must be reinforced on this model: the response to be learned has consequences which 'satisfy' some basic state of need present in the animal at the time at which the response is made. For example, when the animal is hungry, the response to be learned results in its arrival in the presence of food (food here being the reinforcing agent). This implies that all learning is subject to the Law of Effect as manifested by typical animal experiments – at least for animal subjects and perhaps, in a more complex and subtle way, for human learning as well. In order that a response shall be learned, it must be reinforced by an effect of that response which satisfies or reduces some dominant need or 'drive'. This generalization goes far beyond the evidence provided by typical experiments of Thorndike and his successors. One type of animal-learning does conform to the law, but does all learning? Thorndike is constructing a theory of animal-learning which requires much more thorough investigation before it is confirmed or confuted. The importance of Thorndike's work in animal-learning, and his theory of learning, is the influence it had on systematic psychology in the next decade or so. Taken in its broader, speculative, theoretical sense, the Law of Effect became a basic principle in the Behaviourism of both B. F. Skinner (b. 1904) and C. L. Hull (1884–1952), two of the leaders in the Behaviourist schools of the 1930–45 period (see Chapter 12).

More immediately, Thorndike's work had a powerful impact on American psychology in the years immediately prior to the First World War. In the first place it initiated an active movement, in which psychological laboratory experiments used animal subjects as well as humans. Experimental psychologists have often been criticized for spending more time researching with rats, cats, dogs and monkeys than with humans; yet there are obviously some advantages in the study of animal behaviour. The environment and repertory of animals is much simpler than those of humans and so more conditions can be controlled and varied by the experimenter. It is sometimes possible to regulate the life history of each animal subject, so that previous learning can be known; in addition, the simple responses of an animal can often be observed, described and measured with considerable accuracy. However, specialization in this field is perfectly legitimate.

One of the earliest psychologists so to specialize was R. M. Yerkes (1876–1956), though he has an importance quite apart from his work with apes. Yerkes, after studying at Ursinus College, proceeded in 1897 to Harvard. Münsterberg encouraged him to combine zoology with psychology in his graduate studies, and so train as a comparative psychologist. Many of his earlier papers were frankly zoological, but he soon emerged as one of the most distinguished researchers in animal behaviour. He remained at Harvard until 1917 when he went off on war service as psychologist in the U.S. Army – he had had experience of psychometric work for several years when he worked in the Boston State Hospital Psychopathic Department. From 1910 he collaborated with a young psychologist working at Baltimore, J. B. Watson (pp. 163 ff.). Watson was engaged in the comparative study of vision in animals. He was impressed with Yerkes's psychological work with animal subjects, its objectivity, scientific rigour and effectiveness in achieving definite results. The year before the start of their collaboration, Yerkes had translated, with the help of a Russian student, S. Morgulis, some of the papers of Pavlov, reporting his discovery of the conditioned reflex. This was reported in an article in the *Psychological Bulletin* (1909) by Yerkes and Morgulis. Important as was Yerkes's early work on reptiles and amphibians, his greatest work, carried out in collaboration with his wife, did not come until after the First World War, when he was at Yale. At this stage, therefore, his influence on Watson may have been his most outstanding contribution.

It is necessary to digress by referring briefly to the important work of the Russian, Pavlov, which Yerkes first introduced to English-speaking psychologists in 1909. Pavlov's work is well known in its own right. However, what concerns us here is his contribution to the shifting in psychological theory and methodology which occurred in America just before, and immediately after, the First World War. Pavlov was interested in the digestive secretions involved in the utilization of ingested foodstuffs. Using dogs as experimental subjects, he noticed quite by chance that salivation, which is a purely reflex action occurring when food is felt in the mouth, often appeared before the dog was actually fed. Many stimuli associated with feeding – the sight of the food container, the smell of the food, the footsteps and clanking of the food container as it was being brought down a corridor to the animals' room – all these were sufficient to set off salivation. This led Pavlov to conduct his celebrated experiment. Every time that food powder was placed in the mouth of a dog this 'unconditioned stimulus' (food) was paired with the sounding of a buzzer ('conditioned stimulus'). Of course the animal salivated to the food ('unconditioned response') and the amount of saliva was measured. After a number of pairings of food with buzzer, the buzzer was sounded alone. The dog salivated as a response to the buzzer ('conditioned response') – the salivation to the buzzer is conditional upon its being paired with an unconditioned stimulus.

The experiment suggested how a simple form of learning takes place. Conditioning is a process whereby a reflex is modified, so that a hitherto neutral stimulus comes to evoke a specific response and so form the basis for a new habit. No process of mental association was needed to explain such 'learning' or 'habit formation'. Like digestion, the process of conditioning depends solely on the reflex arc.

Whether or not he was fully conversant with Pavlov's work through his association with Yerkes, J. B. Watson certainly made full use of the concept of conditioning in the later formulations of his new programme for psychology.

Other influences which affected him were the studies in animal psychology which had been going on steadily since Darwin's day. Watson accepted Lloyd Morgan's maxim that it is unwise to 'infer' what might be going on in an animal's consciousness when simpler explanations will suffice. Thorndike's experiments and Law of Effect confirmed and extended the application of this principle. All that one can strictly observe is selective-discriminatory behaviour on the part of the animal. Certain environmental events seem regularly to elicit or confirm specific reactions from the animal. Stimuli, responses and physiological data concerning the sensory-perceptual-motor apparatus are the only factors needed for any description and explanation of what animals do and how they do it. This ensures that the psychologist deals with observable and checkable facts. It occurred to Watson that these methodological principles which worked so well with animals might apply to human beings as well.

Thorndike had worked out the basis of a new form of associationism which he called 'Connexionism'. 'All psychological processes consist of the functioning of native and acquired connexions between situations and responses.' Any habit or skill which an animal uses in escaping from a puzzle box or learning a maze is based on the connexion between stimuli from the environment and specific responses. Thorndike replaces associations between mental contents with associations between environmental events impinging on the sensory apparatus and motor activities. Thorndike was not immediately concerned with the physiological connexions underlying the linking of discrete stimuli with discrete response factors: it is sufficient for the psychologist to discover such correlations, and the environmental and internal conditions under which such correlations occur. Thus, adaptive behaviour is to be regarded as the associative shifting between situation (or stimulus) variables and response variables. Thorndike's work gave rise to the first formulation of a stimulus–response model for psychology. His Law of Effect supplied the basis for a theory of 'motivation' in terms of the arousal and satisfaction of primitive 'needs' or 'drives'.

The raw materials of Behaviourism were rapidly being assembled in the early years of the twentieth century. It was Watson who presented a formal and systematic exposition of the new approach to psychology. In the *Psychological Review* (1913), he published an article 'Psychology as the Behaviorist Views It', and followed this by his book, *Behavior: An Introduction to Comparative Psychology* (1914). In the *Psychological Review* for 1916 appeared his article 'The Place of the Conditioned Reflex in Psychology', while his major work *Psychology from the Standpoint of a Behaviorist* was published in 1919 (2nd edition 1924). Thus, although the main impact of Watson's theory was not felt until after the war, the thinking-out of his position and his first statements came just before, and thus belong to the early period of American psychology.

Watson had studied at Chicago under Angell and began work as an 'animal psychologist' in 1903. He went to Johns Hopkins in 1908 as professor and continued his researches into the visual sensitivity of animals to colour. He became interested in fundamental problems concerning the scope, methods and aims of psychology as a science, and the results of his analytical thinking were the books and papers outlining a new conception of psychology. In 1920 he was involved in a divorce action and resigned his appointment, entering advertising and eventually becoming the president of a successful business organization. He died in 1958.

Watson's Behaviourism was concerned with the question what sort of a science psychology ought to be. It rested on a few simple postulates:

(1) Psychologists should no longer take the 'field of consciousness' as their data. Conscious experience has proved vague subject-matter, difficult to fixate and describe accurately. Overt behaviour should be the data. Nearly all psychological functions can be described in terms of responses, since they are involved with the business of adaptation to environment. Even if there is an 'inner aspect' (which Watson did not deny) this can be ignored without loss by the psychologist.

(2) It follows that introspection as the method of psychological 'observation' must be discarded. Controversies over 'imageless thought' and the basic properties of sensations reveal the futility of trying to make introspection exact. Instead, the psychologist should observe and measure (where possible) the responses of his subjects.

(3) The study of mental events (sensations, images, mental acts) should be replaced by the study of behaviour, and behaviour could be analysed in terms of connexions or correlations between visual, auditory, tactual, kinaesthetic and other types of 'stimuli' and the 'responses' which are made to them. In his later papers, Watson argued that the mechanism con-

trolling such association between stimulus (S) and response (R) variables was the conditioned reflex – and its refinements in the nervous system.

(4) The aim of psychology to be completely objective and scientific is thus to be achieved by reducing psychological studies as far as possible to physiological studies. 'Mental' science must change into 'physical' science. Movements of limbs, secretions of glands, electrical discharges in nerve tissue, verbal utterances, blushing, grimacing, tensing of muscles, are the proper data of behaviour – together with environmental events which may evoke or influence such 'responses'. Thus, sensation and perception are studied in terms of discriminatory responses to specific stimuli; imagery is reduced to kinaesthetic reactions; memory and learning are habits developed out of conditioned responses; thinking is sub-vocal speech-habit, etc., etc. The difference between physiology and psychology is one only of emphasis: physiology is more molecular in its approach to the functioning of the organism; psychology deals with that functioning at a more molar level of description.

This viewpoint involved a change in the techniques and methods of psychological research as well as in its systematic theory. The methods of experimental physiology could be more vigorously and directly applied than in the era of Wundt and his Functionalist rivals, to whom introspection and the analysis of consciousness was still of primary importance.

Watson's programme made an enormous impact on American psychology in the early 1920s. Although his 'naïve Behaviourism' was not widely acceptable, nearly everybody began to develop subtler and more sophisticated forms of Behaviourism based on the S–R formula. Hunter, Weiss, Lashley, Holt, Kuo, Guthrie, Skinner, Hull, Tolman, Osgood – all developed new varieties within the broad concept of Behaviourism between 1920 and the late 1950s (Chapter 12). Moreover, Watson had predecessors who contributed to the basic postulates of this complicated movement. The English philosopher Thomas Hobbes (1588–1679) has some claims to be the first Behaviourist; Auguste Comte (1798–1857) attacked introspection; William James in his article 'Does Consciousness Exist?' (*Journal of Philosophy*, 1904) and in another, 'Theory of Emotion' (*Mind*, 1884), reduces mental phenomena to internal sensations; and James Rush (1786–1869), an American who had studied at Edinburgh University, wrote a materialistic psychology in his *Brief Outline of an Analysis of the Human Intellect* (1860), a motor theory of behaviour emphasizing the importance of voice muscles in thinking.

However, the fact that many of his ideas were touched upon by predecessors and elaborated by successors does not diminish the historical importance of Watson's writings. He consummated the development of American psychology which, from its beginnings, moved steadily away from the 'new psychology' of Wundt and his German associates. It is fitting that the radical change, rejecting introspection and consciousness and reducing psychological explanation to a strictly physical set of concepts, should come just before the First World War. It brings to a significant climax the dynamic and vigorous approach of Americans to the developing science of psychology.

It is true that the Behaviourist schools, which were the dominant systematic force in America in the period 1919–39, did not have it all their own way. Other rival theories concerning the nature and scope of psychology arose simultaneously and commanded considerable following. The psycho-analytic movement, the Gestalt school from Germany, and the various groups offering new dynamic theories of personality all made the literature of psychology look as if a regression towards philosophy had suddenly occurred. After the First World War, psychology no longer appeared as a relatively coherent, integrated science, but rather as a number of different *kinds* of psychology, each with its own systematic viewpoint, characteristic interests, special techniques, private terminology and limited scope. This development was inevitable. The theoretical orientation of the 'new psychology' and the range of problems it defined was too narrow, too timidly restricted to seventeenth-century and eighteenth-century traditions of psychological thinking. It was largely the Americans who were adventurous and experimental in trying to widen the scope of the new empirical science, and in doing so they forced it into a new age of speculation, trial and error and uncertainty. It was also the Americans who accepted psychology as a legitimate branch of science with a confidence perhaps lacking elsewhere. Large university schools of psychology, well-endowed research institutes and the employment of psychologists by the State and by industrial corporations were all features of American life long before they were in Europe.

CHAPTER SEVEN

The Influence of Physiology 1870–1914

EXPERIMENTAL psychology in Germany was based
on the theory that descriptions and analyses of the contents of consciousness ultimately required explaining by
reference to underlying neural processes. Progress in
neurophysiology, although far from rapid, was sufficient
to continue to interest psychologists from 1870 onwards.

The study of the nerve cell was advanced by vastly
improved histological methods. For the first time, the
structure and function of many types of cell were revealed.

The upshot of this progress was the refutation of the
earlier view that all parts of the nervous system are connected anatomically. Nerve cells were found to be anatomically discrete; there were no fibres connecting them
to each other. The influence of one cell on another was
now explained in the 'Neurone Theory' formalized by
Waldeyer in 1891. Each cell lives by itself as regards nutrition, self-repair and other metabolic functions. However,
there is a junction-point through which a nervous impulse may discharge from one cell to an adjacent one.
The dendrites on each neurone can receive such stimulation from any one of a large number of other neurones.
Hence, nerves are formed into pathways or inter-
connected systems, but not in any rigid or fixed arrangement. Whether or not an impulse goes in one or another
direction from A to B, or from A to D or F, depends on
the particular properties at the junction-points at any
given moment. Relatively stable inter-connexions
amongst a chain of individual neurones might thus be the
basis for 'habit', while the reorganization of pathways
might underlie the flexible behaviour manifest in 'learning' new habits or skills. Thus the building-up and

breaking-down of resistance to impulses at various junction points, and the overall plasticity of the nervous system, became an interesting new 'model' for psychologists.

This work began in Germany, but it was in England that it was taken up and developed. The British had not been outstanding in physiology since the days of Charles Bell and the early anatomists. However, one really able man served to bridge the gap between the early period and the 1870s. This was Hughlings Jackson (1835–1911), a Yorkshireman who settled in London in 1859 as a neurologist and physician at Queen Square Hospital.

Jackson combined astute clinical observation with skill in exact systematic reasoning. He believed that the nervous system was essentially a sensory-motor machine. Centres should not be categorized as sensory or motor – all nervous activity resulted in sensory-motor coordination. It was Jackson who first corrected the error of Flourens in thinking that movement is the work of lower neural centres and that the cerebral hemispheres and cerebellum were not concerned with movement at all. Prior to its demonstration by Ferrier, Jackson postulated a 'motor cortex'. He came to regard the nervous system as having three levels of organization: the reflex, the middle centres, and the voluntary centres. The highest level did not only handle the most intricate coordinations; it also inhibited the lower centres. In brain pathology, it is always the higher mental functions which disappear first. He applied these general conceptions with considerable success to the study of aphasia and epilepsy. He showed, contrary to Broca, that loss of speech is not due to damage in a highly localized brain centre. Various levels of neural activity can control speech; but it is the most highly complex forms of speech which disappear first while other speech habits remain.

British physiology began a new lease of life in 1870, when Cambridge University appointed Michael Foster as its first teacher of physiology. A scholar of his subject rather than an active researcher, Foster did a good job. He wrote a brilliant textbook (1877), founded the Physiological Society (1876), and founded and edited the *Journal of Physiology* (1878). His teaching produced a group of able physiologists and it was their research which advanced the physiology of the nervous system in the years before the First World War.

In these years, the work of Gaskell and Langley on the autonomic nervous system provided the first clear understanding of the anatomy and basic functions of the part of the nervous system closely associated with emotional response. J. N. Langley's *The Autonomic Nervous System* was not published until 1921, but much of the work came out earlier in scientific papers. More directly of interest to psychologists was the research of Keith Lucas (1879–1916) and E. D. Adrian on the conduction of the nervous impulse, work which filled a gap in our knowledge of the sensory processes.

Knowledge of sensory conduction had made slow progress since the Bell–Magendie law (pp. 38 ff.) distinguished sensory from motor nerves. Something was known during the nineteenth century about motor conduction, since one end of a motor nerve is muscle which gives measurable twitches. The end of a sensory stimulation is the experiencing of a sensation – a more elusive phenomenon. In the twentieth century, apparatus such as the capillary electrometer, the cathode oscillograph and, later, more sophisticated devices for measuring frequency, amplitude and wave-form of amplified currents, all made investigation of sensory conduction in nerves possible for the first time.

In 1886, Bernstein had demonstrated that the nervous impulse is a 'wave of negativity', as he called it, passing along a nerve. He put electrodes at successive points on a nerve and found that the surface of the nerve, at the point where rapid impulses are moving, is always electrically negative in relation to those parts of the surface immediately ahead and behind the impulse. Since the wave of negativity had a measurable duration, the next step was to find the rate at which impulses succeed each other.

In 1874 Bowditch had found that, for the heart muscle, if a second impulse comes too soon after the first, it fails to excite the muscle. Marey coined the term 'refractory phase' for the interval during which the second impulse is totally ineffective as a stimulus. Soon it was shown that nerves, like muscles, have a refractory phase.

In 1912 Adrian and Lucas succeeded in plotting curves for the recoverability of sensory nerves after stimulation. They proved: (1) There is first an absolute refractory period, during which no stimulus is strong enough to excite the nerve. (2) This is followed by a relatively refractory period, during which the excitability returns gradually to normal. Bowditch had also shown in 1871 that any stimulus produces in any muscle either the maximum response or none at all. The reaction is of an 'all-or-none' kind. Once the threshold for excitation is exceeded, the response is adequate. Lucas and Adrian, in 1912, showed that this all-or-none principle applies to nerves as well as muscles. The healthy nerve reacts if the stimulus reaches a certain threshold, and fails to react if the stimulus falls below. Thus the whole problem of sensory conduction was opened up.

In the 1920s, precise measurement of sensory action potentials became possible, and knowledge of sensory processes advanced considerably. Thus, even the peripheral nervous system was beginning to be described adequately only in the first quarter of the twentieth century. The anatomy and functions of the higher 'central' processes remained obscure and speculative (and still do). Hence neurophysiology remained, in a sense, lagging behind the requirements of physiological psychologists, and psychologists often had to speculate far beyond the range of known facts to offer 'neurological' models for explaining the results of behaviour experiments. The speculative nature of much psychological theory derived from this slowness in the development of the physiology of the nervous system.

Perhaps the most outstanding product of Cambridge physiology under Foster was Sir Charles Sherrington (1857–1952). He was Professor of Physiology at Liverpool University (1895–1913), where he did much important work, and later professor at Oxford (1913–35). Sherrington is one of the great men in the history of physiology. He was interested in experimental psychology as a related discipline, and while at Liverpool arranged for a lectureship in experimental psychology to be established in his own department. H. J. Watt of the Würzburg group held it in 1906 and Cyril Burt from 1907 to 1912. Sherrington's interest in psychology is apparent in his popular talks and writings, although he espoused a dualism which fitted neither his own contributions nor the prevailing outlook of his times.

In his physiological researches he had a maxim: 'Behaviour is rooted in integration'. His book *The Integrative Action of the Nervous System* (1906) illustrates this thesis. Integrated motor activity – selecting one activity at a time and carrying it out – is the basis of all behaviour. The complex, conscious, higher functions of the brain (intelligence, memory, etc.) simply make motor integration and control more comprehensive and intricate, and enable the organism endowed with such functions to control the environment more thoroughly. Sherrington wanted to give a physiological account of the integration of nervous activity.

He took the reflex arc as his basic mechanism for the nervous system. He pointed out that the 'reflex' is simply an abstract concept. Reflexes occur in diverse fashion. The 'synapse' (Sherrington's word for the junction-point between neurones) is capable of quite complex organization. Stimuli may summate at a single synapse from several directions simultaneously; stimuli may be inhibited at a synaptic junction; long before the muscular system is activated, many nervous impulses are integrated and organized in the motor nerves, and the reflex may be constituted in any one of a number of ways; it is not a simple mechanism. Sherrington became interested in the way reflexes control posture and muscle tonus. He postulated two systems of stimulation for the muscles – one specializing in the maintenance of muscle tension and posture, the other controlling action and movement. In the course of these studies, he found that many nerves to the muscles are afferent and serve to supply the brain with a 'feedback' of information concerning what movements are achieving or failing to achieve in the overall activity of the organism. Thus posture and movement were regulated partly through signals or stimuli from the actual muscles involved in maintaining posture and mediating actions – a sensory-motor integration of a kind hitherto unsuspected.

The synapse is engaged in facilitating and inhibiting nervous impulses, and plays its part in the control of higher processes or levels in the nervous system. Indeed, motor-coordination may be the basis for higher mental processes. This view attracted psychologists of the Cambridge school in the 1930s, especially F. C. Bartlett, who made the analogy between properties of motor-skills and thought-processes the starting point for his discussion of 'thinking'. Sherrington's work, of considerable importance in the history of physiology, thus had much of interest for psychologists.

While progress in the physiology of the nervous system was slow but impressive, it did not provide the psychologist with the correlations of mental and behavioural data with neurological processes that was demanded by the theories of the time. However, it stimulated the thinking of the psychologist – especially in helping him to turn away from concentration on sensory processes and the contents of consciousness and to re-direct his interest to the study of motor-activity.

CHAPTER EIGHT

British Psychology 1870–1914

B R I T I S H psychology got off to a slow start. One of the earliest British psychologists to emerge was James Sully (1842–1923). He held the Grote Chair of Logic and Philosophy of Mind at London University from 1892 until 1903. He had studied under Helmholtz at Berlin in 1871–2, and was well acquainted with all the developments of his time. Although not an original thinker – he owed much to Darwin and to the traditional associationism – he did branch out into new fields of inquiry. He published *Studies in Childhood* (1895), much of the material of which was produced by the British Association for Child Study, which Sully helped to establish. This was the first systematic study in England of the development of children's behaviour. He wrote a number of textbooks which were prescribed texts in the U.S.A. as well as in Britain in early psychology courses – *Outlines of Psychology* (1884) and *The Human Mind* (1892). These were scholarly and well informed.

Although he was no experimentalist, Sully established a laboratory in University College, London, in 1897. W. H. R. Rivers came from Cambridge to conduct the first courses. William McDougall (pp. 177 ff.) was another assistant who carried out the experimental part of the work of Sully's department. Sully was thoroughly scientific in outlook: his *Illusions* (1881) is a detailed analysis of existing knowledge of perceptual illusions, dreams and hallucinations. Although not so original, he played a corresponding role in England to that of William James in America, and made the transition from mental philosophy to scientific psychology a smooth and precisely orientated one.

Equally important in helping to make the transition was James Ward (1843-1925). Ward originally trained for the ministry of the Congregational Church. He became minister of the congregational chapel in Cambridge, but resigned in 1872, just over a year later. He then entered Trinity College and read philosophy and psychology. After a period in Germany studying physiology, he was given a lectureship in philosophy at Cambridge in 1881 and a professorship in 1897.

His influence on psychology was in two different fields. He wrote an article on psychology, which was of considerable influence, for the ninth edition of the *Encyclopaedia Britannica* in 1885. It attacked the associationist approach to the study of consciousness. Ward emphasized that sensory and motor 'presentations' occur in a complex continuum which cannot be analysed into sensory and ideational units. He insisted that the ego, or self, is a fundamental factor: it is the subject of experience, the unifier and integrator of the continuous stream of experiences, and is always related to objects and events other than itself or its states. 'Attention' is the single subjective activity which functions in different ways under different conditions.

Ward's article, written in a rather teutonic style, seems abstract and remote to the modern psychologist. Yet it served to turn philosophical psychologists in a direction more congenial to the arrival of the 'new psychology'. More important than his ideas was Ward's active support for experimental psychology. In 1877, and again in 1882 and 1886, Ward tried unsuccessfully to persuade the University of Cambridge to found a laboratory for the study of psychological problems. In 1891 he eventually succeeded in getting a grant for the purchase of apparatus and a room in the physiology department for the exclusive use of experimental psychology. Ward used his influence to encourage psychology, although he believed only in the validity of strictly psychophysical experiments, and he frequently discussed experimental problems with the earliest students in Cambridge. In spite of his essentially philosophical interests, several psychologists have acknowledged that Ward made useful suggestions in the field of empirical research.

G. F. Stout (1860–1944) was more directly influential in the field of psychological theory, although completely unempirical in his discussions. He studied under Ward at Cambridge in the early 1880s, was a fellow of St John's College from 1884 until 1896 and then went to Oxford until 1903 as Wilde Reader in Mental Philosophy – the only psychological appointment in Oxford University, and one devoted to systematic psychology. He left Oxford to become Professor of Logic and Metaphysics at St Andrews University in 1903, remaining there until 1936. His *Manual of Psychology* (1898; 5th edition 1938) was a textbook for generations; while his *Analytic Psychology* (1896) remains a major work in the philosophy of mind even today. Stout's significance lies in his criticism of associationism; his anticipation of certain Gestalt ideas; and his insistence on the primacy of 'strivings towards satisfaction' over reasoning, an emphasis which gives his system a functionalist orientation. 'The stream of consciousness, though its course is perpetually controlled and restricted by extraneous conditions, has nevertheless a current of its own.' Instincts, sentiments and attitudes are more fundamental than associations, or even the apprehension of 'wholes' in perceptual experience. The effort and strivings of the individual in adapting needs to environmental conditions supply the factors which explain the unity and continuity of experience. Stout also emphasized the importance of the development of basic psychological functions. In discussing perception, he argued that human beings have to learn to discriminate between objects of different shape, size and distance, and that motor activity is as important as sensory mechanisms in this process. Thus, in spite of his introspectionism and disregard for experimental data, Stout was forward-looking in his views and acted as an important transitional thinker in the move from mental philosophy to strictly empirical psychology.

WILLIAM MCDOUGALL

A systematic thinker of the early days of British psychology who was much more closely related to modern psychology was Stout's successor as Wilde Reader at Oxford – William McDougall (1871–1938). McDougall had an entirely different background from those of Sully, Ward and Stout. He read science at Manchester University. He then studied physiology, anatomy and anthropology at Cambridge, graduating in 1894, and finally qualified in medicine at St Thomas's Hospital, London, in 1899.

He went with the Cambridge Anthropological Expedition to Borneo and the Torres Straits in New Guinea (1898–1900) and then spent a year at Göttingen studying experimental psychology under G. E. Müller. At first he assisted Sully and Sully's successor, Carveth Read, at University College, London, as demonstrator in experimental psychology. From 1903 to 1914 he was at Oxford, where opportunities for experimental psychology were provided only through a private arrangement with a friendly physiologist. After a period of war service in which he assisted in the treatment of shell-shock cases, McDougall left England in 1920 and settled in America. He worked at Harvard until 1927 when he made a final move to Duke University.

Although a scientist by training, McDougall moved steadily away from scientific work and in his American years became a prolific writer of popular books. His earliest work was in the field of visual sensation. He performed a number of excellent experiments, for example, on the effects of muscular activity on the fading of visual impressions. He also surveyed the relevance of physiological knowledge to psychology in his book *Physiological Psychology* (1905). This was an influential and stimulating work in its day – asking questions and defining problems in the light of the most recent researches of Sherrington on cortical synapses.

However, he moved on to theorizing, leaving behind his researches on the effect of drugs on fatigue and his psychophysical experiments. His *Introduction to Social Psychology* (1908) was an attempt to present a new conception of psychology. It was not only influential among psychologists, but proved a best-seller with the general public: indeed, it still flourishes as a paperback in 1965. 'Psychologists must cease to be content with the sterile and narrow conception of their science as the science of consciousness, and must boldly assert its claim to be the positive science of mind in all its aspects and modes of functioning, or, as I would prefer to say, the positive science of conduct or behaviour.' McDougall's attack on the descriptive and analytic psychology of consciousness – which even Ward and Stout only partially modified – was vigorous and positive. It replaced the old approach with something new. The book is difficult to characterize, since it is not what it appears to be on the surface. It is a functional and dynamic psychology which takes as its starting-point the concept of man as a purposeful, striving, goal-seeking animal. McDougall regarded the tendency in psychology to explain behaviour mechanistically as mistaken and misleading. 'The essential nature of mind is to govern present action by anticipation of the future in the light of past experience.' This places the emphasis on *intelligent*, purposeful, goal-seeking behaviour. The positive side of McDougall's system is that he classifies the general kinds of goals towards which much intelligent means-end behaviour is directed – he describes and classifies basic 'motives' in man. However, McDougall confused this line of thinking and vitiated what would otherwise have been a sound systematic psychology by making a number of dubious moves:

(1) He argued that explanations in psychology are teleological ('effects precede and determine their causes'),

which raised metaphysical worries quite needlessly about explanations in terms of typical motives.

(2) He argued that the 'energy' required to activate a human being into purposeful, goal-seeking behaviour was provided by 'instincts', thereby suggesting some special 'mechanism' at work within the organism.

(3) In *Body and Mind* (1911) he attacked all mechanistic explanations of behaviour, and put forward an animistic view of the human mind. He argued that the unity of conscious experience implies a soul or psyche which cannot be explained in terms of mental elements or reflexes. This return to the popular viewpoint of the seventeenth century shocked McDougall's contemporaries and did much to discredit him as a progressive psychologist.

The latter aspect of McDougall's writing can be placed firmly outside the scope of psychology – it was an incursion into metaphysics. However, his other two basic moves may be seen as a mixture of confused thinking and genuine psychological insight. McDougall realized that in discussing man's purposeful, goal-directed behaviour, one must accept explanations which refer to a person's reasons for acting in one way rather than another. Reasons cannot be reduced to pushes from behind or pulls from immediate environmental stimuli. Yet, in spite of this realization and his attempt to devise an explanatory model which would allow for rational motives, he contradicted himself by bringing in instincts as the mechanisms controlling purposeful strivings. However, McDougall is extremely confused in his use of the term 'instinct'. Hunger and sex needs are instinctive, but so is the tendency to acquire wealth and social influence. Some instincts have an emotional partner – the instinct to escape from danger arouses 'fear' responses, and the instinct to repel or reject some situation or object arouses 'disgust' reactions. Yet are there characteristic emotional responses for seeking nutritious substances? If instincts are often a combination of reflexes, and are often merged with habits, and if we utilize and modify habits in the process of carrying out a plan, it is difficult for McDougall to make clear distinctions between these concepts of 'instinct', 'reflex', 'habit', 'motive', etc. In fact, his term 'instinct' is vague and his thinking about the springs of conduct confused.

In later writings, McDougall replaced the term 'instinct' by the ambiguous term 'propensity' – a half-admission that his earlier concept had been a mistake. If one tries to extract from McDougall's *Social Psychology* (getting rid of technical definitions of 'instinct') a straightforward descriptive classification of the chief goals towards which human activity is directed, and the relationship of these goals (a) to characteristic means-end behaviour, and (b) to typical emotional and ideational responses associated with each specific goal-category, then, as R. S. Peters has suggested, one has the basis of a plausible – and relatively non-controversial – model for 'motivation'.

McDougall's personality theory is also relatively free from controversial or metaphysical ingredients. He borrows A. F. Shand's concept of a 'sentiment' which the latter defined in his book *The Foundations of Character* (1914) and earlier in an article 'Character and Emotions' (*Mind*, 1896). Shand defined a sentiment as an organized system of emotional reactions associated with an object or concept. Words like 'love' and 'hate' refer to typical sets of related emotional responses, organized round a person or situation or idea. A personality McDougall conceived as an organized and integrated system of sentiments – although he used the term 'character' instead of 'personality'. Such terms as 'disposition', 'temperament' and 'mood' were all defined in relation to the basic concept of 'sentiment'. A person's disposition is the sum total of his dominant 'goals'; his temperament is the sum total of the effects of metabolic and chemical changes on mental life; while mood is the tendency of specific emotions to persist. Intelligence and cognitive skills form another system of tendencies which, together with 'character', define the individual self. The influence of some of these conceptions, in a refined form, may be found in later theories of personality.

McDougall wrote *Outline of Psychology* in 1923, *Group Mind* in 1920 and *Outline of Abnormal Psychology* in 1926. However, his main thinking occurred before 1914, and his influence on psychology depends mainly on his earlier writings. He may not have had many followers; but he added his weight to the outlook among British psychologists which resisted conversion to the more extreme theories of the Behaviourists. Again, although his discussions of instinct, emotion and character prepared the way for psycho-analytic discourse, his more commonsensical and less controversial approach to motivation helped to keep British psychologists cautious and sceptical. More positively, he presented a clean break with traditionally English habits of thought in psychology – rejecting the associationist, introspectionist, analysis of 'consciousness', in favour of a psychology which was directed towards the description of behaviour, and whose explanations should be in terms of a vigorously functional and dynamic model. Much of his thinking was confused and metaphysical. Yet we can sift the wheat from the chaff and still find in his somewhat neglected writings – so far as academics are concerned – some conceptions which are worth re-examining.

EXPERIMENTAL PSYCHOLOGY AT CAMBRIDGE:
RIVERS AND MYERS

British psychology in the years up to 1914 was not all a matter of theory. Empirical work and the teaching of experimental psychology were begun in earnest. The most active centre was at first the University of Cambridge. In 1893 Sir Michael Foster, by now Professor of Physiology, decided to include a course on the sensory processes in man and physiological psychology. He appointed a medical graduate, Dr W. H. R. Rivers (1864–1922), as lecturer. Between 1887 and 1891, Rivers had engaged in neurological research with Sir Henry Head and had become interested in the physiology of vision. This led him to study experimental psychology with Hering, the distinguished physiologist and pupil of Fechner.

Rivers was well equipped to teach experimental psychology and, in 1897, the title of his lectureship was changed to 'Experimental and Physiological Psychology'. His early papers on visual perception were based on the use of psychophysical methods, although later he broadened the basis of his experimental work and studied the effects of various drugs on fatigue from working at manual tasks. In 1898 A. C. Haddon led his celebrated expedition to the Torres Straits, and Rivers went in charge of the psychological research – with McDougall and C. S. Myers as associates. This expedition was a crucial experience for Rivers, since he became passionately interested in anthropology. In 1902–3 he researched in Southern India. In 1908 he resigned his lectureship and, from 1909 to 1914, and in 1914–15, conducted two expeditions to study Melanesian society.

In his period as lecturer, however, he moved the Cambridge department first to three unused rooms in the pathology department in 1901, and next – in 1903 – to a cottage in Mill Lane. When he returned in 1915 he joined the Royal Army Medical Corps. He did much pioneer work in applying psychological methods of healing to war neuroses, having studied the methods of Janet and Freud.* After the war, Rivers returned to Cambridge to his fellowship at St John's College, but with no official psychology post. From 1919 to his sudden death in 1922 he taught and wrote. Two of his books introduced psychoanalytical ideas to British psychologists – *Instinct and the Unconscious* (1920) and *Conflict and Dream* (1921). His third book of this period, *Psychology and Politics*, was

* Siegfried Sassoon describes Rivers as a war psychiatrist in *Sherston's Progress*.

published posthumously. His eclectic interests – social psychology, the psychology of primitive peoples and psycho-analytic theories – never overruled his original adherence to strictly psychophysical methods and the use of measurement in psychological experiments.

In 1909 Rivers handed over the psychology laboratory to C. S. Myers (1873–1946), who had graduated in medicine at Cambridge in 1898, having read physiology in the first degree course. He was invited to join the Torres Straits expedition by Haddon, who had taught him physiology, on the strength of his having attended Rivers' earliest lectures on experimental psychology. After his return, he worked for a short period at St Bartholomew's Hospital before returning to Cambridge in 1902. From 1904 to 1906 he acted as demonstrator in experimental psychology under Rivers and in 1906 was appointed University Lecturer in Experimental Psychology. In 1912 he was appointed Director of the newly built laboratories which he had planned – and largely financed out of a legacy left him by his father. It was here that the first generation of Cambridge psychology students were trained by Myers in the years preceding the First World War.

Myers distrusted systematic theories in psychology. Experimental psychology was a precise discipline: its results, even when numerical, had to be treated with sharp logic in order to avoid false generalizations. He taught and used statistics, yet was guarded in his attitude: 'Statistics serve, as a rule, to establish and ... give a measure of observable differences. Statistics cannot inform you that one community has broader noses, darker skins, more curly hairs ... than another. ... And if this be true as regards physical characters, it holds yet more strongly in respect of mental characters, in as much as they exhibit still wider individual variation within a community. For those reasons, we must be chary against expecting from statistical manipulations more striking results than from the very nature of the data they are capable of yielding.' While urging pupils to experiment with meticulous quantitative accuracy, Myers insisted that experiments could not be applied in all fields of psychology.

Myers was a skilled musician, being a talented amateur violinist. This may account for his interest in auditory sensation. During the Torres Straits expedition, he made studies of the music of the natives. He studied their ability to discriminate between noises and tones, to discriminate differences in loudness, pitch, duration and quality of different tones, and made similar psychophysical measurements. In 1908 he published a well-known paper on factors influencing the capacity of subjects to localize the source of a specific sound-stimulus. However, his work between 1904 and 1914 was largely a matter of teaching and organizing a new laboratory.

He also published a *Textbook of Experimental Psychology* (1909). This was the first textbook to include an introduction to the use of statistics in psychology, and was more than a laboratory manual in that it discussed the wider implications of experiments. It was popular in the U.S.A. and remained the basic English textbook for many years. Myers' insistence on context, configuration and structure greatly influenced Wertheimer and Koffka, who began to translate the work into German until interrupted by the outbreak of war. Something of the Gestalt, as distinct from the structuralist approach, emerges from the text, and gives Myers an unexpected place amongst those who influenced the changes in systematic psychology which were brewing round about the 1914–18 period. Among his pupils were F. C. Bartlett (in charge of Cambridge Psychology 1922–57); C. A. Mace (Professor of Psychology at Birkbeck College, London, and previously at St Andrews); W. H. Sprott (Professor at Nottingham); and C. W. Valentine (Birmingham). There can be little doubt that Myers trained the first generation of British experimental psychologists admirably.

In 1914 he joined the Royal Army Medical Corps. He

had to organize psychiatrists used to the dull routine of the county asylums, and a handful of psychologists, to deal with hitherto unknown forms of neurosis, and to persuade the High Command that these cases were not cowards and malingerers. At his hospital centre at Le Touquet, he employed hypnosis and abreaction-suggestion therapy to treat his cases. Later, he organized mental hospitals back in England to give longer-term psychotherapy to war cases. Although more critical of the ideas of Janet and Freud than perhaps was Rivers, he nevertheless used some of the new techniques, and thus trained psychiatrists in psychotherapy based on the newer methods of psycho-analysis. Again, Myers trained and taught new psychological methods. Later he did research on the selection of operators for submarine-detecting 'listening devices' and helped to improve listening apparatus to fit the average auditory discriminations of naval ratings.

On returning to Cambridge after the war, Myers became disillusioned with academic life. Psycho-analytic theories had reached the sheltered world of Cambridge and antagonized some of the dons against psychology. Moreover, Myers had become interested in the applications of psychology to practical problems. As director of the new National Institute of Industrial Psychology, 1921-40, he directed original research in industrial psychology and dealt with many problems presented to the Institute by individual firms. His work in industrial psychology is a story in itself and belongs to a later period. It serves to indicate the versatility and vigour of the man who did so much to establish psychology at Cambridge.

Thus, Rivers and Myers, with the august philosopher James Ward giving support on the Board of Studies for Moral Science and supplying a cover of 'respectable' theoretical psychology, set the mark on the quality of Cambridge psychology. This was a tradition of sound, sane and sober psychology, primarily experimental but not unsympathetic to empirical studies in psychopathology or anthropological psychology. If no striking original work emerged during the early days, this was probably due to the fact that much energy was given over to teaching and administration. Also, the British were breaking away from their traditional ways of thinking: not merely was the associationist, atomist, introspectionist approach being replaced by strictly experimental psychology, but the Cambridge way of thinking was moving away from that of the 'new psychology'. Myers, given less sheer work, might have anticipated most of the Gestalt insights before 1914; while Rivers' incursions into anthropology and psychotherapy broadened the scope of psychological interests.

CHARLES SPEARMAN AND THE UNIVERSITY OF LONDON

Cambridge was not the only centre of psychological research and teaching. The University of London was at work in the same year, 1897, as the beginning at Cambridge. In that year, Sully introduced experimental teaching at University College, with Rivers and McDougall conducting the courses. Beatrice Edgell, trained by Külpe at Würzburg, taught psychology at Bedford College for Women from 1897 onwards. Some teaching was carried out at King's College (with Myers travelling from Cambridge as Visiting Professor between 1903 and 1909).

It was at University College that Psychology became most vigorously established in the years before 1914. Sully retired in 1903. Carveth Read, a philosopher sympathetic to psychology, succeeded him until 1911. The department began to exercise some authority when Charles Spearman (1863–1945) arrived as Reader in 1907. Spearman succeeded Read as Professor in 1911. The title of his chair was not officially changed to that of psychology until 1928, but he worked along strictly empirical lines from the start. J. C. Flugel (1884–1955) was appointed lecturer in 1909 and S. F. J. Philpott (1888

1952), a physicist who moved into experimental psychology, became the third psychologist to join the young department. F. A. P. Aveling (1875–1941) also worked in Spearman's department before 1914.

Spearman was a man of considerable drive. His influence gave London psychology a different orientation from that of Cambridge. Taking Galton as its ancestor, London psychology concentrated on problems of human ability and personality, developed statistical and psychometric techniques for accurately measuring individual differences, and was less interested in experimental work and theories derived from experiments.

Spearman was an unusual man. He began his career as a regular officer in the Royal Engineers, and was on active service in the 1890s. In 1897 he left the army and began to study at German universities – Würzburg, Göttingen, Berlin and Leipzig. He researched on spatial perception under Wundt. How Spearman became interested in intelligence and its measurement it is difficult to discover. The Germans were not interested in this problem; yet it was from Germany in 1904 that Spearman sent his article 'General Intelligence Objectively Determined and Measured' to the *American Journal of Psychology*.

Spearman's interest seems to have originated in an attempted verification of Galton's hypothesis that differences in sensory discrimination are correlated highly with differences in intellectual powers: that the more intelligent a person is, the greater is his ability to make fine discriminations between, for example, different degrees of pitch or colour. Spearman experimented with primary school children, finding very high correlations among the school marks of the children in various subjects and their sensory discrimination scores. Since a contradictory result had emerged in an analysis of similar investigations by Cattell, there was a problem. Spearman came to the conclusion that the correlation coefficient between two measured variables suffers a spurious decrease in apparent size as a result of random errors of measurement. He devised a method for estimating the amount of this decrease, and found it was sufficient to explain the low correlations obtained by Cattell. Moreover, Spearman noted that there were systematic interrelations to be discovered in the correlations calculated from school marks and test results in his research. He called these 'hierarchical', because the table of correlations could be arranged with the highest values in one corner and with other values regularly decreasing in both a horizontal and vertical direction.

An analysis of these tables led Spearman to conclude that the hierarchy of correlations, or 'system', could occur only when two factors combine for each tested ability, one factor being common to *all* the abilities in the system, the other being specific for each ability. Spearman then produced a device for measuring the 'general' factor (g). By measuring any large number of different abilities and averaging the results, the specific factors tend to cancel each other out, since they vary in a random fashion from one measurement to the next. Since the 'g' factor is involved in every measurement, it must dominate in any average. Thus, the average must approximate towards a measure of 'g'. Spearman thus postulated a unitary dimension or factor equated with 'general intelligence' or 'general ability'. He claimed that tests could be devised to measure this accurately.

Spearman developed a test of a kind which proved influential. Each subject was given a book with a number of different tests. Little writing was involved: the subject merely had to underline a word or answer from a number of alternatives as 'correct'. The scoring of the test could be the same for each candidate. Analogies, synonyms, mixed sentences, classifications under specific categories were the basis of 'verbal' tests; and there were in addition numerical tests, tests for correct inference, tests based on ability to interpret a code message, etc. The results could be statistically analysed, results of separate testings averaged, and the test score correlated with that of other types of 'intelligence' test. Spearman thus began a British interest in the construction, validation and application of tests for general intelligence – and of tests of all kinds. He also stirred up considerable controversy in the U.S.A., where Thorndike and Terman radically disagreed with his 'two-factor' theory of intelligence. This controversy stimulated great interest in testing intelligence and interpreting tests, and made testing a central interest in psychology.

Before 1914, then, empirical psychology became firmly established in Britain, chiefly in the universities of Cambridge and London. The earliest psychologists had broken clear of the traditional English theories in philosophical psychology without submitting to any alternative systematic position. Experimental psychology was well established; yet other interests – anthropological, psychopathological and psychometric – were given equal place. This eclecticism, together with a refusal to place empirical research too obviously within a theoretical framework, remained a feature of British psychology as it moved towards a late maturity in the 1950s.

CHAPTER NINE

French Psychology 1870–1914

THE main French contribution came from the psychiatrists Charcot, Janet and Bernheim (see Chapter 10). Even the elder statesman of French psychology, T. A. Ribot (1839–1916), was best known for his *Maladies de la mémoire* (1881) and *Maladies de la personnalité* (1885). A champion of British associationism, his *Psychologie anglaise contemporaine* (1870) and *Psychologie allemande contemporaine* (1879) did much to communicate its main theories and experimental results to European intellectuals. He taught experimental psychology at the Sorbonne from 1885, and in 1889 established the first laboratory in France under Alfred Binet (1857–1911). Binet is celebrated in history as the man whose researches resulted in 'intelligence tests' as we know them today. However, as Dr Wyn Reeves has shown in her book *Thinking about Thinking* (Chapter 7), Binet had interests in personality (individual differences – in 'suggestibility' and handwriting – as well as in basic general ability), and did much original research outside the field of test construction. He also founded the first French journal of psychology in 1895.

Binet had worked on devising objective measures of individual differences in motor skills, judgements of visual space, attention and comprehension; and he had plotted correlations between test scores and such 'objective' criteria as school attainment level, teacher's estimates of comparative ability, age, etc.

In 1904, the French Ministry of Public Instruction appointed a committee to inquire into the education of mentally defective children. Binet was asked to devise a standardized test for detecting defective children in primary grades, so that they could be placed in special schools.

With Simon as collaborator, he produced in 1905 the first Binet–Simon scale – the first intelligence test. It was designed with a simple and limited objective in view – to extract from the school population those children who were subnormal in general intelligence and unlikely to benefit from normal schooling. Binet produced a standard scale consisting of a series of tests of increasing difficulty, each of which matched a specific developmental level – all tests at a given level were capable of being solved by any normal child in a specific age-group. There were thirty tests, using a variety of methods – naming objects in a picture, digit span (the number of digits a person can recall after being shown a long list), word definition, etc.

The standardization on this was not adequate. Binet took only ten children in each of five age groups selected by teachers as 'average' for the group. The scoring was rough-and-ready; for example, idiots were those who could not get beyond test 6 and imbeciles those who could not get beyond test 15. However, this was a turning-point in psychology. A new type of test had been produced in which the average level of performance was the criterion, and in which test contents were correlated carefully with other criteria (results of school examinations, assessments of teachers, etc.). In 1908 a revised scale was produced. The tests were now classified by the levels at which normal children could pass them at each age-level from 3 years to 13 years. Children were thus assigned a 'mental age', corresponding to the age at which most children in a given age-group passed all the test items but one for a given test. Thus, some children were above the average for this group and could pass tests which the average child could only master two or three years later; others were less than average in comparison with the mass of their own age-group.

A means was thus available for comparing the general level of ability in children. In 1911, just before his death, Binet published a third revision. There were now five tests at each level and a reorganization of test materials in the light of Binet's extensive research. The 1911 Binet–Simon scale was more accurate in its assessments of general ability and it was this 'test' which proved the model for intelligence tests for many years.

Two improvements were introduced into 'intelligence tests' before 1914 which may be mentioned here. Binet's tests were given verbally by the tester and the candidate's responses were also verbal. This was time-consuming, and made for mistakes. Cyril Burt, the British psychologist, following Spearman, introduced paper-and-pencil tests in 1911: the candidates now gave simple written responses to a printed set of tests in book form (often 'Yes' or 'No', or scoring out or underlining a word or figure), a practice which is universal today. In 1912, the German, W. Stern, proposed the 'intelligence quotient' index for scoring. The mental age of a child on a test was divided by his actual chronological age. Thus, a 10-year-old who passed tests which are characteristic of the average 13-year-old would have an intelligence quotient (or I.Q.) of $\frac{13}{10}$ or 1·3 (the average I.Q. being 1·0). It became conventional to multiply this by 100, so that 100 is average, and the child mentioned above would have an I.Q. of 130.

Binet's scales proved highly successful in practice. They not only detected subnormal children, but also provided approximate measures of individual differences in 'general intelligence'. It was found empirically with large samples that children who tended to get high scores on such tests (high I.Q.) tended also to do well in a wide variety of intellectual tests (school subjects, other types of problem-solving test, etc.), while those who were average or weak in tests were also correspondingly average or weak in a wide variety of cognitive tasks. The Binet–Simon scale had no zero: it merely provided an ordinal ranking among individuals so that they could be placed in order of merit in relation to each other. The test did not strictly measure any attribute of the individual. Yet it did enable accurate predictions to be made about performances in jobs requiring mental agility and persistence. Binet insisted that the test did not assess a single dimension of personality, but simply assessed an average level of performance which was the result of the blending of a large number of separate functions – memory, concentration, reasoning skills, mechanical aptitudes, verbal facility. He argued that intelligence tests must sample a wide range of different aptitudes and skills in order to get a sound estimate of 'general ability'. Thus Galton's concept of 'general ability' was accepted, but was given a different meaning by Binet and Spearman, a move which began a theoretical controversy over the nature of 'intelligence' (or what it is that intelligence tests succeed in assessing with some considerable degree of accuracy).

Binet was a highly gifted psychologist. His studies of hypnotism have been unjustly neglected, as has also his research on thinking processes, in which he studied empirically the reasoning of famous chess players and arithmetical prodigies, as well as his daughter's reasoning powers. His collaborator at the Sorbonne laboratory, C. S. Féré, was also a man of merit. He conducted some of the earliest studies of the effect of fatigue on industrial workers and devised an effective instrument for measuring muscular energy. He also conducted early studies in the physiological processes involved in emotion. Henri Piéron, who was a pupil in this school, continued the tradition, and was one of the most inventive experimentalists of the 1920s.

However, the contribution of the French in the years up to 1914 will always be regarded as constituting two major advances: (1) The definition and early investigation of a new kind of disorder – the neuroses (through hysteria); (2) the perfection and application of the first and most influential form of intelligence test, which is still with us today.

CHAPTER TEN

Psychopathology from Pinel to Psycho-Analysis

EVEN today, there is some confusion in the minds of many people between the respective subject-matters of psychology and psychiatry. This may arise partly out of the use of such expressions as 'mental illness' and 'mental disorder' to describe the group of maladies which psychiatrists treat; and partly from the influence of the Freudian school, which presents a purely psychological account of such disorders, extending the theory to form a systematic psychology which would explain the whole of human behaviour.

The study of 'mental illness', and the therapy related to it, is a field which presents a strange and somewhat unhappy history. Because this field of investigation has influenced the development of psychology, and because it overlaps with it at certain points, it is necessary to give a brief account of medical psychology.

At the end of the eighteenth century, medical psychology lagged far behind academic psychology. As late as 1775 a woman had been executed for witchcraft in Bavaria; and the theory that lunatics were possessed by evil spirits had lingered on in certain parts of Europe. Mostly the insane were regarded simply with fear and disgust, and were thrust into prison-like asylums to be left to the mercy of brutal and ignorant keepers. It was only at the end of the eighteenth century that humanitarians were moved to reform the madhouses and secure decent treatment for their inmates. Esquirol, one of the pioneers of reform in France, described how the typical European asylum contained naked, ill-fed wretches who slept on straw in filthy, unventilated and unlit cells. The quarters resembled dungeons, and the more disturbed patients were frequently chained. In England lunatics were often exhibited like animals in a side-show for the amusement of the public.

The first step away from this insensitive cruelty was simply towards humane and decent treatment. This move occurred simultaneously in England and in France. The mysterious death of a Quaker lady in the York asylum led the Society of Friends in York to erect a hospital for the treatment of those normally confined to asylums. The York Retreat became a model mental hospital, in which kindness and understanding, clean quarters and good food, fresh air and gentle exercise in pleasant surroundings were the principles of treatment. The fact that many patients made progress and some recovered, together with the fact that nobody suffered from this tolerance, made a considerable impression.

In 1815, the House of Commons appointed a committee to investigate the conditions in 'madhouses', and their honest, hard-hitting report revealed a terrible state of affairs. This began a movement for reform. Much of the earlier part of the nineteenth century was given over to planning, building and staffing the new asylums, in which patients were treated at least humanely, if not always with any great therapeutic insight.

PHILIPPE PINEL

In France the reform produced something more than a humanitarian attack on cruelty and squalor. One of the great reformers was also one of the first great psychiatrists. Philippe Pinel (1745–1826), after studying mathematics at Toulouse, qualified in medicine at Montpellier. He came to Paris in 1778 but did not become interested in insanity until 1785.

He was given charge of the Bicêtre asylum in 1793 and decided immediately to remove all fetters and chains, giving patients as much freedom as possible, wholesome food and light occupation. In spite of the suspicions of the Commune (which was still fighting for its security) he got his way. The resulting improvement in the behaviour of many of the patients encouraged him to pursue further reforms. The seemingly obvious principle on which Pinel worked was that his patients were sick people, and that his job was to restore them to normal health if possible. To do this, he studied his patients regularly and methodically, making notes after his daily visits and building a collection of the first 'case histories' ever to be put together. He instructed some of his more trustworthy attendants to supply information and soon had enough material on which to reflect.

In 1795 he was transferred to the Salpêtrière asylum (so called because the saltpetre for the army's gunpowder had previously been manufactured there). Here too he reorganized the administration of patients on humanitarian lines. It was his work as an administrator of hospitals that transformed psychiatry: arrangement of rooms, duties and supervision of attendants and other staff, diet, exercise and therapeutic occupations all received his attention. Agitated and violent patients were segregated from melancholics and other quiet cases; idiots from the rest of the hospital community. Quarters were made clean, light and warm. Nourishing food was given to all patients, and their physical health carefully nurtured. Patients were encouraged to work, either out of doors at gardening or in workshops at basket-making and other crafts. A routine approaching as closely as possible to a normal and useful life was established for each patient. A humane and medical approach was encouraged in all the hospital staff. The aim of the work of the hospital was to treat and mitigate and, if possible, cure these ailments of the mind. The hospital was run by physicians and not by a 'governor' or 'warden' as the former 'madhouses' were. The hospital existed, in Pinel's view, to provide an environment conducive to recovery, not simply as a repository for broken and troublesome lunatics. He opposed such primitive treatments as bloodletting, ducking in cold water and the indiscriminate use of drugs. His therapy was based on kindness, commonsense and re-education towards normal activities. In many respects Pinel was far ahead of several succeeding generations of psychiatrists, and many of the principles of organization and administration in progressive modern hospitals can be traced directly to his reforms and experiments.

However, he also laid the foundations for a new approach to psychiatric theory. In his treatise on insanity (1801), he lists what he considers to be the main causes of mental disorders, regarding psychological factors as of prime importance. The emotional reactions of a patient are often disturbed and abnormal before the actual attack occurs. Environmental influences, such as a bad upbringing or an irregular way of life, seem to contribute to the onset of mental disorder. Again, physical factors such as severe head injury, fevers, and other severe diseases seem to be a causal factor. The main symptoms, however, are disorders of emotional reaction. Patients are disturbed by extreme rage or fear, or by excessive grief or remorse. Conflicts between passions are common. Perception of the environment and thought processes also become disturbed in some cases (demented states). Thus Pinel accepted both physical and environmental factors as causes of mental disorder, and emphasized the need for both psychological and physical treatment of patients.

His ideas were simple and unsophisticated. However, coming at the beginning of the nineteenth century, they clearly emphasized that lunacy and related disorders were diseases on a par with other illnesses; and that organic factors, as well as unfavourable environmental stresses, were the causes of these mental and behavioural breakdowns. Hence medical treatment and proper hospital care were necessary in order to mitigate or cure such disorders. This was a revolutionary change from the approach to insanity which had been commonplace until Pinel's reforms. It made insanity the business of scientific medicine rather than a matter for the department in charge of prisons. Pinel was, therefore, remarkable chiefly as a reformer, but also as one of the first to suggest that psychology not only has a part to play in the study of insanity, but could also learn about human nature through the systematic observation of abnormal behaviour. Abnormality was no longer simply equated with moral depravity or criminality. It was a disorder, the causes of which merited objective and sympathetic study.

Pinel's contribution also included the training of younger men in the methods of medical psychology, and his pupils worthily carried on the new tradition in psychiatry. The most celebrated was perhaps Jean Esquirol (1772–1840). Esquirol was a careful observer and collector of case-material. He was one of the first to employ a statistical approach to clinical data. He argued that 409 out of 1,500 male and 580 out of 1,940 women patients had developed mental illness as the result of psychological stress. He categorized the most common precipitating factors – financial anxieties, disappointment in love, bereavement – and attempted to relate these to typical symptoms. He was the first to use the term 'hallucination' as the product of brain disturbance in which the patient sees or hears what is not there. He isolated depressed states as a separate category. His work as a reformer of hospitals and teacher of advanced clinical methods established the work of Pinel more widely throughout France and Europe. Not only did he found new hospitals based on the humane-medical approach, but he was instrumental in getting laws passed to protect the rights of the insane.

A succession of able pupils gave French psychiatry a supreme position during the first half of the century – and indeed down the years. Their work was primarily that of improving conditions in hospitals, systematically observing and statistically analysing clinical data, and trying to find organic causes for mental disorders. Unfortunately, physiological progress was not such as to further the latter objective. Understanding of the causes of mental illness remained obscure and a matter for speculation. Much of the energy of psychiatrists down to the 1870s was given over to strengthening and expanding the work of Pinel and Esquirol in France and Tuke in England.

MOREL AND DEGENERATION

In the absence of physiological progress, various theories of mental illness of a dubious character greatly impeded the progress of psychiatry and kept it a Cinderella amongst the branches of medical science. One of these theories in particular seemed to gain some vague support from Darwin, and became very popular for over seventy years. This was the degeneration hypothesis put forward by B. A. Morel (1809–73). 'Degenerations are deviations from the normal human type which are transmissible by heredity and which deteriorate progressively towards extinction.' In his *Traité de dégénérescences* (1857), Morel suggested that apart from unfavourable variations, intoxication from alcohol, malaria, food poisoning and social corruption could contribute to degeneration in an individual. This would produce immediately a 'nervous disposition'. In the next generation what today would be called 'neurosis' would appear, in the next a psychotic breakdown, and finally idiocy in the children of psychotics.

This pessimistic theory was accepted by many psychiatrists, whose hospitals were filled with chronic patients whom they did not know how to cure. Mental illness was a form of regression. For decades this view tended to dominate psychiatry, criminals and men of genius being also regarded as different types of degenerative: geniuses produce results which are socially acceptable, criminals produce behaviour which is socially suppressed, while the insane and neurotic fall into an intermediate category. It was not until Mendel's genetic studies became widely known after 1900 that research in genetics completely discredited the degeneration hypothesis. Even Pierre Janet was still under its influence in papers published in the 1920s. This theory proved a hindrance both to research into the causes of mental disorder and to new attempts at improved treatments. It is largely due to this theory that psychiatry at the start of the twentieth century had made little progress since the pioneer work of Pinel.

PSYCHIATRY IN GERMANY: GRIESINGER AND KRAEPELIN

However, some sorting-out of clinical data had taken place. German psychiatry in particular concentrated on systematic work. Wilhelm Griesinger (1817–69) argued that the brain and its pathology is the essential factor in all mental illness. Psychological reactions may be the overt sign of reflex actions in the brain. He recognized that he could not prove this thesis, yet he put it forward as a maxim, to the effect that too much attention to psychological description and classification might be futile in medicine. Griesinger nevertheless gave rigorous descriptions of mental pathology – to the effect that typical disturbances of mood, of motor activity, of logical thinking, are common to cases which otherwise exhibit considerable individual differences. Just as a 'headache' may be a symptom of any one of a number of different complaints, from tumour to influenza, so a depression or a manic attack may be the effect of any one of a number of different brain accidents – lesion, poisoning of tissue, etc.

The classification of disorders in terms of symptoms was highly misleading; for Griesinger the key to any 'mental disorder' was damage or disease to brain and nervous system. There are many similarities between normal and insane people. When intoxicated, a normal person often speaks and acts like an insane person; in dreams – as in certain delusions – the gratification of unfulfilled wishes in indirect, symbolic forms may be seen. Presumably there are physical causes for these similar reactions, the brain being released under alcohol or sleep from certain inhibitions. Griesinger's views were not accepted universally; but he did set a fashion of theorizing about the physiology of the brain in relation to mental disorders.

Unfortunately such speculation was of little use in diagnosis and treatment and offered no genuine explanation. 'Brain mythology' and 'speculative anatomy' were terms which contemporary physiologists used to describe much of the psychiatric writing of this period.

One of two figures, however, stand out in this stagnant period. Emil Kraepelin (1856–1926), who held chairs of psychiatry at Heidelberg and Munich, laid the foundations of modern descriptive psychiatry. He was determined to make psychiatry strictly scientific and to follow what he conceived to be the methods of the biological sciences. Kraepelin studied thousands of case-histories, travelling to India, Java, Mexico and the U.S.A. in search of material. He was not interested in symptoms as such. He believed that the patient's history before the onset of illness, and follow-up studies after discharge from hospital, were necessary to provide a complete clinical picture of the illness. He aimed at plotting the course of the illness from its obscure origins to its final pattern of recurrence (if indeed there was more than one 'attack').

Like Griesinger, he believed that symptoms could be the result of a multiplicity of causes, and thus the pattern of events within each case was the thing to study. His aim was to establish the laws governing typical clinical 'pictures' and, although he studied individual cases in great detail, he was less interested in individuals than in the statistical analysis of large numbers of similar cases in order to define clinical categories or 'syndromes'. His observations, statistical tables and analyses led him to postulate two major psychoses: dementia praecox and manic-depressive psychosis. Kraepelin regarded dementia praecox as an illness caused by internal factors – probably some form of metabolic dysfunction. He regarded it as likely to end in permanent disability and marked deterioration. Manic-depressive psychosis was characterized by swings of mood (elation–depression) with periods of normality. Patients might recover from such attacks and Kraepelin regarded external factors as being the cause of this type of psychosis.

Prognosis – the final outcome of the course of the illness – was of great importance to Kraepelin. He used the very dubious device of using prognosis as a check on diagnosis. If the disease ended in the way predicted, then this confirmed the diagnosis. This was a retrograde step, since it encouraged the notion of 'unfavourable prognosis': thus if a patient were diagnosed as a case of dementia praecox, he was not expected to recover. This was all the more unfortunate in view of the vagueness of Kraepelin's clinical categories. He admitted that 13 per cent of his dementia praecox patients recovered completely. But if such illness ends in deterioration, what is one to say of such exceptions? Again, the third group of 'paranoids', which Kraepelin was forced to postulate, exhibited swings of mood and occasionally deterioration towards a dissociated state.

In fact Kraepelin was simply trying to tidy up the loose ends left by his predecessors. The term 'dementia praecox' was invented by Morel in 1860, and several psychiatrists had previously described the symptoms and course of illness in the terms used by Kraepelin. Kraepelin's division of psychoses into two main groups has remained part of descriptive psychiatry, although the subdivision of these groups has been undertaken since his time to complicate the clinical picture of insanity. The main objective of Kraepelin's system was to demonstrate not merely that mental disorders were *diseases* in exactly the same sense in which tuberculosis and cholera were, but also that mental disease could be dealt with as a branch of medical science. Psychiatry became integrated more completely with medicine through Kraepelin's work than at any previous time. His systematic presentation is an attempt to show that mental illness, in common with any other known disease, runs a typical course from onset to conclusion. It must therefore be the result of organic dysfunction – endocrine conditions, metabolic dysfunction, toxic invasion, or the like. Orthodox medicine could therefore absorb psychiatry, which hitherto had been a peculiar domain in which reform and hospital administration were the chief activities.

This general idea forms the core of the creed of many present-day psychiatrists (the 'orthodox clinical psychiatry' schools), however much they may otherwise differ. Some day, they believe, improved knowledge of brain physiology, genetics and the biochemistry of the nervous system will enable doctors to cure mental disorders by employing orthodox forms of medical treatment: the administration of drugs, electrical treatments and perhaps neurosurgery. Until then, patients who are seriously ill can be taken to well-organized hospitals and given such care as makes their situation as tolerable as possible.

That Kraepelin's systematic presentation of basic 'mental' diseases was no more than a summary of the basic work undertaken during the nineteenth century is evident from the series of modifications in the classification, symptomatology and aetiology of mental disorders which followed, and which has continued in psychiatry down to the present day.

Eugen Bleuler (1857–1939) revised the whole concept of dementia praecox. He introduced the term 'schizophrenia' to denote a group of psychotic reactions, rather than a straightforward type of disease, and distinguished between a number of different kinds of schizophrenic disorder. His monograph, *La schizophrénie*, published in 1911, is still a classic in psychiatric literature. Bleuler characterized this group of psychotic reactions as predominantly cognitive disorders. The patient's capacity for organized, outer-oriented thinking is impaired; instead, his thinking is bizarre and inefficient, fantasy-producing, and disrupted by disturbed emotional reactions. Also the schizophrenic is withdrawn from all kinds of contact with the environment: he no longer responds to stimulation by producing normal adaptive behaviour. There is a disintegration, not only of specific functions (thinking, feeling, etc.), but of all normally integrated functions in behaviour. The personality is 'split' into a number of disconnected and disorganized reactions. The category of 'dementia praecox' thus covers a wide variety of individual cases, the origin and course of which differ considerably from each other. This emphasis on individual differences had been more or less ignored in Kraepelin's system, with its emphasis on statistical analyses of large samples of patients, and the establishing of generalizations about each disease.

Adolf Meyer (1866–1950) was trained in Zürich and went to the U.S.A. in 1892. He taught psychiatry at Cornell (1904–9) and Johns Hopkins (1910–41). His emphasis was perhaps too exclusively on the individuality of each patient; yet he corrected the bias in Kraepelin and made a great impact as a clinical teacher. He approached each patient as an individual and not simply as a case with specific symptoms. The activities of the patient as a whole were important. A detailed study of each individual's history, a thorough analysis of physical, psychodynamic and environmental factors, was essential for each case: in fact, a psychobiological study of each individual had to be undertaken. Meyer rejected the concept of simple disease entities. The unity of physical and mental reactions, and the uniqueness of the individual, were two precepts of Meyer's approach. This did not prevent him from systematizing results and classifying various psychopathological reactions as commonly going together in individual cases. Nevertheless, he departed radically from the somewhat rigid and cut-and-dried system of illnesses presented by Kraepelin. Textbooks of psychiatry, accordingly, vary along a Kraepelin–Meyer dimension regarding their approach to symptoms and syndromes.

NEUROLOGY IN FRANCE : CHARCOT, BERNHEIM AND JANET

Alongside the attempt by German psychologists to systematize the results of psychiatric observations and bring psychiatry within the scope of orthodox clinical medicine, the French tradition continued to prosper. During the course of the nineteenth century neurology in France had made considerable progress and much was known concerning epilepsy, multiple sclerosis, infantile paralysis and other diseases of the nervous system. However, the consulting-rooms of neurologists were crowded with patients suffering from vague complaints that their 'nerves' were disordered. In 1868, George Beard (1838–82) published a list of these complaints, and we can easily recognize neurotic and psychosomatic symptoms among these. 'Neurasthenia' was the word he used to designate this group of complaints – the first recognition of neuroses as distinct from psychotic disorders.

J. M. Charcot (1825–95), a distinguished neurologist who worked at the Salpêtrière Hospital, had researched with success into the causes of multiple sclerosis and tabes. He isolated a complaint which he labelled 'hysteria'. Patients came to him with apparent paralysis of the limbs, contractures and anaesthesias of parts of the body. Others complained of epileptic seizures or other types of convulsive fit. On studying their reflexes and nervous systems in general, he could find neither structural damage nor organic disease. Charcot was puzzled and confused by this phenomenon. He regarded the complaints as somehow connected with epilepsy – perhaps a very mild form whose physical causes were obscure. However, he hit upon the practice of hypnotizing hysterical patients. He falsely believed that hypnotism was exclusively associated with hysterics and he seems to have used hypnotism as a diagnostic device for isolating hysterics from other types of patient. His importance lies in his isolating of hysteria as a phenomenon, and in the fact that he had as his pupils

Janet (see below) and Freud, both of whom were to study hysteria and proceed to a new conception of mental illness.

Even more fruitful investigations were being carried out at Nancy. A. A. Liébault (1823–1903), a general practitioner, had discovered that some of his patients benefited by being hypnotized and given reassurance while under the physician's influence. He published a monograph in 1866 in which he suggested that the 'suggestibility' of patients under hypnosis was the key to the success in his treatment of 'nervous' complaints.

His work remained unread until the Professor of Medicine at Nancy, H. Bernheim (1837–1919), became interested in psychological methods of healing. Bernheim's *De la suggestion et de ses applications à la thérapeutique* (1884) argued that most human beings can be hypnotized and that certain kinds of illness can be cured through hypnotic suggestion. Hypnotism is a condition close to sleep, in which a subject will accept and act upon suggestions which, in the waking state, would be hindered by thinking and by attitudes opposed to guidance from another person. Bernheim carried out many experiments with subjects under hypnosis. He produced blisters, rashes and swellings in hypnotized subjects simply by telling them that they were so affected, and he also produced hallucinations. He discovered that when he made a suggestion to a patient under hypnosis – for example that when the clock struck four he would put up his umbrella – the patient carried out this meaningless act (when no longer hypnotized), but could not recall being asked to do so. He invariably offered a spurious explanation (rationalization) for his odd behaviour. Many cases of 'paralysis', writer's cramp, 'bed-wetting', gastric disorders, were cured by Bernheim – perhaps the first group of neurotic complaints to be cured by psychological methods of healing.

Bernheim and his associates of the Nancy School, together with Charcot at the Salpêtrière, were making the study of neurosis a branch of medical psychology. No longer did psychiatry confine itself to the study of psychosis – insanity requiring hospital care.

This move was one of the most significant in the history of psychiatry, and one which was to bring medical psychology much closer to academic and applied psychology; so much so that 'psychopathology' was to become a part of the academic studies (under the title of 'psychology') in university degree courses. The final stage of this movement came through the work of a young neurologist from Vienna who studied both under Charcot and under Bernheim – Sigmund Freud. However, before considering psycho-analysis and its derivatives, two other important contributors to the new developments within psychological medicine must be considered.

Pierre Janet (1859–1947) also investigated neurotic behaviour under hypnosis. By 1889, Janet had an established reputation as a neurologist and, although attached to Salpêtrière, he was not an adherent of Charcot's teaching. He discovered that patients under hypnosis could reproduce in detail memories of events which in their waking state they could not recall. These events had associations of an unpleasant kind; for example, one of his patients could recall the death agonies of her mother whom she believed she had wrongly treated during her last hour, so contributing towards her death. If such memories were elicited under hypnosis and the physician successfully suggested that their recall would take place under normal waking conditions, then the disturbed neurotic behaviour which seemed to be an indirect product of the lost memories could be cured. This method of treatment Janet called 'catharsis' and it was adopted by Freud, although it was his early associate Breuer who had, independently of Janet, discovered this trick.

Janet regarded 'dissociation' of consciousness as basic to many neurotic disorders. The memory with unpleasant associations becomes dissociated from normal consciousness; the somnambulist often does or says things during 'sleepwalking' which reveal forgotten and disturbing memories, and there is also the phenomenon of dual and alternating personalities with 'fugue states'. In these latter cases, a person loses all sense of self-identity and all memories of his past: he usually disappears from his normal surroundings and turns up in a strange town under an assumed name, where he lives a normal but alien existence. William James (p. 125 of *The Principles*) describes the case of a clergyman, Anselm Bourne, who drew money from his bank and disappeared. For several months he hired a shop and carried out a successful trade in another town. Suddenly, one night, his old sense of identity returned and he awoke in a state of panic, wondering how he came to be living in a strange place. He had automatically forgotten everything about his second personality and his activity as a shopkeeper. Janet was the first psychiatrist to investigate such cases, although his American pupil Morton Prince (1859–1929), who specialized in this field, is often regarded as a greater authority.

Janet also noticed that some of the traumatic memories recalled by his patients while under hypnosis dated back to childhood times, and that others were of a sexual nature. Janet refused to over-generalize about these results, although he regarded them as clinically interesting.

Janet regarded hysteria as only one species of neuroses. Depressions, compulsive reactions, phobias and obsessions were more common than hysterical reactions. Unfortunately, Janet was addicted to the degeneration hypothesis. He regarded all these symptoms as the result of a lack of energy. The inability to carry out normal adaptive behaviour is the product of fatigue and exhaustion in the brain and nervous system which, in its turn, is due to basic degeneration of the total bodily system. He classed all these reactions under the heading 'psychasthenia'. Stresses involved in one's job and in family life could initiate exhaustion, and so elicit behavioural symptoms. Thus Janet was committed to an erroneous theory, and this – together with his failure to draw the full implications of his astute observations of hysterics (that forgotten memories are inhibited or repressed by some kind of specific reaction, that they function below the threshold of consciousness, etc.) – resulted in his being eclipsed by Freud and his followers.

Nevertheless, Janet was an accurate observer. He noted that fear of taking any kind of action was a common neurotic trait; that the neurotic lost his capacity to love and command others, therefore resorting to devious means of winning affection, attention and interest. He noted that the tension produced by typical neurotic situations leads to impulsive attempts to escape – through excessive sexual activity or heavy drinking of alcohol. Kleptomania is another releaser of neurotic tension. Treatment should provide stimulation and the canalization of impulses into positive socially acceptable channels. Rest and quietness may be necessary, but the neurotic needs to be educated towards more positive adjustments. The patient must be trained to live within his 'small or reduced psychological capital'. In an eclectic fashion, Janet assembled many observations which, although confirmed by others, have become commonplace in the clinical descriptions of neurotic behaviour. His use of the concept of 'dissociation', as illustrating what is common to many otherwise distinct symptoms, is still worth employing. Freud acknowledged the usefulness of Janet's work, although he regarded the Frenchman as having failed to grasp the implications of his acute observations. More than anyone else, Janet contributed to the definition of 'neurotic' disorders and so widened the scope of psychopathological studies.

HAVELOCK ELLIS

Another contemporary of Freud's who influenced and was influenced by him is the English writer Havelock Ellis (1859–1939). After schooling in London, at the age of 16 Ellis went to Australia, where he completed his education in a primitive school in the bush. Returning to

England at the age of 20, he studied medicine at St Thomas's Hospital. A small legacy helped him to qualify as a doctor, but he also supported himself during his medical training by editing the famous 'Mermaid Series' of lesser-known Elizabethan dramatists. Ellis never practised medicine. His writings and editorial jobs kept him going. He had no academic or official medical position and lived the life of a lonely, isolated figure – except for a series of extraordinary love affairs. His main work is the seven volumes of *The Psychology of Sex*, published between 1897 and 1928. Medical, anthropological and historical data, as well as information obtained by Ellis through interviews and questionnaires, are brought together to provide a mass of detailed information. Ellis wanted if possible to collect all the facts concerning sexual matters. He approached his subject-matter objectively and scientifically. His was the first major work to deal with normal sexual behaviour in human beings and animals, as well as sexual pathology. Krafft-Ebing had dealt with sexual abnormality – or 'perversion' – in his *Psychopathia Sexualis* (1893); but Ellis covered every aspect of the topic. His was the first English work to investigate homosexuality; indeed it was because of this that his work had to be published in America, and even there it was accessible only to medical men until 1935. Ellis also discovered auto-erotic phenomena: that certain zones of the body and the sensations located there which are not anatomically or physiologically parts of the sexual-reproduction system nevertheless are associated with sexual feelings.

Ellis tackled a wide range of topics in his seven volumes – sadism and masochism, erotic symbols, the psychological reactions involved in pregnancy, the significance of perfumes, the contents and meaning of dream imagery. He recognized the sexual content – often disguised – of dreams, but regarded dreams as being more than an expression of repressed desires. He also considered the reaction of all the sensory modes in sexual behaviour.

Although parts of his work have been replaced by new research, Ellis's study still remains a source-book for any serious knowledge of sexual psychology. Apart from *The Psychology of Sex*, Ellis wrote on criminology, dreams, the effects of drugs on behaviour and the development of men of genius. His approach was that of the natural historian, collecting and sifting and classifying his data, making cautious generalizations and avoiding systematic theorizing. Partly because of his thorough and unspectacular work (which was nevertheless written in an attractive style), and partly because he appeared as a counsellor rather than a theorist, Ellis has not received the attention he deserved. Also, his works were banned in England throughout the greater part of his lifetime, while psycho-analytic literature was readily accessible. Yet the beginning of psychological counselling on sexual matters – as can now be obtained in marriage-guidance clinics – came, in England, through the reading of his works by medical practitioners. Thus, Ellis contributed much to the psychological discussion of the part played by sex in a healthy and normal marriage. His refusal to speculate enabled him to stand as an authority on psychological problems involving sexual behaviour. It is noteworthy that Freud generously acknowledged his debt to the writings of Havelock Ellis.

SIGMUND FREUD

Sigmund Freud (1856–1939) was born in Moravia, but moved with his family to Vienna at the age of four. He lived in Vienna until driven into exile by the Nazis in 1938, when he came to England, dying in 1939. In 1873 he entered Vienna University and specialized in physiology in the Medical School. Qualifying in medicine, he did some research and came near to being the discoverer of cocaine as an anaesthetic. Although anxious to pursue an academic career, Freud was too poor and had to take to medical practice to earn a living. He came to know another practitioner in Vienna, Josef Breuer (1842–1925), who was a scientist of some distinction. Breur had discovered the function of the semi-circular canals of the ear, and was deeply interested in neurophysiological theory. He propounded the theory that a certain amount of nervous energy is required to keep the brain working efficiently. Rest and sleep allow the build-up of energy to normal level, while if energy exceeds the threshold it must be discharged in activity. The young Freud was deeply impressed with this notion of the brain as a physical energy system.

In 1885–6 Freud obtained a travelling scholarship and visited both Paris and Nancy, where he studied hypnotism as a means of investigating hysteria under Charcot and Liébeault. On his return to Vienna, he found that Breuer had been studying hysteria for some years and had evolved a method of treatment which appeared successful.

Breuer had hypnotized his patients and encouraged them, while hypnotized, to talk. Under these circumstances, not only were forgotten incidents recalled, but the patient displayed strong emotional reactions. The working-through of these emotions associated with forgotten materials seemed to bring relief through the disappearance of neurotic symptoms. This discharge Breuer called 'catharsis', using the same term as Janet without borrowing it, and he regarded it as the key to the cure of hysterics.

In the early 1890s Freud and Breuer collaborated, applying hypnotic cathartic treatment to hysterical patients. Freud came to develop an elementary theory of hysteria in these years, which he generalized to other neuroses. This theory interrelated the cause of hysterical symptoms, the characteristics of the symptoms and the therapy – the first psychogenic theory of a mental disorder. Breuer accepted Freud's views, and their joint book, *Studien über Hysterie* (*Studies in Hysteria*, 1895), stated the theory and gave case-histories to exemplify it.

Thus the clinical discovery of the French psychiatrists that there were powerful processes at work hidden from the conscious mind, together with the cathartic method evolved simultaneously by Janet and Breuer, were exploited by Freud to answer the question 'What is a mental illness?' The answer was a theory of the development of the pathological functioning of orectic processes (impulses, desires, emotions, sentiments, motives) which come unconsciously to organize complex behaviour.

In this early form of his general theory, Freud put forward the hypothesis that unconscious dynamic states must be repressed by a special 'mechanism', which serves as a defence for the ego against painful or frightening memories, emotions, desires. Attempts to evoke these repressed contents meet with resistance. Only if the patient is hypnotized or specially treated, and so enabled to relive imaginatively the original shock-situation giving rise to painful feelings, can release from tension ('abreaction', in Freud's terminology) occur.

Freud came quickly to be dissatisfied with hypnotism as a therapeutic technique. He adopted Galton's 'free association' method for eliciting ideas. He persuaded his patients to lie prone and relaxed on a couch in a quiet, dimly lit room. The patient let his mind wander without control from one image or topic to the next, prompted only by questions from Freud. It was found that 'repressed' material often emerged as easily as under hypnosis. The attempt to interpret the data of free association, and of dreams reported by the patient, Freud called 'psycho-analysis' – a new form of therapy and a new method for studying the operations of the mind. In time, the word came to be applied to Freud's theories as well as to his techniques and, strictly speaking, 'psycho-analysis' means Freudian theory and practice.

In 1897, Freud undertook a rigorous self-analysis, using free association but also carefully recording his dreams. He noted that his patients had often talked about their dreams during analysis and he concluded that unconscious processes are more thinly disguised in dreams than in waking conditions. As a result of his early experiences as an analyst and of his own self-analysis, Freud reached certain further conclusions. (1) He came to believe that unconscious wishes revealed in analysis have their origins in infantile experiences. It is between birth and the age of three that many basic strivings, emotional conflicts and motives have their beginnings; present personality problems must be traced back to early childhood experiences. (2) The orectic factors in neurosis are always related to sexual interests. (3) Some kind of trauma or 'shock' experience is involved in the origin of neurosis. For example, Freud came to believe that round about the age of six, children have passionate sexually coloured love directed towards the parent of the opposite sex, coupled with jealousy and aggressive impulses directed towards the parent of the same sex. This situation arouses feelings of fear and guilt, all the more terrible because the child cannot understand the nature of the conflict which it suffers. The emotions involved are repressed, and the way in which the repression works out determines much in the future development of personality. Earlier crises probably leave equally significant unconscious residues important for development.

This new addition to the theory offended Breuer, who had already been upset by a female patient who had shown erotic interest in him while he was treating her, and so the collaboration with Freud ended. For the next few years Freud worked alone – conducting analyses, thinking, writing notes. In 1900 he published his views in what is probably his best book, *Die Traumdeutung (The Interpretation of Dreams)*. In 1904 he published *Zur Psychopathologie des Alltagslebens (The Psychopathology of Everyday Life)*, which applied his theory to normal everyday phenomena, such as 'slips' of the tongue, inability to recall names, and the point of typical jokes.

These early books did not attract much attention. Between 1900 and 1908 only 600 copies of *The Interpreta-*

tion of Dreams were sold. However, as a result of these books Freud soon emerged from his isolation. From 1902 onwards, a group of friends met each week in his house to discuss his theories – Adler, Stekel, Reitter and Kuhane being the original nucleus. Shortly the group grew and became officially the 'Vienna Psycho-Analytical Society', with a constitution, officers and a library. In 1907, C. G. Jung, a Swiss psychiatrist from Zürich who had read Freud's early writings and had corresponded with him, visited the Society, as did Karl Abraham, a psychiatrist from Berlin. In 1906, *The Journal of Abnormal Psychology* in the U.S.A. published a number of articles on psycho-analysis, and in 1908 a congress of psycho-analysis was held at Salzburg at which Freud, Jung, Adler, Stekel and Abraham all read papers.

Through the influence of A. A. Brill, who had also visited Freud, Stanley Hall invited Freud to America in 1908, to attend celebrations marking the anniversary of the foundation of the psychology department at Clark University. Freud accepted and, with Jung and Ferenczi, visited the U.S.A., giving lectures, meeting distinguished Americans (including the ageing William James) and receiving a doctorate. This international recognition and acclaim was encouraging. His views had met with scornful rejection from orthodox Viennese psychiatrists, and some philosophers had denounced him as perverted and obscene. The stigma was to rankle, but his visit to America did much to reassure him.

The year 1908, therefore, was a high-water mark in Freud's life – the peak of acclaim and recognition. Soon his new movement, centred on the Vienna Psycho-Analytical Society, was to be afflicted with internal dissention and rebellion against his teaching. Annual congresses were held, but at each tensions grew, and the views of its members began to diverge. The Jewish–Viennese members had from the start been jealous and resentful of the reception given to Jung, a Christian and Swiss, who had been made a high official. At the same time, neither

Jung nor Bleuler (who had joined with him) was ever quite in step with all of Freud's views.

In 1911, Bleuler resigned, and Alfred Adler also left to found a rival group on the basis of his own theories. Freud took Adler's deviation to heart and regarded 'Individual Psychology' as a threat to the development of psycho-analysis: the first heretic had appeared. In 1912, after five years of close collaboration, Jung left Freud's movement amidst considerable bitterness. Both Adler and Jung originally left psycho-analysis proper because of Freud's insistence that sexual drives were invariably involved in the origin and development of neurosis. However, once free from the Freudian influence, they each produced radically new theories of mental disorder (see pp. 256 ff., 263 ff.) and of personality development. Others followed their example and, taking Freud's work as a starting point, developed similar kinds of theory – blends of clinical experience, theory construction and criticism of Freudian hypotheses. Thus a number of 'derivatives' from Freud's psycho-analysis appeared from 1911 onwards, emerging in final form in the years 1918–40 as alternatives to Freud – Otto Rank, Karen Horney and Harry Stack Sullivan being examples.

Thus the psycho-analytic movement crystallized between 1902 and 1911 and thereafter split into rival schools – those of Jung and Adler being the most influential. This sudden collapse of what had seemed a strong school of medical and general psychology had important results.

It made Freud more defensive, inducing him to systematize his views into an orthodox set of dogmas. He gathered a group of faithful adherents round him who taught his methods and theories and he established an orthodox school of Freudian psychology which ultimately came to have recognized branches in the U.S.A. and in England (under his daughter, Anna Freud, and Ernest Jones, his early disciple). The rival schools developed their ideas freely and without reference to Freud.

Medical psychology was offered new kinds of therapy for neurotic patients, and a new clinical literature grew up, giving accounts of case-histories, treatments and explanations of neurotic reactions in terms of Freudian, or Jungian, or some alternative theory. Moreover, the literature did not confine itself to strictly clinical issues. The new movements recognized that a new type of psychology was being developed which applied outside the clinic and the mental hospital to normal subjects. Psychiatry was invading the territory of psychology with new techniques of investigating the mind and new theories about human personality.

The new movements were thus, from the start, a centre of both interest and controversy. Both orthodox psychiatrists, trained in the tradition of Kraepelin and Bleuler, and academic psychologists were suspicious, if not openly hostile. Freud became a somewhat notorious figure, teaching strange and unacceptable theories. Up to 1914 few people were well acquainted with psycho-analysis. It was only after the First World War had given the authorities innumerable 'shell shock' and war neurosis cases to deal with – and physicians had found some of the psycho-analytic techniques useful – that more adequate accounts of the original literature became available; and it was not until the 1920s that Freud's name became widely known in America and England – and even in Germany. It was then that his theories began to influence psychologists on a wider scale. In the years immediately following the First World War, Freud's psycho-analytic theories and Watson's Behaviourism began to disrupt accepted ideas about the scope and methods of psychology.

However, the foundations of psycho-analysis had been built long before the 1920s, although Freud in 1918 still had much work to do. Between 1918 and 1938 he wrote many of his most celebrated books and articles, drastically modified his earlier theories, and continued to teach his pupils and treat his patients. His younger rivals did most of their work after the war and only established their reputations in this later period.

One effect of this movement was to bring psychiatry and psychology closer together than hitherto. Clinical data of all kinds became of interest to psychologists instead of being regarded as the specialized preserve of a branch of medicine. Psychologists themselves carried out investigations as researchers in the clinics, and later trained as 'clinical psychologists' to assist psychiatrists in their work. Psychological tests and psychological experimental techniques were brought into the psychiatric hospital as additional research instruments. The two disciplines came to exchange information and to collaborate in studying both pathological and normal subjects. Another effect of the psycho-analytic movement was due to Freud's insistence that the origins of unconscious conflicts could be traced to infant and childhood crises – hence the importance of studying children in the interests of tracing the origin and development of adult traits. The psycho-analysts had not themselves studied children in their early days. As a result of Freud's teaching, child psychology received a great stimulation to go forward along many new lines of investigation.

The influence of Freud, Jung, Adler and their successors did not remain part of the story of psychological medicine, but rather became part of the study of psychology in general after 1918. As such it shall be treated.

CHAPTER ELEVEN

Retrospect: Psychology in 1914

THE year 1914 draws a line across European, if not world, history. The impact of the terrible and tragic war disrupted, and turned off in new directions, almost every kind of human interest. What had happened to psychology down to this dividing line?

In the 1880s and 1890s, psychology was in an expansionist mood, self-consciously breaking away from philosophy and setting up as a new scientific discipline. The physiological psychology of Wundt was ascendant, the study of sensory thresholds, reaction times and memory being dominant topics. The study of animal behaviour had been initiated by the British, and was soon to be taken over by Thorndike, Yerkes and Watson. Attempts at child and developmental psychology had begun, and the psycho-analytic movement had just started.

The conceptual framework was simple. Darwin's general ideas were widely accepted as a vague background, while mental processes (for example, emotions) were still regarded as real entities. There was little concern with improving empirical methods and techniques. The psychophysical methods of Fechner and the Wundtian experimental methods were simply taken for granted, but not developed much. The 'new psychology' down to 1898 presented a harmonious and united appearance without any signs of radical disagreement. It was accepted that psychologists were beginning to provide adequate descriptions of mental processes, and that the application of psychology to practical problems would come about in a few decades.

By the turn of the century, this situation had changed. By 1910 there was a bitter clash between the Structuralist and the Functionalist rival 'schools' over fundamental principles in experimental psychology. Freud's views had been formulated and published and were arousing controversy, not merely between him and Adler, but between supporters of psycho-analysis and its critics, who denied the existence of unconscious drives of a sexual character. By 1913 Watson had published his first version of Behaviourism – attacking 'mental processes' as the data of psychology and 'introspection' as a valid and objective method. Empirical research, to judge by the contents of journals, diminished in favour of theoretical disputes about fundamentals. Just before the war, the Gestalt school began to formulate yet another basic 'system' of psychology, and the subject appeared to be reverting to a philosophical phase. However, the general opinion seemed to be that these theoretical differences would resolves themselves and a unity would be restored such as existed in the early days of Helmholtz and Wundt.

The war did not merely disrupt academic work. Psychologists in all the countries involved were drafted into the war-effort and required to deal with the practical problems of soldiers, sailors, industrialists and politicians. Theoretical disputes were set aside and pure science was diminished. In order to select the most able men for training in specialist techniques or for positions of responsibility, intelligence testing was developed. Tests of mechanical aptitude and skill were devised to pick the recruits most likely to benefit from training for technical jobs. Some weeding out of mental defectives and neurotics was needed to form military units with sound morale. Problems of adapting men to machines were posed for the first time, while the need to reorganize industry and make it more efficient turned industrial psychology from an interest in the hands of, literally, one or two pioneers into an everyday business for psychologists. This profoundly affected the development of psychology – mental testing and the application of psychology to industry became two major fields of activity after the war.

However, the old theoretical disputes between the new rival 'schools' were not forgotten: differences over first principles, methods and techniques and disagreements about the proper subject-matter for psychology came to the fore once the war and its problems were over.

PART TWO

Psychology between the Wars

CHAPTER TWELVE

Behaviourism 1918–40

IN the period between the two world wars the New Psychology, which had developed during the nineteenth century, greatly expanded in scope and activity. It also presented an entirely new 'image'. In spite of some arguments over fundamentals, the new psychology had appeared as a relatively coherent and consistent science. It had confined itself to the study of consciousness and had employed methods of experiment adapted directly from physiology.

Especially after 1890, many new ideas about psychology were being developed in embryonic terms. The main impact of these developments did not come until the 1920s. During this decade, psychologists began a period of theory-construction and systematic thinking about basic aims, methods and concepts. The result was that rival theories of psychology grew up simultaneously. They were designed to provide basic methods for dealing with empirical problems in psychology and a conceptual framework within which the results of research could be related to each other.

The new science appeared as a field of dispute between various schools. Philosophical differences cut across the growing corpus of knowledge acquired by the patient application of scientific methods for studying experience and behaviour. These different schools led some editors, Murchison for example, to publish books with such titles as *Psychologies of 1925*. The new science appeared to be splitting up into a number of different versions.

It is necessary, in this and the three following chapters, to discuss the principal systematic theories which arose during the period between the wars, since the basic ideas developed within each provided the stimulus for specific empirical researches.

Already in 1913, the main principle of Behaviouristic theories had been defined by J. B. Watson (pp. 163 ff.). After the war he wrote *Psychology from the Standpoint of a Behaviorist* (1919). As we have seen, in 1920 he became involved in a divorce action and resigned from Johns Hopkins University. From then onwards he worked in the advertising business. Although he continued to write articles to popularize his views, his main work was over.

Watson's attack on introspection and the study of mental life as the characteristic approach to psychology received support from several contemporary sources. A. P. Weiss (1879–1931), born in Germany but living in the U.S.A. as a child and graduating in psychology at Missouri in 1912, became a respected teacher at Ohio University (1912–31). He wrote a number of articles in the early 1920s which were brought together in his influential book *A Theoretical Basis of Human Behaviour* (1925). Weiss argued that psychological data ought to be reducible to descriptions of physiochemical processes in the living organism, complicated by consideration of social relationships. Weiss agreed with Watson's basic postulates. More sophisticated support came from a respected philosopher E. B. Holt (1873–1946), a Harvard man. His *Concept of Consciousness* (1914) attacked the assumption that a scientific study of individual experience is practicable.

In *Animal Drive and the Learning Process* (1931) he summarized his earlier teachings, and put forward the objective study of the 'response relation' as the basis of psychology. However, 'response' for Holt was a broader category than the muscular contractions of the radical Behaviourism of Watson. Holt initiated the concept of 'molar behaviour', later to be adopted by E. C. Tolman and others dissatisfied with the limited scope of early

Behaviourist programmes. Acts such as 'opening the door' were counted as units of behaviour – admitting goal-following purposeful activities as a proper subject for observation. Holt also argued that a human being knows what is happening, or is about to happen, in virtue of the fact that the response meets the requirements of the context in which it is made. There is a feed-back of information from motor activity, which gives clues that the 'meaning' of a perceptual judgement is more or less correct, or that an intention is being actualized successfully. The cognitive aspect of perception and the intimate interaction of sensory and motor systems were thus emphasized in Holt's thinking. This was a reminder that Behaviourism required modification and refinement beyond the scope of Watson's 'reflexology'. Nevertheless, Holt assisted in shifting the interest of description in psychology away from the scientific description of consciousness to the scientific description of behaviour.

Watson's exploitation of Pavlov's conditioning as the mechanism for explaining how stimuli and responses come to be linked led to some interest in Russian physiology. I. M. Sechenov (1829–1905), who had preceded Pavlov at the Moscow Institute, had put forward a version of Behaviourism in his *Reflexes of the Brain* (1863). Sechenov had maintained that intelligence is a function of the reflexes of the cortex, and even the psychology of the higher mental functions should be reduced to the study of neurophysiological mechanisms. V. M. Bekhterev (1857–1927), another member of this school, also argued, in his *Principles of Human Reflexology* (1917), that mental concepts in psychology should be abolished, and physiological methods and concepts substituted. These views became known to American psychologists, encouraging the development of a 'stimulus–response' (S–R) model for psychological science, and the adoption of a technical jargon from physiology.

When Watson moved out of academic psychology, the leadership of the new movement was assumed by W. S.

Hunter (1889–1947). He had studied at Chicago under Angell and Carr up to 1914 and he later became professor at Kansas. He wrote a number of theoretical papers attacking the 'mentalism' of the older experimental psychology. He also asked in one article for a list of those psychologists who accepted the views of Watson and Weiss, seeming anxious to collect a recognized 'school'.

Hunter's main contribution was as an experimentalist who exemplified the ideas of the new school. He devised a type of study which was greatly exploited: the delayed response experiment. In this, an animal is shown food being placed in one of a number of similar boxes. A screen is then placed between the animal and the boxes and the animal is restrained for a period. If it goes straight to the correct box on release, how does it retain the information received earlier? Hunter argued that animals do so only in virtue of being able to hold a bodily 'set' or 'orientation' in which they remain pointing towards the correct box. This conclusion was challenged by Gestalt psychologists, who maintained that rats can retain information for as long as four hours. The controversy sparked off a number of experiments on the 'delayed response' and other aspects of animal learning. In the 1920s, adherents of Behaviourism experimented rather than theorized. The main aim was to demonstrate that a wide variety of animal-adaptation could be achieved in terms of conditioning experiments, in which the animals' response is controlled through the presentation of stimuli, suitable according to the laws governing the establishment, strengthening and inter-connexion of conditioned responses.

E. R. GUTHRIE

In the 1930s, new forms of Behaviourist theory were developed. Within the strictly Watsonian tradition, that of E. R. Guthrie was perhaps the most celebrated.

Guthrie's article 'Conditioning as a Principle of Learning' (*Psychological Review*, 1930) and his book *The Psychology of Learning* (1935) state as coherent a thesis for radical Behaviourism as any available.

'All that the most sophisticated organism can do in any situation is to contract his muscles in some order and pattern.' The sophisticated behaviour of a human being is simply the result of having developed a large number of new orders and patterns relating to a wide range of stimuli.

Guthrie believed that psychology must seek to establish rules or generalizations of which particular descriptions of this or that behaviour are instances. These 'laws' describe the observable conditions under which any particular example of behaviour takes place. Since we cannot observe, record and control *all* the conditions under which behaviour occurs, and since we cannot describe every detail in any sample of behaviour, it is therefore best to select observable stimuli and observable responses. Conditioning as described by Pavlov presents a good model for psychological observation and description. We can isolate stimuli, which Guthrie defines as: 'any change in physical energy which activates a receptor and sets up afferent impulses in the nervous system'. We can isolate responses which the stimuli evoke: responses being the movement of any muscle or group of muscles, or the secretion of any glands. Movements are the basic data for psychology.

Guthrie makes an important distinction between movements and acts. When we talk of a person walking towards a door, opening a door, sitting down, we are describing 'acts'. He argues that psychologists cannot describe behaviour in terms of acts. Attempts to do so end in inaccuracy and vagueness. Psychology can only hope to achieve accuracy by observing and predicting movements. Nerves connect sense organs to muscles and glands, and not directly to doors or chairs. The movement of organisms, studied by the use of techniques adopted from experimental physiology, is the main task of psychology.

The operation of organisms on the complex environment cannot profitably be made the aim of a scientific psychology.

This is as clear and as consistent an account of 'radical Behaviourism' as any available. Responses are the result of stimuli impinging on the receptors, which then activate the central nervous system and ultimately produce the contraction of various muscles and the secretions of various glands – the immediate causes of overt behaviour. In studying the way in which stimuli and responses are connected, conditioning and habit-formation ('learning' processes) are the key. In Guthrie's theory of learning, the essential condition for 'learning' was contiguity in place and time between the conditional stimulus and the response to be acquired or strengthened: the acquisition or strengthening of a specific S–R bond. Guthrie's writings give us a clear picture of the dominant creed of Behaviourism in the mid-thirties.

SKINNER AND OPERANT CONDITIONING

B. F. Skinner (b. 1904) was educated at Harvard, taking his Ph.D. in 1931. After working at Minnesota for nearly twenty years, he returned to Harvard in 1948 and has been responsible for many new developments (research on teaching machines, for example). In 1938 he published *The Behavior of Organisms*. The conclusions of his experimental and theoretical work in the period 1930–45 appeared in his *Science and Human Behavior* (1953). He has also written a novel called *Walden Two*, which is an exemplification of Skinnerian theory in a sort of Behaviourist utopia.

Skinner has always maintained that psychologists ought to be primarily interested in behaviour which has some effect on the environment, especially if this impact in its turn produces a feed-back of information which influences future behaviour (for instance, learning and adaptation). He also holds the Behaviourist thesis that psychology should seek to establish empirical laws which describe regular and precise relationships between independent and dependent variables, showing how a specific response is a function of a given class of stimuli. Given a particular stimulus, the psychologist should be able to predict what response will follow.

Skinner claims that in his experimental work he has discovered techniques for the precise control of 'reinforcing' effects so that he can accurately shape the behaviour of his subjects. It is possible to train animals to perform three or four well-defined responses in any experimental session. These techniques have been developed on the basis of a new type of conditioning which Skinner discovered in the 1930s and which he called 'operant conditioning'. Skinner's conditioning situation differed from that of Pavlov. Pavlov took a hungry animal and paired a previously neutral stimulus (sounding a buzzer, for example) with the giving of food to the animal. In time the buzzer alone evoked anticipatory food-taking reactions, such as salivating. Skinner, on the other hand, waited for an animal to make a specific response spontaneously and then stepped in with a reinforcing agent such as food.

Thus a hungry rat in a box comes eventually to press a lever sticking out from the wall. This immediately releases a pellet of food. The rat 'learns' to press the lever in order to produce food pellets. Thus, the animal has to learn to make a specific response (or a series of responses in more elaborate experiments) in order to produce the reinforcement. The method is called 'operant' because the animal has to operate upon its environment in order to be reinforced. The laws of conditioning apply equally to the Pavlovian or classical type of conditioning and to operant conditioning. Skinner has simply applied Thorndike's Law of Effect (p. 159) in order to modify the Pavlovian situation. The thirties and forties were devoted by Skinner to studying in detail the conditions which control operant behaviour, and a vast experimental literature evolved from this thorough and systematic work. It substantiates Skinner's claim to be able to invent training schedules which mould the behaviour of animals, training them to perform quite elaborate tricks (his pigeons 'dance' elaborate step-sequences and play 'ping-pong' with each other).

Basic to Skinner's type of conditioning is his distinction between 'operant behaviour' (which is spontaneous) and 'respondent behaviour' (all responses directly elicited by known stimuli: light sources which cause the pupil of the eye to contract; pressure which causes the patellar tendon to contract, producing a 'knee jerk', etc.). When the rat in the Skinner-box reaches up and presses down the lever for the first time, it is not obviously being 'stimulated' by a specific external stimulus. The sight and smell of the lever must have some part to play; but why it sets off the 'pressing' reaction just at a particular moment is not clear.

This is the point of an old joke which appeared in a student journal in which one rat says to another: 'Oh boy, have I got this psychologist conditioned. Every time I press the lever he gives me a pellet of food.'

However, Skinner insists that the key to learning and adaptation (and hence to understanding 'behaviour' in general) is the way in which specific responses are controlled by the presentation of stimuli which have the property of serving as 'reinforcing agents'. He believes that the specific laws of conditioning and habit-formation as revealed in the study of operant behaviour give the answers to this basic problem.

Nor does he hesitate to explain human behaviour in terms of his theory. He talks of an industrial manager reinforcing the work-behaviour of his employees with high wages and good conditions. The efficient work and lack of absenteeism or strikes are controlled responses in answer to these reinforcements provided by the management. This line of thinking is open to theoretical and methodological objections of a kind which prevent many psychologists from accepting a strictly Behaviourist theory. However it is important at present to expound Skinner's version of Behaviourism simply, without subjecting it to criticism. The theory does claim to provide a basis for a complete psychology for dealing with all aspects of human behaviour and not simply to explain the way animals learn.

Skinner operates in terms of a strict stimulus–response model. He has often been characterized as the champion of the 'open organism'. He does not want to speculate or even to utilize existing physiological knowledge in order to suggest how the brain and nervous system mediates between stimulus variables and response variables. By performing experiments in the laboratory, the psychologist can discover correlations between certain environmental variables and specific response-factors. Laws of conditioning are simply inductions: generalizations applying to innumerable particular instances, in which environmental conditions correlate with each other and with specific responses. The physiologist may ultimately supply data to explain why these conditions between independent and dependent variables are what the psychologist demonstrates them to be, but such an explanation belongs to physiological psychology. Skinner's psychology is purely descriptive. His concept of conditioning simply states a lawful correlation between stimulus and response. Like Watson's, his approach has affinities with the old associationist psychologies. Instead of analysing consciousness into sensations and images, and studying correlations between these mental events, or between mental events and environmental events, he analyses behaviour in terms of associations between overt stimuli and overt reactions. Analysis into elements and their correlations is the basic method of psychology. From this point of view, Skinner has remained within the basic postulates of radical or orthodox Behaviourism, which derives from Watson and Pavlov, with modifications from Thorndike's

Law of Effect. Other Behaviourists have deviated from this tradition.

TOLMAN'S PURPOSIVE BEHAVIOURISM

E. C. Tolman (1886–1959) introduced considerable flexibility into Behaviourism. He was influenced by Holt at Harvard, where he took his Ph.D. in 1915. After 1918 he worked at the University of California at Berkeley. The influence of Holt is evident in his magnus opus, *Purposive Behavior in Animals and Men* (1932).

Throughout his career Tolman was an active experimentalist. His rats were as hard-worked as those of Skinner, and he provided the textbooks with many interesting accounts of place-learning and latent learning experiments. However, he was not satisfied with explanations in terms of the conditioning of S–R bonds. He was influenced by psycho-analytic literature and McDougall's interest in 'instinct'. He was not unsympathetic towards the work of the Gestalt school. He had never forgotten his teacher Hugo Münsterberg's emphasis on 'purposeful' striving as a facet of behaviour. Yet he adhered to the view that psychology should be objective and avoid mentalism. The result of his experiments and reflections was a theory which provided a more complex analysis of animal as well as human behaviour, and which, while claiming with some justification to be a version of behaviourism, also greatly influenced subsequent theorizing by other behaviourists.

Tolman introduced the concept of 'intervening variables' (I.V.s) into Behaviourist terminology. He argued that between stimuli and their ultimate responses we must use variables in terms of which hypotheses about hereditary and past learning may be constructed. He divided these intervening variables into three types, and insisted that there is nothing mentalistic about their meaning. They simply specify functional properties which must be postulated if S–R relationships are to be adequately described. Tolman used such un-Behaviouristic concepts as 'demands' and 'expectations' in defining his I.V.s; yet his claim that they can be objectively defined in terms of operations can be defended.

A 'demand', for example, is defined in terms of such observations as that the animal persists in trial-and-error activities towards a specific goal; by observing the actual selection of responses from its repertory which serve as a means for reaching a specific goal; by the changes in the environment resulting from its behaviour; and by the fact that it shows capacities for learning how to reach the goal through a number of 'problem-solving' situations. Again, an 'expectancy' is the information which an animal collects about the character of a distant goal (for example, Tolman claims to show in his experiments that animals learn direction and distance of goal from starting-point, as also the type of means required to achieve a goal).

Tolman's basic generalization was that animals learn that one pattern of stimuli (sign) is related to another pattern (significate). Thus, animals can often react towards the significate (or even the last in a series of signs in recurring order) whenever the sign is presented in the absence of the significate. It can display a 'means–end readiness' to meet a situation which is signalled but not yet actual. Animals learn 'what leads to what': they build up 'cognitive maps' of recurring situations, and of the way things and events relate to each other in a familiar environment. They do not simply learn muscular movements in relation to stimuli; they learn sign-significate *Gestalten*.

Tolman supported his theories with original experiments using rats. He demonstrated the fact that 'latent' learning occurs. If one group of rats (A) are placed in a maze for several days or nights and fed regularly in the goal-box, they explore the maze casually. However, when deprived of food for a period and placed at the starting-point, they quickly take the shortest route to the goal-box.

A second group (B), with no experience of the maze, have to undergo considerable trial-and-error learning before they take the quickest route to the goal-box for food when hungry. Some kind of information about the layout of the maze seems to have been acquired, retained and utilized by group A during their casual and unrewarded explorations of the maze. They have learned the maze and can apply this learning when set the problem of getting food urgently and quickly.

Again, a number of 'place-learning' studies by Tolman suggested that rats which were trained always to go to the same place in a maze by different routes on different occasions learnt more quickly and permanently than rats trained always to take a specific sequence of turns (right–left–right–left) and who learnt a series of movements. The former exploit a rat's capacity to learn direction and distance, changing its movements to get to the goal to suit changed routings, obstacles and other difficulties.

Was Tolman strictly within the Behaviourist tradition? His concept of expectancy has some affinities with Gestalt thinking, since sign-significate relationships are structured within a field of variables influencing behaviour. Nevertheless, Tolman operates within a conceptual framework in which stimuli related to responses are the key factors. He disagrees with Guthrie and Skinner in thinking: (a) that the S–R relationship is much more complicated, in so far as intervening variables are required to provide an adequate description of what is observed to be taking place, (b) that there is more than one kind of learning, so that conditioning models fail to account for all the available data.

Yet many of his apparently deviant conceptions are not alien to Behaviourism. 'Demands' are the product of physiological states (cf. 'drives') *plus* prior learning. Sign-significate relationships are involved in a type of association between stimuli and response, linked by a set of intervening processes. Such relationships are strengthened by the confirmation of the significate appearing, and weakened by its non-appearance: a type of 'effect' principle. The frequency, recency and temporal contiguity in the pairing of a sign with a significate are factors which strengthen a particular association – all of which notions are familiar to Behaviourists.

Where Tolman clashed with other Behaviourists was in his denial that the presentation of a reinforcing state of affairs was a necessary condition for the acquisition of learning. Reinforcing agents for Tolman simply facilitate established learning – the utilization of what is already acquired. Learning can occur without the operation of reinforcing stimuli, since it is 'cognitions' or 'meanings' which are learned, and not responses.

Tolman's writings in the thirties had two main results. (1) Other Behaviourists adopted his conception that 'intervening variables' are useful in accounting for S–R associations. This added a new dimension in theory-construction. (2) In opposition to the heretical tendencies in Tolman, more orthodox Behaviourists attempted to 'improve' Behaviourist doctrines to meet his criticisms. In particular, C. L. Hull developed a sophisticated theory which provoked a controversy between Tolman's followers and his own – a controversy which enlivened both the study of animal-learning and theorizing in the period between 1930 and 1949.

Tolman had a stimulating effect on American psychology, and it is somewhat surprising that this shy, charming, humorous and open-minded man, who seems to have found psychology an amusing as well as a fascinating profession, should have been the cause of a major split in the Behaviourist school.

C. L. HULL

Clark L. Hull (1884–1952) did not graduate from Michigan until he was 29, owing to illnesses. He took his Ph.D. at the age of 34 from Wisconsin. Originally destined for engineering, he switched to psychology and became a great theorizer as well as an active experimenter. In 1929 he settled at Yale. He died at the age of 68 before completing his work.

From 1929 until his death, he was engaged in the construction of a theory of behaviour. From 1929 to 1943 he performed experiments and formulated basic concepts and 'miniature' formalizations of parts of his theory. These appeared in the *Psychological Review* between 1931 and 1939. His book *The Principles of Behavior* (1943) summarized his work. Towards the end of his life, he revised his ideas in *The Essentials of Behavior* (1951) and in the posthumously published *A Behavior System* (1952). Hull's system, in its most influential form, is obviously in the Behaviourist tradition. He adopts Thorndike's Law of Effect and accepts much of Pavlov and Watson, together with the ancient doctrine that living creatures seek pleasurable stimuli and avoid pain – a theory held in common by the Greeks, the utilitarian philosophers and the evolution theorists. Hull, nevertheless, moves away from radical or orthodox Behaviourism.

Watson's Behaviourism was the sketch of a programme for psychology, a policy of reform correcting the faults of early experimental work. It aimed at getting more accurate empirical data with which psychologists could work, by getting rid of ineffective introspective methods within the laboratory, replacing observation of the individual's conscious states by observation of overt responses and their environmental conditions. S–R variables were put forward as the only legitimate ones for science: 'Given the S, predict the R: given the R, predict the S.' Conditioning – a correlation between S–R factors capable of precise experimental investigation – seemed a good model for associative laws connecting stimuli and responses. This gave a strong emphasis on peripheral determinants of behaviour (stimuli, the operation of receptors visual, auditory, etc.), and utilized the traditional interest of experimental psychologists in the sensory processes. All behaviour must therefore be analysed in terms of S–R connexions.

Hull did not accept all of this. Instead, he adopted Tolman's view that intervening variables should be postulated to mediate between the S variables and the R variables. Nor did he accept Pavlovian or Skinnerian conditioning as adequate to account for all S–R connexions. Habits and serial responses constituting simple skills required more elaborate description and explanation. Eventually, Hull produced a highly formal theory. This was modelled on the logical structure of theoretical physics, in which postulates and axioms were related to empirical laws within a rigid system, while logico-mathematical formulae were used to suggest the possible quantification of the basic processes. We need not concern ourselves with this highly idiosyncratic presentation. Nobody else seems to have adopted it, and Hull's ideas have been accepted by a large number of followers without all their trappings. His theories are straightforward enough.

Hull takes a strictly biological view of behaviour. From birth, the organism begins a dynamic relationship with an active environment. The possibility of studying this complex and dynamic relationship depends on the fact that stimulus-factors in the environment are subject to natural laws as discovered by physics, while the internal environment of the organism is subject to natural laws discovered by physiology. Psychology has the task of linking the two other sciences by discovering 'molar behaviour laws', the ultimate explanation of which depends on physics and physiology. The way to arrive at such psychological or behaviour laws is to consider the structure and function of a living organism in the Darwinian terms of evolution and survival. Survival depends on the reduction or elimination of basic primary needs – getting food and drink, shelter and protection, a mate and offspring. Much animal behaviour (and, less obviously, much human behaviour) has the effect of satisfying survival needs. Secondary needs, not essential for survival but evolved out of the process of meeting primary needs, also become central and demand satisfaction.

Hence, much motor activity has the function of satisfying 'drives' or 'needs' (which arise because of an inner state of disequilibrium, caused usually by some lack of a physiochemical agency or a gap in the organism's inner economy); or, it promotes conditions in the environment which make the easy satisfaction of needs possible. The concept of 'drive' or 'need' is essential for Hull, and is an 'intervening variable' (I.V.). Another key I.V. is 'habit', which, for Hull, is not simply the regular occurrence of a specific type of response whenever certain environmental changes occur, but a complex state of the nervous system – a readiness, or 'set', to react in a highly specific manner, provided a number of conditions are satisfied. Habits are related to each other in a system, so that if one habit is not selected, another, second in order of probability according to a complex balance of forces, will come forward to fit the environmental-plus-motivational requirements of the moment. I.V.s like 'drive' and 'habit' refer to processes which cannot be observed, but which may be plausibly inferred (a) in relation to observable S–R connexions, (b) in relation to our knowledge of physics and physiology.

Thus, when a stimulus evokes a response, Hull requires ten concepts to describe what is happening (physical stimulus, afferent neural impulse, habit strength, generalized habit strength, reaction potential, reaction, reinforcement, etc.). This scheme is necessary, because Hull recognizes that once the stimulus in the environment has caused the receptor (eye or ear) to react, afferent impulses in the nervous system are set off, which continue to reverberate after the stimulus has ceased at the periphery. These afferent impulses (persevering stimulus traces) interact with on-going nervous activity, and are modified by such activity before producing a final modification at some crucial centre. Moreover, the afferent nervous activity arouses central nervous centres (those responsible for storing prior learning, the hierarchy of 'habits') which are both active and subject to variables other than those signals coming from the peripheral sensory system. Before a specific 'habit', or tendency to react, is selected, and before it evokes motor systems to produce an overt reaction, rapid interactions among internal states have to work themselves out. Finally, the reaction occurs (the observable R) and produces effects on the environment. These effects, in turn, provide stimuli which impinge on the organism, and certain such stimuli have the effect of setting off inner processes which eliminate a 'drive' state (restoring equilibrium in some previously disturbed centre). 'Whenever a response process is closely contiguous to a stimulus process, and this association occurs, near in time, to a reduction of a drive, then the association is strengthened.' Reinforcement is therefore a necessary condition of learning.

Hull's research work was chiefly concerned with the conditions under which reinforcement operates to strengthen habits and simple skills. His theorizing was concerned with speculations concerning the way in which 'intervening variables' must be defined in order to allow for the mediation of the nervous system between S and R variables. His conception of the processes involved in mediation was a strictly mechanical one. For example, as we shall see later, when he tried to explain how an animal learns to make a precisely selected response to a 'cue', he thought in terms of arithmetical increases in 'reaction potential' building up bit by bit from one learning trial to the next.

Hull is therefore a Behaviourist who sticks closely to the S-R model, who utilizes both Pavlov's studies and those of Skinner on conditioning, and who adheres to Thorndike's Law of Effect as the basic law of learning. However, he introduces an elaborate set of postulates and laws to explain how intervening variables mediate between S and R, and it is usually in terms of these hypotheses that he seeks to interpret the data of both animal and human studies of learning-operations. Hull maintained that intervening variables were simply logical constructs designed to relate S–R variables, and that, accordingly, their usage should be firmly linked to overt, observable facts or to generalizations confirmed by observation. It seems to most interpreters of his ideas that his concepts operate rather as 'hypothetical constructs' – they serve to suggest the general function of unknown factors (mechanisms and organizations within the brain and nervous system).

Hull and Tolman set a fashion in the devising and use of hypothetical constructs in the theoretical side of experimental psychology. Many eminent American psychologists within the Behaviourist tradition have contributed to this literature. Two notable examples of more recent times are K. W. Spence of Yale, who followed and developed in several new directions Hull's line of thinking, and C. E. Osgood of Illinois, whose 'mediation hypothesis' is both a development of Hull and an attempt to incorporate Gestalt criticisms of Behaviourist models. (See K. W. Spence: *Behavior Theory and Conditioning*, 1956, and C. E. Osgood: *Method and Theory in Experimental Psychology*, 1953.)

CHAPTER THIRTEEN

Gestalt Psychology

NEARLY all those concerned with the formation and development of Gestalt psychology were born and educated in Europe. Most of them were of Jewish origin and were ultimately driven by the Nazis to the U.S.A. in the 1930s. They were gradually absorbed into American psychology and the 'movement' as such ceased to exist. The influence of this group, in experimental psychology at least, proved considerable in the 1920s and 1930s.

Max Wertheimer (1886–1943) was born in Prague and took his degree there. He became a Ph.D. at Würzburg as a pupil of Külpe. He became interested in the perception of movement. During a holiday he left his train on impulse at Frankfurt and, after discussing the ideas which were exciting him with a former teacher of his who was professor there, he was offered research facilities and stayed on for several years. It was his researches which led him to the simple thesis that the perception of movement is a given 'whole' in experience, and cannot be reduced to compounded sensory elements.

Kurt Koffka (1886–1941) and Wolfgang Köhler (1887–1967) were both in Frankfurt from 1910 to 1913 while Wertheimer was researching, and both became interested in the work. Koffka had taken his degree at Berlin, under Stumpf's supervision, in 1909. He carried out experiments on 'apparent movement', distinguishing five types of this species of optical illusion. Together with Wertheimer, he then became interested in the phenomenon of 'figure' as contrasted with 'background' in perception of shapes. Both men were agreed that in perception the whole is not merely the summation of its distinguishable parts. The whole has properties of its own, so that the parts and relationships within the whole are largely a product of the entire 'configuration'. This opposed the assumptions of associationist theories from Mill and Bain down to Wundt and Titchener.

Köhler had been born in Estonia, but received his education at Berlin with Stumpf. He had also studied physics with Max Planck and was an expert on acoustics. He readily accepted Wertheimer's theories. In 1913, he left Frankfurt to study apes on the island of Tenerife. He was interned there during the First World War, although allowed to continue his research. His book, *The Mentality of Apes*, shows the influence of early Gestalt ideas. He attempts to show that animals do not respond to isolated stimuli; they react in terms of perceived relations between objects. 'Insight' or the sudden perception of 'means–end' relationships is as common as trial-and-error learning.

Köhler returned to Germany in 1920 and succeeded Stumpf as professor in Berlin in 1922. By this time Wertheimer had returned to Berlin and the association begun in Frankfurt was renewed. In 1921 Wertheimer, Koffka and Köhler founded a periodical, *Psychologische Forschung*, which continued until 1938, when the Nazis suppressed it. It was the main organ of the experimental work and theories of the movement. The members of the group remained in complete harmony with each other throughout their lifetime. There were no dissentions and no diverse developments. They specialized in different aspects of psychology (Köhler in auditory perception and animal learning, Wertheimer in problems of thought and judgement, etc.).

The Gestalt school was highly influential between the two wars. The theory may be vague and abstract yet the experimental work it inspired in the fields of perception, learning and reasoning has supplied textbooks of experimental psychology with many familiar studies. The theory also created a shift in the general thinking of psychologists away from common assumptions of the

pre-1914 era, and even modified the extremes of Behaviouristic thinking in the late 1930s.

William James, Oswald Külpe and Lloyd Morgan had
all insisted that analysis of experience into elements was
mistaken. The view that 'wholes' have emergent
properties, not derived from the sum of their parts, was
not new. Whereas Wundt and Helmholtz had maintained
that spatial relations have to be learned, Hering and
Stumpf had argued that these are perceived immediately
and that human beings have built-in mechanisms for
grasping such *Gestalten*. Stout and Myers in England also
anticipated some basic Gestalt concepts. There were even
experimental anticipations of Gestalt results. In Sweden,
David Katz (1884–1953), who became an adherent of
Gestalt psychology, produced some experiments on
colour perception in 1912. He distinguished three kinds
of perceived colours. (1) Surface colour, which is bi-
dimensional, localized at a distance, and usually attributed to a given object as a property. (2) Volumic colour,
which is tri-dimensional and is usually of such trans-
parent things as coloured liquids or air illuminated by
artificial light. (3) Film colour, which is without localization or spatial characteristics as in a spectroscope. Katz
demonstrated that surface colour can be reduced to film
colour if viewed through a small hole in a screen. It then
loses its surface properties – distance, constancy under
shifting illumination, etc. Thus 'field' or 'context' determines the fundamental properties of colour as we
perceive it.

In spite of such anticipations of the movement, it is
doubtful if they would have made such an impact without the organization of a 'school'. What, then, were the
main characteristics of Gestalt psychology?

The German word *Gestalt* means, roughly, 'shape' or
'form'. The use of the term emphasizes that what is given,
the basic data of consciousness, is grasped immediately
in organized, structured and dynamic 'wholes'. In perceiving a melody we grasp a melodic form and not a

sequence of separate tones. Changes of key, of tempo, or even rhythm and stress, do not destroy this unitary characteristic of the 'tune' we hear. Perceptual wholes are more than the sum of their parts. They emerge and have characteristics of their own. This basic conception of Gestalt psychology was thus opposed to the well-established tradition in psychology, that of analysing experience into sensory elements connected by laws of association.

Many 'laws' govern the organization of such 'wholes' or 'configurations'. These laws were partly generalizations from typical Gestalt experiments and partly theoretical models. For example:

(1) A perceptual field tends to become organized in terms of a specific *Gestalten*. Parts are connected in relation to the dominant 'form'.

(2) A fundamental feature in this organization is the structuring of the field into 'figure' and 'ground'. The former is central, the latter peripheral.

(3) A good form tends to impress itself clearly on the observer and to persist or recur (basic geometrical shapes such as square, circle, triangle, are 'good' *Gestalten*). These resist disintegration by scrutiny or analysis).

From these, and many other laws governing the organization of 'wholes', certain basic generalizations emerge. (1) Perceived objects tend to remain constant in size when their distance from the observer varies. Even when the retinal image is known to vary, the observer still regards the object as remaining constant. Constancy applies to every attribute of an object – shape, weight, etc. It is probably the effect of an innate, central organization in the brain. (2) The perceptual field is shaped by interacting forces or vectors on the analogy of an electrical field. There must be some innate organization which imposes such dynamic fields over all kinds of human experience. Not merely our perceptions but our thinking and striving seems to be organized within a field of such forces. (3) All such psychological 'fields' correspond to underlying neurophysiological patterns. In the perception of apparent movement, for example, two adjacent separate fixed points of light, perceived in darkness, appear as one point moving in a specific direction if illuminated in succession. The Gestalt theory assumes that there must be a dynamic relation between two centres in the brain such that one area influences the other by a process similar to the flow of electricity across a poorly insulated gap. Thus, a dynamic field of energy, with a physical basis, is the explanation of this phenomenon. There is no separate movement of discrete sensory elements. This type of explanation was called 'isomorphic'.

This somewhat abstract theory stimulated much interesting and fruitful experimental research (Chapter 17) into problems of perception, learning and remembering.

Otherwise the main effect of the Gestalt school was to attack atomism and associationist assumptions; to replace introspection by demonstrations of a more operational kind in the laboratory; and to insist that what we experience is the result of highly complex, innate and *centrally* organized processes in the brain. A general movement away from old assumptions did not necessarily imply an acceptance of Gestalt hypotheses, so that many psychologists who did not accept the views of the school nevertheless accepted their criticisms of the older schools. Perhaps the main contributions to experimental psychology were (1) the realization that problems about how we perceive were relatively separate from problems about the functioning of the sensory nervous system, (2) the improvement of experimental method for studying perception. The Gestalt psychologist, instead of trying to measure the attributes of sensory elements, asked such questions as, for example, whether the observer reports movement of a red line from left to right under specific conditions of intensity of stimulus, time of exposure to stimulus, distance of stimulus, etc. The perceptual data were rendered operational and correlated with measurable, controllable changes in the stimulus-situation.

Once the German refugees of the Gestalt school emigrated to America, their views tended to blend and be compromised with other points of view – even with the less rigorous types of Behaviourism. Thus the school has been absorbed and integrated with other theoretical models in the thinking of more contemporary psychologists and to some extent has disappeared in more recent years. In the twenties and thirties, however, it was an active, coherent, united and quite militant school. In theory and experiment a new way of thinking was presented and many new interests were introduced by this group. The importance of the Gestalt theory cannot be over-estimated.

CHAPTER FOURTEEN

Psycho-Analysis and Its Derivative,

FREUD AND PSYCHO-ANALYSIS

ALTHOUGH Freud did much of his basic thinking and published some of his most important writings between 1890 and 1914 (see Chapter 10), he developed his system in a series of famous books, continuing his work right down till his death, in London in 1939. Indeed, it was only after psychiatrists' experiences with war neuroses, and the translation of Freud's writings into English and languages other than the original German, that psychoanalytic theory began to influence psychology. The emergence of psycho-analysis as a major force in the literature of psychology occurred in the 1920s. Even *The Interpretation of Dreams* was translated into English only in 1913, and most of his writings appeared, in English, in the mid-twenties. Moreover, the rival theories of Jung and Adler appeared in English either in the later years of the war or in the 1920s, many of Jung's influential and popular works appearing only in the 1930s. Karen Horney, Erich Fromm and Harry Stack Sullivan published in the late thirties and forties, so that it would be true to say that the main impact of this kind of psychology came very much within the 1919–39 period.

The life of Freud within this period was less dramatic than in the early days or during the stormy times of the pre-1914 Psycho-Analytical Association. Until 1938 he lived in Vienna – treating patients, writing, keeping in touch with those psychiatrists and psychologists who accepted a Freudian viewpoint, and struggling with sickness. This period ended with his humiliation by the Nazis and his exile to England in 1938.

It is impossible to deal with Freud's ideas in detail;

apart from their complexity and voluminous content, Freud shifted his position during the last twenty years of his life – as he had every right to do. However, certain theories came to be accepted as 'Freudian' and influenced, as drastically as any have ever done, the course of psychology.

Between 1900 and 1910, Freud began to formulate some new theories. In the 1890s he had believed that neuroses were due to the repression of memories of actual and painful events, usually sexual seductions in childhood. Only 'abreaction' – the release of emotions associated with the original shock – could relieve tension. He accepted Janet's view that dissociation had occurred. Unconscious memories and associated feelings had become cut off from the rest of the personality. Freud changed his mind after finding many cases in which no actual seduction or shock could have happened in the past history of the patient. Why was the patient inventing fictitious experiences?

Freud had already noted in his early writings that dream contents, slips of the tongue, lapses of memory, as well as neurotic symptoms, were governed by unconscious factors. Moreover, fears were often the overt expression of unconscious desires or needs. On the basis of these early observations, he developed two new theories to account for his puzzle: (1) the hypothesis of infantile sexuality; (2) the theory of the Oedipus complex.

There were, Freud concluded, two basic drives or instincts which were important in all human personality. The drive for self-preservation and the drive to procreate. The latter Freud called 'libido' or 'sexual energy'. This natural instinct is often thwarted by social constraints and conventions, and so leads to tension. Sex, however, is not simply the urge to have intercourse. It is associated with a wide variety of pleasurable sensations relating to bodily activity, and it begins, not at puberty as was commonly supposed, but at birth. Infants experience and gratify libidinal impulses in sucking, food taking, urination and defecation, rubbing of genitals and other erogenous zones of the body. Libidinal energy, in adults, is also associated with the mouth and the anus as well as with the genitals, and it is sublimated into various channels by expressions of emotional tenderness, making friends, etc. What the Buddhists appear to mean by 'desire' seems closer to Freud's use of the term 'sexual energy' than the narrower connotations of the term. His use is therefore a somewhat unconventional one, although it covers sexual impulse in the common meaning.

Infants are subject to sexual disturbance and to libidinal pleasures. At first this instinct is associated only with the mouth. This is the primary organ of desire, pleasure, satisfaction, to the infant. Food taking, breast contact, sucking the thumb act as a substitute – all these are outlets of libidinal energies. This pleasure remains throughout life: kissing, smoking, eating and drinking and many pre-sexual acts retain something of the oral phase of libidinal expression. Up to the age of six months, oral pleasure is passive. Once teeth appear, aggressive impulses develop and the libido becomes outer-oriented.

Freud's chief disciple, Karl Abraham, developed the libido theory in a series of papers, and the Freudian teachings about infantile sexuality owe as much to him as to the originator himself. As a result of Abraham's contribution, Freud came to regard libidinal energy as being organized differently at different stages. At the oral phase, the infant begins to be aware of other people dimly for the first time and to form basic relationships with its mother. At about 2 years the libidinal outlet of satisfaction is shifted to the anus (anal phase). Toilet training involves a compromise between instinctual gratification and the rules and requirements imposed by society. Here the child must learn to give up immediate satisfaction in order to please and influence others and so gain more remote favours. Defiance–submission patterns, give-and-take attitudes, love–hate relationships, all develop during this phase.

At 4–5 years the phallic phase begins. Libidinal gratifications are now centred on the genitals. Boys tend to feel sexually coloured attractions for the mother, together with feelings of jealousy directed towards the father. This obscure set of impulses also generates guilt and fear (the father is loved and is powerful). This 'complex' experience Freud names the Oedipus complex, after the classical myth. The way the conflicts generated in the Oedipus complex are resolved is important for future personality development. If resolved successfully, the boy accepts the repression of his sexuality, since he fears he may lose his masculinity if he continues (castration fear).

Girls pass through an Electra complex. Libidinal gratifications are centred on the clitoris, and the inferiority of this organ to the male penis leads to envy of the male and a desire to be like a boy. Attachment to the father takes place, and only after she has renounced masculinity and accepted the female role does the complex resolve. There follows a period of sexual latency after these crises, which lasts until puberty (that is to say, no libidinal development takes place until then).

Up to 1910, Freud believed that each neurosis is the result of the repression of libidinal energy, and results in a regression towards an infantile mode of coping with sexual impulses. Hysteria is a form of regression to attitudes and strategies of the phallic phase, obsessionals regress to the anal level, etc.

This theory, however, was drastically modified as the result of discussions with the Psycho-Analytic Society and disagreements and conflicts among members. Alfred Adler left Freud's following in 1910. His views will be briefly discussed later. His main influence on Freud was to convince the latter that the ego, the conscious and accessible part of a personality, plays a large part in generating neurosis (that is, a disorder of the total personality). Freud also came to accept Adler's suggestion that non-sexual factors might produce an unconscious conflict. These were drastic modifications. His experiences with war neuroses during the First World War also convinced Freud that his earlier theories were not sufficiently developed to deal with all the facts. He studied the ego – the total personality – instead of concentrating on self-preservation and procreative instincts. The result was his division of a person into three separate but related systems (ego, super-ego and id); a new theory of life and death instincts; and a new theory of the importance of 'anxiety' as a key factor in behaviour. *Das Ich und das Es* (*The Ego and the Id*) and *Jenseits das Lustprinzips* (*Beyond the Pleasure Principle*) (both published in 1922) presented the results of Freud's clinical work and theorizing between 1910 and the end of the war.

Eros (life instinct) is the libidinal energy plus the impulse for self-preservation already discussed. Thanatos (death instinct) is an impulse towards aggression and destruction which is often directed against the self. Inwardly directed aggression requires defences in order that the personality is not damaged or destroyed. Freud became interested in accidents and diseases as unconsciously self-inflicted, and also in self-destructive addictions, and in sadistic and masochistic 'perversions'. Although agreeing that aggression is an important factor for investigation in neurosis and in normal personality, Freud's followers found it hard to accept all of Freud's theorizing. Even Fenichel, an orthodox and loyal Freudian in most respects, found his Thanatos theory confused and implausible.

In *The Ego and the Id*, Freud argued that the ego – that part of the mind concerned with adjusting efficiently to external realities – required a place in his theory. The ego is concerned in self-preservation as a system of organization and control against neurotic conflicts and the demands of the id. Also, a system of sentiments and values has its part to play in the development of the total personality. Sooner or later the child must have the ability to make judgements and decisions about what is right or wrong, fair or unjust. At first it accepts the external authority of parents or guardians; but later (about the age of 6) there is a positive adoption and identification ('internalization') of the parental codes. The super-ego is the system of beliefs and attitudes which develop out of this major change. Freud thought the change was closely related to the Oedipus complex in boys. The sense of guilt and the fear of punishment involved are incorporated into the super-ego to reinforce the rules and orders the child gives himself. 'Conscience' is part of this system. Thus, the personality develops as the result of these three systems of reactions which may conflict and produce tensions to be worked out in the course of development.

In the 1920s and 1930s, Freud worked on the concept of the ego. In doing so, he made a final shift in orientation. This was away from a theory explaining behaviour mechanically and causally in terms of forces or energies from the 'Unconscious', and towards a more purely descriptive psychology, simply showing what sort of functions, for example, neurotic behaviour serves. The crudely topographical conception of 'repression' as some sort of 'mechanism' actively opposing energies striving for conscious expression was modified. Instead, 'repression' was simply a stratagem of defence against unconscious tendencies or conflicts.

Freud's thinking tended to turn towards the problem of anxiety and the ways in which a person struggles to deal with it. The main source of anxiety comes from the id – the impulses which threaten to overpower the rational, moral self and which are held in check only tentatively. The ego develops strategies of defence against threats and dangers to the personality which arouse anxiety. Repression is, in Freud's later thinking, simply such a strategy. The person simply develops a trick for not discriminating his own instincts, desires and goals: a skill associated with the earlier 'dissociation', in which a person could be unaware of part of his experiences (like Janet's patient Irene, who could recall painful memories of her mother's last illness under hypnosis, but never in normal waking consciousness).

Again, 'projection' is a technique for attributing one's own (unconscious) attitudes to other people. X may regard Y as jealous and spiteful, when in fact it is X who is jealous of Y. Again, aggressive impulses towards Y may be inhibited and replaced by excessive overt reactions of an opposite kind – gentleness, consideration, etc. Freud discussed a variety of 'defence mechanisms', and other theorists have suggested many more. This aspect of his work has in many respects been the most fruitful in making us aware of aspects of our behaviour which had not hitherto been discussed systematically by psychologists. Freud was able to show that neurotic behaviour (and some normal behaviour), although superficially serving a given function or directed towards a specific goal, can in fact be seen to be directed towards a completely different goal and to serve quite different functions once it is examined in relation to the life-history, development and total context of the agent. Freud's system gave a new way of observing and describing behaviour so as to reveal these hidden features.

This rough sketch of some of the main ideas in Freud's thinking cannot do justice to the subject. However, it is sufficient to indicate the radically new approach to psychology implied. At first (from about 1910 onwards) Freud's views penetrated slowly into psychological circles. By the early 1920s his name was world-famous, and so widely were his ideas spread that few educated people were without some conception of his teaching. For many, Freud's psychology was regarded as the whole of what modern psychology contained, and for many years a psychologist was regarded as an investigator of the unconscious motives of human beings, who attempted to show that apparently harmless thoughts and emotions were disguised forms of the sexual appetite!

In fact Freud's influence has never been extensive in psychology. Physiological and experimental psychologists, who form the bulk of academic psychologists holding university appointments, have proved very little influenced by any of his theories and less by his methods of investigation (which most of them regard as unscientific and hopelessly inaccurate). Applied psychologists, in the fields of educational and child psychology, have had among them some Freudian-minded investigators, but there are as many who have followed other orientations. Industrial psychology does not appear to have benefited much from psycho-analysis. Even within the field of psychopathology in which Freud worked, the majority of psychiatrists have been suspicious of a theory which offered a purely psychological explanation of mental disorders (although Freud did not deny the possibility of organic factors producing these breakdowns). Moreover, the revolts of Adler and Jung and Rank were followed by the establishment of several independent schools of theory and therapy on psychological-individual lines (by Horney, Fromm, Sullivan, Alexander, Reik, Suttie, to list a few of the more original deviants). The orthodox Freudians have constituted an influential and active, although also a relatively isolated, school viewed in the context of the whole of psychology during and after Freud's lifetime.

Nevertheless, the impact of Freud even within academic psychology has been considerable, if only as a point of reference in defining differences of method, technique and theory. Psycho-analysis and its derivatives constituted such a unique approach to psychology that the limitations of other schools and methods are at once defined.

JUNG AND ANALYTICAL PSYCHOLOGY

Before meeting Freud, Jung had worked in Zürich as a psychiatrist. He had independently reached the conclusion that unconscious mental processes were at work in mental disorders, and his association tests were designed to elicit crucial clues to unconscious processes. At first Jung eagerly welcomed Freud's theories, and between 1907 and 1913 was a collaborator. From 1909 onwards, Jung was a freelance, treating patients in his own clinic, writing and travelling. He visited primitive tribes in North Africa, South America, the U.S.A. and India, collecting anthropological data and acquiring a life-long interest in comparative religion, folklore and mythology as additional sources of information about unconscious processes.

Jung's main period of activity was from 1914 until his death in 1962. He was not only a brilliant and successful psychiatrist but also a man of enormous erudition. His intellectual interests and thinking could not be confined within the conventional limits of psychopathology, or even psychology – to which fields he made distinguished contributions. The breadth of his interests and his distinctly personal approach have given Jung a somewhat unusual position. Within orthodox psychiatry and academic psychology, he has been regarded as an erudite eccentric with a dubious taste for mystical literature. Outside the field of psychology, however, Jung has found many admirers, particularly among humanist scholars and writers who find his insights more meaningful than the offerings of academic psychologists.

In psychological literature, even those not predisposed to accepted psycho-dynamic theories give Freud due attention, often to the neglect of Jung. In Boring's *History of Experimental Psychology* Jung receives only four lines; while a scrutiny of examination papers set to candidates for degrees in psychology in British universities shows that Freud gets a question or two, but Jung is rarely included. While it is true that Jung's writings cover philosophical and religious topics, it is also the case that he has produced an original psychological system and incorporated generalizations from a long lifetime of clinical experience and observation. It is possible that, in spite of comparative neglect from many academic psychologists, Jung's ideas will receive attention for many years to come, and may yet prove one of the most prolific sources of psychological inquiry originating in the first half of the twentieth century.

It is not possible to do justice to Jung's intricate theory. However a sketch of some of his main generalizations will show the extent to which he deviated from Freud. Jung begins by asserting that the evidence for unconscious reactions is extensive: hypnosis, dream-analysis and free association produce plenty of data. Like Freud, Jung thought in terms of energy being organized at different levels and requiring discharge in activity ('libido' being a general term for such nervous energy). However Jung did not regard unconscious processes as being invariably infantile, animal or pathological. Some unconscious processes do have the characteristics of Freud's 'id' system, but other energies and strivings which are unconscious are the source of positive and creative activity, and are important for the growth and development of the mature and well-adjusted personality. The 'ego', the system of conscious responses, collects information and registers decisions. It is the unconscious factors which are of crucial importance in the organization, control and development of the personality.

Unconscious processes are regarded by Jung as belonging to two systems:

(1) The 'personal' unconscious is formed as the result of repressed infantile impulses and desires, forgotten traumatic experiences and the like. It is highly idiosyncratic to each individual and depends on his unique personal history. Its contents can be aroused into consciousness – sometimes in dreams and fantasies, sometimes only as the result of analytic therapy.

Usually, unconscious material emerges into consciousness in the form of a 'complex'. Jung's concept of a 'complex' has some affinities with Shand's notion of a 'sentiment': a concept or idea with associated attitudes and emotions. Such 'complexes' have the capacity to initiate and organize behaviour. For Shand, a 'sentiment' is usually conscious, whereas a 'complex' is for Jung usually unconscious. The definition of a person's basic set of 'complexes', therefore, informs the analyst about his probable goals and strivings.

(2) The collective unconscious is a purely Jungian conception. Evolution has predetermined the human brain to react in terms of basic principles derived from the experience of many generations. The tendencies to react and to apprehend or experience life in a manner originating from the remote past of the human race Jung calls 'archetypal' tendencies: 'archetypes' are 'congenital conditions of intuition'. Archetypes are manifested in imagery and symbols common in the dream life of human beings of widely different cultural groups and of different periods of history. These emerge from the deepest levels of the unconscious mind, and are never directly accessible. Archetypes bear traces of their primitive origins: the basic experiences of mankind, involving birth and death, mating, danger and escape, food, drink, the cycle of the seasons, night and day. Elementary hopes and fears, triumphs and disasters, seem to have left residues out of which archetypes have developed. These emerge in crises involving danger, awe-inspiring experiences, conflicts. Dream symbols often refer to archetypes and have affinities with the data of folklore and mythology of all cultures and races. Dreams, mythology, folk-tales show how human beings react to critical experiences in terms of common archetypal responses. These are clues to the working of the collective unconscious in shaping basic patterns of adaptation. Hence not merely the data of individual analyses and dream interpretation but the examination of folklore, myths and religious symbolism give the psychologist insight into the working of unconscious processes.

Jung's analysis of the conscious aspects of personality

is based on two main assumptions. Jung believed that people tend to react to a wide range of different experiences in terms of two basic attitudes. The 'extraverted' attitude is characterized by an out-going orientation, in which the individual is interested in and governed by environmental factors; such people are sociable, practical, involved in inter-personal relationships and the manipulation of people and things. The 'introverted' attitude is one of withdrawal from the environment. Such introverted individuals are unsociable, shy, preferring reflection and inner aesthetic experiences to action. There are mixed and neutral types; but Jung believed that most people tend towards one or other of the two extreme poles. Tests designed to measure individual differences in respect of specific 'traits' are regarded as showing which clusters of specific traits tend towards an extra- or intro-verted personality-type.

Jung also regarded behaviour as being classifiable under the headings of different basic 'functions': the sensory-perceptual; thinking; feeling (emotion-sentiments); intuition. Individuals tend to specialize in having one function developed more than the others, so giving a further bias to the total personality. Some individuals may succeed in obtaining a degree of balance between operations of the various basic functions, but most people are lop-sided.

Adaptation to the environment is in terms of personality bias (extraversion, introversion and dominant function). In meeting the demands of education and society, many traits and dispositions are repressed and remain active in the personal unconscious. The outward compromise which the individual presents to society Jung calls the 'persona' (after the mask worn in Greek drama). The roles which the individual acts out in the family circle, at work, in social activities, in the expression of conventional beliefs, etc., constitute the 'persona', and this is a long way from being the whole personality.

The repressed dispositions form an aspect of the total

personality which Jung nicknames the 'shadow'. Often the tendencies of the shadow are the opposite of those of the 'persona'. The well-known defence strategy of 'projection' (in which a person dislikes and condemns attitudes or other characteristics in another which are in fact part of his own shadow or repressed self) illustrates this basic opposition. However, Jung regards the shadow as a necessary counter-balance to the artificial and imposed dispositions of the persona. It is possible to come to terms with the inevitably existent repressed material in our make-up and in fact we must do so. In neurosis and psychosis the shadow-aspects have not been sublimated and integrated with the outer mask. Within the 'shadow', each sex, according to Jung, has some of the basic traits of its opposite. Males have a set of female traits (the anima) and females a masculine set (the animus). These contrary sex characteristics are related to archetypes which in men, give rise to innate capacities for producing images and emotions related to women, while women tend to have archetypal symbols of the ideal male. Everybody tends to project archetypal images on to individuals of the opposite sex – hence 'complexes' related to the opposite sex make for difficulties in emotional relationships. Human beings are never rational, objective and common-sensical about members of the opposite sex, and this is why sex-life, courtship, marriage and child-rearing are so dogged by problems.

The 'self' Jung conceives as a centre or organization within the personality which seeks to develop towards a goal of maturity and integration: the harmonious balance of conscious and unconscious dispositions. The 'self' is rarely complete or balanced, and its basic instability is revealed in dream symbols (the 'child' or the 'jewel' being a symbol of the unified harmonious 'self' image).

Jung's therapeutic techniques, although similar to those of Freud ('free association', 'dream interpretation', etc.), have a different aim. Jung aimed at the growth and development of the personality through 'individuation' or 'integration'. Sometimes circumstances might prescribe limited aims – for example, dealing with sexual pathology or neurotic strivings for power. However, Jung regarded psychotherapy as attempting something more than the sterilizing of psychic conflicts. Psychotherapy should achieve a more positive and capable personality in which potentialities hitherto unexploited could be made explicit, and all the positive factors integrated and placed under the control of the knowing self. Treating neurosis was not a negative affair – merely getting rid of awkward emotions and tendencies. It was an indication of one-sided development requiring correction, and even pointing to new possibilities for healthy growth. Sexual greed, aggression, anxiety, guilt, selfishness, were not the only factors to be considered in neurosis. Other types of need could engender frustration and disharmony – including complex ones which can only find an outlet in 'religious' life. Whereas Freud conceived neurosis and its treatment as a matter of restricting and re-channelling powerful, primitive 'instincts' and so mitigating troublesome symptoms (a somewhat pessimistic view of human nature since the sources of neurosis are in-built and indestructible), Jung has an optimistic outlook which regards man as capable of changing positively into something 'better' than he was before therapy. Another basic difference was that Freud believed the roots of neurosis to lie in infancy and childhood, while Jung believed that factors in the present adult situation might be as crucial. Obviously such more immediate factors could be more drastically dealt with than the residues of remote infantile trauma.

These are only the outlines of Jung's theory as expressed in such early writings as *Collected Papers on Analytical Psychology* (1917) and *Psychologische Typen* (*Psychological Types*, 1921). Jung went on elaborating his theory, and such works as *Einführung in das Wesen der Mythologie* (*Introduction to the Science of Mythology*, 1949) and *Psychologie und Alchemie* (*Psychology and Alchemy*, 1944) opened up new vistas for the development of analytical psychology. However, Jung's influence was marked from the end of the First World War onwards. For example, those interested in psychological tests, without subscribing to the whole of Jung's theory, were prepared to try to analyse – in terms of test results – the precise differences involved on an extraversion–introversion scale. Many Jungian concepts achieved a wide currency in psychological as well as in general literature. Jung was the first to offer an alternative to those who could not accept the basic assumptions of Freud's teaching, but who were attracted by its attempt to explore the unconscious aspects of human personality. Perhaps he attracted interest because of his distinctly more optimistic and forward-looking attitude. Freud's view of human nature seems pessimistic and cautious. All that we can hope to do is to sublimate powerful instincts and remedy some of the damage done by the traumatic experiences of infancy and childhood. Jung believed that unconscious processes can be the basis of 'positive' expansion and achievement for the personality. The unconscious is the source of creativity and of tendencies which can lead to greater integration than that achieved at ego level.

ADLER AND SOCIAL PSYCHO-ANALYTIC THEORIES

Freud and Jung had both regarded neurotic conflict as arising from basic built-in factors in human nature. Variations in the energy-system responsible for assisting the human organism to adjust to environmental requirements led to some individuals becoming less well adapted than others. However, some who began work within the original psycho-analytic schools became dissatisfied with Freudian 'instincts' and Jungian 'archetypes' as main explanatory concepts. It was felt that the environment and the many social influences peculiar to human life must have some bearing on the development of personality, normal and abnormal.

The first to break away and insist on a social orientation was Alfred Adler. Adler was born in 1870 in Vienna and died in Aberdeen while on a lecture tour in 1937. He graduated in medicine and specialized in psychiatry. He was one of the charter members of Freud's Vienna Psycho-Analytic Society and was its president for a year. In 1911 he broke with Freud and formed his own group in Vienna. After serving in the Austrian army during the war, he became interested in the child-guidance movement, founding clinics and a special school in Vienna in the 1920s. In 1935 he emigrated to the U.S.A., becoming Professor of Psychiatry at Long Island College of Medicine. He founded a Society for Individual Psychology in America which has continued his work. Adler's books proved extremely popular, *The Practice and Theory of Individual Psychology* (1927) and *Social Interest* (1933) being his two major works.

Adler believed that human beings were more influenced by ambitions, hopes and the striving towards future goals than by built-in drives or the residues of past experiences. Healthy people have realistic and social goals; neurotics unreal and egocentric goals. Adler thought that aggressive reactions were more characteristic than instinctive (sexual) ones: a striving for conquest, mastery and security was basic to much human activity. At the centre of this was a need to master oneself, to achieve self-realization through the perfecting and exercising of abilities and skills. This goal is influenced by the fact that during infancy and childhood human beings are weak and inferior to adults. A sense of inferiority (incompleteness) leads to efforts to remedy or compensate. In healthy individuals this is an aid to normal development and growing-up. In neurotics an 'inferiority complex' develops, which takes the form of exaggerated anxiety and unrealistic beliefs about personal deficiencies together with wild strivings to 'overcompensate' for these real or imagined weaknesses. In healthy people, the realization that there are limits to what the individual can achieve by himself leads to compensation in the form of 'social interest'. The human being socially trained from birth learns that the individual can only mature to the fullest extent through merging self-interest in cooperation with others, enjoying inter-personal relations, affection and trust, and work for the benefit of all. Striving and aggression, through becoming socialized, are sublimated and turned to useful ends, civilized life in society. Social ideals replace egocentric needs. The neurotic fails to make this adjustment and remains an outsider.

Adler believed that each personality is unique. (Apart from William James, few psychologists seem to have believed this, most of them preferring to think of men as subject to 'laws' of behaviour.) In early childhood, each person develops a style of life: all traits, habits, motives, strivings, come to have characteristic and idiosyncratic features. This style is determined by the peculiar set of 'inferiority feelings' and social circumstances to which the individual was subjected in infancy and childhood. However, there are many ways of striving to similar goals, and the priorities among one's basic goals may be shifted. Hence each man may create his own personality by modifying his style and attaining some self-realization through the 'creative self'.

In studying neurosis and the origin of the style of life, Adler attached importance to (1) relationship of parents or guardians to the child, (2) order of birth among the siblings – 'only' children, eldest children, youngest, etc., each having special problems and 'inferiorities' partially arising from their 'position' in the family, (3) types of 'inferiority' experience in childhood – he believed that the earliest memories of childhood produced by individuals exhibit their basic conflicts about their own childhood inferiority-feelings.

Adler played down the 'unconscious'. He did not believe in 'repression' or the inaccessibility of basic goals.

Patients might need help and training in discriminating and defining their inner life, but this was not due to Freudian unconscious processes or 'censors' at work. Adler's views thus emphasized social environment and inter-personal relationships in personality development. Although scorned as 'superficial' by orthodox Freudians and Jungians, Adler did point to the need to consider the social context in normal and pathological personality, and to the fact that the present environment and inter-personal network may affect neurotics as much as the remote past.

Erich Fromm (born in Frankfurt, 1900) was another analyst who emphasized man's social character. He graduated in psychology and sociology at Heidelberg and Frankfurt, then trained as a psycho-analyst in Munich. He went to the U.S.A. in 1933, practised as an analyst in New York and lectured at the Chicago Psycho-Analytical Institute. His book *Escape from Freedom* (1941), published as *The Fear of Freedom* in England, produced a considerable impact. Fromm argued that the freedom and responsibilities imposed upon the individual in the modern democratic state are sources of stress which lead to neurosis. He argued that revolutionary periods (the transition from feudalism to capitalism, the industrial revolution, the Nazi revolution) produce neuroses and personality-types peculiar to themselves. Social organization and its stresses affect personality development intimately.

Perhaps Karen Horney (born Hamburg 1885, died New York 1952) may be taken as typical of many deviants within the psycho-analytic movement. She regarded herself as a neo-Freudian – a critic and corrector of errors, who nevertheless simply developed Freud's insights. Graduating in medicine at Berlin, Horney was analysed by Karl Abraham, Freud's lieutenant in the 1920s. She practised at the Berlin Psycho-Analytic Clinic in 1918–32 and went to America in 1932. After two years at the Chicago Psycho-Analytic Institute, she settled in New

York, practising as an analyst and founding the American Institute of Psycho-Analysis in New York.

Horney believed that anxiety is a basic emotion in human beings. In childhood we are all helpless and isolated in an environment which is too complex to cope with. Many factors increase this basic anxiety and determine our strategies for trying to deal with it. In particular, relationships with parents and family influence this process: dominating parents, indifferent parents, overprotective parents, unjust parents, quarrelsome parents – each presents the child with stresses and problems which aggravate the basic anxiety-situation.

Children react in different ways. Some attack and become over-aggressive; others are over-submissive; others withdraw within themselves from contact with other people; others make excessive demands for love and attention. If any of these strategies is strongly reinforced, the basis for a neurotic personality is established. Horney lists ten basic 'strategies' for reducing anxiety which can develop, and round which a personality 'type' begins to form. All such strategies are ineffective. Based on unrealistic inter-personal relationships, on unreal attitudes, they tend to produce problems, difficulties, conflicts, which only serve to increase anxiety and so lead to further incompetent attempts to adjust. There is thus a 'vicious circle' effect in neurotic strategies. However, these orientations are exaggerated forms of needs and inclinations which most people have. It is the environmental situation which has led to the neurotic exaggeration and produced conflicts. Not only childhood influences but present social factors enter into the neurotic situation. As Horney put it: 'The person who is likely to become neurotic is one who has experienced the culturally-determined difficulties in accentuated form, mostly through the medium of childhood experience.'

Horney accepts unconscious motives through repression and other defence strategies, and the irrational, emotive basis of many neurotic goals. However, she also accepts many of Adler's views on the social origins of anxiety and conflict in neurotic – and normal – behaviour.

These views were published in *The Neurotic Personality of Our Time* (1937) and *New Ways in Psycho-Analysis* (1939), although Horney had, like Fromm, published papers and taught psychotherapists before the publication, in English, of her books. They confirmed the trend within the psychotherapeutic movement to be critical of Freud, to modify, revise and develop some of his ideas along new lines, while also deviating into new conceptions.

Nevertheless, Freud and Jung remained the dominant figures within this tradition throughout the period from the end of the first war to the end of the second. Further deviations occurred. Harry Stack Sullivan's 'interpersonal theory of psychiatry', Carl Rogers' theory, both of which emerged towards the end of the Second World War and were influential in the 1950s, and Ian Suttie's *The Origins of Love and Hate* (1938), a work critical of Freudian assumptions, were landmarks in the tendency for psychoanalysts to strike out on independent lines.

THE INFLUENCE OF PSYCHO-ANALYSIS

In the years between the two wars, the theories of Freud, Jung, Adler and their successors were influential and popular. In fact, to the layman, the term 'psychology' was practically synonymous with 'psycho-analysis', and psychologists were all regarded as disciples of the mysterious Germans. Such views were erroneous and misleading. This group of theories was only one of several schools or systems of psychology in a period of speculative theory – construction on a wider scale than had hitherto been attempted in psychology.

The influence of the movement, however, was noticeable, even on those who were critical or hostile. The psycho-analytic movement emphasized the importance of studying infants and children. Even without accepting any of the special theories of the rival schools, it was obvious that more important things tend to occur during the 'formative' years than most psychologists had realized; moreover, our understanding of children was obviously extremely limited and required much research and re-thinking in child-psychology before serious limitations and gaps within the science could be dealt with. In addition, while physiological and experimental psychologists on the one hand and psychometric (or 'testing') psychologists on the other dealt minutely with abstracted, analysed aspects of human behaviour, the Freudians and Jungians were attempting to deal with the personality as a whole, and approached the person as a dynamic and developing system. However necessary abstraction and analysis might be in the interests of an exact experimental science, it was evident that some idiographic and 'wholist' approach to human beings was required.

In the 1930s, Kurt Lewin (1890–1947), a member of the Gestalt school specializing in child psychology, produced a dynamic theory of personality exploiting and extending Gestalt concepts (*A Dynamic Theory of Personality*, 1935); in 1937 G. W. Allport (b. 1897), the distinguished Harvard psychologist, published his individual and dynamic system in *Personality: A Psychological Interpretation* (see pp. 382 ff.). This was the beginning of a series of theories of personality – systematic psychologies constructed round empirical data from experiments, test results and research, clinical material, case-histories, etc. Henry A. Murray's *Explorations in Personality* (1938), Kurt Goldstein's *The Organism* (1939) and *Human Nature in the Light of Psychopathology* (1940), N. E. Miller and J. Dollard's *Social Learning and Imitation* (1941) and *Personality and Psychotherapy* (1950), and Gardner Murphy's *Personality* (1947) were all major works which attracted·adherents and led to disputes concerning the basis of psychological research into human personality. Whatever these diverse theories owed to the psycho-analytic movement, they all aimed at providing alternative systematic frameworks for studying the dynamics of personality.

The psycho-analysts had developed clinical methods of investigation in getting information. The clinical interview, the clinical case-history, the clinical approach to behaviour as 'symptoms' requiring diagnosis, aetiological description prognosis – this was the model for studying human behaviour. The free-association technique during the analytic session of treatment, the recall and interpretation of dreams, and the dynamic interchange between patient and analyst introduced a mixture of old and new. There was something of the old method of armchair introspection in dream-recall, but free-association had novel features: the presence and stimulus of the analyst, the *active* production of verbal responses and the analyst's interpretation of the individual patients' material during and after each session. Emotions, sentiments, attitudes and desires were being expressed in an unstructured and dynamic situation. The methods and techniques involved were open to criticism – where were the controls, what were the safeguards against subjectivity and against bias and error in 'observation' and 'interpretation' on the part of the analyst? However, many psychologists recognized that in addition to laboratory experiments, or standardized tests, or questionnaires, clinical methods originating in medical or psychiatric practice might be capable of being modified and adapted for use in psychological research. The individual personality – in addition to being the subject of laboratory experiments or tests, or case-history reports – might be approached in a dynamic, free-flowing, unstructured situation, in which spontaneous activity might reveal aspects of personality which more formal and restricted situations would not reveal.

Finally, the psycho-analysts put forward hypotheses which challenged acceptance, denial or modification in the light of any objective and empirical research of which psychologists were capable. The stimulation of their ideas in the fields of social psychology, personality theory and by psychometrics was considerable, and even experimental psychologists occasionally tested a hypothesis derived from psycho-analytic sources.

The psycho-analytic movement presented theories and a view concerning the nature of psychology which corrected the bias of other schools – the Behaviourists in particular. In spite of novelties and some 'shocking' views, it also represented the continuation into the twentieth century of older traditions. The insistence on 'individual' and 'dynamic' psychology and clinical methods are present in William James, in Janet and in Morton Prince. Herbart and Schopenhauer had both insisted on the unity of the person, and the latter had produced a theory which anticipated Freud's views on the unconscious character of basic wishes and motives. Indeed, recent studies have shown the extent to which Freud's ideas were anticipated by earlier thinkers. Nevertheless, the vigour and boldness of psycho-analysis in attempting to apply its theories to the treatment of neurosis, and to offer an account of aspects of behaviour hitherto left unexplained, gave it a central place in the psychology of the first half of the twentieth century.

CHAPTER FIFTEEN

Dynamic Psychological Theory

R. S. WOODWORTH

R. S. WOODWORTH (1869–1962), the author of one of the leading textbooks on experimental psychology (*Experimental Psychology*, 1938, revised with H. Schlosberg 1954), was a prominent figure in the inter-war years. As head of Columbia University psychology department he exercised influence in many fields. In 1918 he put forward a systematic psychology in his *Dynamic Psychology* (republished in 1957). This was a modest but distinctive theory which offered a middle way between Behaviourist and other dominant views.

Woodworth insisted that there was nothing new in his system – he was making explicit what good psychologists had always done even in pre-scientific times. Psychology had always dealt both with experience and behaviour; it had always employed both an analytical and a molar approach to its data, and both development and structure had been important. The basic aim had always been to explain the particular event by showing it to be an instance of a general law for which there is empirical evidence; it had always been held that theories can be postulated to relate laws to each other.

Woodworth held that a knowledge of stimulus–response relationships is the base from which psychological studies advance. He began with responses, and was interested in a wide variety of antecedent conditions, rather than in the control of the response by specific stimulus variables. The stimulus, he believed, is only one factor among several: the structure of the organism, its store and organization of physical energy, progressive activities at the time of the stimulus, are a few of the other factors to be considered. Stimulus–Organism–Response is a better formula than S–R. He regarded the reflex as too simple a mechanism to serve as a model for behaviour. Reflexes are evoked by different stimuli, are capable of being mediated through a variety of different neural mechanisms and are subject to cortical control. In any case, complex behaviour may not be built up of small units compounded together. Hence radical Behaviourism is naïve and misleading.

Moreover, a purely reductive psychology in neurophysiological terms cannot describe all features of behaviour. Just as geologists discuss facts at a molar level which are not accessible to physicists, so psychologists can discover truths not available to physiologists. The facts of consciousness are important in psychology. Which of two patches of colour is brighter, or which of two objects in space appears nearer to the observer, are simple facts of introspection. Earlier psychologists such as Wundt and Titchener made the mistake of trying to analyse consciousness into mental elements; Fechner's and Ebbinghaus's work in trying to measure individual differences in sensory discrimination was more useful. Woodworth's principle, in dealing with both conscious and motor activity, was firstly to relate performance to its conditions and then to evaluate performances in terms of success in goal-directed action.

In what sense was Woodworth concerned with the dynamics of behaviour? He made a distinction between 'mechanisms' and 'drives'. Mechanisms help to explain how an action is performed. Drives help to explain why an action is performed. In the case of a pitcher in a baseball game, 'the problem of mechanism is how he aims, gauges distance and the amount of curve and coordination in his movements to produce a given result. The problem of drive includes such questions as why he is engaged in this exercise at all, why he pitches better on one day than another, why he rouses himself more against one batter than another. ...' Motivational complexes must be included in the S–O–R formula. However, the distinction between mechanisms and drives is not absolute. A drive may be regarded as a mechanism or organization of the nervous system facilitating some actions and inhibiting others (as in a swimmer 'set' at the start of a race to dive and swim a particular stroke once the whistle sounds). Mechanisms can serve as a basis for drives. Once activated, a specific skill tends to run on its own. A child who has learned to read will want books, buy them, join a library, and express the skill in actions. Goal-directed strivings, as well as habits, skills and perceptual structurings, must be explained.

Woodworth did not think of 'drives' as a special set of activities or a special source of energy. Like mechanisms, they are simply descriptive of basic functions in behaviour. He took issue with McDougall over this. McDougall had insisted that instincts supply the 'drive' or 'energy' for all goal-directed behaviour – a principle he shared with Freud. Woodworth on the contrary thought that, although innate tendencies might reinforce motivated behaviour (aggressive, curious, anxious reactions), such orectic factors were not necessary conditions for goal-directed, purposeful activity.

Thus Woodworth's *Dynamic Psychology*, with 'learning' as its central topic, was a systematic work without dramatic theories or hypotheses. Empirical and common-sensical, it put forward the view that there is a scientific psychology independent of any 'school': a corpus of knowledge which is the product of observation, experiment, psychometric research, reflection and generalization. This body of knowledge has grown slowly and goes back beyond the origins of scientific methods; it is always being corrected and amplified by patient, methodical research and criticism. Woodworth presented some of this knowledge in his large textbook in 1938 (it has over 800 pages), which still remains a handbook for students.

This neutral, cautious and plausible point of view

offered an alternative to psychologists who found the various 'schools' of the twenties and thirties unacceptable in detail. It helped to modify extreme opinions and to keep many psychologists critical, cautious and open-minded in relation to systematic theories about the scope and methods of psychology.

MCDOUGALL'S HORMIC PSYCHOLOGY

We have already met McDougall as a force in British psychology in the years before the First World War (pp. 167 ff.). After the war he emigrated to the U.S.A., teaching first at Harvard and later settling at Duke University, where his interest in psychical research led to the founding of one of the largest centres of scientific investigation into para-normal psychological phenomena. His basic theory had already been stated in *Social Psychology* (1908). His *Outline of Psychology* (1923), *The Group Mind, The Energies of Man* (1933) and *The Frontiers of Psychology* (1934) elaborated his systematic psychology and kept his views in the public eye.

McDougall's theory begins with the postulation of a number of inherited instincts. These are modified on both the sensory and the motor side by learning. They also become combined through the operations of intelligence into complexes called 'sentiments' – emotionally-toned attitudes and beliefs (love of parents, patriotism, self-respect, for example). Thus one's attitudes and beliefs to-wards oneself are energized by instincts of self-assertion, self-control, etc. It is a group of complex psychological factors which are the basic motives for activity, although the energy behind these complexes is organized through primary instinctual drives. Behaviour is controlled by loves and hates, interests, and enthusiasms, and the emotional-impulsive aspect is the most important one for psychologists to study. Purposeful goal-striving is the essential characteristic of behaviour. The analysis of the various factors involved in the selection of goals and the means adopted to reach them is the main job of the psychologist.

McDougall criticized the Behaviourists for oversimplifying the picture and attempting to reduce behaviour to the learning of stimulus–response connexions reinforced by the reduction of organic needs, and the operation of glandular controls. Motives for acting in humans at least are much more complex and much more fundamental than the Behaviouristic models. 'Purpose', the active striving towards often distant goals, is the main characteristic of behaviour. In propounding this thesis, McDougall attacked 'mechanistic' explanations of behaviour, and defended a teleological view of psychological explanation. Behaviour can only be understood in terms of the ends towards which it is directed. This raised philosophical arguments about the nature of explanation in science which obscured the essential issue, that of giving adequate descriptions of goal-directed activity, a problem which psychologists have always found difficult.

McDougall's theory of instincts was unquestionably open to criticism. Yet his emphasis on the need for a dynamic psychology to account for the complex motivation of behaviour, and to take account of orectic factors, was influential in making psychologists aware of the weak spot in the new Behaviouristic theories. Even if he remained a peripheral figure in America, his books were widely used in Britain and Europe, and he remained a best-selling psychological author with the general educated public.

The systematic writings of Woodworth and McDougall, together with those of the psycho-analytic schools, offered a different orientation from the two leading systems of Behaviourism and Gestalt psychology in the 1920s and early 1930s. They bridged the gap between the earlier systematic psychology and the emergence of personality theories in the late 1930s and 1940s, contributing to the inter-war period of grand-scale system-building and theory-construction.

It was within this new tradition of psychology as a subject divided into rival schools of thought that the empirical researches of the period were undertaken. It became difficult for psychologists to interpret the results of thousands of researches – experiments, psychometric investigations, anthropological field studies, clinical research, investigations in industry, education, child study, etc. – without relying on hypotheses or concepts derived from one or other of the comprehensive systems available. Yet a corpus of knowledge, the result of applying sound empirical techniques, grew rapidly during this period. What were the main types of investigation undertaken by psychologists in the years following the First World War? Psychology flourished greatly in these years: investigating new problems, devising new techniques for studying familiar problems, interacting with other disciplines, and developing entirely new branches of inquiry hardly recognized by the psychologists of the pre-1914 era.

To these empirical investigations we now turn, keeping in mind the theories which stimulated the ideas of those in laboratories and clinics and applied fields of research.

CHAPTER SIXTEEN

Physiological Psychology 1918–40

IN the pre-1914 period, physiological psychology had meant psychology involving the use of methods characteristic of physiological experiments. However, the neurological mechanisms underlying behaviour had always interested psychologists, so that invasions of the territory of physiology, especially in studying sensory processes, were not uncommon.

A dominant influence in the 1920s was Charles Sherrington, whose earlier activities we have already mentioned (pp. 172 ff.). Psychologists were inclined to interpret Sherrington's work on the functional interdependence of reflex systems as suggesting that complex behaviour should be reduced to simple structures, and that the theory of naïve Behaviourism (that the 'conditioned reflex' was the key to 'habit') was confirmed by his and Pavlov's work. Sherrington's writings hardly sanctioned the exploitation by Watson of the conditioning of reflexes as the model for all adaptation.

During the 1920s, Sherrington concentrated on excitation and inhibition at the synapse. Inhibition appeared to be an active process, not merely the interference or blockage of on-going impulses, or the total cessation of impulses. He studied the specific motor units, each of which can control hundreds of muscle fibres, and the way in which such 'motoneurons' react to a single stimulus. His research is summarized in *The Brain and Its Mechanisms* (1933). This book emphasized the importance of integrated motor control, and echoed Hughling Jackson's overall view of the nervous system as a sensory-motor integration organized at different levels. 'The brain seems a thoroughfare for nerve action passing on its way to the motor. It has been remarked that life's aim is an act, not a thought. Today the dictum must be modified to admit that, often, to refrain from action is no less an act than to commit one, because inhibition is – coequally with excitation – a nervous activity.'

Sherrington became the leading authority on the nervous system during this period, and his work was accepted as the basis for most textbooks of physiological psychology.

Adrian (p. 171) continued to work on the conduction of the nervous impulse and published his results in *The Basis of Sensation* in 1928. Both Adrian's writings and those of J. T. MacCurdy, of Cambridge, emphasized the importance of patterns of excitation and patterns of physico-chemical reactions in the central nervous system as a basis for behaviour. The actual specific reactions of sensory nerves, reflexes and specific neural circuits may not seem to be related to behaviour when they are isolated as units for neurophysiological description. However, these units are organized into complicated overall patterns of nervous activity which probably provide the basis for behaviour patterns. This idea, although rather vague, was a conception which guided much subsequent thinking in physiological psychology. Thus, the known reactions of a drug on specific cells and centres in the brain may not be directly related to the effect of the drug on behaviour: the parts affected by the drug may be involved in a much wider pattern of activity which is related to behaviour.

In the 1920s this view of the nervous system as a structure built up out of simple elements was challenged. The first major criticism came from S. I. Franz, a physiologist who had also graduated in psychology from Columbia University in 1899. Franz was interested in discovering what parts of the brain, and how much of it, functions during learning. He devised the method of comparing the ability of animals to learn before and after the destruction of specific parts of the brain by surgical operation, and also of comparing performances of animals so treated with those of normal animals – a refinement of the Flourens techniques of a century earlier.

Franz investigated the function of the frontal lobes in relation to the learning of 'escape habits' of cats and monkeys, using a version of the familiar Thorndike puzzle box (p. 159). He trained animals to escape for a food reward by pulling a loop and thus opening a door. After learning was complete, the frontal lobes were disconnected from the rest of the brain by operating. The animals were re-tested after recovery from the operation. They were found to have lost their ability to escape, although old habits were retained. Franz next trained his control-group animals over a long period in escape problems until their skill appeared thoroughly overlearned. After destruction of their frontal lobes, these animals were found capable of solving escape problems. Thus only recent learning depended on the frontal lobes.

In another experiment animals were given the operation before being trained to escape, and these were found to be as capable of new learning as normal subjects. Franz concluded that one part of the brain must be able to take over the work of another part, either vicariously or by substitution. There did not appear to be a specialized part of the brain serving as a centre for learning and retention. Franz believed that a patient he had known at St Elizabeth Hospital, New York, confirmed the findings of his experiments with animals. This patient had suffered severe damage to the temporal lobes, with the result that his right side was paralysed and his language habits disorganized. He could speak only in jumbled sentences, he misnamed objects and used non-existent words. Franz trained this man to name objects correctly, learn short poems and recite scriptural passages. Over three months of training, his score improved from 44 per cent to 96 per cent correct responses on each test. In spite of damage and impairment, he was able to re-learn skills he had lost.

K. S. Lashley (1890–1958) graduated in zoology and physiology at West Virginia and Johns Hopkins. He studied experimental psychology, and finally became a pupil of Franz while working at St Elizabeth Hospital. Franz set Lashley off on problems of exploring brain function in relation to behaviour. Lashley's subsequent work at Minnesota, Chicago and Harvard was a major influence in physiological psychology. His *Brain Mechanisms and Intelligence* (1929) is a classic – although most of his work was reported in journals.

Initially, Lashley studied the capacity of rats to learn discriminations between stimuli of different brightness. By removing portions of the rat's occipital lobes he demonstrated: (a) that the occipital lobes are normally active in brightness discrimination; (b) that the removal of the lobes shows that no part of them is necessary for discrimination; (c) that *any* part of the cortex can take over the function of the destroyed lobes.

Next, Lashley studied the effects of brain injury on various motor habits. Again the extirpation of specific motor centres did not result in loss of previous learning or the capacity to acquire new habits (e.g. negotiating mazes). Lashley found that it was the amount of cortex rather than the specific part which was correlated with loss of learning.

He concluded from these experiments that learning and retention do not depend on precise pathways, specific localized brain structures, or the formation of specific synapse connexions. The activity of the brain as a dynamic and interrelated whole seemed to be essential for the higher functions. He coined the term 'equipotentiality' to indicate this capacity of the brain, as a whole, to take over functions often handled by a specific part, if that part is destroyed or damaged. In attempting to trace behaviour functions to specific regions of the brain, physiologists had lost sight of the overall plan of the organism. Of course, Lashley did not deny the fact of localization of function. The parietal lobes are the seat of sensations in specific parts of the body; motor areas are located in the frontal lobes and injuries there lead to loss of voluntary movement; areas relating to vision, hearing, taste and smell are well established, and articulate speech is connected with structures in the parietal and temporal lobes. However, Lashley argued that, in spite of such localization, two generalizations hold: (1) Intelligent and learned behaviour has no neural centre or structure; (2) The destruction of some neural centres which specialize in controlling a specific function does not necessarily mean the loss of that function: other parts of the brain can take over the work. Localization within a complex organization working as a unity was the new axiom.

Lashley had his critics, but other evidence seemed to support his view. In 1923 Sir Henry Head, a British physiologist, published *Aphasia and Kindred Disorders of Speech*. War casualties with injuries to the brain had stimulated Head's researches. He produced clinical data in his book which refuted Broca's extremely narrow theory of localization of speech in a highly specific region. It was in this book that Head put forward his concept of 'vigilance' – a high-level organization in which the total organism is ready to respond to any stimulus, internal or external. Overall states of the nervous system, as well as specific structures, control behaviour. Work on soldiers with brain injuries had also been conducted by Gelb in Germany and by Goldstein in the U.S.A. This had shown that if part of the visual area was destroyed or damaged, the whole visual field could still be retained. The region serving the fovea, for example, could be totally destroyed, yet another part of the brain obviously took over the work of controlling focusing and figure-ground differentiation. This work on human subjects seemed to confirm the view of Franz and Lashley.

This new orientation received a systematic exposition in G. E. Coghill's book *Anatomy and the Problem of Behaviour* (1929). Coghill argued that discrete responses always emerge out of larger, more complex patterns of behaviour by a process of 'individuation'. It is the larger 'total' behaviour-patterns which are primary, and these are not the result of the integration either of discrete responses (such as reflexes) or of partial patterns. This theory provoked discussion and stimulated embryonic and foetal studies to test its implications. Coghill's evidence was largely behavioural, although he produced anatomical correlations for simple organisms. 'Individuation versus Integration' has disappeared as an issue – both processes are now known to occur. However, Coghill's work confirmed the trend against reducing the complex to the simple in physiology, and encouraged the Gestalt theorists against the Behaviourists.

THE PHYSICAL BASIS FOR EMOTION

W. B. Cannon (1871–1945), of the Harvard Medical School, had published *Bodily Changes in Pain, Hunger, Fear and Rage* in 1915 – an enlarged edition appearing in 1929. This work investigated the hitherto neglected autonomic nervous system – the ganglia and fibres which control 'vegetative' processes, such as the action of the heart, lungs, stomach and internal glands. Its two branches, the sympathetic and parasympathetic, had been known. Cannon offered evidence to suggest that the sympathetic is active in such emotional reactions as fear and rage, while during pleasant emotions of joy and tranquillity it is the parasympathetic system which is dominant. He removed the entire sympathetic system from cats, thus cutting off internal stimulation to the viscera. After this operation, the animals still displayed behaviour characteristic of fear and rage when appropriately stimulated. Thus the sensations or feelings present in emotion are not essential or primary factors. Adrenalin was discovered to be secreted into the bloodstream in fear and rage. Cannon injected adrenalin into human subjects. The effect was a feeling of tension and excitement but without either the overt responses or the feeling-tones characteristic of being angry or afraid. He pointed out that physical changes in fear and rage are very alike; yet the total behaviour and feelings involved are quite different. There must be an interaction between cognitive responses and the autonomic system in emotion. He put forward the theory that emotions are the result of the interaction of the cerebral cortex and the diencephalon (inter-brain).

One of his associates, P. Bard, located the hypothalamus as a crucial region. He postulated that it sends impulses to the cortex and to the motor system in an 'emotional' reaction. The arousal to activity comes from the autonomic system, but the 'meaning' of the situation determines whether fear or rage – or some other total response of the organism – is appropriate. The theory was both over-simplified and not sufficiently specific; yet it opened up a new approach to the study of emotion and, especially, of the acute emotional disturbances encountered in psychopathology.

In 1937, J. W. Papez, in a celebrated paper, proposed a neurological mechanism for emotion. The hypothalamus, the anterior thalamic nuclei, the gyrus cinguli and the hippocampus seemed to constitute the essential mechanism which controls emotion. The central process – of cortical origin – may be built up in the hypothalamus and transferred to the manillary body, and thence through the anterior nuclei of the thalamus to the cortex of the cingular gyrus, from which the process might spread to other regions of the cortex. H. Kluver and P. C. Bucy offered evidence, in 1939, which squared with the Papez model. Operations on the brains of rhesus monkeys which disrupted the circuit described by Papez produced marked behavioural changes. The monkeys were curious about their environment. In fact they approached any object (such as a dangerous snake) without hesitation and examined it. There was an almost total lack of fear, anger, resentment or pleasure in appropriate stimulus-situations. One monkey approached and licked the fangs of a snake and did not display any marked response when severely bitten. Kluver and Bucy had shown that the removal of some of the essential parts of the Papez system resulted in total loss of the capacity to respond emotionally. This was the beginning of interest in the 'limbic' system involving hippocampal and cingulate gyri in relation to behaviour. This line of research has stimulated much activity in physiological psychology and is much in evidence in the 1960s.

This account of physiological psychology, selective as it is, may give the impression of sparseness. In a sense this impression would not be misleading. In spite of much admirable work in physiology during this period, there was not much which could directly throw light on behaviour. At the same time, psychologists were inclined to be less concerned with physiology than in earlier, and later, periods. The behaviourists had techniques for discovering correlations between measurable changes in stimuli and changes in response-measures. Some, like Skinner, openly advocated an 'open organism' psychology, which set aside the details of intervening neurophysiological processes until the physiologist could confidently supply them. The business of developing and applying tests, devising new statistical techniques for analysing test results, initiating new types of applied research in industry, education and child development, together with psycho-analytic theorizing, absorbed the energies and captured the interests of many psychologists. To this extent, there was a tendency for physiological basic research and psychological research to diverge, and for physiology not to have quite such an impact on psychology as it did in the early days of experimental psychology, or as it does at the present time.

CHAPTER SEVENTEEN

Experimental Psychology 1918-40

PERCEPTION

IN the period between the wars experimental psychologists made new approaches to the problem of how human beings experience their environment. A vast amount of experimental work was carried out on the structure and functioning of the sensory processes involved in seeing, hearing, touching, smelling and exercising the muscular systems. Much of this overlapped with the physiology of sensation, and psychologists contributed to our knowledge of the structure of the eye and eye movements, the discrimination of visual stimuli of different degrees of intensity, and the factors involved in colour (in the field of visual processes), and they also extended the work of Helmholtz in the field of hearing (through studies in the localization of sound, measurement of different sensations of pitch, etc.). This work constituted a whole branch of experimental science, and provided a background for studies in perceptual organization. The sophistication and rigour of this work can be judged from any standard textbook of experimental psychology (see, for example, Chapters 22 to 32 in S. S. Stevens' *Handbook of Experimental Psychology*, 1951).

It is impossible to select from and summarize this massive achievement. The excuse for not attempting this, however, is neither the distorting inadequacy of any such summary, nor the cowardice of the author. For in a sense such work is peripheral to more purely psychological interests. Perception is partly dependent upon the operation of the peripheral sensory mechanisms of the eye, ear, nose, etc., and the sensations to which the stimulation of these organs gives rise. But the complex action of the central parts of the brain, which 'interpret' and coordinate the information from the receptors, are equally, if not more, important. About these central operations physiologists and psychologists still do not have much knowledge. In studying perception, psychologists collect information of a kind which gives facts and generalizations which physiology has still to explain, though it does provide knowledge useful in itself.

The problems of perception are, therefore, more strictly the province of experimental psychology, and arise out of the earlier history of psychology. It was these problems which the experimenters explored so thoroughly between 1918 and 1945. We cannot discuss all of them. An arbitrary selection will serve.

The philosophers had raised the problem of the validity of our perceptions. How accurate or true a representation of objects and events in the environment do our visual, auditory and other perceptual responses give? We know that it is possible to suffer illusions, and be mistaken about what we see and hear; we know that some mental illnesses involve hallucinations, and even ordinary people have vivid dreams which for some minutes after waking are hard to discredit. Do we ever register the environment with the clinical accuracy of a camera, or is there always some degree of distortion and inaccuracy? Much evidence has been accumulated to show that perceptions are not passive and accurate registerings of external happenings, but are highly selective and 'processed' by the central parts of the brain. This being the case, there exists the problem of how to describe and explain the exact nature of the discrepancies between what is perceived and what is 'there' in the environment. The psychologist also wants to discover what factors in the stimulus-situation and what factors in the responses and general make-up of the percipient determine the precise contents and characteristics of typical perceptual experiences.

Some knowledge of the sensory mechanisms is required

in answering questions of this kind; but a knowledge of the physiology of sensation is not enough – hence the distinction between experiments on sensory processes and experiments in problems of perception which was made explicit in the twenties and thirties. In the absence of detailed knowledge of the central processes, some theorizing was inevitable.

The Gestalt school accepted the fact that perception owes something to external stimuli, but emphasized the view that there are inherent organizing factors in the nervous system which are of fundamental importance. These are not influenced by learning.

Empiricists in England, following Sir Frederic Bartlett of Cambridge, argued that perception is the product of prior learning interacting upon physical stimuli and intrinsic organization. Humans categorize and automatically 'interpret' incoming information, in terms of a system of 'concepts' or 'schemata' produced by the central brain as a result of learning, remembering and other cognitive reactions. Behaviourists in the U.S.A. also emphasized the crucial importance of learning in determining what is selected and related in acts of seeing or hearing.

To look ahead somewhat, it is relevant to mention that since 1945 other theories have further complicated the picture. Some psychologists maintain that what we perceive is also a function of personality. Dominant attitudes, sentiments, emotions also structure our perceptual reactions and influence the selection and interpretation of the information provided by the receptors. Again, other psychologists, on the basis of existing neurophysiology, speculate about what sort of processes in the brain might translate information into elaborate and meaningful perceptions. These viewpoints have tended to come closer together in the 1960s, but twenty or thirty years earlier psychologists tended to be guided by Gestalt or empiricist biases in devising hypotheses to test.

In spite of this lack of theoretical foundations, much

patient, systematic and useful empirical work was done on a vast array of problems. As with the field of sensory processes, only a comprehensive textbook can adequately review all the problems investigated. In an excellent survey, *A Further Study of Visual Perception* (1952), the author, M. D. Vernon, complains that far too much experimental work between the two wars was devoted to the study of apparent movement. However, this work has been of considerable importance. It was Wertheimer's studies (see also pp. 243 ff.) which provided the basic concepts of Gestalt psychology. His theory, supported by experiment, caused the emphasis to be shifted away from analysis of perceptual experience into sensory elements and from explanations in the form of association – a major change which benefited the study of perception. The work also scotched for ever the old 'constancy hypothesis', the view that we perceive only what is there and that perception attempts to approximate exact reproduction. These studies also led to new insights into the sort of variables which control perceptual responses. And even if the Gestalt view (that built-in organizing processes are basic) was one-sided, it provoked other experimentalists into producing alternative hypotheses. Many new variables, important for any understanding of perceptual processes, were identified and studied separately from the big issues.

Wertheimer became interested in explaining our perceptions of movement – of real movement, of the apparent movement of stationary objects, of the failure to perceive movement when it is actual and of the perception of movement when only successive phases are exposed.

He placed two lights along the edge of a table. Between these and a screen on the wall, a thin rod was erected. If the lights were switched on and off alternately, the shadow of the rod seemed to move backwards and forwards between two positions, provided the interval was about 60 milli-seconds. If the time was reduced to 30 milli-seconds, the two shadows from each of the rods appeared simultaneously. If the interval was increased to

200 milli-seconds, less distinctive movement was observed. Under favourable conditions, the apparent movement of the shadow A——>B, B<——A, is as 'real' as if something was moving. Again, if a light is flashed through a window-slit in a black screen in a dark room and the window is closed, then followed by the opening of a similar slit to the left, the phenomenon of one light moving from right to left is seen. Wertheimer elaborated his experiment to study the influence of the order of presentation of stimuli; the effect of distance; form and colour of objects on apparent movement.

Attempts to explain these phenomena by attributing the illusion to eye-movement were invalidated. The time required for movement is less than the minimal time required for eye movement (130 milli-seconds). In further experiments fixation was so controlled as to prevent eye-movements, yet the phenomenon still occurred. And finally, Wertheimer demonstrated that several apparent movements, in different directions, can be seen simultaneously, a fact which precludes explanation in terms of eye-movements. In these experiments, little or nothing is seen of the lights or lines – the movement is of something indefinite and it cannot be analysed into static elements of any kind. Since there is an experience of movement, there must be a dynamic process in the brain which mediates this. The experience is a 'whole' (or Gestalt) phenomenon incapable of analysis into sensory units. The perception of movement is a unified, integrated unity, and this is characteristic of all perceptions.

Wertheimer had been studying the effect of controlling distance and time factors between stimuli in relation to the perception of apparent movement. In 1919 Korte summarized the results of the early experiments by formulating three laws, which state that there is a direct relationship between measured time and distance, an inverse relationship between time interval and intensity of the stimuli, and a direct relationship between distance and intensity.

A rigorous study of the conditions of apparent movement was performed by W. Neuhaus (*Archives of Gestalt Psychology*, 1930). He investigated the variables over a wider range, and with improved equipment. He found that if exposure time and distance between stimuli are kept constant, a choice of temporal interval is necessary if the subject is to report movement. There is a large range of temporal interval values within which changes in this variable have little effect. For certain values of stimuli and time exposure, optimal movement may be seen over a range of 80 to 400 milli-seconds – which undermines Wertheimer's general estimate of 60 milli-seconds. He confirmed Korte's third law, but contradicted the first and second laws (by showing that variation of stimulus intensity over a wide range does not necessitate change in the other variables). He also investigated states of the subject as well as stimulus conditions. Practice enables subjects to report apparent movement under controlled conditions which produce reports of simultaneity or succession in unpractised subjects. Training assists in the production of the perception of apparent movement. The effect of instructions is also relevant. Direct instructions to see movement enable subjects who had previously failed to report it to do so.

This emphasis of learning and 'set' had been made by an earlier investigator, P. Linke, who in 1901 had argued that apparent movement only occurs when a subject identified the two stimuli as referring to the same 'object'. He pointed out that we are constantly subject to disparate stimulations of the visual apparatus, many of which have a degree of similarity in size, brightness, shape and hue. Perceptual learning has to be taken into account before we can explain those cases in which apparent movement is attributed to the successive presentation of separate stimuli. Helmholtz's view that 'unconscious inference' occurs in our perception of movement is involved in this interpretation.

These studies – and we have selected only a few illustrations – therefore raise big questions concerning the function of peripheral and central determinants of perceived movement, the function of experience as opposed to Gestalt factors, and the fundamental and unknown working of the neural mechanisms involved. C. E. Osgood (pp. 243–8 of *Method and Theory in Experimental Psychology*, 1953) gives a plausible explanation in terms of 'perceived movement as change in the location of contours' which evokes a neurological model. Such an explanation, however, was not characteristic of the earlier period when the pioneer work was being done.

Another aspect of perception which received considerable attention from experimental psychologists between the wars was 'perceptual constancies', a field of research which had its origins in the assumption of philosophers, and certain earlier scientists, that experience approximates closely to the data supplied by the peripheral receptors. The problem of constancy arose because psychologists demonstrated that the attributes of size, shape, colour and brightness of objects perceived remain apparently unchanged in spite of considerable variations in peripheral stimuli. For example, when a blue paper is placed in a yellow light (of a certain intensity) and viewed through a small hole in a screen, it appears as grey – as one would expect from the laws of colour-mixing. But when observed without the screen (under 'normal' viewing) it appears as blue paper under yellow light. Brightness, size and shape constancy are also easily demonstrated.

The old nativist *v.* empiricist controversy re-activated by the Gestalt theory also contributed. Is our perception of a three-dimensional world, in depth and filled with objects all of which display relatively consistent attributes, determined by built-in neural principles, or learned through experience?

The results of the work of this period demonstrated that perception is a complex affair. We do not simply perceive objects against a background: objects are perceived in a spatio-temporal context such that an observer has an immediate and implicit grasp of the relation between the appearance of objects and the conditions of their stimulus context. He assumes both a constancy for certain attributes and allows for lawful changes in the stimulus-situation. He has built-in mechanisms for making constant adjustments between basic attributes and changes in the stimulus conditions.

Many generalizations, much more specific, were established about constancy:

(1) It was found that neither perfect constancy nor perfect matching of stimuli occurs when we perceive: there is a sort of compromise between the two 'ideals'. Brunswik, who had strong orientations towards Gestalt conceptions, succeeded in devising a measure of the degree of constancy in his subjects. If a subject matched exactly according to the measured intensity of the stimulus then he would show a zero tendency to colour constancy. If, on the other hand, a subject matched according to the colour of the object, he would show 100 per cent colour constancy. However, most subjects' actual judgements could be assigned a per cent value, according to position on this continuum, one end of which conforms to the 'stimulus' and the other to the 'object' properties. Thus, if a grey mixture on a colour wheel has 30 per cent white and 70 per cent black, its object value is 30. If the wheel is lightly illuminated, and an observer alters the mixture on a second colour wheel, in an illumination 10 times as high, then a strict matching with the stimulus would be one-tenth of 30, that is 3, which is the stimulus value. However, if the actual matching of a particular subject is 15 – that is, if the observer makes the more brightly illuminated wheel match the dimmer one by mixing 15 per cent white with 85 per cent black, then his constancy is measured thus:

$$\frac{15-3}{30-3} = \frac{12}{27} = 0\cdot 44$$

Therefore, if A is the numerical value for the object, S the numerical value for the stimulus and R the numerical value of the actual match, the ratio is:

$$\frac{R-S}{A-S}$$

This gives an approximate measure of the degree of approximation to the 'strictly objective' perception of the object.

Many experiments have been performed to measure and compare the constancy in the perception of different individuals for colour, shape, size and brightness characteristics. Ratios over a wide range *never* reach either 0·00 or 1·0. In other words there is *always* a compromise between sensory data and object reference. R. H. Thouless of Cambridge made this clear in an article (*British Journal of Psychology*, 1931).

(2) It is further established in many experiments of these years that the degree of constancy increases with the absolute stimulus difference between standard and comparison objects. Brunswick reported his celebrated investigations of size constance in the *Psychological Review* (1940). He used 13 cubes of various sizes from 30 mm. to 90 mm. a side. The standard blocks (50, 55, 60, 65, 70 mm.) were placed singly, at varying distances from the experimenter, and the comparison blocks were placed further from the subject. The subject had to select the block, from among the comparison ones, which appeared equal in size to the standard block in the foreground. Brunswik proved that the further apart the standard blocks (hence the greater discrepancy in the visual angle) the greater the degree of constancy achieved in the matching. Thouless had results on size constancy (in his paper of 1931) which confirmed this. The experiments demonstrated a psychological fact, but raised a problem. Why should objects show greater constancy effects, as the objects

compared deviate more radically in terms of 'absolute' stimulus values? Such problems as this can generate many series of investigations and keep pure scientists happy for years.

(3) The more aids an observer has in identifying standard and comparison objects as the 'same', the greater the constancy effect. In 1931 Burzlaff, a Gestalt worker, used two sets of 48 grey papers as the basis of a simple experiment. One set was in strict order of shading from near-white to near-black. The second set was mounted with the shades in random order on a medium-grey 'blackboard'. The irregular set was placed near a window where the light was twenty times as intense as that part of the room with the blackboard. Pointing to a particular paper, the experimenter asked his subjects, standing by the irregular set, to judge which of the distant papers was a perfect match. Near-perfect constancy was achieved by a large sample of both child and adult subjects.

Katz, the eminent Swedish psychologist already mentioned for his work on colour perception (pp. 245 ff.), performed studies with animal subjects and showed that many animals display a high degree of brightness and size constancy. For instance, he trained chickens to select white rice grains and leave yellow-stained grains. When given the two under strong yellow light, the chicks selected the white. In a comparative study, chimpanzees showed as much brightness constancy as human adults and children.

This suggests that innate neurological mechanisms are responsible for constancy phenomena rather than learning, since some of the animals are limited learners.

This has proved a wide field for experiment. Measures of constancy in relation to controlled changes in the environment was a common project in the 1930s. Moreover, other topics were stimulated by this research. Jaensch in 1920 suggested that brightness and colour constancy might be 'contrast' phenomena in a special setting. Since contrast effects of brightness differences or colour differences within a perceptual field cannot be separated from 'contour' phenomena, a great deal of experimental work resulted from the constancy studies.

Another topic of investigation was figure-ground relationships. In most visual perceptions, we see 'objects' against a background which is formless and featureless. Rubin was one of the earliest to investigate this basic fact. Rubin used black and white ambiguous figures – so that white forms against black ground could be changed for black forms against white ground. He suggested that: (1) Figures have form; the ground is relatively formless. (2) The ground appears to extend beyond the figure and is not interrupted by it. (3) The figure has the character of an object while the ground appears as unformed 'material'. (4) The 'contours' (or boundaries) belong to the figure, not the ground.

Wever (*American Journal of Psychology*, 1927), demonstrated that while the figure has definite localization in space, and has surface texture, the ground is weakly localized and has filmy texture. Wever, by exposing the ambiguous black and white figures for different times (from 10 milli-seconds upwards), showed that, with very brief exposures, no figure-ground effect occurred. It was only with longer times that contour began to appear (at about 11 milli-seconds). Good contour with good brightness difference between figure and ground came at 14 millisecond exposures. With longer exposures, the subject 'identified' the ambiguous shapes as 'objects' such as birds or human profiles. Ehrenstein (1930) discovered that the greater the intensity of illumination and the greater the brightness difference between figure and ground, the shorter was the exposure time needed to give figure-ground differentiation. Also, the more symmetrical and the more meaningful the figure, the less was the exposure time required.

Koffka maintained that figural organization is a dynamic process, in which energy is discharged in fixating a particular percept, and put forward the hypothesis that the density of this energy is greater within the figure than the ground. Several corollaries of this hypothesis have been tested experimentally. When coloured sectors are used for reversible figures, the portion serving as figure should have more colour than the ground. In *Principles of Gestalt Psychology* (1935) Koffka reported that when a pattern is made of alternating grey and green sections, the green loses saturation (measurable quantity of hue) when it shifts from figure to ground, and the grey adds contrast red as it becomes central.

These experiments led to many others. The stability and instability continuum for figures under various conditions of observation were investigated. The factors which produce this form or that in a visual field were studied. People blind from birth, who had their sight given to them through surgical operation, were studied by Senden (1932) in order to trace the extent of innately given organization, as against the amount of learning needed before different shapes could be easily recognized. Contour formation on the basis of differential rates of excitation, contrast in terms of brightness and colour, attention and discrimination mechanisms were all investigated in relation to the formation of figure-ground effects.

We have discussed only three fields of study which were opened up through experimental work in the 1920s and 1930s, yet many more aspects of perception were investigated – space perception (depth and solidity, relative and absolute distance), after-images, binocular vision, the organization of hearing (e.g. the localization of sound) and many others. Perception provided psychologists with a full-time study quite apart from anything else. The Gestalt school provided the lead, but not all psychologists accepted their theories. Towards the end of the 1940s the role of experience and learning, of motivation and attitude, and of 'personality' variables in perception were being studied as well as the intrinsic organization imposed by the nervous system.

The older psychologists of the German schools of Wundt and Kulpe (when they were not introspecting for sensory elements of mental acts) often stuck to psychophysical methods – to measuring the degree of sensory modalities (brightness, pitch, etc.). The Gestalt school, while often controlling and measuring variables in the environment with precision, were interested in the totality of perceptual experience – with what we see, hear, feel, taste, as an organized whole. This necessitated the study of the response side of the process, and introduced new kinds of experiments demanding design, techique and apparatus different from the 'brass instruments' of the earlier pre-1914 workers.

The present study is not the place to trace the influence of physicists, electricians and engineers in providing the basis for better equipment – and hence improved techniques of experimental procedure. Some day, a history must be written of the factors which from the 1930s onwards went to make improvements of this kind possible.

We have concentrated on the way in which theories (the main sources of stimulation in the years between the two great wars) changed interests and raised new problems, thus enabling psychologists to do new types of psychological experiment. Many of the Gestalt experiments were aimed at demonstration, producing qualitative rather than quantitative results and yielding new descriptions of what happens when we perceive, rather than at establishing elaborate psychophysical formulae. It is this 'new look' in the study of traditional interests that is the main feature of the work done.

LEARNING OPERATIONS

The main impact of Behaviourist theories was to stimulate psychologists to investigate simple learning operations experimentally and, since animals (especially rats) were used, to develop new fields of animal research. The word 'learning' did not appear in Baldwin's encyclopedic *Dictionary of Psychology* (1906). Titchéner's textbook (1909) simply mentions 'learning' in the chapter on association, and he excuses himself from discussing it because it is too complex. Even the word 'habit' occurred only twice, and then cursorily, in his vast and learned book.

It was the possibility of studying conditioning in the laboratory that turned experimental psychologists towards the study of learning operations for the first time. A very large and varied literature appeared in the journals, and for many psychologists this provided the basis for research and writing to the exclusion of all other interests.

At first, the main activity was in studying conditioning more exactly, and discovering the environmental and response variables involved in the acquisition, strengthening, extinction, modification and linking of specific conditioned responses. Much valid scientific knowledge was accumulated about conditioning, and about its function in the formulation of simple 'habits'. Then, under the stimulus of theoretical disputes (especially between Hull and Tolman and their followers), certain empirical problems arose which psychologists attempted to solve by experimenting. The literature connected with these experiments is so vast that we can consider only one or two illustrations of the sort of work involved. *Conditioning and Learning* by E. R. Hilgard and D. G. Marquis (1940) gives a lucid account of work on conditioning; while B. R. Bugelski's *The Psychology of Learning* (1956) describes the earlier work on problems arising from theoretical controversy, as well as giving accounts of more recent studies.

The experimental studies of learning operations and the theories constructed to explain their results formed a large and coherent subject-matter from the late 1920s down to the 1950s. The traditional topics and problems are still a subject of interest in several university research institutions, although new approaches to the study of learning were made after the Second World War. In spite of new development, the enormous output of those interested in learning during the past forty years has left its mark on the textbooks of experimental psychology, and many specific researches remain in contemporary accounts.

Much of the earlier experimental work was principally concerned with finding out more about conditioning and its refinements as a simple model for 'habit' formation. There were basic questions to be answered to which a study of conditioned responses seemed appropriate. First, how does a new response emerge for the first time, since the situation is new and the precise response may never have been made before? Second, once a useful response has emerged, how does it persist and recur just when the occasion demands it? Responses do not have to be acquired over and over again.

The study of the conditioned stimulus seemed to give an inroad into the study of animal learning, since it can serve as the sign of something other than itself. At first, psychologists worked at classifying different types of conditioned response, and the functions each could serve in behaviour. Even the Pavlov type of conditioning could serve a variety of behaviours – dogs conditioned to salivate to a buzzer show all kinds of food-taking anticipatory reactions, such as going over to the food bowl, looking at the door or hatch through which food usually arrives, wagging the tail. Skinner's operant conditioning provided an even more flexible situation, capable of being exploited as the basis for all kinds of training (reward, escape, avoidance, secondary reward, etc.), in which precise relationships between stimulus and response variables could be studied (for example temporal relations between unconditioned and conditioned stimulus: presentation of CS simultaneously, after a delay, after cessation of US).

In all this preliminary experimental work, three topics especially received considerable attention: reinforcement of the conditioned response; extinction and strengthening of C R; and generalization and discrimination phenomena.

Extinction

It was obvious from the start that C Rs do not disintegrate easily. Disuse over long intervals does not eliminate the ability of an animal to produce the C R to its C S. To what process is elimination of a C R due? Pavlov studied what he called 'inhibition' – the reduction of C Rs resulting from positive rival stimuli. Two main types of inhibition were discovered in the earliest researches: (a) 'Adaptation'. If a C S–C R relationship is repeated to the point at which the nervous system suffers fatigue, the response is eliminated. (b) 'Interference'. Here reduction results from the elimination by another and incompatible response evoked simultaneously with the C R. The degree of inhibition depends on the nature and intensity of the interfering responses, and also on the temporal relations between the two responses. Pavlov's research concentrated mainly on adaptation, while E. R. Guthrie favoured interference as the basis of extinction. The facts discovered are summarized in G. H. S. Razran's article 'The Nature of Extinction Process' (*Psychological Review*, 1939). His main conclusions are:

(a) Decrement by repetition is the most widespread factor in extinction.
(b) The restoration of the original response to the C S after extinction is a slow process and gives time for new adjustments.
(c) Conditioning to some new factor arising in the course of the extinction 'treatment' sometimes occurs and assists in the extinction.

Although the experimental data were not without ambiguities, some generalizations about extinction were well established.

Strength of Conditioning

The problem of how CRs vary in their resistance to extinction exercised the attention of researchers. This work established a distinction between the response strength (referring to the magnitude, frequency and persistence of a given response) and strength of conditioning. The strength of a response is always positive, since it refers to an overt occurrence. The strength of conditioning can fall to zero. This had an important influence on learning theory, since it turned the concept of 'conditioning' into a hypothetical construct – a reference to an inner (neural) process inferred from overt muscular activities. The business of trying to measure indirectly the strength of a specific conditioned response proved difficult: the force with which movement was made; the length of delay between CS and CR; the number of trials before CR is extinguished; the probability of a given CR occurring (percentage of CRs over 100 trials); the number of repetitions without reinforcement; the amount of reinforcement required to keep the CR going; the attempt to measure 'drive' (degree of hunger, thirst, etc.) – all these variables were investigated, without producing clear and accepted criteria for measuring the strength of conditioning. However, psychologists did succeed in producing new variables relevant for the functioning of a conditioning process.

Reinforcement

As we have already seen, the fact that certain environmental stimuli have effects which appear to strengthen a CR was discovered by Thorndike. Skinner (in the 1930s) and Hull investigated reinforcement more comprehensively and thoroughly. Reinforcement proved a much more complicated process than it had first seemed from the earlier studies, since many elusive factors in a learning situation can serve as reinforcing agents for a reaction. In fact, the experimental data gave rise to a number of 'problems' which not only stimulated experiment but provoked theoretical controversies (see p. 307). Ultimately the whole problem of the 'motivation' of animal behaviour arose out of this specific investigation.

Generalization and Discrimination

Pavlov had discovered that when a subject has been conditioned to make a specific response R to stimulus S_1, other stimuli, S_2, S_3, etc., will elicit the response without necessarily having been conditioned. This is the phenomenon of sensory stimulus generalization. Response generalization also occurs, so that a specific stimulus S_1 comes to elicit R_2, R_3, etc., without further training. It is obvious that this degree of flexibility must hold. Even in the artificial conditioning situation, the buzzer sounds each time in a different context of changing background noise. Again, when an animal responds, it does so in a slightly different receptive state and with some variation in its motor performance, however slight. No habit could work without some 'spread' on both stimulus and response side, and no learning could occur without generalization, since learning is largely the modification of former habits or reflexes to meet new requirements.

Generalization insures similar, or equivalent, responses in spite of slight changes in the stimulus-situation. It was not surprising that sensory and response generalization should become a subject of experimental investigation.

A typical study is C. I. Hovland's papers in the *Journal of General Psychology*, 1937, 'The Generalisation of Conditioned Responses'. Hovland demonstrated how a response, conditioned to a particular stimulus, is generalized to other stimuli. He selected the galvanic skin response as the one to be conditioned. In 1890 a Russian physiologist, Tarchanoff, found that any two parts of the skin of a human being, if connected through a galvanometer, show a difference of potential. When two terminals from the galvanometer are placed on the skin, a weak current passes through the instrument and is measured. This current can be neutralized by an external current from a battery passed in the opposite direction, thus bringing the needle on the galvanometer to zero. Now, having obtained this neutralizing effect, a further deflection of the needle can be produced if the subject is presented with a stimulus – the sounding of a buzzer, the flashing of a light, or even a 'mental' stimulus. All these changes are the result of currents generated in the skin through the activities of the sweat glands, and are known as galvanic skin responses. Such responses can be measured and are easily conditioned to neutral stimuli.

Using an electric shock as the original stimulus (U S) to which a change in galvanic skin response was the U R, Hovland then used a pure tone of 1,967 c.p.s. as C S. After the galvanic skin response was strongly conditioned to this tone, the magnitude of the response to other tones of varying frequencies was measured. The response was strongest for 1,967 c.p.s. and decreased for magnitudes both above and below, in a systematic form.

Using the same experimental design, Hovland demonstrated the generalization of pitch, selecting four tones separated by 25 just-noticeable differences measured by established psychophysical techniques (153, 468, 1,000, 1,937 c.p.s.). Having equated them for loudness, the tones thus represented a scale of approximately equal units on a dimension of 'similarity of pitch'. Next, one group of subjects was conditioned to the lowest tone and then tested on the others to find the extent of generalization. A second group was conditioned to the highest tone and tested on the three lower. It was then possible to pool the results for all subjects into a single curve, representing the generalization exhibited in tones separated by 25 j.n.d.s. The results of two other experiments in which tones separated by 50 j.n.d.s and 75 j.n.d.s were added. The resulting curve showed how neatly the degree of generalization *decreases progressively* with *increase of pitch* (see figure –

after Holland, 1937). The demonstration of the fact of stimulus and response generalization and laws governing the amount of generalization became an important research topic.

However, it is obvious that in experimental work generalization must not spread too widely, and there are occasions where the opposite tendency is required: a very precise response must be made only to one specific 'signal'.

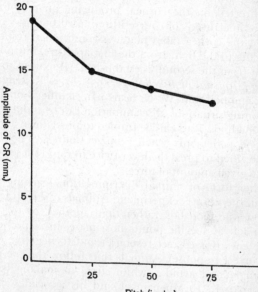

The mechanism for curbing generalization and for making very refined S–R connexions possible was called 'discrimination'. This term has usually been used to indicate a situation in which a subject has been trained to respond to a number of distinct, but similar, stimuli as equivalent, and is then required to discriminate between these, for example, by making the response to only *one* stimulus, or by making different responses to each of the stimuli.

Methods of training subjects to make exact discriminations were worked out, and the variables involved in controlling discrimination-learning were studied. Within the framework of Pavlovian conditioning, the 'method of contrasts' was applied. A specific response is reinforced to one stimulus while similar stimuli, to which the response tends to generalize, are not reinforced. In one experiment, two apertures in a screen are illuminated equally. When the subject looks through one aperture, a puff of air is directed on the cornea, producing an eye-blink: the other aperture is of course illuminated but no stimulation of the cornea takes place. A conditioned response of blinking to the light from the first aperture, but not to the light from the second, is established. (Reported in the *American Journal of Psychology*, 1938, by E. R. Hilgard, R. K. Campbell and W. N. Sears.) In Skinner's operant conditioning situations, discrimination can be induced by similar methods. Rats can be trained to press down a lever for a food pellet only when a buzzer sounds. They can also be trained to press the lever twice in rapid succession, or with a given amount of force.

Another form of animal discrimination learning was shown in the 'choice' experiment. Animals can be trained to choose one food box rather than another, or to turn right or left at specific points in a maze, in response to positive cues (for correct response) and to negative cues (for incorrect response). Animals thus follow the cue of a red triangle and avoid a white circle in making for a distant goal. K. F. Muenzinger and his associates, in a series of articles in the *Journal of Comparative Psychology* (1935–7), describe several typical researches of the time (for example, on the influence of delays in rewards and punishments before choice, at moment of choice, and after incorrect choices).

These are a few samples of the experimental investigations into conditioning and its refinements as the basis of habit which psychologists undertook in the 1920s and 1930s. Stimulated by the work of Pavlov and Thorndike and influenced by Behaviourism, they aimed at studying the basic features of elementary animal learning. However, the foundation work developed into the study of certain empirical problems about the nature of learning which provoked a certain mild controversy. Differences of theoretical bias led to the different interpretation of experimental results, and in trying to test the adequacy of specific hypotheses – derived from this or that theory – a different kind of investigation into learning processes developed in the 1930s. Is reinforcement the necessary condition of all kinds of learning? Is there such a thing as latent learning without reinforcement? Are there several kinds of learning, or are they reducible to one set of operations elaborated and refined in various ways? Do animals learn movements only, or, in a primitive form, the 'meaning' of signs? These problems rose chiefly out of the realization that even in the simple conditioning situation, used as a model for habit formation, a number of 'intervening variables' had to be postulated to conceive the total and complex situation.

CONTROVERSIAL PROBLEMS IN THE EXPERIMENTAL PSYCHOLOGY OF LEARNING

Hull's learning theory is based on the model of an organism driven by such needs as hunger, or by a secondary need associated through conditioning with a primary need. Only if the need is satisfied does reinforcement occur and a habit become strengthened. For learning to take place at all, a drive has first to be aroused, and then reduced through the effects of the response to be learned.

Tolman, on the other hand, argued that learning can occur without reinforcement, as in 'latent' learning. Here, bits of information are acquired and stored for later use, as the result of associating stimuli, so that S_1 comes to suggest S_2.

In an experiment to demonstrate learning without reward, H. C. Blodgett (*University of California Publica-*

tions in Psychology, 1929) used three groups of rats in a six-unit maze. All animals had one trial each day. The control group A were fed following each trial run from the beginning. Group B were fed on the third day and every following day. Group C were fed on the seventh day and every day afterwards. Blodgett tested the latent learning for B and C groups by comparing the fall in errors for the control group A between the second and third days with those for group B between the third and fourth days and those of group C between the seventh and eighth days. He claimed that reductions in errors were greater for groups B and C than for group A – the latent learning groups had learned the maze without reward.

Hull and his supporters argued that it is impossible to prove that no reinforcing stimuli are operating in this or in any other 'latent' learning experiment. Curiosity urges may reinforce the learning of the maze. It was pointed out later that in an experiment by Culler and Brogden in 1935 (*Journal of General Psychology*), in which a buzzer was used as a substitute for a shock, it was necessary to bring back the shock occasionally as a reinforcer for the conditioned stimulus. Also Grindley, a Cambridge psychologist, demonstrated in a monograph (1929) that while the sight of food can function as a conditioned stimulus, it loses its effect unless the animal is allowed to eat the food from time to time.

This controversy concerning the proper interpretation of latent learning experiments has continued from the 1930s to the present. Is an obscure reinforcing stimulus present or not? Tolman and Gestalt experimenters have not been able to disprove Hull's basic law of reinforcement conclusively, although their many experiments have suggested that Hull's concept of reinforcement is too stringent. Animals do learn under the stress of hunger, thirst, sexual deprivation, shock, provided their behaviour satisfies the 'need' for food, drink, a partner, escape. But when such obvious control is absent, what is the substitute for the reinforcing stimulus? At least this controversy defined the problem.

Another dispute was over the explanation of discrimination-learning experiments. As we have seen, when an organism has learned to give a response to a given stimulus S_{1A}, it is easily demonstrated that other stimuli S_{1B} and S_{1C}, which are similar to S_{1A} but not identical, can evoke the response without training or reinforcement. This is 'stimulus generalization'. 'Response generalization' is also a well-known occurrence, in which a specific stimulus comes to evoke any one of a number of similar but not identical responses to the one which has been conditioned to the stimulus. Since S and R factors always vary slightly, generalization serves to keep S–R bonds adjusted to an approximate 'mean'. Also generalization allows new adaptations to arise on the basis of established associations without undue rigidity in adhering to old ways of reacting. However, accurate adaptations are sometimes required, and these depend on the control of generalization. Animals and humans must be able to 'discriminate' between similar but different stimuli in the selection of only one among a number of like responses. How do animals discriminate accurately on both the stimulus and the response side?

Hull's theory of discrimination-learning is clearly stated:

(1) Reinforcement strengthens the required reaction tendencies: non-reinforcement weakens.
(2) Just how much the magnitude of any increment in the strength of a reaction tendency is, on any trial, depends on the amount of habit-strength at the time of reinforcement.
(3) Both excitatory and inhibitory tendencies within the nervous system generalize.
(4) These excitatory and inhibitory tendencies at each point along the stimulus summate algebraically to yield effective reaction potential.

(5) Which of two competing reaction tendencies to the same stimulus has the greater reaction-potential will win.

(6) The amplitude, probability and latency of a response is a function of the effective reaction-potential (presumably a state of the nervous system).

This is a mechanical theory, in which nervous energy is conceived as building up to a climax when a specific 'firing' of certain pathways and centres produces a specific overt response. This Hullian theory was opposed by psychologists within the Gestalt school. Of these, J. Krechevsky and Lashley of Harvard (pp. 280 ff.) produced experiments to dispute Hull's conclusions.

Krechevsky held that, when they make discriminations, organisms select and abstract certain aspects of the total stimulus-situation. Only those aspects selected at a given moment are affected by reinforcement or non-reinforcement. Discrimination is, therefore, not a continuous process: differentiation in terms of relevant cues only starts once the subject has already selected and fixated these cues. Hull, on the other hand, maintained that reinforcement produces a cumulative increase in the strength of specific reaction tendencies, while non-reinforcement weakens any specific tendency. Hull postulated a mechanically continuous process behind the learning to discriminate a cue for action. This continuity–non-continuity controversy led to much experimental work in support and refutation of rival hypotheses following from the two theories.

For example, Krechevsky studied the behaviour of a white rat learning to select a black door, as opposed to a white door, as a cue for food. He argued that there were two distinct phases in the behaviour of the animal: a pre-solution phase and an activity phase. The reactions during the former were of a distinctly trial-and-error kind, during which incorrect solutions were eliminated. There was no steady, bit-by-bit building-up of the correct response from trial to trial, but rather varied, oscillating behaviour. Once the correct response was selected there came a sudden change. Thenceforward the rat tended to stick rigidly to the correct solution.

Krechevsky performed 'reversed cue' experiments to establish his thesis. During the pre-solution period, in an experiment in which a rat had to learn to discriminate S_1 from S_2, S_1 was always reinforced and S_2 not. However, just before the shift to the solution phase, the cues were suddenly reversed, so that S_2 was now reinforced and S_1 not. According to Hull, learning should have been disrupted. Krechevsky attempted to show that this was not the case. He subjected one group of rats to this reversed cue, comparing them with another group which had simply continued to learn S_1 as the correct cue without any reversal.

He used a Lashley jumping stand. In this apparatus a small platform is fixed at the top of a pole from which rats leap, over a short space, towards a box with two doors. One door opens to a food reward, the other is locked and so forces the rat to fall into a net. Each door can be given a distinct visual cue. By comparing one group with two 'reversed cue' groups, Krechevsky was satisfied that his non-continuity theory was confirmed. There were no more errors for the reversed cue group than for those subjected to the simpler training. These results were questioned by Hull on the ground that the cues selected by Krechevsky were too difficult for the rats. The relevant cues were not at first received by the animals because they were probably fixating other aspects of the stimulus.

Another experiment by Krechevsky (*Journal of Experimental Psychology*, 1938), however, posed something of greater difficulty for Behaviourist theory. Group A rats were given training on a very different discrimination problem. They had to distinguish between horizontally and vertically arranged patterns of black squares on a white background. The spatial arrangement of the squares determined whether the pattern gave a predominantly vertical or horizontal *Gestalt*. Half of the group were trained with positive reinforcement for horizontal discrimination, the other half for vertical. Group B were given a much easier problem. They had to discriminate between the same horizontal *or* vertical pattern, on the one hand, and a triangular pattern of squares on the other. Finally, the horizontal or vertical patterns that had been positively reinforced were paired with horizontal or vertical solid lines. For the Group A rats there was a preference for the solid lines – but not for the Group B rats.

Krechevsky interpreted this result as follows: 'These forces [of attraction among the squares due to proximity] thus generated are of such a nature and of such a strength as to make for a perception which results in a preference of the organism for a stimulus-complex where the discontinuous members do in fact coalesce, as opposed to a stimulus complex where the members are still, in some degree, discontinuous.' The difficult discrimination pattern forced the animals to pay attention to the relevant cues. This presents a difficulty for continuity theory, since the positive stimulus was not preferred subsequently against a new cue.

However, most of the controversy over discrimination-learning with animals failed to reach a definite conclusion. Lashley provided several 'reversed cue' studies and 'training on a single stimulus' studies. Hull's followers provided experimental data which plausibly claimed to produce contradictory results. (See T. C. McCulloch and J. C. Pratt, 'A Study of Pre-Solution Period in Weight Discrimination by White Rats' (*Journal of Comparative Psychology*, 1934) and K. W. Spence, 'An Experimental Test of the Continuity and Non-Continuity Theories of Discrimination Learning' (*Journal of Experimental Psychology*, 1945).)

This ambiguity in experimental results is characteristic of nearly all these controversial problems in the field of learning. The control of variables is crude. It is possible to give a qualitative description of the animal's molar behaviour: on the Lashley Apparatus, the rat jumps first towards one door and then towards the other, and finally jumps consistently towards the door which opens. But how does the experimenter verify the stimuli which operate? This is always a matter of inference. Similarly in a maze: the experimenter can describe the sequence of turns selected on each run, and demonstrate that the number of 'wrong' turnings up blind alleys is reduced; but he cannot demonstrate or observe anything of the processes of stimulus-selection – this again is an inference.

It is noteworthy that Krechevsky and Lashley got their results in experiments using the Lashley jumping stand, while the Hullian experimenters got their results by using the Yerkes discrimination box (in which visual cues are provided for turning right and left at the end of runways). The food reward is considerably delayed after the animal makes the required response at the choice points in the Yerkes box, but no punishment is involved, other than delay in reaching the food, for an incorrect response. In the Lashley jumping stand experiment, the animal is immediately rewarded for each correct response, but is 'punished' by hitting a closed door and being knocked down into a net, involving a fall of about one foot.

How *exactly* these differences might influence the behaviour of the animals is a matter of speculation. There is evidence, of course, on the effect of 'reward' and 'punishment' on learning, but from experiments involving different apparatus, different species of animal, different conditions of training, different methods of scoring 'errors', etc. The interpretation of experimental results has tended to be in terms of the theory favoured by the experimenter, and hence neither side in the controversy has succeeded in producing convincing evidence.

One final example will serve to illustrate the interests of psychologists in the 1930s in the psychology of learning. Tolman's contention that animals can form a 'cognitive map' of a situation has been mentioned. Once a need arises, the schema can help the animal to locate the significate, utilizing whatever movements are available in the situation to reach the goal. Tolman implied that animals learn to go to a particular place rather than to make a series of movements in response to cues. Several experimental designs were used to test Tolman's theory:

(1) Animals were trained to run a maze along one route and then given the opportunity to take a more direct route to the goal.

(2) Having learned one method of getting to the goal (e.g. running), an animal was tested to see if it could adopt alternative behaviour (such as swimming or climbing through a totally different environment).

(3) A situation could be devised such that learning to go to a particular place conflicted with learning to make a specific response. Do animals follow 'place-learning' or 'response-habit' models?

The experimental results did seem to establish the fact that animals can learn to locate things in specific directions. Does this necessitate accepting Tolman's theory? The crucial question is: 'What is the mediation process which represents this spatial relationship?' 'Are purely S–S associations formed, or must all associations be S–R relationships?' It might be further asked whether *neither* type of relationship, but some more subtle central process, is involved.

All of this indicates the preoccupation of the learning psychologists of the period with hypothetical constructs and pseudo-physiological models. It may be argued that experiments designed to resolve conflicts between highly speculative theories were largely time-wasting. Is reinforcement the essential condition for learning? Is discrimination a step-by-step increase in the strength of a specific habit, or a non-continuous process involving selection of cues before formation of regular response to a given signal? Do animals learn movements or some kind of schemata? Is there one basic learning process or are there several distinct ways of learning?

Towards 1950, theories such as C. E. Osgood's 'mediation hypothesis' (see R. Thomson, *The Psychology of Thinking*, pp. 121–31) attempted to reconcile Hull with Tolman and both with Gestalt conceptions – smoothing out the extremes. Even so, Osgood's theory cannot be established by unequivocal reference to experimental data. The problems themselves may not be as important as they appeared to the experimental psychologists of this period. Nevertheless, even if the situations are far from being free of ambiguity, the research covered a great deal of ground and enabled psychologists to discover in general terms just what animals can do. The over-simplifications of the dominant Behaviourist theories were at least challenged and modified by the experiments of Tolman, Lashley, Krechevsky and others. Behaviourism began to find the old S–R formula of Watson and Guthrie inadequate to deal with the complex situations of animal problem-solving. After the Second World War, new approaches to the study of animal-learning were made and the clear-cut outlines of the earlier literature on 'learning operations and learning theory' (so neatly structured round conditioning experiments and the Hull–Tolman controversies) became displaced.

The whole of this enterprise (involving large laboratories, animal houses and keepers, the publication of thousands of articles and many books) constitutes a subject matter on its own. It is very much 'pure science', divorced from any of the human interests of the period, or the requirements of human societies. If only for this reason, it deserves a place as an example of a dominant interest of academic experimental and theoretical psychology between 1920 and 1950.

THE HIGHER MENTAL FUNCTIONS
Remembering

As early as 1885, Ebbinghaus had produced the first experimental study of remembering (p. 75). It was remarkably successful in making a number of discoveries about remembering and forgetting, and it established a tradition in this field which was closely followed by most researchers for the next forty years. In spite of its positive contributions, the Ebbinghaus method of studying the recall of nonsense-syllable lists had its limitations. It derived from an over-simplified conception of memory as the storing-away of data and the bringing out of storage certain items for use when needed.

F. C. Bartlett, Professor of Psychology at Cambridge University, conducted research into 'real life' recall situations occurring in the First World War and throughout the 1920s, and an account of it was published in *Remembering* (1932). Although lacking the precision of Ebbinghaus's work, with its standardized procedures, Bartlett's book revealed new facts, and made psychologists take an entirely different overall view of the function of remembering. Bartlett's researches, mainly qualitative experiments illustrating the distortion of data in recall, rejected the 'storehouse' model of memory. People do not passively record what is presented to them; they select and interpret in terms of present attitudes and interests. Nor, in recall, is the original data simply reinstated. It is treated to a process of selection, modification and construction in relation to the context of recall and the subject's activities at the time. In the intervening period, whatever is 'stored' has not remained unchanged, but has assimilated elements from on-going experience. 'Remembering is not the re-excitation of innumerable fixed, lifeless and fragmentary traces. It is an imaginary reconstruction, or construction, built out of our attitude towards a whole active mass of past experience' (p. 213).

Bartlett used the term 'schemata' to indicate groups of related concepts built up from our past experience. These are active, cumulative organizations which assimilate new information. Not only do schemata absorb new relevant experiences: they affect the way we interpret the events we meet. It is in terms of such schemata that we recall our past, and in doing so we construct a present image out of fragmentary data in the light of present attitudes and needs.

Bartlett demonstrated the extent to which the activity of recalling a past situation is 'inaccurate' and 'reconstructed' in terms of developing schemata. We interpret what we recall in terms of present interests and attitudes, and also in terms of *accumulated* past experiences. The fragmentary stored datum is related to dynamic, changing schemata, so that recall is a constructive, active process and no mere inspection or reinstatement of a 'copy' image of a past experience.

Bartlett gave his experimental subjects a picture, story or prose passage to learn. He tested reproduction by making subjects recall the original data at intervals – a week, a month, six months. With variations in the 'repeated reproduction' method, Bartlett traced the ways in which the original material was altered. If there were short intervals (for example, if the subject was tested every week over several months), the material rapidly approximated to a fixed form – although simplified and altered. If long intervals occurred between tests, the material continued to be transformed almost indefinitely. Interpretation occurs in both forms. The subject reacts to the original interpretation in terms of some specific schemata. If he has to recall a face presented with a square jaw, he may think 'that is a determined and grim face'. The jaw becomes a symbol for determination, and the face, originally presented full, may be recalled as if in profile so that the jaw-line is emphasized. Other details are omitted, and the concept of 'firmness' may lead to added details, the eye, mouth, etc. being of the type associated with strength and perseverance. The initial schemata structures all subsequent recalled material. Rationalization also occurs, connecting what was not related in the original data, simplifying in terms of some dominating 'idea'. The individual always contributes much to what is reproduced.

The Gestalt school contributed to the changed attitude towards remembering. Koffka (in Chapters 10 and 11 of *Gestalt Psychology*) puts forward a theory of remembering supported by experimental data from Köhler, Lauenstein and Von Restorff. It is a trace-theory: 'The temporal dimension of experience is transformed into spatial dimensions within the brain field and is thereby rendered interpretable by the same principles that apply to perception.' The theory is complex and controversial, but the data supplied in the experiments led to two widely accepted generalizations:

(a) Remembering cannot be a simple, isolated function of the brain. Like perceiving, learning and thinking, it is an abstracted aspect of a complex and dynamic activity involving the whole personality.
(b) A human being, as a dynamic unity, is in a constant state of change. His motivation changes and shifts, and acts of recall and recognition are part of a much more complex dynamic and changing situation.

The view that remembering is the selection of an image or concept out of storage for inspection or reinstatement was demolished by the work of Bartlett, Köhler and other experimentalists during the period under review. A further reinforcement in this direction came from the clinical work of Freud and his associates. 'Repression' was seen during the 1920s as a defensive strategy, whereby a person develops a 'set' not to remember a particular event. Recall might arouse painful emotions or stir up a conflict between incompatible tendencies to react. Here, complex motivational reactions affect capacity to recall, and remembering is shown to be part of a complicated dynamic situation involving the total person.

In addition to these new approaches to remembering, much experimental work along more traditional lines was done. Various quantitative methods for measuring the amount of retention were investigated. C. W. Luh ('The Conditions of Retention', *Psychological Monographs,* 1922) compared four different indices of retention. The analysis of his results showed conclusively that each method measures something different, and that no method of measurement does more than evaluate a part of a complex of skills involved in learning-and-recall – even when nonsense syllables are the materials used. Other experiments (e.g. J. A. McGeoch and A. W. Melton, *Journal of Experimental Psychology* 1929) showed how learning different tasks (learning nonsense syllables as compared with tracing a maze blindfold with a finger) makes for different conditions of learning and recall. The topic of 'remembering' gave psychologists the opportunity to display the greater sophistication and flexibility of experimental design and technique available since the First World War. The scope of experimental psychology was increasing, and the variety of problems amenable to investigation was far greater than in the days of Stumpf and Titchener.

In no field of investigation was this more evident than in experiments on thinking.

Thinking

After the experiments of the Würzburg group, the investigation of thinking centred largely upon 'problem-solving'. These studies had their origin partly in the work of Thorndike and partly in the writings of John Dewey (pp. 149 ff.). Dewey's book *How We Think* (published in 1911) pointed out that we do not think as long as things run along smoothly. Habit, impulse and well-practised skills help us to adjust in much of our work and play. It is only when routine is disrupted by the intrusion of an obstacle or difficulty that we are forced to stand back and think what to do. The troublesome problem-situation can be either transformed or avoided by action. Not all thinking results in overt behaviour; sometimes we inhibit all activity and postpone tackling the difficulty. 'Thinking', however, is covert, symbolic activity imposed by circumstances and is a complex reaction to environmental factors. This view proved attractive to experimental psychologists, who could arrange to form problem situations in the laboratory and observe their subjects reacting to them.

The first task was to provide descriptions of typical problem-solving behaviour. Can activities be described in terms of the 'methods' which organize responses into means-end patterns? How is behaviour structured, and in response to what environmental variables? On these problems the Gestalt school did much experimental work.

Wertheimer's contributions during this period did not appear until his book *Productive Thinking* was published posthumously in 1945, although his pupils benefited from the work. One pupil, however, Karl Duncker, published a celebrated monograph *Zur Psychologie des produktiven Denkens* (*On Problem-Solving*) in 1935. Duncker gave his subjects a series of mathematical, logical and practical problems and instructed them to speak what they were thinking. An account of each subject's strivings was recorded and the reports analysed. The problems were such as to leave little scope for idiosyncratic methods – there was a 'correct' solution, and the subject had to take specific steps to discover it. Duncker was concerned with heuristic methods common to different subjects, and with gross environmental factors which either facilitated or inhibited the acquisition of the right moves. In mathematical problems, the objective was to analyse the data so as to define the basic propositions from which deductions follow to establish the theorem constituting the 'problem'. The extrapolation of the steps from premises to conclusion is then a matter of routine. With practical problems, the subject often had to analyse the goal, defining the requirements which had to be worked out in order to reach it. Impracticable or irrelevant moves had to be avoided and misleading presuppositions exposed.

Duncker identified what he called 'functional fixedness' as a common snare. For example, if, in constructing apparatus, a subject is looking for an object to serve as a holder for a pin, he may not realize that a cork would serve his purpose if it is performing its usual function as the stopper in a bottle. If the cork is left lying on the bench apart from the bottle, subjects are more likely to see it as a possible holder, since its usual function is not so obviously suggested. Again, if subjects are given six matches and told to construct four equilateral triangles having one match for each side, they find this difficult to achieve. They assume that the triangles should lie in a plane on the surface of the table. But in fact a tetrahedron solves the problem, there being no principle ruling out a three-dimensional model.

Duncker was interested in finding what features of the problem-situation tend to encourage 'functional fixedness' and what arrangements are required to overcome this tendency. Thus the question was raised: 'How do specific types of difficulty affect behaviour?' Fixation difficulties provided an interesting category to investigate. Some fixations appeared to depend on the perceptual characteristics of the data or on the conceptual characteristics of the goal state. Other fixations seemed more dependent upon 'personality' variables, specific habits, attitudes or assumptions due to prior learning. Other difficulties were primarily associated with the behaviour required – the operations involved in working out the steps to be taken – and here 'interpolation' or 'extrapolation' or 'analytic' thinking each seemed to involve special snares.

N. R. F. Maier of Michigan University carried out experiments to determine the role of 'set' on problem-solving behaviour. He began with Duncker's finding that subjects often fail to solve a problem by persisting with a stereotyped mode of attack, without asking whether it is practicable or not. How rigid are such blockages? Presumably, if some 'direction' or 'hint' is provided simply to vary methods, and if subjects respond effectively to such aids, the 'set' is stimulated by the characteristics of the data. Maier therefore gave a series of problems both to a control group (who simply were set the problems) and to an experimental group, who were given instructions to vary their mode of attack. The results were not satisfactory. In only one problem did the experimental group perform more efficiently than the control.

In a further set of experiments, Maier substituted demonstrations of 'part-solutions' for verbal warnings to the experimental group, and in this case the experimental group benefited markedly from the 'directions'.

It was from this early work that many investigations of *Einstellung* effects in problem-solving derived. *Einstellung* is supposed to be a 'determining tendency' which influences associations. It originates in a specific task and generalizes to other tasks of a similar kind. It was suggested that practice at a certain kind of problem forms an *Einstellung* which organizes future methods of working. In some cases a negative transfer might result, and subjects fail to adjust to differences in new task-requirements. A whole literature of experiments developed, centred on the attempt to study this elusive type of 'attitude', and culminating in the celebrated monograph by A. S. Luchins, *The Mechanization of Problem Solving* (1942).

Not all studies were centred on such inhibitory factors as 'functional fixedness', 'set' or *Einstellung* effect. In particular, Wertheimer attempted to define some of the positive aids to successful problem-solving, although his concepts of 'restructuring' of data and of 'resonance' were somewhat ambiguous. These experiments owed much to the Functionalist and Gestalt ideas about the scope of psychology, and if they were qualitative experiments the results of which were not precise, at least they served to broaden the scope of experiment.

Another type of investigation was into 'concept formation'. How do human beings acquire basic categories in terms of which perceptual data is interpreted? Hull's study of 1920 assumed that concepts are formed through abstracting common features from a large number of particulars. He showed his subjects a series of twelve packs of cards, each card having a complex Chinese character. Nonsense-syllables were attached to a particular prominent element in different configurations, and the subjects had to learn which characters were called 'oo' or the like. Hull found that the learning of the nonsense syllables on the basis of a common visual sign was typical of discrimination learning.

Smoke argued, in 1932, that such concepts are learned on the basis of common perceptual relations. He presented his subjects with a series of geometrical figures associated with nonsense-syllables. All circles with two dots were 'dax', all other circles were not; 'mib' was a triangle with a line extending at right angles from its shortest side. Thus, common relations and *not* recurring identical elements were the basis for Smoke's artificial concepts. Whether such studies are investigations of concept-formation, or studies in perceptual discrimination-learning, is an open question. Nevertheless, they were fashionable and provided scope for another attempt to investigate cognitive processes experimentally.

Experimental psychology was a thriving discipline between the two wars, and many different 'fields' were explored. For example, psychophysical experiments continued to flourish. The work of S. S. Stevens and J. Volkman culminated in a study (*American Journal of Psychology*, 1940) in which they successfully investigated the dependence of pitch upon frequency for the purpose of erecting a scale by which pitch, as a perceived aspect of tones, could be measured. Their resulting scale (in mels) was used to measure the subjective size of musical intervals, such as octaves and fifths. They demonstrated that the pitch extent corresponding to a given interval varies with the frequency-region in which the interval occurs. Thus, octaves and fifths increase in subjective size as we go up the musical scale to about the fourth octave above middle C. They also demonstrated that frequencies separated by equal intervals of pitch excite the basilar membrane at points of approximate equi-distant separation – an important physiological discovery. Thus psychophysics continued to make progress.

Another traditional topic, transfer of training, was also a popular subject for investigation. Steady progress was made and earlier work corrected and amplified.

However, it was the sensory processes, perception and learning that were the main interests of experimental psychologists during this period, and the majority of important publications fell within the scope of these fields.

CHAPTER EIGHTEEN

The Development of Tests 1918–40

THE intelligence test had been firmly established as a new instrument of psychological research with the publication of the Binet–Simon scales of 1905 and 1911, and by the early tests of Charles Spearman in England (see Chapter 8). However, it is doubtful if mental tests would have become such a prominent feature of psychological research in the 1920s had not the Americans quickly seized on the new techniques and made considerable use of them after the entry of the U.S.A. into the First World War in 1917. The obvious success of the application of tests in the U.S. Army convinced not only academic psychologists but also politicians and businessmen that psychology had techniques which were worth encouraging with grants for research.

The great period of the 'test' began only after the war, although the pioneer work of Galton, Cattell, Binet and Thorndike had been well done. The earliest Binet–Simon scale had been translated into English shortly after publication by Lewis M. Terman (1877–1956), who had taken a Ph.D. at Clark University under Stanley Hall. Terman had been a schoolmaster in country schools and did his Ph.D. thesis on the subject of 'mental tests' in the years 1904–5.

In 1910, after a further period of teaching, he went to Stanford University, where he began a thorough research project into the new Binet–Simon Scale. Using 2,300 schoolchildren, Terman tried out modifications on the scale – dropping some items, introducing new ones, modifying others; he assigned many items to different age-levels from those chosen by Binet, and carefully correlated his revised tests with external criteria of ability. In 1916 he published the results of his work in *The Measurement of Intelligence.* This made a considerable impact on American psychologists. His revised 'Stanford–Binet Scale' was a greatly improved version of Binet's 1911 scale and was the basis for the applications of intelligence tests in the U.S.A.

When America entered the war in 1917, R. M. Yerkes (pp. 160 ff.) was asked to organize American psychologists to assist the military authorities in whatever ways they could. The result was a highly efficient organization, which conducted research into the use of tests in helping the military to select personnel and devised new, highly successful tests. The objectives of the scheme were to segregate the mentally incompetent, to grade recruits according to general ability, and to select competent men to train for positions of responsibility. By December 1917, 31,520 men had been tested. Low-grade individuals were either discharged or drafted into units engaged in manual labour of a simple kind; incompetent officers were either discharged or given simple tasks; men of high intelligence or with specific abilities were sent for specialist training. Also, the reactions of some subjects suggested instability and unsuitable recruits of this sort were eliminated after psychiatric examination. A rapid and reliable method of sorting out thousands of recruits was thus available. In the end, 1,750,000 men were tested; 8,000 were discharged, 10,000 were sent to 'labouring' battalions and 10,000 selected for special training.

Two tests were devised: the Army Alpha (for literates) and Beta (for illiterates). In preliminary trials, groups of students, high-school children and officer-cadets were used to validate the A-tests; while patients in homes for the mentally defective were used for B-tests. The test scores on the new tests were checked against Stanford–Binet test scores, school work record, estimates by teachers. Correlations between A-test and various external criteria varied from ·5 to ·8. The A-test had items testing ability to follow instructions accurately, arithmetic, synonym-autonym recognition, number series completion, analogies, scrambled sentences and general knowledge. The items were arranged progressively in order of difficulty, and time limits were set to prevent all but the fastest class of worker from finishing. Five forms of the particular test were constructed. The B-test involved maze-drawing tests, cube analysis, digit symbols, picture completion, geometric constructions, etc., designed to test native ability rather than school knowledge. They were steeply graded in difficulty, so that there were easy items for the average person but difficult tests for the intellectually able. The scoring was simple, rapid, objective; the answers were brief and straightforward, so that ambiguity in marking was avoided.

The result of this work, published by Yerkes in 1921 in *Psychological Testing in U.S. Army* (National Academy of Sciences Memoirs, Vol. XV), was to put intelligence testing on the map as a technique which could be trusted to achieve its objectives. The governments of the Allied powers became interested in employing psychologists to help with education and civil-service selection. Industrialists realized that psychology had an applied and practical aspect that could assist in the personnel side of industry. Universities were prepared to support research into the possibilities of extending the scope of psychological tests.

Thus, the work of Binet and Simon, Terman and Spearman had achieved a workable set of scales for comparing the general ability of individuals with respect to tasks requiring mental agility and accuracy. In the 1920s Terman, now head of the Stanford psychology school, carried out extensive research on testing. The National Intelligence Test, the Terman Group Test of Mental Ability and the Standard Achievement Test were the result. A group of able psychologists grew up at Stanford largely interested in developing intelligence tests, studying gifted children and defectives, and developing tests for assessing individual differences in personality. In 1937 Terman, with his colleague Merrill, published a further revision of the Binet–Simon scale. They retained the basic age-scale arrangement, provided two forms of the test, and extended its range to cover a mental age measurement of two years to twenty-two. The construction and standardization were the result of massive and patient work based on a very large sample. The test was used widely in the U.S.A. and elsewhere to select entrants for higher education and for jobs requiring high intelligence. It answered a need for a quick, efficient and reliable means of testing large numbers of individuals, and follow-up studies demonstrated that it worked well in practice.

In Great Britain test-construction and validation flourished. Spearman continued to be an active figure in the years between the wars. His *Nature of Intelligence and the Principles of Cognition* (1923) and his *Abilities of Man* (1927) were theoretical works, but his pupils produced a flow of empirical results. Twelve out of the first twenty of the Monograph Supplements to the *British Journal of Psychology* were by his research pupils. When he retired in 1931, his successor in the chair of psychology at University College, London, was Cyril Burt.

As we have seen, Burt had been a pupil of McDougall's at Oxford. In 1909 he had published an article 'Experimental Tests of General Intelligence' (*British Journal of Psychology*). He did research into the measurement of intelligence at Liverpool (1907–12), and was then appointed psychologist to the London County Council in 1912 – the first full-time applied psychologist in Britain. His work was original and distinguished. Although Yerkes and the Americans first exploited the written group test in the First World War, it was Burt who had earlier devised it. He worked out tests using analogies, sentence-formation, syllogisms, reasoning, and other items which have become standard. His research activity in constructing new tests and adapting existing ones while working as an educational psychologist culminated in his book *Mental and Scholastic Tests* (1923). This includes not only a revision of the Binet–Simon scale, but special tests for educational attainment in reading, spelling, composition, arithmetic and other basic subjects. Burt disagreed with Spearman on the interpretation of tests. He did not believe that the test scores measured a general factor 'disturbed' by specific factors, the influence of which the test must iron out. He regarded human ability as functioning at different levels: sensory-motor; perceptual; associative; relational. Furthermore, he regarded factors in terms of which basic ability is analysed as logical constructs rather than causal agents: factors serve simply to classify the correlations consistently reached between the scores on different tests.

The idea that Spearman's single-factor method of explaining test results was wrong, and that correlations should be explained in terms of several factors, was put forward by L. L. Thurstone (1887–1955) of Chicago University. His classical books *The Measurement of Intelligence* (1925) and *Multiple Factor Analysis* (1947) introduced a new technique for constructing tests of intelligence. Thurstone introduced 'factor analysis' – the statistical analysis of postulated factors determining performance in a series of different tests – into research in mental testing. (As clear an explanation of this technique as any is given by R. D. Tuddenham in 'The Nature and Measurement of Intelligence', which he contributed to Leo Postman's *Psychology in the Making*, 1963).

Multiple factor-analysis techniques proved stimulating in so far as new specific dimensions admitting of measurement were suggested. Thurstone's Tests of Primary Mental Abilities were widely used in the 1930s. Seven primary abilities were involved in measuring 'intelligence': verbal comprehension, word fluency, number manipulation, space visualization, associative memory, perceptual speed and logical reasoning. The PMA battery yielded separate scores for most of the factors, thus providing a much more complex description of the individual's ability than a single-score test. There were different versions for different age groups.

Factorial-analysis testers claimed that they were isolating the basic 'powers' or 'faculties' of the mind – primary source traits or basic abilities. However, not everyone could accept this claim. Godfrey Thomson criticized this view in his *Factorial Analysis of Human Ability* (1939). He was Professor of Educational Psychology at Edinburgh for many years and a research worker of outstanding ability in the field of mental testing. Thomson argued that it is not in virtue of any psychological laws, but simply as a result of the laws of chance that it is possible to analyse ability into a few common factors. The mind works as if it *were* so composed. Our ability to solve a set of tests depends on a wide range of variables – inherited genes, acquired information, well-exercised skills, habits of thought. Thus, correlation coefficients between performances in tests will tend to show the same relationships with each other that they would have done had ability been the result of a number of common 'factors' (plus specifics). We may have such 'factors', and they may have a neurological basis. But on the other hand we may not; the postulation of factors is purely speculative and hypothetical. The 'sampling theory' was never a dominant one, although many psychologists seem to have been attracted by its commonsense.

The result of this work in theorizing, constructing and validating tests was that intelligence tests became widely used – by those wanting to select people for special places, to detect subnormal individuals, or to predict performance. Educationalists, industrialists, clinical workers and the military all used psychologists to test personnel.

Moreover, research moved in new directions. If general intelligence could be successfully assessed, why not other human traits and characteristics? The psycho-analytic movement and its derivative schools made the study of the human personality from the orectic point of view (the functioning of emotions, sentiments, attitudes, desires) an important aspect of psychological inquiry. It was natural that psychometric techniques should be thus extended, though the testing of personality proved to be a more controversial matter.

Some psychologists have believed that traits, attitudes, etc., can be analysed, defined and subjected to psychometric techniques of assessment. Others have argued that 'personality' is so complicated that to break it down into a number of 'factors' for measurement is to caricature and falsify the whole. What is essential in human personality is still missing after the results of factor analysis have been worked out.

The two approaches are evident in different theories of personality which have appeared in the literature of psychology over the past forty or fifty years. An intuitive, clinical, ideographic approach is put forward in G. W. Allport's *Personality* (1937), in H. A. Murray's *Explorations in Personality* (1938), and in Kurt Goldstein's *Human Personality in the Light of Psychopathology* (1940). A strictly analytic and psychometric approach, on the other hand, is advocated by Godfrey H. Thomson, by R. B. Cattell's *Description and Measurement of Personality* (1947), and by H. J. Eysenck's *Dimensions of Personality* (1947), a book which follows in the tradition of the earlier *The Vectors of the Mind* (1935) by Thurstone.

The two approaches are not necessarily opposites or incompatibles. Hypotheses to be investigated and ideas for composing tests come from clinical observations; while clinical judgements can be corrected or amplified by psychometric studies. However, the testing movement in its earlier phases reflected considerable differences in theoretical bias and orientation.

One of the earliest lines of thought was that there might be a correlation between personality traits and physical characteristics. In 1925, E. Kretschmer published *Physique and Character*, in which he stated that in his experience as a clinical psychologist the majority of schizophrenic patients were tall, thin and pale (leptosomes) while the majority of manic-depressives were round, florid and stocky (pyknic). He thought that normal people were extended along a similar scale. 'Schizothymics' tended to be quiet, sensitive and reserved while 'pyknics' or 'cyclothymics' tended to be genial, sociable and emotionally labile.

Later investigations have not confirmed Kretschmer's somewhat ambiguous descriptions. However, his book stimulated research. Cyril Burt in 1938 argued that there was a correlation between introvert–extrovert ratings, and physical distinctions between macrosplanchnic individuals (with predominance of trunk over limbs) and microsplanchnics (with predominance of vertical over horizontal body measures). In 1940, W. H. Sheldon's *The Varieties of Human Physique: An Introduction to Constitutional Psychology* put forward a more elaborate scheme based on a correlation between clinical data and bodily measurements. On his scale, endomorphy (roundness, softness of body build) is correlated with sociable, affectionate, comfort-loving types; mesomorphy (hardness and muscularity) with vigorous, assertive, physically active types; ectomorphy (linear physique with weak visceral and somatic structure) with reserved, mentally active, withdrawn types. Rigorous and extensive studies of these generalizations failed to confirm them, and physical characteristics do not seem to be closely related with personality.

The work done along this line has, however, deflated an ancient hypothesis – going back to medieval psychology and greatly enhanced in the early nineteenth century by the popular craze for phrenology – that physical characteristics (facial physique, body build, skull formation, etc.) are clues to temperament and character.

Instead of pursuing this traditional conception, psychologists concentrated in the 1920s and 1930s on four main types of personality test: (1) Ratings and judgements of a person by people who know him well; (2) self-ratings; (3) assessment of basic attitudes and interests; (4)

'projective techniques'. Let us consider briefly each of these in turn.

RATINGS OF PERSONALITY

Galton appears to have first conceived such tests and was the originator of the first rating scales (Chapter 5). As we have seen, the U.S. Army investigations under Yerkes in 1917 used questionnaires in which observers were required to rate trainee officers in order of merit for specific traits, such as 'leadership', 'quickness of reaching a decision', etc. From these beginnings innumerable tests were developed in the years after the First World War. Their aim was simply to elicit opinions and judgements on a person, and convert these into numerical estimates of his basic traits. This work was useful if only because all sorts of techniques for constructing, validating and correcting psychological tests emerged.

It was soon discovered, for example, that raters tend to err in idealizing one or two traits and interpreting all of a person's characteristics in the light of these – the 'halo' effect. Thus, if X is regarded as 'jovial' and 'friendly', all of his characteristics will be said to be sociable and amiable – whatever his actual characteristics. Such ratings therefore lack objectivity, and a large number of ratings of a given personality are required in the attempt to diminish and estimate error. Ratings can only be a contributory source of information about a person. However, the techniques developed to make such ratings of some practical use in assessment have justified the whole venture.

C. L. Hull, the Yale psychologist eminent in learning theory (pp. 237 ff.), developed a 'paired comparison' technique. Here, the rater is given every possible pair in a group of, say, 40 people, and asked to judge which of each pair is the higher in a specific trait ('dependability', for example). Hull's tables convert the rankings into normally distributed scores (*Aptitude Testing*, 1928). It is possible to combine or average raters whose rankings produce different results.

In 1923, Max Freyd published his Graphic Rating Scale, in which each step was defined as concretely as possible. Instead of trying to assess in terms of a quantitative scale or apply some standard, the rater simply answers a question (for instance, 'Does X need stimulating or does he go forward with his work without being directed?') by ticking one or other of a number of possible replies, ranging from 'Needs much stimulation' to 'Seeks and sets additional work for himself'. Several questions can be set for each 'trait', and the rater is not required to think in terms of abstractions such as 'initiative'.

These were only the beginnings of numerous devices for improving the reliability of rating scales which research in test-construction produced. Relative ratings were found to be better than absolute ratings. If a rater is told to put all his subjects in four grades, A (top 10 per cent), D (bottom 10 per cent), with grade B and grade C taking the rest, greater agreement can be reached than if all the individuals are compared in absolute rank-order. Graphic scales like Freyd's produce better results than those in which individuals have to be graded according to a numerical 'mark' or letter-scale. Traits should be defined concretely and unambiguously – and so forth.

SELF-RATINGS

It is only to be expected that an individual's rating of his own traits tends to be inaccurate – the result of aspirations and ideals rather than objective appraisals. However, psychologists wanted to know how an individual sees himself as a person and to elicit genuine self-appraisals. Most of the tests appear to derive from three prototypes: R. S. Woodworth's Personal Data Sheet (1920), the Freyd–Heidbreder Introversion–Extraversion Test (1924 and 1926), and G. W. and F. H. Allport's Ascendance–Submission Reaction (1928).

Woodworth selected 116 items derived from psychiatric descriptions of neurotic symptoms. He constructed direct questions requiring a 'Yes' or 'No' reply, such as 'Did you have a happy childhood?'; 'Do you know anybody who is trying to do you harm?'; 'Does it make you uneasy to cross a bridge over a river?' Thurstone's *Personality Schedule* (1929) contains most of Woodworth's items. Thurstone correlated the scores of a large number of subjects with clinical data available for each subject, and drew up percentile norms for the test.

The Freyd–Heidbreder test simply aims at classifying subjects on the Jungian introvert-extravert dimension. Questions are designed to discover to what extent the subject day-dreams, prefers reading rather than activity, keeps in the background or enters into social occasions, etc.

The Allport study attempts to elicit responses on concrete items which are supposed to manifest ascendant or submissive tendencies. A typical question is: 'A salesman takes trouble to show you a quantity of merchandise. You are not suited. Do you find it difficult to say "No"?' The subject chooses one of a number of set answers: 'Yes, as a rule'/'Sometimes'/'No'.

One of the most widely used tests was S. R. Hathaway's and J. C. McKinley's Minnesota Multiphasic Personality Inventory (MMPI). In this, 550 statements are presented on separate cards which the subject sorts into one of three boxes labelled 'TRUE', 'FALSE' and 'CANNOT SAY'. The statements relate to basic interests, social attitudes and emotional traits. The tests were constructed with 500 normal subjects and 800 patients in mental hospitals as experimental aides. The scores were correlated with objective data about each subject's interests, attitudes and emotional dispositions; and certain 'profile' scores seemed closely associated with normality, hysterical syndrome, paranoid tendencies. In 60 per cent of the cases the test interpretations agreed closely with psychiatric diagnoses. Hence the test was developed as a method of diagnosis – sorting people into normal or abnormal with considerable reliability, and to a lesser extent suggesting the *sort* of abnormality which mentally disturbed subjects might have.

How accurate and useful were these early personality questionnaires? Psychologists were anxious to evaluate their tests as critically as possible. Articles by R. B. Smith in *Archives of Psychology* (1932) and R. T. Stetto in the *American Sociological Review* (1936) reported studies in which it was evident that most subjects tend to react to questions which imply the existence of socially unfavourable traits or reactions with defensive or hostile attitudes. They were unlikely to admit that such characteristics applied to them. Items which implied socially acceptable characteristics provoked a greater variety of response. They also demonstrated that different tests for measuring the same trait, given to subjects on different occasions, had poor agreement. In 1946, A. Ellis ('The Validity of Personality Questionnaires', *Psychological Bulletin*, 1946) provided an even more rigorous study of the difficulties in eliminating the influence of subjects' attitudes to the test as a test, or controlling 'halo' effects. However, it seems generally agreed that, with all their known weaknesses, such questionnaires – if used with due caution and in combination with other data – can be of some use in collecting information.

MEASUREMENT OF ATTITUDES AND INTERESTS

Techniques which worked badly in attempts to elicit emotional dispositions seemed to be more successful when applied to social attitudes and opinions and to basic interests. Whether individuals are conservative or radical in political outlook, are religious or sceptical, or are strongly nationalistic, can be assessed. More deep-seated attitudes, sentiments or complexes seemed less accessible to testing – defence strategies might be too well organized to allow them expression. On fairly general attitudes most subjects can be assessed. In testing for a person's attitude towards religion, such questions as the following help to place him on a scale: 'Do you belong formally to any denomination?' 'How many times a year do you attend a service?' 'How many religious books have you read in the last twelve months?' 'Do you accept completely dogma "X"?' From a large number of such questions it might be possible to rate a person as strongly, averagely, weakly, pro or con religious beliefs and practices.

Thurstone's Scales for the Measurement of Social Attitudes (1930) attempted to assess attitudes towards war, Negroes, communism, capital punishment, etc. H. H. Remmer's Attitude Scales (1934) were designed to assess children's attitudes towards various school subjects (algebra, modern languages, etc.). In all these tests, statements expressing an attitude are presented, and the subject ticks those with which he agrees. In the questionnaires of T. F. Lenz (1935) and G. B. Vetter (1938), the subjects select any one of about six answers to a given question or statement. These multiple-choice tests may be contrasted with the Thurstone-type scales. It is not difficult to analyse results so that an individual's answers are placed on a scale with the average set of attitudes in the middle and opposite extremes at either end. The difficulty with such tests proved to be the wording and selection of statements or questions, which were usually based on a variety of sources such as newspapers, essays, conversations or talks on radio – samples of real-life judgements expressing a specific attitude towards a given topic or institution. Once selected, items were usually assessed by a group of judges who rated each item for favourableness or unfavourableness towards the subject. Thurstone had an elaborate system for scaling each item, so that extremes were avoided and the items selected were not so middling as to fail to elicit variations in response on one side or the other.

In evaluating individual differences in a person's 'interests', E. K. Strong's Vocational Interest Blank (1927) attempted to construct a test on the basis of an interesting research programme. Strong attempted to discover the basic likes and dislikes of representatives of several occupations with reference to a large number of miscellaneous items (420 altogether). Groups of doctors, architects, schoolteachers, farmers, etc., were given a questionnaire. Typical patterns for each occupational group were extracted, and this provided a 'key' for each profession. That is, individuals who on the Interest Blank produced a pattern of scores typical of, say, the schoolteaching profession were regarded as having 'interests' suitable for that occupation. For instance, if a subject's score falls within 75 per cent of an occupational group he gets a top-rating for this occupation. In situations in which a candidate is seeking vocational guidance and wants to know what occupations he is most likely to find congenial, such tests have some use, since the candidate is likely to be truthful and careful in his answers. For selecting candidates for training, however, such tests have proved unreliable.

PROJECTIVE TECHNIQUES

Freud's concept of 'projection', a defensive strategy whereby a person defends himself, unconsciously, against repressed material by attributing his hidden wishes or emotions to other people, was the inspiration of a new type of personality test. Gestalt theory, with its emphasis on the totality of a personality, was another influence.

Some psychologists regarded tests of specific, isolated traits as too limited. They felt the need to be able to evaluate the human person as a whole in a 'test' situation. Thus, tests using projective techniques are totally different from most other mental tests. While they do not measure specific variables and are therefore non-quantitative, lacking in controls, and liable to individual differences of interpretation, it has been claimed on their behalf that they allow better opportunities for individual differences to emerge unrestricted by self-conscious, critical attitudes and the exact 'structuring' of tests involving statements or questions. Jung's Word Association Test (1918) was probably the first to use a projective technique. However, the two most influential were the Rorschach Test and the TAT (Thermatic Apperception Test).

From 1921 onwards, the Swiss psychiatrist H. Rorschach devised and improved a series of tests which began from his chance observation that patients looking at ink blots, or other ambiguous or meaningless configurations, often reported seeing different objects in them. He argued from this that patients – and normal subjects – react to such ambiguous stimuli by projecting their attitudes and complexes in their 'interpretations' of the shapes. He decided to attempt to construct a test to evaluate such reactions. He gave trial tests to a large number of patients, and interpreted their reactions partly in the light of clinical data, partly in terms of Jung's theories of neurosis and psychosis. From this he developed a set of 'ink blots' and methods for scoring reactions to them.

In the Rorschach test, the subject is presented with the ambiguous shapes and encouraged to produce as many free associations as possible. His statements are recorded and his reactions described by the testers. After the completion of the test, the subject is asked to elucidate his remarks. The test is scored under three headings: (1) Mode of apperception. Did the subject react to the whole shape, to ordinary details or to unusual details? (2) The determinant. Did the subject react to the shape aptly or in some unusual way? Did his responses imply movement in the configuration, or did he see it as static? How did he react to coloured parts? (3) Content. Was his reaction commonplace or original? Was the shape architectural, geographical, animal, human, etc.?

Numerous rules were worked out for scoring and interpreting the 'profile' on the tests. Since no category or trait is considered in isolation, it has been difficult to assess the test for validity or reliability, but it has proved immensely popular. In 1937 a Rorschach Research Exchange was established to coordinate information and results of research, and a journal was founded devoted to researches with the test. In 1950, Sen reported a factorial study in which three main components (associative fluency, intelligence and neuroticism) seemed to emerge from various scorings. Correlations of approximately 0·5 were obtained between these three 'factors' and independent ratings by clinical observers. In spite of its ambiguous character, the test, if used by trained and skilled investigators, appears to have validity in the differential diagnosis of mental patients. This, after all, was its original purpose. As a method of making predictions or assessments about normal people it seems much more dubious.

The Thematic Apperception Test (TAT) was published in 1935 by Morgan and Murray. Pictures and photographs were presented to the subjects. Each was asked to make up a story describing the situation and the events leading to it. They were also asked to suggest the thoughts and emotions of the people in the pictures. The subject was encouraged to identify himself with these people and thus project needs, frustrations and conflicts on to the dynamic test-materials.

The interpretation of the results of this test presented considerable difficulties. Cyril Burt devised a scheme in terms of level of organization (coherence), degree of observation of detail, verbal fluency and introversion–extraversion categories, whereby the results could be scored. R. Harrison (*Journal of Psychology*, 1943) argued that the interpretation of the same test result by different testers was reasonably consistent in his researches; also he claimed that the interpretations matched independent clinical data reasonably well. Like the Rorschach test, the various TATs have developed over the years into useful supplementary methods for diagnosing psychological disorders – differentiating neurotics from normal subjects, and suggesting which syndromes fit each individual case.

These tests of ability and personality-characteristics, constructed and assessed by research and applied to large numbers of people, were a new development in psychology. Quite apart from the fact that they provided psychological tests for use in education, mental hospitals and clinics, or industry, they led to the development of new techniques and skills in psychological research. It was not so much in the administration and scoring of tests but in the research in construction and validating them that progress was most profitably made. The research techniques involved testing the adequacy of tests actually constructed. A test must be valid to a certain degree – it must measure or assess objectively what it sets out to evaluate either quantitatively or qualitatively. If it is valid, its diagnostic or predictive interpretations will square with independent judgements. Thus, if a set of test results suggest that X is neurotic with a bias towards hysterical symptoms, the test is valid if psychiatric interviews, observations of the person in hospital, examination of detailed case-history, and psychotherapeutic treatments all arrive at a similar diagnosis. An intelligence test which gives X a high I.Q. is valid if X passes a large number of school and university examinations with a high grade, is assessed by teachers who know him intimately as one of their brightest pupils, and is then successful in a career demanding 'brains'. The external criteria confirm the test prediction. Psychologists had to devise accurate methods for assessing the validity and reliability of tests.

The business of selecting specific items for inclusion in a test was partly a matter of judgement and partly an empirical matter of seeing how well the item correlated with objective criteria; but statistical skills were also involved. Much work by statisticians had preceded the test movement in psychology. G. D. Yule's *An Introduction to the Theory of Statistics* (first edition 1912) made available quite sophisticated techniques. In the 1920s and 30s psychologists working in the field of psychometrics developed statistical methods, and adapted them for their own purposes with considerable ingenuity.

The upshot was that, even if tests had their limitations, the precise degree of error involved at each stage of constructing, administering and scoring of tests was known. The research side of testing became a matter of considerable expertise, even when many tests could be used only with caution and in relation to data obtained by other means (clinical observation, interviews, examinations other than tests, etc.). Moreover, the techniques and methods of psychometrics influenced general and experimental psychology. Experimental psychologists became less interested in discovering empirical laws applicable to all, and more sensitive to the range of individual differences. Subjects for experiments were chosen only after careful sampling of traits likely to influence the experimental result; experiments were designed involving an experimental group, subject to special experimental conditions, and a control group, for whom these conditions were removed from the experiment; the use of two groups often produced data in the form of two means, and this involved techniques for discovering whether the difference was significant or not; again, correlation techniques were applied to paired scores, representing changes in a dependent (response) variable in relation to changes in an independent (stimulus) variable – in tests, correlations were usually discoverable between two (or more) sets of dependent variables.

Perhaps the most significant work done on providing a statistical basis for psychometric research was that of R. A. Fisher (1890–1962), a Cambridge-trained mathematician who worked at an agricultural research station in England. Fisher was critical of the existing statistical techniques, however much had been achieved through their application. He saw that many research workers are concerned with small samples. Existing methods of statistical analysis and inference were based on the use of large samples. Fisher's work on exact sampling distributions led to the possibility of treating all the distributions involved in testing 'null hypotheses' – hypotheses to be excluded as accounting for observed data. One application, known as the 'analysis of variance', came to be of great use to psychologists.

However, Fisher's improved statistical techniques did not stand on their intrinsic merits. He was interested in the use of statistics in the design of scientific experiments, and his book *Statistical Methods for Research Workers* (1925) included an analysis of the logical structure of experimental design. Such concepts as randomization and level of significance were introduced, and the social sciences as well as the physical were shown to be capable of employing sophisticated experimental procedures. A further book, *The Design of Experiments* (1935), amplified Fisher's highly original thinking about the wedding of statistical procedure and experimental research. Fisher became Galton Professor at London University in 1933, applying statistics to research in genetics, and from 1943 to 1957 held the chair of Genetics at Cambridge. His methods did not influence psychology until after the Second World War. However, as Hearnshaw has pointed out, R. H. Thouless, the Cambridge psychologist, referred to Fisher in an article in 1932, and used analysis of variance in a study published in 1937. The influence of statistical techniques on experimental psychology was prepared for by the example of psychological testing in the 1920–40 period, when the fundamental research from which tests emerged was based on the most advanced statistical knowledge then available.

It was the testing movement that gave psychology its most characteristic aspect. Ryle argues, in *The Concept of Mind*, that psychology has no subject-matter which is unique to it, resembling geography in this respect. He says that geographers have one activity, however, which is exclusive to geography – the construction of maps – while psychology has no unique psychological techniques. This is not true. The construction (indeed invention), validation and application of various kinds of test has been exclusively an activity of psychologists – or a special branch of psychology. Experimental psychologists may overlap with and borrow the methods of physiologists; social psychologists may often be hardly distinguishable from anthropologists; clinical psychologists may intrude into the preserves of psychiatry; and psychological theory may get entangled with philosophy of mind. Psychometrics, however, has always had an independence from other behaviour sciences which has made the psychologist a separate species of exploratory animal.

CHAPTER NINETEEN

The Rise of Industrial Psychology

BEFORE 1914, attempts had been made to apply psychology to practical problems in industry. Hugo Münsterberg, as we have already seen (pp. 133 ff.), carried out several pioneer studies which were published in 1913 in *Psychology and Industrial Efficiency*. The first 'time-and-motion' study was attempted in 1911 by F. B. Gilbreth, of whom we shall have more to say in this chapter.

However, there were scattered and isolated efforts. It was only during the First World War that psychologists were called in to help with the reorganization of industry and with the armed forces. This work really gave 'industrial psychology' its start and earned its recognition as a promising enterprise.

In Great Britain, the Health of Munition Workers Committee (1915–17) organized much of the earlier research until it was replaced in 1918 by the Industrial Fatigue Board. The Board was required 'to consider and investigate the relation of hours of labour and other conditions of employment, including methods of work, to the production of fatigue, having regard both to industrial efficiency and to the preservation of health among the workers'. Under the guidance of H. M. Vernon, the Board carried out research on the effect on efficiency of different hours of work and different conditions of lighting and ventilation. After the war was over, its work continued. The cotton industry, the iron and steel industry, the boot and shoe industry, the laundry trade, among others, employed the Board to conduct research into problems of health and efficiency. In 1921, for reasons of economy, it was proposed to wind up the Board. However, owing to protests from members of parliament and trade-unionists, its survival was insured as part of the Medical Research

Council. In 1928 it was given the title of the Industrial Health Research Board and continued to do good work for many years.

The work of American psychologists in the war has already been described in Chapter 18. In addition to the application of intelligence tests, several trade tests were used and these were published by J. C. Chapman in 1921. The work of psychologists during the war was sufficiently encouraging for industrial psychology to become an organized profession immediately after the war. In 1921, in England, C. S. Myers (see pp. 183 ff.) founded the National Institute of Industrial Psychology. In the same year, J. M. Cattell (see pp. 137 ff.) in the U.S.A., founded the Psychological Corporation. Both these institutes had a similar function. They were both to carry out psychological research of a kind likely to be applicable in industry, and to carry out specific investigations as consultants at the request of firms or industries. In these early days, the two bodies also had the task of training industrial psychologists in the special skills required for professional practice. London University cooperated with the National Institute by providing a diploma in industrial psychology, which the students of the Institute could take. Soon a journal reporting the general research of industrial psychologists appeared, and the work of the N.I.I.P. became an integral part of psychology in Britain.

In the U.S.A. the Federal Government quickly recognized the value of applied psychology. In 1923 they established the Bureau of Public Personnel Administration in Washington under the guidance of L. L. Thurstone (see pp. 329 ff.). This body was to make psychological assessments in the selection of personnel for all government departments. In 1924 the U.S. Civil Service appointed the first psychologist to work in a state department. American industrialists were quick to follow the lead of the government, and industrial psychologists found it easy to obtain employment.

What work was done in these early days of industrial

psychology? The novelty and success of mental tests encouraged industrial psychologists to apply psychometric techniques on a wide scale – in selecting applicants for jobs, in assessing employees for specific skills required in new trades, in guiding those leaving school and wanting to enter industry.

Another obvious field of inquiry, which developed out of the wartime interest in the problem of fatigue, was into the factors liable to decrease the efficiency, health and safety of workers in specific jobs – lighting, ventilation, temperature, length of shift, etc. Time-and-motion techniques led to the more precise study of posture and movement, the arrangement of tools and materials, the distribution of periods of effort and rest – and to the more detailed 'job analysis' studies, in which descriptions of the skills involved in different tasks were analysed so that selection tests, training methods, design of machinery, organization of factory layout, etc., could be improved in the interests of greater efficiency, comfort and safety. Later, more specifically psychological factors (incentives to work, inter-personal relationships within working groups, grievances, boredom, accident proneness) were investigated, and the field of research and guidance expanded enormously as more and more types of industrial, commercial and military unit employed industrial psychologists to deal with their problems.

In Britain the National Institute of Industrial Psychology, although supported by grants from industrial firms, had nevertheless to earn its living by carrying out fee-earning investigations at the request of customers. Problems of selection of staff, training of skilled apprentices, time-and-motion studies, methods of work, advertising and marketing, personnel-organization, all came its way. Much of the work done became the confidential property of the firm which had engaged the Institute's psychologist. A vocational guidance unit was established under Cyril Burt, and this, under such psychologists as F. M. Earle and Alec Rodger, was to flourish greatly and lead to several major research projects. The journal published by N.I.I.P. from 1922 onwards (since 1958 known as *Occupational Psychology*) provided an outlet for research reports. The other British body – the Industrial Fatigue Research Board (becoming the Industrial Health Research Board in 1929) – also did excellent work. H. M. Vernon, E. G. Chambers, T. Bedford and May Smith were a few of the distinguished psychologists who served it.

At first the influence of the war years was strong – hours of work, environmental factors (light, heat, ventilation, noise), design of machinery in relation to operators, time-and-motion studies, and similar 'ergonomic' projects were the main interests. In the 1930s, the closer connexion with M.R.C. led to studies of mental health in industry – indeed a chair of Medical–Industrial Psychology at the London School of Hygiene was closely associated with this work. However, in spite of the quantity and quality of the work done by N.I.I.P. and I.H.R.B., government departments in Britain did not employ their own psychologists until during and after the Second World War. Nor were many industrial psychologists to be found in industry. There were notable exceptions, such as the Quaker firm of Rowntree's of York, whose psychological department did notable research work in the 1930s. In America, industrial psychologists were employed on a grander and more comprehensive scale. However, what the British lost in amount and spread of effort, they gained in having a more systematized national service for industrial psychology, in which intensive research within selected fields and co-ordination of the work of all applied psychologists in the country made for considerable results with fewer resources.

Much of the work of the earliest investigators was concerned with the use of psychological tests. Also many of the personality tests were used in selecting personnel. In particular, rating scales, such as Freyd's Graphic Rating Scale (p. 334) and Strong's Vocational Interest Blank (p. 338) were widely used. Special tests were constructed and developed for use in industry. Trade-tests designed to measure the skills involved in a specific trade were widely used, so that the best men could be selected for work demanding care and precision. Apprentice tests designed to evaluate the progress being made by learners at different stages of training; proficiency tests to help employers decide whether or not an apprentice was sufficiently skilled to qualify; promotion tests intended to select trained men for more skilled or responsible jobs – all these were designed for a wide range of trades. Other tests for mechanical or clerical aptitude were designed to select school-leavers for training in different occupations. These tests were all limited to specific jobs, often in specific local conditions of work, and so were the result of 'on-the-spot' investigations, made usually at the request of a particular firm or factory. For example, Max Tagg's analysis of engineering skills (1923) led to tests for perception of forms and space, for memory of form and size, motor ability, accuracy of detail, attention and ingenuity in problem-solving. Such tests were usually of considerable validity in selecting good workers and eliminating those lacking skills and aptitude for a specific set of operations.

However, in attempting to select candidates for managerial or overseers' posts, or for salesmanship, industrial psychologists had to rely on modifications of conventional 'personality' tests with poor validity. One result of systematic research (analysis of a number of independent ratings by different individuals) was to cast grave doubts on the usefulness of interviews as a method of selecting people for jobs. Even if tests were of limited value, the traditional method of selection was shown to be even less valid.

The First World War had stimulated interest in the problems of fatigue and efficiency. Factory workers producing munitions were required to work for longer hours than in peace-time and under different conditions. It had been found that production or output was not substantially increased by introducing twelve-hour shifts. The

Industrial Fatigue Research Board established in 1918 set out to study the operation of fatigue-effects on work, and the circumstances in which fatigue is likely to increase. This work continued after the end of the war, in the interests of the health of workers and the attainment of maximum output.

Vernon in 1920 studied the charging of blast-furnaces in iron and steel works. In the same year Elton studied weaving operatives. It was clear from their studies that production per worker fell off towards the end of each shift through fatigue. Experiments in which workers were tested on a 'tape dotting machine' (a) between 9 a.m. and 10 a.m., (b) between 5 p.m. and 6 p.m., revealed that each group tested had over 10–20 per cent more errors in the evening – towards the end of the shift. Accidents also were known to occur more frequently during the later parts of a shift. In the war, the recommendation that shifts should be reduced by two hours was accepted and output increased. Vernon's researches also recommended short rest pauses after $2\frac{1}{2}$ hours of continuous work – one in the middle of the morning shift and one in the middle of the afternoon between lunch-break and going off. This led to a further rise in output. The effect of environment on fatigue and efficiency was also studied during the war and afterwards.

Lighting, heating and ventilation were found to have an effect on the worker. Careful studies of the brightness needed to avoid visual strain for different types of work; the contrast required between working area and adjacent areas; the colours most helpful in avoiding visual discrimination (between different parts of a machine, for example) – these were studied and accurate results obtained. R. J. Lythgoe's 'The Measurement of Visual Acuity' (Medical Research Council, 1932) was an outstanding example. As a result, lighting engineers designed lighting to assist in minimizing fatigue or strain in factories.

Similarly, too high or too low a temperature was found

to have an adverse effect on health and efficiency. Bedford's work in 1935–6 studied the effect of temperature-change within a number of different industries (aircraft production, dressmaking, paper-bag manufacturing). In spite of a range of individual differences and the obvious effect of amount of muscular activity, body build, type of clothing, age, most workers were satisfied and worked with high efficiency at temperatures of 64–66° F. Statistical data had shown that accidents tend to increase above or below the range 65–69° F., so that Bedford seems to have discovered the safe working-temperature for most jobs. Heavy muscular activity might require a lower temperature. Ventilation also must be considered, and industrial psychologists carried out innumerable experiments to discover the necessary amount of fresh air, the movement of air currents per foot per minute, and the relative humidity for efficient and healthy work in different types of occupation.

As well as studying physical environment, length of working hours and relation of work to rest periods, psychologists also studied the effect of monotony and boredom on efficiency. In 1929 Wyatt and Fraser attempted to discover how to mitigate the boredom of repetitive tasks in cigarette-making. Interest was increased (and output) by alternating cutting tobacco with making cigarette rolls – one of many examples of improvement.

As early as 1911, F. W. Taylor's *The Principles of Scientific Management* had argued that many movements and actions performed in industrial work are wasteful of energy. Taylor was the first to attempt an accurate observation, description and analysis of all the actions involved in working tasks, beginning by a careful time-and-motion study of men loading pig-iron. He noted exact timing of movements. Taking experimental subjects – on extra pay – he gave detailed instructions on what movements to make, when to rest, etc. Output amongst the 75 men trained increased from $12\frac{1}{2}$ tons per man, per day, to $47\frac{1}{2}$ tons.

F. B. Gilbreth developed 'time-and-motion' study in the U.S.A. and Miss A. G. Shaw did similar work in England. In his book *Applied Motion Study* (1919) Gilbreth reported a study of the building trade which he made in 1917. He took photographs of bricklayers at work, noting that the average craftsman executed fifteen distinct movements in order to lay one brick. He invented a scaffold which could be speedily and easily altered to enable the bricklayer to operate at a level convenient to his task, so that stooping was eliminated; he trained labourers to inspect the bricks and carry them to a number of layers; he suggested that two hands instead of one should be used for certain operations; that bricks be laid on the scaffold in certain ways. Thus, the average number of movements was reduced to eight and the average number of bricks laid per man, per hour, was increased from 120 to 350.

Gilbreth also invented the chronocyclograph. This device consists of a small electric light bulb which is attached to a finger or hand or leg; by photographing the path of the light with a stereoscopic camera, the motion of the operator can be traced in three dimensions. The cyclographic records can be used to measure time, speed, acceleration, direction. Models can then be constructed exhibiting the pattern of movements involved in a skilled performance, precisely, for each worker – wasteful movements being instantly revealed and both 'correct' and 'erroneous' parts being defined.

Gilbreth also devised a scheme for analysing all manual operations in terms of basic types of action ('grasp', 'hold', 'release', 'inspect', for physical aspects; 'position', 'search', 'assemble', 'rest,' etc., for psychological aspects). These were named 'Therbligs' (his own name spelt backwards). This breakdown of working-activity into specific units enables precise observations to be made and 'process charts' (descriptions of orderly sequences of movements and pauses) to be devised for many different jobs. Such questions as 'Is this movement really necessary?' or 'Is the order of operations maximally efficient and economic of effort?' could be asked. Gilbreth himself initiated several studies which led to simpler, more efficient methods – in laundry work, moulding of metals, chocolate manufacturing, etc. Time-and-motion study thus became a new type of investigation. It led not only to discovering the most economical way of performing specific work tasks, but also to the improvement in equipment used by workers, the re-designing of machinery in the interests of the human operators, and the more logical layout of factory and workshop in which tools, benches and machines were related so as to make work both safer and more efficient. The early suspicions that such studies had the aim of simply getting more out of the workers were soon dis-pelled by results: work could be made less strenuous and fatiguing, more pleasant, and often safer. This approach – the exact description and analysis of behaviour in a work-ing environment – led to many later developments.

Accidents at work have always been a problem. Guards on machines, careful machine-design and elaborate rules and regulations all help to prevent accidents or to limit them. But there are psychological factors involved as well. H. M. Vernon's studies of accidents in munitions works, mines and the shoe-making industry (1920) con-centrated on fatigue-effects from long hours of working, excessively high and low temperatures, bad lighting, and awkward machine design, as contributory causes. Farmer and Chambers (1926–39) studied the interesting pheno-menon known as 'accident proneness' – the fact that only 10 per cent of the total working population accounts for 56 per cent of the accidents over a period. Tests given to workers prone to accidents revealed poor coordination of movements, abnormally slow reaction-times, weak visual acuity and other basic deficiencies. Time-and-motion study techniques showed clearly that accidents (and mistakes leading to damage to work product rather than to oper-atives) tended to occur at specific stages of a work se-quence. This was the point at which the key factor

– whether awkwardness in operator or bad machine design, layout, or lighting – tended to intrude most into the situation.

It was also obvious that emotional factors played their part – being rushed, irritated or distracted often upsets control and concentration as much as fatigue, or badly coordinated movements.

Another field which psychologists explored was that of training for skilled work in industry. Before the rise of industrial psychology, apprentices were often simply put beside skilled workers and, by a mixture of watching the skilled at work and casual training, gradually picked up the job. This was a long and wasteful method, taking years to complete, and distracting to the skilled man. Time-and-motion studies enabled exact descriptions of improved skills to be given and schemes for imparting such skills through formal practical training to be drawn up.

Shaw's *Training of Workers* (1936) gives an account of the research which resulted in early training schemes for industrial workers. Properly selected and trained instructors could be provided to give trainees basic training leading to organized practice and supervision on the actual job. The arrangement of materials, the layout and handling of tools and equipment, simple assembly, the stages of the tasks, the timing of coordinated movements – all these could be taught, and the reasons for the recommended methods explained in systematic courses. Errors and basic awkwardness could be eliminated before the apprentice qualified as 'skilled', causes of accidents could be made clear and good habits for safety inculcated at the beginning. All this was only possible as the result of knowing more exactly what is involved in the performance of a specific job – the result of time-and-motion study, fatigue study, the application of trade tests, etc. Industry was somewhat slow to realize the importance of training workers for their jobs – it was regarded as the business of schools to supply the basic training for life and work.

Only since the Second World War, which necessitated rapid technical training for vast numbers of people, did industrial training become widely accepted.

Although these fields of research and interest (from which only a few examples have been cited from a very extensive literature) were the main ones, there were others. Industrial psychologists studied mental health in industry – the incidence of mental disorder in different groups; the extent to which absence from work is due to nervous disorders; what factors appear to contribute to stress and breakdown, or upset workers of 'nervous' temperament. 'Motivational' subjects such as incentives to work, factors which make for 'interest' in and 'liking' for a job or working-conditions, were studied. Inter-personal relationships, both within work-groups and (especially) between managers, supervisors and rank-and-file workers, and the psychological factors contributing towards good 'communication', understanding and cooperation, or towards misunderstandings, grievances and tensions were considered. However, the earlier stages of industrial psychology were primarily concerned with the development of psychological tests for selection of personnel, training of apprentices, time-and-motion and job-analysis techniques, and the study of factors leading to efficiency and safety at work.

On the whole, the results were impressive. Efficiency, safety, health and welfare did appear to improve. Industrial psychologists were able to solve the practical problems of industry and commerce, otherwise they would not have survived. Industrial psychology has made important contributions to industry – helping to fit the man to the job, the machinery and the factory organization to the man, to increase production and limit the number of serious accidents, to provide healthier and happier conditions of work for many. However, the influence of this new field did more than change industrial organization and provide a new outlet for the employment of psychologists; it also presented them with new problems, and new methods and techniques for dealing with them had to be devised.

In the field of psychometrics, industrial psychologists did perhaps more than any other group towards perfecting rating methods and scales. Graphic rating-scales owed much to the Scott Company (personnel consultants), while forced-choice technique and methods of checking errors in rating seem to have been the result of research carried out in industry. In time-and-motion study and work-analysis, a type of exact observation, description and analysis of human behaviour was evolved which was quite different from that of the physiological and experimental psychologist or of those primarily engaged in psychometrics. Work in industrial psychology influenced the Cambridge University academic psychologists. F. C. Bartlett's experiences in both the world wars clearly influenced his ideas. His book *Thinking* (1957 – the result of work spread out from 1919 onwards) suggests that thought processes develop from, and have many of the characteristics of, motor skills. The approach of Cambridge experimental psychologists to the study of learning-operations during the post-Second World War period obviously owes much to studies of industrial skills undertaken by the department during the war.

Industrial psychology, concerned with the solution of practical problems arising literally on the factory floor, or at the office desk, or in the cockpit of an aircraft, opened up a new source of stimulation. Hitherto the speculations of philosophers, the researches of physiologists, the clinical work of neurologists and psychiatrists, had been the chief external sources of psychological problems. The practical world of workers and management and of military organizations now impinged upon psychology – and with this new invasion came new sources for financing psychological research.

However, it is a safe generalization to say that the influence of industrial psychology on general psychology was not very considerable in the years between the world wars. Although industrial psychologists were men with a first degree in psychology, the academic world kept aloof from industry and the researches of university departments were usually directed to traditional problems in perception, memory and learning. It was only after the upheaval of the Second World War that applied psychology and pure psychology became closely linked, and that their respective fields of research came to overlap at certain points.

CHAPTER TWENTY

Child Psychology between the Wars

T H E study of children by psychologists and attempts to apply psychological knowledge to education in schools has a history going back beyond 1914. Stanley Hall, as we have seen (p. 136), made a bold beginning in the 1880s. Thorndike (pp. 156 ff.) had moved into educational psychology at Columbia University by 1903. Binet's work in France (pp. 190 ff.) had produced the first reliable mental tests – the result of research with child subjects. In England there had been great advances towards the establishing of a national system of education through the setting up of the Board of Education (1899), the local education authorities administered by county or borough councils (1902), and the establishment of local secondary and technical schools and teacher training colleges under local education authorities in 1902. In 1912 Cyril Burt was appointed psychologist to the London County Council Education Authority. Great interest was being shown in the problems of training and educating children, and educationalists as well as psychologists were anxious to base reforms and improvements on sound child studies.

In Germany during the last two decades of the nineteenth century the Froebel Society had been experimenting with *Kindergarten* for pre-school infants, claiming that children under 5 years require early schooling to assist natural growth of intellect and character. Montessori, an Italian psychiatrist who specialized in teaching subnormal children, devised a system for normal children as well, which condemned the regimentation and formality of classroom teaching. These new ideas led people to examine and criticize established school methods and find fault with education and training along conventional lines. These early movements, however, were further reinforced by the impact of the psycho-analytic movement and its derivatives. Freud, Jung, Adler and their successors all agreed that infancy and childhood were crucial years for the development of the human personality and that many things which go wrong in the early years can lead to serious mental pathology in adulthood. Child study became of overwhelming importance in the exploration of human behaviour.

The years between the two wars saw the expansion of psychological studies of children to an enormous extent. This work was somewhat haphazard and uncoordinated. Psychiatrists and psychologists became interested in 'problem' and 'delinquent' children as exhibiting the early stages of psychopathology. Subnormal and mentally defective children received special care and training. Educational re-organization led to the demand that psychologists should study individual differences in ability (both general and specific) and in personality, with a view both to selecting children for higher education and to recommending changes in teaching and organization which would meet the needs of different classes of child. A few psychologists wanted to do research less related to practical problems, and to discover facts about the growth and development of basic human dispositions at different ages. From the mass of work done with children in this period it is not easy to select the main achievements.

Perhaps the most characteristic was the attempt to study children systematically and objectively. Certain aspects of behaviour, for example, activity day by day and week by week in learning to walk or speak, were isolated for scrutiny, a large sample of individual children being observed in any given project. Detailed notes were made, films were taken, apparatus devised to make the 'facts' as clear as possible. With regard to any specific behaviour, a child subject might be observed in different contexts – at home, at school, at spontaneous play, during 'organized' play. The child would be observed while alone, with other children of the same age, in a mixed age group of children, with adults, while changes in behaviour under changing environmental conditions would be noted. Again, a child would be closely observed at the same time each day over a long period, and certain specific responses during the period – outbursts of rage or aggression, for example – noted in relation to the stimulus factors. Anecdotal data was replaced by more systematic observations. Methods were far from being exact, but much more information was obtained than hitherto.

In 'pure' research, psychologists were interested in describing the characteristic stages of growth which most children exhibit with regard to such specific dispositions as motor activities, perceptual acuity, speech and language habits, 'social' orientations.

Arnold Gesell at Yale carried out systematic observations on individual children from birth to 5 years of age. He was especially interested in the first year of life and hazarded the generalization that there are three growth periods – 0–4 months, 4–6 months, 6–9 months – during which it is possible to establish average reactions for large samples of observed infants. Tests which present objects for the infant to fixate and reach out towards indicate that while only 40 per cent are persistent in reaching towards an object at 6 months, 65 per cent do so at 9 months. At only 16 weeks, most babies can 'pick up' an object with their eyes although they cannot yet pick it up with their fingers. This description and classification of what most children do, and of the range of individual differences with regard to basic perceptual, motor and 'social' actions, was the work of such early investigators as Gesell in such books as *Infancy and Human Growth* (1928) and *The Feeding Behaviour of Infants* (1937).

Another investigator, Charlotte Bühler, in *The First Year of Life* (1930), described tests given to infants to determine what reactions infants are capable of at specific ages, and how one compares with another in rapidity or slowness of all-round development. If two sticks are placed in front of an infant, one of various characteristic reactions occurs: either nothing is done with the sticks except to stare at them; or the sticks are picked up and hit against each other; or they are waved and other objects are hit; or they are placed so that they form one continuous line. (The latter reaction is 'advanced' for a one-year-old, but characteristic of two-year-olds.)

Charlotte Bühler was also interested in determining early signs of excessive timidity and withdrawal as indicative of early pathology. Perhaps the most rigorous early studies of infancy were M. M. Shirley's, whose series of monographs 'The First Two Years of Life' were published between 1931 and 1933 by the Institute of Child Welfare. Shirley observed each infant and tested it daily for the first two weeks of life in the maternity hospital. After leaving, the child was visited each week by a paediatrician and a psychologist, given tests and examined. Records of basic physical measurements, nutrition and health were kept. Tests were given for sensory development, motor coordination, vocal development and reactions to different types of events. Nurses and parents were given regular questionnaires eliciting facts capable of observation. Out of a mass of data only items which occurred in 75 per cent of a very large sample were selected as common or general features of child development. Shirley then concentrated on the day-to-day development of specific features of motor development and speech during the first two years of life.

In Switzerland in the early 1920s Jean Piaget of Geneva University, with the Institut Jean-Jacques Rousseau (a large clinic for children) at his disposal, began his monumental studies. Piaget was ambitious in wanting a complete description and a theory to account for the whole developmental process from birth to maturity. In the U.S.A., Gesell at Yale and Shirley at Minnesota were interested in detailed analysis and tracking specific behaviour sequences. Piaget was interested in a general psychology of the child 'mind'. His earliest book, *Le language et la pensée chez l'enfant* (1923), and his subsequent volumes, *La représentation du monde chez l'enfant* (1926) and *Le jugement moral chez l'enfant* (1932), attempted to explain large tracts of behaviour.

Piaget devised a variety of methods for studying child behaviour – systematic methods of observing play, 'clinical' interviews, experiments and tests of a highly individual kind. His results were presented within a framework of general conclusions. He concluded that younger children cannot clearly distinguish between their own experiences and external reality – they project their moods, wishes and fantasies into their environment. Furthermore, this inclination towards 'animism' is strong – consciousness and volition are attributed to objects and events (such as the wind) other animals and humans. Like 'projection', this tendency goes through various developmental stages until the child can adopt and accept an adult outlook. At first everything which moves is conscious – a ball, a rolling stone. Later, a narrower category of moving things (e.g., the sun, cars, animals) are accepted as 'living minds'. In a final stage only things which move on their own are accepted – a motor car or a scooter are not 'alive' since somebody has to start and drive them, but the sun and moon are alive. At last consciousness and voluntary action are applied only to animals and men.

Piaget thought 4–6, 6–7, 8–10 and 11+ were crucial stages for these basic shifts. He also found successive stages of growth in the use of moral principles and social rules. His general conclusion was that the minds of children below 11 years are quite different from those of adults. They develop from purely primitive, subjective, egocentric, non-logical attitudes and concepts to more objective, realistic, logical, outer-oriented appraisals of self and environment.

Piaget's ideas provoked research and controversy. Victoria Hazlitt, a British psychologist, conducted experiments on children's thinking which she claimed showed no qualitative difference between adult and children's reasoning powers. Hazlitt argued that Piaget had assumed that understanding is identifiable with the ability to express concepts and relations verbally. However, when children have to express ideas concretely, they often show a clear grasp of relationships and logical implication which Piaget denied was within their scope. Studies by J. M. Deutsche (1937) and by W. Dennis and R. W. Russell (1939) on 'causal' explanations and 'animism' suggested that even if children are classified by 'stages' of development, these do not correspond to age groups as Piaget had suggested.

Piaget also stirred up great interest in the development of language. Studies by M. M. Lewis in England (*Infant Speech*, 1936, remains a classic) suggested that there is a period of imitating sounds before language is understood. At about 1 year, children begin to react intelligently to words and even sentences. Comprehension of uttered sentences comes before ability to speak. Lewis made recordings of infant vocalizations from birth onwards, making phonetic analyses of the sounds and tracing variables which shaped them. Much was discovered about how children learn to speak, and what functions language serves in early socialization. Early vocalizations and babblings were carefully recorded; the first words and their situations traced; the development of the use of some three words at 1 year of age to some 900 words at 3 years was studied, and the assimilation of parts of speech, syntax, etc., described developmentally. The relation between general intelligence and the growth of language skills, the differences in development between boys and girls, and the effects of home environment were all subjects of investigation (as, for example, in D. A. McCarthy, *The Language Development of the Pre-School Child*, Minneapolis, 1930).

The emotional development of children was another topic investigated extensively. Watson (see pp. 160 ff.)

had studied the newborn infant at Phipps Clinic, Baltimore, and published a celebrated paper, 'Studies in Infant Psychology' (*Scientific Monthly*, 1921). He concluded that there were only three basic emotions – fear, anger, affection. These appear shortly after birth. Watson's tests revealed that only three types of situation elicited fear reactions – loud noises, painful stimuli and loss of support (dropping the infant a few inches, for instance). Darkness, animals (such as snakes) and people did not elicit fear responses. In testing children between 4 months and 1 year, Watson concluded that children learn through experience to fear certain objects or situations, and many fears are the result of early conditioning. An 11-month child was given a white rat. He attempted to grasp it. When the rat was later presented the child continued to reach out. Now a steel bar was struck with a hammer every time the rat appeared. The child reacted with fear – puckering lips, turning away and whimpering. After a number of such pairings of rat with noise, the child reacted towards the rat by withdrawing and crying. Moreover, the child reacted with expressions of fear to a rabbit, a dog and cotton wool – all resembling the rat in certain aspects. The 'fear' response had 'generalized' to stimuli resembling the rat.

Sherman, in *Journal of Comparative Psychology* (1927), questioned Watson's conclusions. He made photographic and film records of infants reacting to four types of stimuli (hunger, restraint, painful stimulus, being suddenly dropped) and then rubbed out the stimulus. Different groups of subjects were then requested to name the reaction. A wide range of interpretations and low correlation between them and the 'actual' emotion were the result. When others were shown the films with the stimulus left in, there was both greater agreement and correspondence with type of emotional reaction. Sherman argued that most people infer the emotion from the stimulus. But does this give us any insight into the character of the response? How do we know the child is afraid?

The British psychologist C. W. Valentine pointed out that fear may be the result of the maturation of several neural processes. A child of 4 months may not exhibit fear simply because its brain and nervous system have not developed sufficiently. Again, if a child is comforted and reassured after being startled by a sudden noise, the second occurrence of the noise may not disturb it. The context in which an original response is elicited will have some effect on its development.

Thus great interest was aroused in the question of the origin and development of basic emotions. Gesell supported Valentine in regarding maturation as more fundamental than social conditioning in the emergence of emotional reactions. He performed experiments in which infants were observed in an enclosed pen at 10, 20 and 30 weeks. At each stage the reaction was different for most subjects – indifference at the youngest age, next mild apprehension, then crying and agitation at the greatest age. However, whether it is the basic pattern or the capacity for communication which matures seemed an open question. Children's fears in particular – the situations which evoke them, the kinds of behaviour involved and the ways of coping with them – became a subject of investigation. A. T. Jersild's *Children's Fears* (1935) is a typical study.

Freud's daughter, Anna Freud, began to investigate the problems of adjustment in young children. Melanie Klein also became interested in the psychodynamics of childhood and devised play techniques for getting children to express their hidden fears, conflicts and desires. Her *The Psycho-Analysis of Children* (1932) led to a widespread use of psychotherapy both for treating disturbed children and for investigating unconscious aspects of children's behaviour. This also led to the increase in the number of clinics for treating 'problem children'. Not all of these were run by Freudians. As it was, the child clinic dates from 1896, when Witmer began to study children. He was interested primarily in the schoolchild and especially the academically backward ones. He developed his methods between 1907 and 1925 and published the result of his work in his journal, the *Psychological Clinic*. Children were treated individually and elaborate case-histories were developed through interviews, tests and Witmer's own 'diagnostic teaching' techniques. A physician gave a thorough medical examination, a psychiatrist studied children with pathological tendencies, and a social worker obtained detailed information about home background. A 'rounded' picture of each child was thus obtained.

Few clinics existed before 1914. In the U.S.A., the National Committee for Mental Hygiene founded five child-guidance clinics between 1925 and 1929. Witmer's clinic was used as the model. By 1935 there were 233 such clinics in the U.S.A. In England, the London Child Guidance Clinic was founded in 1929, and at least seventeen new clinics were established throughout the country within the next decade.

From clinical records a new source of information about children was opened up. The team of psychologist, psychiatrist, physician and social worker provided detailed and comprehensive accounts of factors involved in educational backwardness, delinquency, 'nervousness', etc. The Institute of Child Psychology in London (1928) offered training for psychologists wanting to work in child guidance, while in the U.S.A. several universities specializing in child study established clinics and training schools. The information obtained applied not only to neurotic but also normal personality development. The psycho-analytic movement (especially the work of Anna Freud and Melanie Klein) was the chief stimulus to this attempt to study personality through the clinic, although many child-guidance psychologists worked outside the theories of the psycho-analytic schools. However, the normal child had not been neglected. The comprehensive theories of child development of Jean Piaget, and the patient analytic researches of Gesell, Shirley, Jersild and others were building up the outlines of what is now known as 'Developmental Psychology'.

In the field of education, psychologists carried out experiments in 'special' schools. Susan Isaacs at the Malting House School at Cambridge, while emphasizing child-oriented teaching and greater freedom of activity, noted that children did not benefit from completely unrestricted school settings. Given as much personal freedom as possible, young children still needed a 'framework of control and routine, and definite help ...'. Isaacs, however, argued eloquently against all forms of drill, training and moulding according to fixed goals. The teacher can only provide situations in which the child has a good opportunity to learn for himself.

Much of the work in 'educational psychology' proper during this period was devoted to research into and the use of intelligence and personality tests. Much basic research was done with children as subjects. Attempts to measure educational and personal growth during schooling by using tests and studies to discover whether test scores were influenced by home conditions, and by type and amount of school instruction, were typical of much research.

The work done in child psychology was heterogeneous, fragmentary and uncoordinated. It was not until after the Second World War that the materials produced over twenty-five years began to be assimilated and sorted out in such books as L. P. Thorpe's *Child Psychology and Development* (1946) and L. Carmichael's *Manual of Child Psychology* (1946). The main achievements of this period were probably all in the direction of working out more objective methods for studying the behaviour of children, moving away from subjective and speculative hypotheses to more exact and objective methods of observation.

The biographical and questionnaire methods of the pre-1914 days were replaced by a number of new techniques for acquiring information. Gesell, for example, while at Yale, constructed a dome-shaped compartment which enabled him to photograph a child from several angles at the same moment. The walls of the compartment were one-way screens, so that the child could be observed by a number of psychologists without its being able to see them. Gesell had rooms in which the child could live a normal life with its own family while being observed and photographed during feeding, bathing, playing. He noted that children at the same age tend to exhibit specific types of response and he plotted a 'developmental' schedule for a specific (e.g. manual) skill. Objective tests were also quickly adopted for child study. In England, at the London Institute of Child Psychology, Margaret Lowenfield used her Mosaics Test (in which children arrange coloured pieces of different shapes to construct designs) and a 'Word Game' test to study children's play. Her book *Play in Childhood* (1935) argued that play in the child serves all the functions covered in the adult by work, art, relaxation, etc. The whole of life is involved in play activities. Psychophysical investigations of acuity of hearing, weight discrimination, reaction time, etc., were also used to measure individual differences in the rate of development at different stages.

The clinical movement – aiming at a complete and balanced case-history of each child investigated – combined the empirical techniques of psychiatrists, physicians, social workers and psychologists in the interest of child development study. Projective techniques of testing were exploited and Klein's diagnostic play techniques proved a new way of eliciting responses from children. Experimental methods were used, although children do not seem to be 'good' subjects. However open to criticism many of Piaget's experiments have been, they are at least interesting attempts to involve children as subjects for laboratory experiment.

Thus, the study of children was not merely developed to an extent far beyond any previous researches during this period: its methods were reformed and improved and its objectives more clearly defined. The task of surveying the many different studies, analysing, evaluating and systematizing the results had to wait until after the war. There was then the possibility of a more organized and rigorous attack on the problems which emerged from this first period of rapid growth in child study.

CHAPTER TWENTY-ONE

Social Psychology 1920–40

U N T I L the beginning of the twentieth century, psychology had been regarded as the study of the individual human, or animal mind. The study of behaviour of men in groups, or the interrelations between men in society, was left to other disciplines: history, jurisprudence, political economy, political science. Some philosophers in their political philosophy discussed the psychology of the individual in order to show how society arises, or how it is necessary for a civilized life (Hobbes) or for developing human aspirations to the maximum extent (the Utilitarians). The study of the human group as a psychological topic, and of the psychological factors in inter-personal social relationships, had a slow and unsteady beginning. In a sense, social psychology did not become sufficiently coherent and technically advanced to receive much recognition until after the Second World War. In his *Introduction to Modern Psychology* (1950), O. L. Zangwill treats social psychology as a possible future field of study rather than as a present field of achievement, and predicts slow progress.

However, the beginnings of social psychology go back beyond the First World War. Wundt regarded the problems of social psychology as belonging to that non-scientific, somewhat speculative 'folk psychology' (based on historical and anthropological data), to which he devoted considerable time (Chapter 3). At the same time, the studies of the hysterical personality by Charcot and Janet in Paris and by Liébeault at Nancy (Chapter 9) gave rise to the idea that since some people are more 'suggestible' subjects for hypnotism there is a natural basis for the leader-follower relationship. G. Tarde's *Les lois de l'imitation* (1890), one of the earliest attempts at social psychology, and G. Le Bon's *Psychologie des foules* (1893), both use pathological data on suggestibility taken directly from the Paris and Nancy psychiatrists. Thus, group behaviour is shown to be blind and irrational in certain situations and, following the Darwinian emphasis on unknown mechanistic factors controlling adaptation, there is the beginning of the hypothesis that much individual behaviour might be socially conditioned. Thus, the individual may have no insight into the fact that his beliefs, attitudes and emotional reactions are the result of social training in infancy and childhood.

A more direct extension of Darwin's influence into the beginnings of social psychology was McDougall's *Introduction to Social Psychology* (1908). As we have already seen (p. 177), McDougall developed the concept of 'instinct' to account for the typical goals which men seek and the reason why a specific goal is selected in a given set of circumstances. McDougall's book, a mixture of genuine insights and confused thinking, became popular. Wilfred Trotter's *The Instincts of the Herd in Peace and War* (1917) carried the application of the concept of 'instinct' (as explanatory of group activity) a stage further. This book had a strong impact, for it was published at a time when rumour, jingoism and nationalistic feeling had been stirred by the war, to an extent unknown in Europe for many years. The irrational moods of whole nations united by the stress of the war seemed to call for explanation in terms of innate, inherited and 'blind' factors in human personality.

The instinctive basis of social life became a fashionable hypothesis in social psychology. However, it equally evoked opposition from those who found the concept of 'instinct' vague and indicative of mysterious but unknown 'powers' or 'faculties'. Knight Dunlap (*Social Psychology*, 1925) and L. L. Bernard (*Social Psychology*, 1925) were prominent critics. This dispute – largely semantic and methodological – was typical of early social psychology.

Equally typical was the argument over the concept of the 'group mind'.

McDougall's book of this title, published in 1920, seems to have started the controversy. Many writers had suggested that the interaction of individuals produces a common manner of thinking, feeling and striving different from the functioning of an individual who does not belong to a group. The interpretation of just what individuals, acting in a united group, have in common was the point at issue. McDougall did not wish to imply that consciousness could exist apart from individuals. However, he argued that the institutionalization of certain beliefs, attitudes and sentiments led to individuals introjecting these beliefs. Thus social institutions become 'parts' of individuals, and people, therefore, share common dispositions to react, in terms of the socialized behaviour – the 'group mind' being what is *common* in individuals so organized. A great deal of argument resulted from this sort of theorizing. F. H. Allport of Harvard led the attack in his *Social Psychology* (1924). 'All theories which partake of the group fallacy have the unfortunate consequence of diverting attention from the true locus of cause and effect, namely, the behaviour mechanism of the individual' (p. 9).

Much confusion and dissipation of energy resulted from disputes over instincts, the group mind and other speculative concepts in the 1920s. This kind of theoretical disputation was aggravated by obscurity in the data and methods of social psychology. K. L. Smoke, reviewing the state of social psychology in 1935 (*Psychological Review*, pp. 537–43), noted the confusion by showing, (1) that the contents of the leading textbooks were so unlike that it would be possible for a reader to understand one thoroughly and yet remain ignorant of most of the contents of all the others, (2) that the topics discussed in books and articles on social psychology down to the year 1934 constituted a diverse rag-bag of unrelated material – psychological factors involved in the origin and development of human society; learning alone compared with learning in a class or group; the origin and propagation of rumours; the factors making for cooperation and efficiency in industries; the motives involved in political activities; the development of the 'Self', etc., etc. Topics which are equally discussed by sociologists, economists, anthropologists, political philosophers and general psychologists were assigned to 'Social Psychology'.

In particular there seemed to be no clear division between sociological questions and social psychological questions. Also, there existed a confusion between psychological research and research aimed primarily at assisting in the development of social services and welfare work. It was not suggested that social psychology should not spill over into neighbouring fields; rather that it should define its aims, methods and problems to make it more strictly a part of empirical psychology. This fuzziness of outline seemed to derive from the origins of social psychology in the folk-study movement of the nineteenth century, with its interest in national, group and ethnic data. The fact that Wundt suggested that language, mythology, art, politics, etc., might be studied in the light of psychological principles, and that early workers such as Lazarus and Steinthal attempted such inquiries, had left its mark on social psychology.

However, some investigations of an empirical character did emerge. Münsterberg (p. 133) had carried out experiments showing that subjects together in a class influence each other's objective judgements (for example, of the number of dots flashed on a screen). Under Münsterberg's supervision, F. H. Allport began a series of experiments on the influence of group-membership on individual behaviour. Allport discovered that associations occur more rapidly in a group-test than when the individual works alone; but that complicated reasoning processes are less accurate when carried on in a group. His results appeared in his book *Social Psychology* (1924). Allport put forward a Behaviouristic approach to the study of social psychology.

Beginning with six classes of reflexes, he argued that social development and the membership of groups depends on the conditioning of these reflexes in early training. Conditioning and 'social facilitation', according to Allport, explain the individual's behaviour as a member of a group. What an individual wants or needs to do *as an individual* is simply facilitated and elicited clearly in the group situation; there is no control of the individual by the group through instincts or group 'mind'. Allport thus reduced social behaviour to individual behaviour. His work was reinforced by the research of H. T. Moore (1921), who introduced a method which became widely used. Moore attempted to estimate the influence of expert opinion on majority opinion, in moral and aesthetic topics. But instead of having experts present, he merely reported their judgements. He showed that verbal, or other, stimulation can 'artificially' arouse pre-existing attitudes in subjects of an experiment (e.g. 'respect' for expert opinions). Thus attempts at objective research into social behaviour began in the early 1920s. By 1931 Murphy and Murphy's *Experimental Social Psychology* reported over 800 studies. Not all of these were well designed or controlled; yet a move towards objectivity was noticeable in spite of the theorizing over fundamentals provoked by McDougall and stimulated by the theory construction of the period, when Behaviourism, Gestalt Psychology, and psycho-analysis offered complete systematic psychologies.

Much writing on social psychology in the 1920s and 1940s reveals the influence of data from the expanding researches of social and cultural anthropologists. The study of the ways in which the culture of a primitive society influence the behaviour of its members, and mould the basic psychological reactions, led to interest in the purely cultural factors on dynamic personality processes.

Malinowski's celebrated studies of the Trobriand

islanders of the western Pacific were published in *Argonauts of the Western Pacific* (1922) and *Sex and Repression in Savage Society* (1927). These books suggested the ways in which unconscious reactions (of the kind postulated by Freud) emerge in behaviour patterns which are quite different, among primitive peoples, from those of people living in a civilized urban society. Margaret Mead's studies also suggested that cultural factors influence personality to a crucial extent. Samoan girls make the transition to adolescence and womanhood without the signs of 'stress and turmoil' characteristic of Westernized young people. The social training provided in infancy by Samoan culture was the key factor in accounting for such differences in adjustment to sex-life and marriage. *Coming of Age in Samoa* (1928) and *Growing Up in New Guinea* (1930) had a striking effect on social psychologists in the 1930s. They recognized that their approach had been on too theoretical and restricted a scale. The findings of anthropology seemed to provide a basic groundwork for an adequate social psychology.

Many social psychologists went over into the field of social and cultural anthropology in their research work. Kardiner's *The Individual and his Society* (1940) was not untypical. Here a clinical psychologist collaborated with anthropologists in fieldwork designed to find out how far both normal and pathological behaviour was moulded by cultural factors in different primitive societies. Reference to cultural differences as the explanation of social behaviour became common. McDougall's appeal for instincts and Allport's use of conditioning as explanatory concepts were left behind.

Another development was the use of psychometrics in social psychology. Tests such as Thurstone's and Likert's attitude scales (see p. 337) gave an instrument for measuring the attitudes of, for example, various groups of white Americans towards Negroes; or the attitudes of children towards parents, other siblings or schoolteachers. Variation in the kind and intensity of prejudices and attitudes in different groups with reference to political (radical–conservative) or religious (acceptance–rejection) attitudes could be assessed roughly by use of questionnaires and tests. Public opinion sampling on a wide variety of social attitudes and interests occurred for the first time when George Gallup in 1932 begun his first studies. How political voting is related to different age-groups, socio-economic classes, educational groups, etc., was studied in public opinion polls; while the influence of specific advertising techniques on the beliefs and attitudes of various consumer groups was studied with the aid of the new inventories.

An influential development which was to define a new area of research came with the publication of *The Psychology of Social Norms* (1936) by Muzafer Sherif, a Turkish psychologist who worked at Harvard. He noted that an individual's perceptual responses are often determined by norms commonly accepted or followed by the social group of which he is a member. Sherif carried out experimental studies derived from this observation. Using the apparent movement of a point of light in a darkened laboratory, he demonstrated that experimental subjects in groups were influenced by group norms in the way they reported movement – individuals changing their response in the direction of a dominant group norm. In perceiving rates of tapping, what the individual perceives also differs when he is tested alone and when he reacts as a member of a group. Autonomy of judgement is abandoned in favour of the central tendency exhibited by the group. Thus the individual's perceptual reactions are often adaptations to cultural norms. Judgements (for example, of the quality of a painting or a passage of literature) were found to be similarly affected.

It seemed that cognitive responses of a complex order can be shown in the laboratory to be subject to interaction with the beliefs and attitudes of other people. From Sherif's work many investigations followed, showing the extent to which and the manner in which thinking and remembering, interpreting problems, etc., are influenced by social orientations structured by group norms.

Another development initiated in the 1930s was sociometric measurement. This was the work of J. L. Moreno, whose book *Who Shall Survive?* appeared in 1934; he also instituted the journal *Sociometry* (1937), following the short-lived *Sociometric Review* (1936). The techniques of sociometric measurement attempt to assess the attractions and repulsions of individuals towards each other within a group. Each member specifies other persons in the group with whom he or she would like to cooperate in a specified activity, and also the persons with whom they would *not* like to participate. Techniques aim to measure the emotional strength of such attachments and antipathies.

Moreno set up explicit requirements for devising sociometric tests. No restriction was placed on the persons chosen or rejected within the group. No limit was placed on the number of choices, though subjects had to indicate the criteria in terms of which each choice was made. The effect of restructuring a group was then studied in the light of choices made on the behaviour of individuals while engaged in specific activities. Subjects could also make their decisions privately – and indeed the procedure could be varied in a considerable number of ways to answer different questions.

The original method used by Moreno for analysing his data was the sociogram. This was a diagrammatic device illustrating the acceptances and rejections within a group. 'Overchosen' members were those who received a large number of choices, no matter what the pattern of choices within the group. The 'isolate' emerged as an individual who received no choices and made none. Some individuals formed mutual 'pairs' or belonged to a 'triangle' within the group. Others emerged as leaders without necessarily being the most popular; certain key choices determined the figure possessing power and authority within the group. Elaborate statistical techniques were employed to calculate 'ratios of attraction'. Sociometrics had developed into a new and sophisticated psychological technique by the early 1940s. It switched the interest of social psychologists for many years to come to the study of small groups.

Another influence from anthropology was the emergence of the cross-cultural method of studying social behaviour. Different cultures throughout the world provided examples of specific kinds of social behaviour, and this data was analysed to support or confute specific hypotheses. E. B. Tylor, a British anthropologist, introduced this method in 1889 when comparing the development of marriage customs. It was revived in the late 1930s and has since become widely adopted. An early example (1939) was C. P. Ford's study of the frequency of certain types of behaviour which seemed directly to derive from biological needs. It was H. G. Horton's celebrated study of the functions of alcohol in primitive societies (1943) which seems to have made cross-cultural studies fashionable once more.

Throughout the period between the two wars it is obvious that there was considerable ambiguity concerning the aims and methods of social psychology. However, the idea that the social characteristics of individual behaviour might be the focus of discussion was beginning to form.

G. W. Allport's definition of social psychology of 1954 would have been too positive for the situation in 1940, although social psychologists were working towards it. He defined it as 'an attempt to understand and explain how the thought, feeling, and behaviour of individuals are influenced by the actual, imagined or implied presence of other human beings' (Vol. 1, *The Handbook of Social Psychology*).

Thus, other disciplines such as political science, sociology and cultural anthropology are less concerned with individual functioning or development than with facts about the social organization within which many individuals live. The distinction is not altogether clear or even defensible. Its purpose is to insist that social psychology must integrate with general psychology rather than with sociology. The individual is so often studied in the laboratory or test-situation, in isolation from everybody except the experimenter. Social psychological studies correct this bias in general psychology by insisting that man is essentially a social animal. How does the individual react in specific social situations? How does he form his social attitudes? How does his behaviour change when he joins a new group? The aims of social psychology were becoming clearer by the late 1930s.

Whatever the shortcomings of its methods, social psychology posed new questions about behaviour and introduced new ways of thinking and writing in psychology. This 'new look' was not always welcomed by physiological and experimental psychologists, since they seemed to introduce less precise, or even distinctly 'unscientific', methods into the growing science.

This attitude has persisted, but without discouraging the growth of social psychology as an active and expanding field. Since the Second World War, social psychology has flourished more vigorously, establishing itself as a field of study destined to develop independently of the social sciences.

CHAPTER TWENTY-TWO

The Study of Personality 1930–40

THE most important body of research in psychology in the period between the two wars was probably within the field of experimental psychology. The principal theories which were advocated and discussed between 1918 and 1940 – Structuralism and Functionalism, Behaviourist theories and Gestalt, and Woodworth's Dynamic Psychology – were all closely related to current experimental research problems.

However, as we have seen, other psychological work had been going on outside this tradition: the application of psychology to problems in industry, education and mental disorders, including the rapid development and use of psychological tests among other 'non-laboratory' techniques; the compiling of individual case-histories illustrating the various psycho-analytic theories; the anthropological studies of psychologists into the influence of cultural factors on individual and group behaviour; the establishment of clinics to treat subnormal, delinquent, or neurotic children, and of psychiatric clinics to help maladjusted adults; the widespread use of 'personality tests' by applied psychologists to assess and compare basic attitudes, interests, opinions of different groups in relation to social issues – all these fields produced a new kind of data on human behaviour.

Except where the material was used by an orthodox Freudian, for example, it tended to be fragmentary and piecemeal – the product of a specific study carried out to deal with a particular practical problem in an industrial organization, or a clinical diagnosis, or an 'opinion poll' survey. It was natural enough that once this heterogeneous and diverse collection of information about human attitudes and interests or basic traits had accumulated, some psychologists should feel the need to survey and analyse it, should begin to ask fundamental questions about the way in which the study of the individual personality might best be conducted.

Much of the work in physiological and experimental psychology had been directed at discovering empirical laws in terms of which particular facts about human sensory processes, perceptual organization, methods of learning, remembering and problem-solving could be explained. In psychometrics, the measuring of traits and other variables was conducted partly to evaluate the range of individual differences, but also in the hope of being able to construct empirically defensible scales against which to evaluate the performance of any individual in relation to a typical and valid sample of his fellows. In social psychology, many studies aimed at generalizations exhibiting the type of factors in a cultural milieu which tend to reinforce specific behaviour in individuals – the emphasis so often seemed to be on the discovery of general statements in terms of which particular specimens of behaviour could be explained.

There had always been psychologists who insisted that the individual personality should be studied as a whole, that the individual should not be forgotten in the interests of scientific methods. William James had done so in the early days of empirical psychology, and Hall had also shown a strong interest in individual development. This tradition had been preserved in the psycho-analytic movement, especially in the work of Jung and Adler – the latter more especially. However, not every psychologist could accept the assumptions and theories of these psychiatrists. Towards the end of the 1930s, a new development became apparent in American psychology. This had a three-fold purpose: (1) To survey, analyse and systematize the diverse data on human nature accumulating within psycho-analysis, clinical psychology, social psychology, psychological testing, child and educational psychology and, indeed, general psychology. (2) To construct theories of personality on the basis of sound first principles, reliable empirical methods and such evidence as had emerged within psychology. (3) To initiate improved types of empirical study of the human personality as a dynamic, integrated unity. In some cases the theorist also attempted to allow for all that is unique and idiosyncratic in the individual.

Reference has already been made to Kurt Lewin of the Gestalt group whose *A Dynamic Theory of Personality* appeared in 1935 (p. 269). This somewhat abstract approach, together with the more empirical *Psychology of Personality* (1936), by Ross Stagner, began the new movement. Psychology journals had already questioned whether the human personality should be studied as a complex whole or through isolated traits, habits and interests. Now systematic books began to define the methods and categories within which a psychology of personality could develop.

One of the most influential of these systematic works was *Personality: A Psychological Interpretation* (1937), by G. W. Allport. Allport (1897–1967) graduated at Harvard in philosophy and economics. In 1922 he took a Ph.D. in psychology there. After studying in Berlin, Hamburg and Cambridge, he returned to America and has taught ever since at Harvard University – with the exception of two years at Dartmouth College in the early 1920s. Most of Allport's work has been in the Harvard School of Social Relations, in which psychology, sociology and anthropology are combined. This school owes much to Allport's ideas about the scope of psychology, and his editorship, for twelve years, of the *Journal of Abnormal and Social Psychology* also indicates his original and independent approach to psychological problems.

In his book of 1937, Allport defined personality as 'the dynamic organization within the individual of those psychophysical systems that determine his unique adjustments to his environment'. His thinking is original and dynamic and therefore difficult to describe. Only a sketch of some of his ideas can be provided here. He begins by emphasizing that 'personality' is a referent. It 'is something and does something'. There is an organization which lies behind specific acts. This is unique to each individual. Like Adler and James, Allport emphasizes that the acceptance of individuality is essential for understanding adjustment: the individual has his own ways of mastering the physical and social environment, or for submitting to its demands. No analysis of the processes involved in perception, learning, problem-solving, etc., is adequate to account for the functionings of the total complex which constitutes the individual. Psychology must somehow devise concepts in terms of which personality becomes a subject for empirical research.

One basic concept is 'trait'. This is defined as 'a generalized and focalized neurophysical system (peculiar to the individual) with a capacity to render many stimuli functionally equivalent, and to initiate and guide consistent (equivalent) forms of adaptive and expressive behaviour'. Traits are similar to 'attitudes'. The latter, however, are tied to specific objects, while traits are more general. Moreover, traits are not tied to 'values', the acceptance or rejection of objects or situations. All traits are unique to the individual, although some are much more like those of other individuals and so may be called 'general' traits. To this extent, psychological tests may measure and compare common aspects of general traits. Not all traits are on the same level. Allport distinguishes cardinal or dominant traits which for some individuals, but not for all, structure the whole personality. Yet even those individuals who are not so biased have a limited number of central traits, which are more crucial than others to the description of personality. Traits also serve a variety of functions which it is the business of empirical research to define.

Traits are important in any attempt to account for purposeful, goal-directed behaviour. In dealing with motivation, Allport believes that present involvements and future goals are as important as past history. Individuals know often what they are trying to do and what are their hopes, ambitions and plans. Prior learning and early development may determine much, but orientation to the present and the future must also be considered in any complete psychology.

However, since traits are learned and are developed through experience, how are they different from habits, skills, or primitive drives or needs? Allport introduces the notion of 'functional autonomy' to answer this difficulty. He argues that a form of behaviour may become a goal in itself whatever its original function or use. Even if no need or adjustment-function is served, the behaviour may be followed for its own sake. Thus, if a man takes up a sport to strengthen a body weakened by illness, or to imitate an admired friend, or simply because he has to (as he might in the army), he may go on exercising it afterwards as a basic trait. An activity may acquire functional autonomy from basic motives, drives or needs. Allport has developed his system to explain why the individual, on this basis, does *not* develop an anarchic and useless system of motives. His later concept of 'propriate functions' has been developed to remedy weaknesses in the original concept of 'functional autonomy' on the basis of an 'ego' concept. It is a basic hypothesis in all his work that, however important the role of past experience and primitive types of organization, these factors have been emphasized at the expense of certain types of motive which exist and which give man relative autonomy to grow away from past determining tendencies. Not all purposeful behaviour is autonomous, but the extent to which a person can change away from his past is a measure of his 'maturity' and mental health. Development towards the full and positive exploitation of personality, whatever the pressures from the past, is possible for some individuals.

Allport does not ignore the biological determinants of behaviour. Indeed, his account of infancy stresses heredity, primitive organic needs, reflexes, etc. However, the modification of the human being is more complicated than the Behaviouristic account in terms of conditioning, learning, the operation of built-in drives, etc. There is an element of intelligent choice in growing towards goals of maturity, self-organization and control.

The first thirteen chapters of Allport's book were devoted to theory. The remaining seven were devoted largely to methodological problems involved in an empirical study of personality: what behaviour to isolate, observe, measure; the relative merits of rating scales, tests, experiments, clinical assessments; the basic techniques to be developed and improved in this field. Allport insisted on idiographic procedures which study the individual as a unique, complex, dynamic entity. However, he did not neglect nomothetic approaches, which take large groups of individuals and compare measures of some specific attribute as isolated in psychometric tests or laboratory experiments. Indeed, Allport's contribution towards nomothetic tests has been considerable, and this readiness to use such methods has counteracted criticisms by some psychologists that idiographic methods are difficult to handle satisfactorily. Allport's advocacy of treating the individual *as* an individual has led to the supplementing of tests by the direct approach in questionnaires, the use of personal documents (records, diaries, correspondence, free expression in essays, etc.) and to new attempts to study 'expressive' behaviour. In Allport and Vernon's *Studies in Expressive Movements* (1933), which was a starting-point for this revival of the study of the individual, intercorrelation of 38 measures for each subject was the basis for an attempt to find a way of studying expressive actions. Allport's pupil, S. Estes (*Journal of Abnormal and Social Psychology*, 1938), carried this work further, and stimulated a new line of research in devising techniques of rating the opinions of a number of different judges who are set the task of assessing individual expressive reactions. Interviews, self-ratings, questionnaires aimed at evoking judgements based on the observation of an individual in innumerable day-to-day situations – all these have been investigated as instruments of research supplementary to standardized tests and experiments.

This selection of a few basic ideas fails to do justice to Allport's adventurous yet sane approach to the problem of studying the individual personality – an approach which has been refined and developed in many subsequent empirical researches and theoretical books. His influence has been greatest since the Second World War, many of his books having appeared in the 1950s. His influence began, however, in the 1930s and indeed several articles ('Concepts of Trait and Personality', *Psychological Bulletin*, 1927, for example) were sketched very early. His book of 1937 has been an influential text, stimulating interest in a new range of problems and correcting the bias of the prevailing 'Behaviouristic' and 'psycho-analytic' theories and methodologies of the interwar years.

Another psychologist in this movement was Henry A. Murray. His article 'Basic Concepts for a Theory of Personality' (*Journal of Genetic Psychology*, 1936), and his books *Explorations in Personality* (1938) and *Manual of Thematic Apperception Test* (1943), give him a place beside Allport among the pioneers of personality study.

Murray was born in 1893 and educated at the patrician academies of Groton and Harvard. He qualified in medicine at Columbia in 1919. After medical appointments in hospitals and a period at the Rockefeller Institute of Medical Research, he studied biochemistry at Cambridge, England, and graduated Ph.D. in 1927. It was only after this that he became interested in psychology through reading Jung's *Psychological Types*. He visited Zürich and had long conversations with Jung which determined him to devote his interests to psychology, and more especially to the study of the personality. Morton Prince, who had founded the Harvard Psychological Clinic to conduct psychopathological research, arranged for Murray to become its Director in 1928. While doing this job, Murray qualified as a psycho-analyst under Franz Alexander and Hans Sachs, completing his training in 1935, and thereby obtaining a type of psychological qualification.

Under Murray's guidance, the Harvard Clinic proved to be a dynamic enterprise. Much interesting, unusual research and treatment went on there – as well as theoretical argument and discussion amongst the able collection of psychologists, psychiatrists and other scientists on the staff. In 1943 Murray joined the American Army Medical Corps and was in charge of a giant programme of clinical examination and psychological testing. (His book, *The Assessment of Men*, 1948, describes this work.) In 1947 he returned to Harvard, and in 1950 was appointed Professor of Clinical Psychology in the School of Social Relations. The work of this remarkably gifted and unusual man – he is also an authority on the literary works of Melville – has culminated in recent times. Here we are concerned with his earlier writings of the 1930s.

Murray's outlook is well characterized in an article of 1940. Speaking of academic psychologists, he says '. . . almost everyone was nailed down to some piece of apparatus, measuring a small segment of the nervous system as if it were isolated from the entrails. . . . The phenomena which intrigued me were not mentioned, since these were not susceptible to exact experimental validation, a standard which rules out geology, paleontology, anthropology, embryology, most of medicine, sociology, astronomy. . . . I had changed because of a consuming interest in other matters, in the problems of motivation and emotion.'

Murray's attempt to remedy this situation began with a classification of those aspects of human personality which required investigation. From this he went on to an analysis of the structure of personality, a description of personality dynamics and a developmental account.

Murray insisted that psychology is always limited both by the human intellect and the concepts it can form, and by the techniques available for observation and analysis. In personality study, we are dealing with a complex which covers a whole life span which we can know only in a series of temporal segments. Hence, any psychology will be only partially successful. In the active person, a number of interacting functions may be expressed simultaneously in the one segment of behaviour – making analysis problematic.

Murray's attempt to provide a systematic framework is, like Allport's, comprehensive and complex. Like Allport, human goal-directed behaviour is a central interest.

Murray regarded the reduction of tension as basic in human strivings. Man not only experiences built-in tensions, which he seeks to reduce; he also generates tensions to keep on the move. Some needs are built-in; others are created as 'stimulants' to behaviour. The concept of 'need' is therefore important. There are criteria for saying a need exists – the kind of object to which the agent responds, the particular behaviour exhibited, the end or result sought, the emotion experienced, etc. The direction and organization of behaviour under the influence of a 'need' is distinctive. Murray classified characteristic needs under twenty headings, ranging from needs for sex, nurture, harm-avoidance and other biological needs to the needs for achievement, abasement, affiliation and other 'social' needs. Murray regarded needs as being of quite distinct kinds (primary, secondary, proactive and reactive, overt and covert, focal and diffused). Some needs are simply satisfied, others require long and complex activities before any results are achieved. Again, the interrelationship of needs is far from simple, and the description of operative needs in a person necessarily complicated: some fuse, others conflict; some are dependent on the prior satisfaction of others; some are prior to others according to a scale of 'values'.

Also, the external factors in a person's environment influence his motives and emotions. Objects, events and persons can assist or frustrate the satisfaction of needs.

The word 'press' was used to indicate factors which frequently 'press' a person to one kind of activity or another in meeting basic needs. Poverty, cultural discords, parental illness, lack or loss of possessions or companions – these are just a few of the factors examined in detail by Murray to illustrate the 'press' dimension. 'Presses' are not simple. Sometimes the objective attributes of a 'press' are dominant (as in the case of a person threatened by a fire); but sometimes subjective interpretations of the object are crucial. The Freudian concept of 'cathexis' and the old term 'sentiment' are used by Murray in discussing the attitudes and emotions involved in 'press' situations.

The term 'theme' is used to discuss the behaviour involved in relating press to need. Themes vary from the simple to the very complex. In a complex theme, a number of needs and presses are related to each other, over a long period, through recurring and evolving motivational patterns. Nor does Murray ignore the physiological aspects of motivation: 'regnancy', the neural basis for molar behaviour, is discussed.

Murray is not limited to an account of motivation and emotion. He is interested in the socio-cultural determinants of personality and has cooperated with Clyde Kluckhohn, the anthropologist, in several studies; both 'complex' and 'unconscious' are basic concepts in his accounts of the development of personality. He uses both clinical and psychometric research to discuss such diverse topics as suicide, marriage, humour, criminal behaviour and religious belief. No summary can do justice to the comprehensiveness of his theory. Like Allport, he emphasizes the uniqueness of the individual and the necessity to bring this into psychology. In his research he has devised experiments, exploited tests and used physiological data. Nevertheless, the emphasis has been on the improvement of clinical methods. Using small numbers of subjects Murray has studied each individual longitudinally and intensively, claiming to find facts which the large sample in the test or laboratory would miss. He insisted that observation of the individual can be improved by pooling the observations of a number of trained observers. The 'clinical conference' was one of Murray's innovations at the Harvard Clinic and has subsequently proved useful.

Understandably, Murray's approach has aroused hostility from some psychologists, who insist on rigorous experiment and statistics. However, his ability to stir controversy and make psychologists consider the possibility of less rigorous empirical methods as at least supplementary or exploratory devices has been an important feature of the last thirty years. Nobody can deny his vigour, originality, unorthodoxy and charm of style. Together with Gordon Allport, he has made the Department of Social Relations and the Harvard Psychological Clinic the centre of a new kind of psychological research, alongside the schools specializing in physiological and experimental psychology.

The work of Allport and Murray stimulated others to produce programmes for personality-oriented psychology. Sheldon's constitutional psychology (1940), Carl Rogers' system and clinical method (1942, 1947) and Gardner Murphy's bio-social theory (1947) were the immediate developments. These theories and methodologies did more than provide alternative systematic psychologies to the 'establishment' theories of Functionalist, Behaviourist, Gestalt and psycho-analytic systems. They stimulated research and applications of personality-tests both in the clinic and in industry. They stimulated basic research in hospitals and clinics which was to make clinical psychology independent of both orthodox psychiatry and psycho-analysis, greatly extending its scope and utility. They stimulated social psychologists to define the basic 'ethnic personality' types within each distinct culture, and so to investigate new socio-cultural factors influencing behaviour. Experiments in orthodox general psychology became increasingly oriented towards personality factors. For example in 'problem-solving' experiments, the experimental group of subjects was often differentiated from the control-group on the basis of personality tests, so that the influence of basic traits, attitudes, etc., on thought processes could be demonstrated.

However, in 1939 all this was in the future. The work of the 1930s was principally a matter of basic systematic thinking: the construction of an outline of theory and method in terms of which new kinds of investigations could begin. Henceforward, developmental psychology, clinical and abnormal psychology, social psychology and personality-studies were to constitute a group of psychological fields which opened up new kinds of problems, exploiting experimental and psychometric techniques, but also devising new methods for studying human behaviour alongside the orthodox experimental and psychometric techniques.

CHAPTER TWENTY-THREE

Retrospect: Psychology in 1940

THE period between the two wars presents a confusing picture. Psychologists appear to be divided into a number of rival schools or philosophies, each with its own view of the scope, methods and aims of psychology as a science. Even within schools receiving the same tag there appeared to be fundamental disagreements; in the Behaviourist school, for example, Hull held 'reinforcement' to be a necessary condition of learning while Tolman denied this principle; Skinner denied the importance of 'intervening variables' and 'hypothetical constructs' between stimulus and response while Hull made these central for his Behaviourist system. Similarly, the psycho-analytic movement split into rival groups, the controversy between the followers of Freud and those of Jung being especially bitter.

Not only were there clashes between Behaviourists and Gestalt theorists, between Freudians and those who favoured 'factor analysis' studies of personality, or between rival interpretations of the nature of 'intelligence' as measured in standardized tests. The subject-matter of psychology appeared to exhibit a variety and heterogeneity which baffled the layman. Some psychologists devoted themselves to studying the behaviour of rats in mazes or cats in puzzle-boxes; others were indistinguishable from specialists in physiological optics; some devised tests for comparing the general intelligence, or basic emotional stability of individuals in large groups; others wrote philosophical papers about the nature of intelligence; some discussed the dreams or free-associations of neurotics; others the environmental factors productive of delinquent children; others studied the effect of lighting or machine-control design on the efficiency of industrial workers; others specialized in the factors responsible for producing optical illusions or errors in perceptual judgements; others studied the behaviour of primitive tribes in relation to their culture and its development; others discussed the logical principles of 'scientific methods' in relation to the problem of psychology. Psychology seemed to have no coherence or order among the topics it discussed and no agreement on a central core of fact or theory. The subject was a veritable Tower of Babel.

There seemed in 'General Psychology' to be a division between those who were primarily physiological and experimental psychologists using laboratory experiments as their basic data and the growing number, towards the end of the 1930s, who insisted that the human personality was recognizably complex and dynamic, integrated into a unity and thoroughly social. Personality theory, personality testing, social psychology, clinical psychology and developmental psychology, in spite of weaknesses of method, were a strong protest against an exclusive emphasis in some quarters on animal subjects and experimental techniques. This division within 'pure' or 'academic' psychology between the biological–experimental and the sociological–clinical–individualistic approach was, of course, complicated by the greater separation between 'pure' psychology and 'applied' psychology. The two types of psychologist rarely collaborated or communicated with each other, the one group remaining within the academic campus and the other in 'back-room' jobs in factories, hospitals, schools, clinics, or the offices of state departments.

Thus Gilbert Ryle, to quote the Oxford philosopher again, described psychology in 1949 as a 'partly fortuitous federation of inquiries and techniques'. This description has been true of psychology since the 1930s at least. Psychology is a group of more or less discrete disciplines, some having intimate inter-connexions with each other, others having hardly any common ground between them (animal behaviour and intelligence testing, for example).

Nor is it possible, when surveying this large and hetero-geneous federation, to decide which are central or basic and which more peripheral. As O. L. Zangwill, of Cambridge University, wrote in 1956, 'Every psychologist has perforce to create his own psychology' – often on the flimsy criterion of personal interest. This view is now widely accepted, but in 1940 there were still psychologists who ignored the facts and hoped that a grand science of human nature could be evolved which would have a co-herent programme and would ultimately achieve a theory or systematic form which would logically relate every pro-position to everything else in the system. Such a science would also, of course, be able to explain any sample of human behaviour.

The state of psychology by 1940, however, seemed to indicate that this dream of psychology as *the* science of human nature was a delusion. Psychology was only one of a number of studies dealing with human activity and the factors which produce it. History, politics, economics, jurisprudence; anthropology, sociology; neurophysiology, biochemistry of bodily processes; genetics and embryology – each contributes some insights by asking and answering different *kinds* of question about behaviour. Psychology too is limited in scope, since its methods and techniques only allow for certain types of question to be attempted. Moreover, the different disciplines within psychology (animal behaviour, psychological tests, the physiological psychology of the sensory processes, the conditions of learning motor skills, the psychogenetic factors in neu-rosis, etc. etc.) each asks different (and limited) questions about behaviour, and applies its own special techniques and conceptions in trying to answer these questions. There need not be any grand summary or synthesis of all the results of these diverse inquiries. The psychologist trying to explain a specific optical illusion; the psycho-logist studying the formation of a maze-learning habit in rats; the psychologist applying a test to two groups of sub-jects in order to compare a range of individual differences

– each is asking a different type of question about behaviour.

However, although by 1940 psychology had become fragmented and diversified, there were still dedicated Behaviourists or Freudians or factorial analysts who still believed that a comprehensive and logically integrated science of behaviour might develop out of their systematic and empirical work. There was considerable confusion about the logic and methodology of psychology – about its basic assumptions, scope and methods, and practicable aims. This confusion and uncertainty was reflected in the 1920s in many articles on methodology in psychological journals. This interest increased rather than diminished in the 1930s. Psychologists studied what logicians and philosophers wrote about 'scientific method', and many books and articles contain discussions on such abstract topics by psychologists worrying about the first principles of their own science. Logical positivism appealed to many Americans, and 'Operationism' was also popular. This was a revision of Behaviourist and Functionalist tenets in the light of logical positivist theories (especially the version of P. W. Bridgman in *The Nature of Physical Theory*, 1936). S. S. Stevens' article in the *Psychological Bulletin* (1939) and C. C. Pratt's book *The Logic of Modern Psychology* (1939) were typical expressions of an Operationist viewpoint. Only those statements about mind or behaviour which can be verified (or refuted) by observable, public and repeatable 'operations' are meaningful in science. Therefore, observable operations by the organism are the basis for any statement about experience or behaviour. Thus if X discriminates between a strong and a weak light stimulus he can be known to do so only if he makes one overt response to the first and another overt response to the second. Again, X's motives are behaviours directed towards different, objectively definable 'goals'.

Thus, in 1940, psychology was an extremely complicated, diversified and ill-defined collection of inquiries, techniques, skills and interests. Psychologists were men and women with a variety of training, interests and technical skills, such that one specialist might have little understanding of the speciality of another. This situation had developed rapidly from the early 1920s onwards, so that by 1940 the 'Tower of Babel' aspect was well established. Henceforward, however, many new links were established between different branches or sections (such as the study of 'neurotic' behaviour in animals); the parts were bound to expand in diverse – and often divergent – directions from each other. The 'loose federation' was not likely to become more coherent or compact – unless the discipline were to break up into a number of discrete 'behaviour' sciences such as 'Physiological Experimental Psychology' as distinct from 'Social Psychology'. However, social psychologists began to perform laboratory experiments; perceptual experiments began to be devised in which subjects were divided into two or more groups on the basis of the use of psychological tests; 'learning theory' began to be used in psychotherapy – and therefore there were sufficient connexions and exchanges between diverse parts to justify the continuation of the federation as a loosely organized 'unity'.

PART THREE

Psychology Today

CHAPTER TWENTY-FOUR

A Sketch of Post-War Developments

ANY history of psychology might end conveniently with the outbreak of the Second World War, which disrupted and re-oriented the work of psychologists. Since the war, psychology has flourished. Between 1946 and 1956 the membership of the American Psychological Association increased by 241 per cent. In other parts of the world, the number of graduates in psychology making a career as 'psychologists' has shown a corresponding increase. With this there has been a complicating of the specialisms and applications of psychology which makes the situation of 1940 seem comparatively simple and the situation in 1914 a mere family affair.

Any attempt to deal with the rapid growth and diversification of psychology, since 1940, and more especially from 1945 onwards, is well beyond the scope of this book. However, some attempt to round off the history of psychology down to 1940 must be made, if only to provide a tenuous link with the active and extremely complex present-day scene. This chapter will mention some of the changes which dominated the post-war generation of psychologists. The bibliography for the chapter will suggest what reading might remedy its sketchiness.

After the experiences of the First World War, it was obvious that the services of psychologists would be mobilized to help with the war effort. In the U.S.A. in particular, psychologists were organized on a large scale in almost every department. The war gave a stimulus to two fields of research which had been somewhat neglected – clinical psychology and social psychology.

During the war psychometric tests were improved and applied to as wide a range of purposes as they could serve – picking the right men for specific jobs, weeding out neurotic personalities who were likely to collapse under the stress of battle, discovering new types of skill needed to operate new kinds of technical equipment (radar, for example). As in the First World War, psychotherapy to treat those suffering from excessive strain was investigated along new lines, since larger numbers had to be treated in as short a period as possible. Within the field of social psychology the interest centred on 'group dynamics' – the small group and its interpersonal relationships. Surveys of public opinion were also undertaken to assess 'morale' and the factors influencing national reactions under war conditions. More strictly empirical and experimental methods of research in social psychology brought this somewhat diffuse branch of psychology more into line with other parts of the subject.

The new apparatus invented to combat aircraft raids on land targets and assist defenders by rendering anti-aircraft guns self-regulating led to a branch of research sometimes called 'human engineering'. In this, machinery is ultimately designed with the limitations and needs of the human operators in mind – the knowledge of human limits being the result of research by psychologists. Conversely, human operators had to learn new skills in order to operate new instruments or machinery invented in war-time. Experimental psychology received some stimulation from this kind of war-time research.

However, not all the new developments arose out of war-time psychology. The break with established problems and techniques produced by the war served, in some instances, to turn the attention of psychologists in fresh directions, so that what were peripheral interests in 1939 had become a main field of research by 1959. Again, not all the preoccupations of leading psychologists after 1945 were in the form of new developments. Many of the problems in the fields of perception, learning and problem-solving which were investigated in the 1930s continued to interest researchers, and so there were continuing traditions, in every branch of psychology, as fundamental as any new interests.

PHYSIOLOGICAL PSYCHOLOGY

In the 1930s, physiology and experimental psychology had tended to drift apart. In the immediate post-war period physiological psychology had become a more active and developing field. It is not yet certain whether the electrical activity of the brain and nervous system is an immediate factor in shaping behaviour. Since the war, the techniques of electro-physiology have improved sufficiently to encourage research into the electrical action of the brain in relation to behaviour. The improved electro-encephalographs for recording and measuring electrical wave forms, for selected brain areas, have opened up new types of research. Electrical (and chemical) stimulation of specific brain areas in living animals (by means of plastic-and-metal implants inserted into the brain) is another new device. The stimulation of specific parts of the brain electrically, and the recording of natural or artificially induced activity, can be correlated with particular behaviour, giving rise to theories concerning the physical basis for psychological states.

Another new field of research has been psycho-pharmacology. The accidental discovery that certain new drugs, originally compounded to treat tuberculosis, had a powerful anti-depressive effect on mood led to their use in treating 'depression' in mental hospitals and clinics. Other drugs were discovered which had the opposite effect – that of calming an over-excitable maniacal state; and yet others were devised which lowered violent, aggressive impulses to the point of harmlessness. The basic research into the effects of such drugs on the brain and nervous system has led to tentative hypotheses concerning the physical basis for psychotic behavioural reactions – acute melancholia, excessive excitement, violent and uncontrolled aggression, acute anxiety. The biochemistry of the brain during acute emotional disturbance has become a new field of research and speculation.

Neurosurgical techniques have gradually improved over the years. The traditional practice of observing behavioural changes after the surgical removal of lesions or tumours in the brain has continued. In addition, the Canadian brain-surgeon Penfield has stimulated exposed portions of the brain electrically during brain-operations in which the patient has remained conscious – a combination of surgery and electrical physiology which has produced new data on the brain and its functions. Several new lines of research have emerged through the application of these new techniques.

(i) It has emerged that in the centre of the central nervous system is a very diffuse organization of cells and pathways. This seems to have the general function of changing the excitability of the entire brain. There are degrees of 'arousal' however, and the study of the mechanisms controlling changes along this continuum open up the possibility of neural bases for attention, sleeping, dreaming and other basic behaviour.

(ii) Experiments by Olds and Milner have established that when electrodes are implanted in a moving animal, it can learn to turn a switch which stimulates that portion of the brain electrically. To stimulate certain areas seems to be 'rewarding'. There are no specific 'pleasure' areas, but several different regions are associated with 'rewarding' self-stimulation. This effect can be a substitute for food for a hungry animal.

(iii) This work, together with evidence from human brain surgery, has stimulated interest in the limbic system or visceral brain. The hypothalamus, thalamus and limbic system are closely related anatomically and appear to be the seat of basic 'drives', 'impulses' and emotional reactions. Different parts of the limbic system would appear to be affected in different 'need' states. A further extension of 'localization of function' research appears to be opening up.

In 1949, D. O. Hebb, a Canadian psychologist, published a book, *The Organization of Behaviour*, based on extensive reading into neurophysiological and neurosurgical literature, which presented a 'model' for the way in which the brain organizes typical behaviour. The brain was conceived as a dynamic system. It is richly endowed with circuits all organized into a network which provides alternative 'routes' for impulses and innumerable possibilities for specific linkages between one network and another. Any stimulation from receptors is fed into this on-going, complex total activity of the brain. Thus, incoming stimulation of the receptors is modified by, as well as having its impact upon, the central activities. Adult learning is not the creation of new neural structures. It is the re-ordering of existing organizations. 'Redintegration', changes within an existing dynamic organization, is the key concept. Hebb re-interpreted the result of earlier experiments on animal and human learning in terms of his system. His re-thinking of the total organization of the mammalian brain has led to further neuro-physiological speculation.

Another type of physiological theorizing resulted from the development of pharma-psychology. Research into the action of new drugs on the brain has led to biochemical hypotheses. It has been suggested that the emotional disturbances characteristic of the psychoses may be the result of hormones such as serotonin, histamine and acetylcholine being displaced from their natural sites in nervous tissue by anti-metabolites. So far, the chemical theories put forward cannot be fully sustained by the fragmentary evidence available. However, sufficient information has been assembled to encourage research into the biochemical factors which disrupt, instead of maintaining, the normal cell processes of the brain. It may be that a neurochemical explanation of hallucinations, aggressive impulses, violent swings of mood, etc., may be forthcoming before long.

Some interesting new beginnings have been made in

physiological psychology since the war. While the psychologist cannot yet offer more than tentative hypotheses about the physical basis of behaviour within the nervous system, this field has revived as a promising one in the last twenty years or so.

ANIMAL BEHAVIOUR

In the years before 1939, experimental psychologists had conditioned thousands of rats in their early investigations of simple learning. They had not shown any great interest in the work of zoologists. However, ethologists, studying the behaviour of animals in their natural surroundings and with minimal human interference, had been working independently, and it was only in the post-war period that this work impinged on psychology. Konrad Lorenz, the German ethologist, had been interested in innate behaviour and, in particular, with the way in which specific stimuli seemed to evoke elaborate reactions in very young animals, flight or defence for example, when the shape or sound of a predator was perceived. His pupil Tinbergen, working at Oxford, published his *Study of Instinct* in 1951 and made the Lorenz-Tinbergen theory of 'innate releasing mechanisms' well known. The reaction of psychologists to the ethological literature was to conduct laboratory experiments on a variety of new-born animals under controlled conditions, in order to find what early experiences most drastically affect later behaviour. What early learning occurs, and what factors influence its development? What behaviour appears unaffected by the environment, if any? Much has been discovered about the mere effect of exposure to specific stimuli, in the early days of life, on later behaviour. (Even being handled by a human being in early infancy seems to improve the later learning capacity of a rat.) Of special interest was the study of 'imprinted attachments'. It was found that newly hatched chicks exhibit approach and following behaviour towards specific objects. Usually the mother hen is the object selected; but, given appropriate exposure, humans or moving objects suspended on wire may be selected for this 'attachment'. 'Imprinting' has become a topic of considerable interest as a new kind of early learning.

H. F. Harlow of Wisconsin has also studied the early affectional reactions of young monkeys. Using two 'dummy monkeys' (or 'mother substitutes') he observed the reactions of the infant monkeys towards these. One was a wire figure from which milk could be obtained; the other was covered with soft cloth. The monkeys showed recognition and attachment reactions to the cloth figure and clung to it when afraid. This preference for the fur-like substitute 'mother' appeared to be an inbuilt survival mechanism. To be able to recognize and cling to the fur of the mother guarantees safety from falls and predators in the jungle.

The interest in 'unconditioned' responses in early life, together with early learning and the stimuli which shape such early behaviour, is a relatively new one in the animal laboratory. In particular, the effects of exposure to specific experiences in early life on later learning is a new field of study.

Another relatively new development has been the study of the factors which appear responsible for abnormal behaviour in animals. Many of these researches are based on the study of the effect of brain lesions or drugs on behaviour, and environmental stress as a factor in promoting behaviour pathology has also been studied in the animal laboratory.

Animals, of course, make useful laboratory subjects in many fields of research. However, so much data has accumulated, both from psychology laboratories and ethological expeditions, that animal behaviour has become a branch of study intermediate between zoology and psychology and almost independent of either.

EXPERIMENTAL PSYCHOLOGY

The work of experimental psychologists has become so much more diverse and heterogeneous in its interests that no summary of recent developments can be other than highly selective. Apparatus has become much more elaborate; techniques of experimental design have become so much more sophisticated than those of twenty years ago; and basic theory has come to rely on more complicated 'models' of behaviour than those of the early Functionalists or Behaviourists.

As Professor Brown points out in Chapter 5 of *New Horizons in Psychology* (1966), information theory has made an impact on experimental psychology in recent years. Information theory was devised by mathematicians to enable engineers to analyse and assess the efficiency of radio and telephone communications. In 1948 C. E. Shannon published *The Mathematical Theory of Communication*, which greatly interested psychologists. The theory seemed to provide both a system of measurement and a language for describing basic human capacities for processing data from the environment. Brown shows how this theory has been applied to the making and interpretation of new types of psychological experiment. The influence of information theory has been pervasive in experimental psychology, without displacing more traditional methods of description and measurement.

Perception

The structure and function of the visual system has benefited from electro-physiological techniques. Some advances have been made in knowledge of the anatomy and physiology of the neural connexion between eye and brain-centres, owing to the increased capacity of researchers to record and measure minute electrical changes in small structures. This work is a refinement of previous knowledge due to improved instruments and techniques.

A relatively new approach is to examine the development of basic perceptual capacities from birth to maturity and the changes which occur throughout adult life in perceptual organization. In particular, the effects of a person's emotional make-up and unconscious conflicts on perception have been topics of interest – another example of the invasion of experimental psychology by clinical techniques and hypotheses.

After being neglected since Titchener's time, there has been a revival of interest in 'attention'. Many forms of behaviour can be investigated without assuming that there is one common mechanism to which the concept of 'attending' refers. One topic to be resurrected is the 'span' of attention, or how much information can be handled by the sensory input systems simultaneously. Another problem is that of the extent to which two or more separate sequences of incoming information can be handled by the brain (for example, two sets of data fed in simultaneously to each of two earphones). Again, the extent to which a person can switch from one sequence to another without losing control of both 'inputs' is another type of problem. Many of these topics have practical applications to machine-control operations. Most of the work has been on the 'stimulus' or 'selecting' side of the process: recently the response side has been opened up by asking such basic questions as 'Can one attend to two responses being made to a single stimulus?' New ways of thinking about the nervous system, new techniques of experiment and improved apparatus have made 'attention' once more a problem for psychologists.

In general, psychologists studying perception have continued to demonstrate that visual and auditory responses are much more complexly determined than was generally thought in the pre-1914 era. Central brain processes organize and 'interpret' incoming information, in terms both of innate mechanisms and prior experiences. The effect of emotional state, dominant attitudes and traits, expectancies, recent 'set', and other 'personality' variables have been demonstrated in experiments, which combine clinical techniques with laboratory experiments. The prevailing objectives of much research since the war seems to have been to link the experimental-psychological study of human perception more closely to personality study on the one hand and the neurophysiological study of the central nervous system on the other.

Learning

Research along traditional lines has continued. Skinner has been continually active in researching into operant conditioning, both as the basis for training animals and in the design of teaching machines for use in infant schools. However there have been several new lines of research. As early as 1930 Thurstone had put forward the idea that learning might be a process of sampling from a collection of possible actions, some appropriate but others inappropriate, to a specific stimulus-situation. The unsuccessful actions would have a fixed probability of being eliminated once learning had begun, and this should be calculable for each succeeding 'trial'. This idea was taken up by R. R. Bush and F. Mosteller in their book *Stochastic Models for Learning* (1955), and by E. K. Estes in an article in the *Psychological Review* in the same year. Complex statistical models have been devised for predicting which possible responses, in a simple conditioning situation, are likely to be eliminated and which retained, at each stage of a trial-and-error sequence. This constitutes a new type of learning theory and it is still too early to judge whether or not it provides avenues for fruitful experiment.

Another new development has been the construction of mechanical models which simulate animal learning. Maze-running machines have been invented which closely simulate the learning behaviour of rats in mazes. It is argued that these models provide a mechanical plan, embodying the minimal basic mechanical functions which a nervous system must have in order to be able to discriminate and select pathways in a maze. J. A. Deutsch's *The Structural Basis of Behaviour* (1960) is typical of this type of work – the earliest application of 'cybernetics' (the study of self-regulating mechanical systems) to psychology. More recently computers have been programmed to solve simple learning and problem-solving tasks of a kind characteristically given to human experimental subjects. The verbal reports of human subjects on their patterns of decisions in performing as subjects, in identical experiments, have been compared with the printed 'trace' of the computer which shows how it worked out the problem. Analogies between the work of the brain and the computer 'information-processing' have been drawn – although it is difficult to assess the value of such investigations for psychology.

More concretely, H. F. Harlow performed a series of interesting experiments with monkeys (1949), in which he demonstrated that monkeys could solve quite difficult problems at the first trial after experience on a range of other and 'similar' problems. A 'learning set' had been formed, a generalized skill at solving any problem within a certain class of problem. Harlow argued that such 'sets' are not explicable in terms of simple stimulus–response associations or generalization. Since the 'cues' used in each trial were different, the monkeys were learning to discriminate in terms of very general criteria. Harlow's work was a sign of the dissatisfaction with established theories of learning. This dissatisfaction was also evident in Hebb's discussion of learning in *The Organization of Behaviour,* in which learning is considered as 'conceptual', and concepts are given a neurophysiological basis. In Hebb's view, the reorganization of dynamic processes in the central nervous system, rather than the formation of new associations between new items, is the basis for mature learning, so that all S–R models are misleading.

Thus, there has been an attempt to break away from the approach to learning which was developed before the Second World War and to find improved theories which account for the complexities of real-life situations.

Skills

During the Second World War it was necessary to train older men and women in skilled trades so that younger workers could be released for specialized tasks. Experimental and occupational psychologists were required to investigate the factors involved in the acquisition and practice of motor skills in various jobs. Although the influence of age on the acquisition of skill was the main interest, it was obvious that older subjects had to be matched with young ones in such investigations – hence much was found out about the learning of skills in general. Although this was partly a major project in industrial psychology, many laboratory experiments were conducted to investigate fundamental variables. A. T. Welford's *Age and Skill* (1958) reports and assesses this work, as well as the post-war developments from it. This was also a study of human learning, a somewhat neglected topic, and the first systematic attack on the important subject of man's motor skills. A new inroad into the study of learning seems to be opening up, and a new topic, 'skill', has appeared in psychological literature.

Cognitive Abilities

The study of 'thinking' has been a field in which considerable interest has developed since the war. Models derived from the theory of games and from information theory have led to new types of experiment. J. S. Bruner and his associates published *A Study of Thinking* in 1956. In Bruner's experiments the subjects are presented with instances of a 'concept' which is defined in terms of a number of attributes, each of which has a number of values. The data were cards on which geometrical figures were painted. Each figure could be given singly or in twos or threes: different colours would change the values of the figures, and each card could further be diversified by having a different type of border. Each instance involved a decision; and a series of decisions (involving a number of exemplars and non-exemplars of a chosen 'concept') were necessary before the subject could define the concept correctly (all cards with two blue circles and a single border, for instance). The process of decision-and-test gave information about the correct attributes and values. The sequence of decisions also could be required to conform to a 'strategy', the objectives of which were to maximize information, minimize strain on memory and inference, and regulate risk of failure rationally. Bruner's experiment revealed the strategies which regulate the specific decisions in each task. Presumably, since subjects were usually unaware of the strategy involved in their behaviour, the selection of a strategy is controlled by inner mechanisms and reveals the functional characteristics of 'thinking'.

Other experiments involving sequences of decisions in relation to a complex task have been designed. These have had two main effects. (1) Psychologists have been able to describe more precisely the environmental factors which facilitate or inhibit efficient reasoning or intelligent decision-making. (2) Psychologists have made new speculations about the operation of the brain in thinking-situations. One development of this new interest in cognitive processes has been the programming of computers to solve problems involving the following of strategies similar to those required of Bruner's subjects. The way in which the computer processes information in the working-out and application of such strategies provides a new model for the general functions of the brain in doing the same job. Whether or not these new ways of thinking about thinking will be adequate to model all the levels of organization involved in the brain remains to be seen. The reception and categorization of the incoming flow of information (the 'perception-translation') seems to be handled quite well. However, motivation, the complex structures from past experience, creativity and value-judgements also enter into human reasoning, and it may be a long time before these factors are capable of adequate treatment by psychologists.

Human Engineering

As has already been mentioned, during the Second World War psychologists were required to cooperate with engineers in problems arising out of the human operation of new and complicated mechanical devices. The application of the techniques of experimental psychology was aimed at discovering how equipment and machinery should be designed in order to allow for human limitations and so minimize errors or accidents in its use. The fitting of the machine to the man was a relatively new problem for the psychologist. This type of research, initiated in war-time, was obviously one to be exploited in peace-time. Thus the problems, methods and topics now included have become numerous. Psychologists have also been involved in training people to operate new kinds of equipment efficiently. P. M. Fitts, in 'Engineering Psychology and Equipment Design' (Chapter 33 in S. S. Stevens' *Handbook of Experimental Psychology*, 1951), gives a thorough account of the origins and early developments in this new field.

These are a few of the more striking new developments in experimental psychology which have appeared since 1940. The list is by no means comprehensive. Moreover, many of the methods and problems defined before 1940 had not been fully exploited in the pre-war period. Much research and discussion since the war has been the refinement of work which was familiar to psychologists in the thirties. Skinner and his assistants have produced very considerable literature on operant conditioning, the result of work done in the 1930s. Visual illusions continue to fascinate psychologists – indeed the kind of illusions to which astronauts in space-craft are subject constitutes an important topic in space research. Those interested in the experimental psychology of the 1930s will find that the work begun then continues to be developed. Not everything is new and exciting, and not everything which is new is necessarily going to turn out to be crucial.

CLINICAL PSYCHOLOGY

Clinical psychology became firmly established only after 1945. As early as 1894, August Hoch had worked as a psychologist in the McLean Hospital, Massachusetts. Witmer had established his clinic in the 1890s and we have already discussed his influence. Clinical psychology remained a tentative venture throughout the 1920s and 1930s. Psychologists worked in mental hospitals, in clinics, in child-guidance centres and in homes for the sub-normal. There was no recognized training and no official professional status. Indeed, the main techniques relevant to clinical work were only being tested for the first time in the inter-war years. In 1927 the Harvard Psychological Clinic gave clinical psychology some kind of status, so that by 1934 there were fifty clinics for the treatment of neurosis in the U.S.A. Attempts to define the proper qualifications for the profession of clinical psychologist failed in the 1930s and standards varied widely from individual to individual.

During the war this situation changed. Many psychologists were engaged in dealing with practical problems. Over 90 per cent of these had been either academics or civil servants before their war service. These psychologists discovered that their training in psychology was capable of new applications to practical problems. Pure psychology was not the only legitimate behavioural science. Moreover, they learned to use such clinical and psychometric techniques as were available, to improve and to come to have a greater respect for these hitherto 'suspect' methods. The involvement of many academics with practical problems had several important results. (a) Since the war there has been more basic research into personality tests, clinical methods of therapy, case analysis, etc. (b) Experimental techniques and psychometric methods have been refined and applied in the field of psychopathology to a greater extent than previously. (c) Clinical psychology as a profession has received recognition and encouragement.

In the U.S.A., the Veteran Administration in 1946 defined the qualifications, up to Ph.D. degree standard, which a clinical psychologist should have. The U.S. Public Health Service also provided a training programme. Universities and hospitals responded quickly by providing new courses. Hospitals created posts for clinical psychologists. Money and facilities were made available for basic research. Clinical psychology henceforward advanced rapidly, and by 1950 about 500 Ph.D.s were graduating each year as clinical psychologists in the U.S.A. Other countries began to follow this example. As early as 1955 clinical psychologists formed a large and respected group. In 1918 the American Psychological Association listed only fifteen psychologists with clinical interests. In 1937 ninety-nine were interested in this field. Clinical psychology has changed from being peripheral and dilettante to being organized and prosperous.

However, the field is still diverse and problematic. Techniques, both diagnostic and prognostic, are imperfect. There is a great variety of therapeutic method. Theories differ considerably. Clinical psychology remains an art rather than a science. But attempts are being made to improve the limitations of clinical work. Basic research into the validity of diagnostic techniques has begun. Research aimed at accurately assessing the results of different therapeutic methods have increased. Progress has been sufficient for general psychologists to become increasingly interested in both the techniques and results of both clinical research and clinical practice. Parallel to the development of clinical psychology towards maturity has been corresponding development in psychometric research and the study of personality.

PERSONALITY

At the end of the Second World War psycho-analytic concepts still dominated the thinking of psychologists, although Allport and Murray had modified the situation. Since the war several new lines of thought and practice in studying human personality have emerged.

Originating in the writings of Spearman, and elaborated in the early thirties by Thurstone, the techniques of factor analysis have come into prominence since the war. A large collection of subjects provide the analyst with a large number of scores from tests, questionnaires, ratings and laboratory experiments. With this data, derived from as many different kinds of behaviour as possible, an elaborate statistical treatment aims at isolating basic underlying 'factors'. A small number of 'factors' (for example, traits) are postulated to explain the variations in the large number of scores. Next, the factor analyst tries to devise psychometric methods of measuring these basic factors and, thus, of measuring individual differences in new types of test. The tests may be used as the basis for new descriptions of personality structure.

In England, H. J. Eysenck, of the London University Institute of Psychiatry, has combined clinical with psychometric and experimental techniques in an attempt to provide a strictly scientific study of personality. From an early study of seven hundred neurotic soldiers, Eysenck isolated, by factorial analysis, the basic dimensions of 'neuroticism' and 'extraversion–introversion'. These dimensions represent regularities among traits measured on a large number of separate scales. Eysenck thus aims at describing and measuring the basic attributes of specific types of personality. Some individuals are extreme types with high or low scores on, for instance, an introversion–extraversion scale: others are between the extremes. Thus Eysenck claims to have objectively demonstrated the existence of two different types of personality which Jung defined on the basis of clinical experience and descriptive qualitative psychological theory. Once factor analysis of innumerable scores has defined the dimension, further experiments, tests, ratings, etc., consistently differentiate individuals along this basic dimension. Further research led Eysenck to postulate dimensions of neuroticism–normality and psychotism–normality. Whatever the criticisms of factor analysis as such, there is little doubt that Eysenck has successfully applied the techniques of psychometrics and experimental psychology to the fields of psychopathology and personality study. He has also developed a theory of personality, Behaviouristic in orientation, and closely related to his empirical and statistical concepts. The large-scale projects he has supervised, the search for objective techniques for discovering basic personality-attributes, his attempts to test his basic hypotheses have introduced a new style of research both into clinical psychology and into personality theory. His anti-psycho-analytic attitudes have also been a feature of his writings.

Not dissimilar has been the work of R. B. Cattell (not related to J. M. Cattell) of Illinois University. Cattell is an Englishman and a London University graduate. After teaching at Exeter University and working as a clinical psychologist in Leicester (England) he went to the U.S.A. in 1937. Since 1944 he has been a research professor at Illinois. Like Eysenck, Cattell combines clinical with psychometric and experimental techniques, although he has not researched as a clinical psychologist but rather as a student of personality. His aim is to use factor analysis to derive, from innumerable scores, a description of basic traits. He has used data from 'life record' sources, as well as from tests, ratings, questionnaires and experiments in order to extract his 'source traits'. His tests for his basic 'dimensions' are well known and he has developed a complex theory of personality based partly on his own researches. Cattell has developed highly sophisticated correlational techniques and demonstrated how these may be used for a variety of 'analyses'. His *Description and Measurement of Personality* (1946) and his *Personality: A Systematic, Theoretical and Factual Study* (1950) have been among the most original publications of the post-war decade.

Like Eysenck, Cattell believes in large-scale projects of research. His later work has not only postulated basic dimensions (tender-mindedness, neuroticism, will-control, somatic anxiety) but has suggested that such factors are primarily the result of environment. Other factors (intelligence, cyclothymia or manic-depressive tendencies, etc.) are largely the product of heredity. Yet others are the product of both heredity and environment. His attempt at psychological genetics (based on studies of 104 identical twins, 64 fraternal twins, 182 siblings reared together, 72 unrelated children reared together, 504 children in the general population randomly chosen) is a new type of investigation.

The emphasis on quantitative methods, strictly operational concepts and statistical analysis has been a new feature of work both in clinical and personality studies. However, factor analysis has been criticized both by mathematicians who detect flaws in basic assumptions and by psychologists who argue that the factors are too abstract (being averages computed from many individuals' scores). It is too early to judge just how useful this new enterprise will be.

Within the more conventional tradition of studying the personality through interviews, case-history constructions and intensive psychotherapy there have been several new lines of thinking.

Harry Stack Sullivan (1892–1949) was a psychiatrist who established his reputation in the thirties through research into schizophrenia. However, he later developed new techniques of therapy based on ideas for facilitating communication within the clinical interview. From his clinical experience he developed a new dynamic theory which was published in 1947 in his *Conceptions of Modern Psychiatry*. Many of his publications have been edited posthumously from his notebooks and lectures: *The Interpersonal Theory of Psychiatry* (1953) is perhaps the best known. Sullivan's major emphasis was on the fact that personality develops largely out of the individual's relationships with other people. Social interactions are important factors in both normal and pathological developments. Social psychology is important for psychiatry. The concept of 'anxiety' is important in Sullivan's account of the 'self' and its mechanisms. Although he obviously owes much to Freud and Horney, Sullivan's concern with the interpersonal – the constant interaction of a person with others (including the analyst with his patient) – gives his theory an original bias. In the 1950s many psychiatrists and clinical psychologists in the U.S.A. became interested in Sullivan's ideas.

Another clinical psychologist who developed a new theory was Carl Rogers (born 1902). After working at Rochester Guidance Centre as a therapist from 1931 to 1940, Rogers became Professor of Psychology at Ohio. In 1942 he published *Counseling and Psychotherapy* and in 1951 *Client-Oriented Therapy*. The main contribution of Rogers in recent clinical psychology, and in personality study, has been the attempt to investigate objectively the efficiency of various counselling and therapeutic techniques. He was the first to obtain recordings of therapeutic sessions – with the full consent of his patients – and from the ensuing transcriptions he attempted methods of classifying, counting and analysing the responses of patients during therapy or interview. In particular, self-approving or self-critical remarks and other expressions of a positive or negative attitude towards the self were studied. The use of psychometric tests and other 'external' assessments helped to confirm the shifts in a patient's attitudes throughout the course of therapy, and thus the development of an individual under treatment could be described in terms other than the reactions of the therapist. What happens during treatment? What therapeutic tactics appear to be most effective in changing the behaviour of the patient towards more consistently normal patterns?

Statistical and psychometric techniques devised by William Stephenson of Chicago University have proved particularly useful to Rogers and his associates. These methods – Q techniques – are designed for analysing the conceptions a person has about himself, as these are evoked by Stephenson's questionnaires.

In his therapeutic methods (which are constantly revised in the light of objective research of the kind he has encouraged) and in his theory, Rogers has come to attach importance to the self-image and the way it changes. Unconscious reactions exist and are important for Rogers. However, he emphasizes the importance of what a person says about himself and his experienced difficulties. In the end, what is important is self-knowledge, and self-development towards mature goals.

However tentatively, Rogers has worked out new therapeutic techniques and a developing theory of personality. Even those who do not follow his ideas accept his attempts to test the adequacy of his assumptions and methods of treatment by reference to psychological investigations external to the theory and the clinical practice. This new approach has been welcomed at a time when clinical psychology is finding its feet. Psychotherapy is no longer a mystery revealed only from the analyst's notebooks, recollections and interpretations. It has become a subject for research and critical examination within psychology.

More recently G. Kelly, of Ohio State University,

an academic who has combined research with a great deal of clinical practice, published a theory of personality with clear applications for both psychotherapy and the assessment of individual differences. Already *The Psychology of Personal Constructs* (1955) has proved stimulating. The theory, the therapy and the tests derived from it spring from a basic idea, that 'a person's processes are psychologically channelized by the ways in which he anticipates events'. Neither his present environment, nor his past history, nor his current motivational state, are sufficient to account for behaviour: human behaviour is primarily 'anticipatory'. Bannister gives a good account of Kelly's ideas in Chapter 19 of *New Horizons in Psychology* (Penguin, 1966).

Besides those engaged actively in clinical work, more typically academic psychologists have contributed influential discussions on the structure, dynamics and development of personality. Gardner Murphy, a distinguished member of Columbia University's school of psychology from 1930 to 1940 and subsequently at City University, New York, has produced two influential books, *Personality* (1947) and *Human Potentialities* (1958). Data from almost every department of psychology were synthesized and related by Murphy to produce an eclectic, functional, 'field' theory of personality. Murphy has been concerned, after considering all the determinants of behaviour, to emphasize potentials for growth and fulfilment. A. H. Maslow has developed this approach in a recent book called *Towards a Psychology of Being* (1962) in which growth, positive mental health, and creativeness are central topics.

In the last twenty years there have been plenty of new ideas about the human personality and how we must study it. However, it might be asked whether empirical methods have improved much. It can be answered that, at least, psychologists have tried to improve their methods of research. Personality tests have been made the subject of much research designed to improve their validity and reliability. Projective techniques, questionnaires, ratings and interviews have all become a matter for basic research. As a result, new tests are constantly coming into use and, in turn, providing new information for analysis.

Apart from psychometric research, the beginnings of a neurophysiological approach to personality are noticeable. Drug therapy, psychosurgery, electrophysiology and psychosomatic medicine provide data of interest to the psychology of personality. Much more knowledge of the physical basis of personality is likely to emerge in the future, as biochemists and geneticists become involved with physiological psychology.

Things have thus moved a long way since Freud's writings were the main source of our ideas about personality. The many different studies and the diverse theories, all thrown together in this particular melting pot, have not yet produced a coherent and systematized view of the human personality. But much is happening to make this kind of psychology lively and progressive.

SOCIAL PSYCHOLOGY

During the Second World War, psychologists in America were exercised with studying 'small groups'. Many crucial military and industrial organizations, such as air-crews, commando units or research teams, were in the form of such working groups. This interest seemed to many, after the war was over, to provide a new centre for the development of social psychology. Laboratory experiments, the use of psychometric methods and the opportunity to observe spontaneous behaviour in the small group seemed to give the psychologist his chance to study social behaviour objectively.

Accounts of this development are given in G. C. Homan's *The Human Group* (1951) and W. J. H. Sprott's *Human Groups* (1958). Many different problems have been investigated with the small group in the laboratory.

The influence of the behaviour of others on that of an

individual required to make objective judgements or assessments (of defective manufactures, for example) has been a familiar type of experiment. 'Stooges' are told off to deviate from correct judgements, and the effect of the 'group norm' on an individual can be observed. It is not difficult to show the ways in which and the extent to which an individual can be influenced by group norms.

Studies in 'group climate' as a determinant of individual behaviour have become extensive. How do individuals react to working in a group when the leader creates an autocratic method, as compared with a democratic approach or a careless, indifferent attitude? What kinds of 'climate' are most pervasive in determining the behaviour of the group?

Problems of 'communication' within a group which is working cooperatively are obviously important. Different forms of organization ('communication networks') clearly involve different kinds of relationship between the members of the group. Studies have been carried out to discover how efficiency can be improved or impaired, at what points breakdowns occur, how frustration and annoyance are created in particular 'links' once a given system comes under strain, and in what circumstances the leader fails to get adequate 'feedback' from points lower down the hierarchy.

R. F. Bates in *Interaction Process Analysis* (1950) studied the complex interactions between individuals in a group engaged in solving a problem or discussing a problem. How can a group work efficiently and avoid disruption or time-wasting clashes? What behaviour contributes positively towards problem-solving, and what behaviour has the function of reducing tension, controlling extreme deviation, holding a mutual attitude of consent? Bates attempted a method of observing, classifying and analysing the interpersonal reactions of the individuals in a group spontaneously working at a problem. This method of analysis has clearly many applications to the problem of the work of committees and to problems in personnel management.

The changing 'structure' of a small group has been another topic to be investigated. Individuals in a group are not all on a par. There is a hierarchy of 'prestige' from leader downwards; the attitudes of individuals towards each other may differ considerably; the participation of each individual will be different from group to group – what each contributes and how much; and thus some groups will be more closely integrated than others. What factors influence the 'structuring' of any group? Although more difficult to study within experimental situations, attempts have been made to study the differences, in the attitude and behaviour of each individual, which influence the total organization of the group.

Much was expected of small-group studies. It was hoped that more objective and controlled studies of social behaviour would be possible. Whether or not these hopes have been fulfilled is a matter of dispute. However, there is little doubt that this development has enabled social psychologists to integrate their studies more firmly within the science of psychology, and to move away from involvement with sociological and social-anthropological types of investigation. Also, many of their researches have been usefully adapted by industrial psychologists, so that a new approach to practical problems has opened out.

Another type of research which has flourished since the war is that known as 'cross-cultural study': what effects do the basic cultural factors have on behaviour? Much of this work has been concerned with psychopathological disorders. Is the behaviour of all 'abnormal' people similar as one moves from society to society, or are some syndromes shaped by cultural influences? Do most people have similar criteria of what constitutes behaviour-pathology? Is there an ethnic personality type for each culture which determines what sort of a personality is regarded as a deviant? In what respects precisely are psychotics similar the whole world over?

In the course of such inquiries, psychological methods have been used. For example, it has been shown that not all subjects, in contrasting societies, react alike in 'optical illusion' experiments (for instance, Murray islanders are less liable to the well-known Müller–Lyer illusion than Europeans). To a certain extent, what we see and how we interpret our visual field is the product of our cultural training. Clearly, the methods of anthropology still play an important part in such comparative studies. However, much information which bears on psychological problems traditionally assigned to 'general' or 'experimental' psychology has come out of such research by social psychologists. These examples are sufficient to indicate a shift in social psychology since the war. It is attempting to deal with individual behaviour in a social context and to throw light on questions crucial to the explanation of behaviour. It is more strictly involved in psychology and less involved with other social sciences. It is for this reason that social psychology has expanded since the war. A considerable number of research institutes devoted to social psychology now exist in the U.S.A. The number of articles, monographs and books has increased to such an extent that specialization within the field is inevitable. Before the war, in spite of its confused subject matter, it would have been possible for an individual to keep abreast with most of the relevant publications. Thus, social psychology appears to have developed into something of a major department of the science.

OCCUPATIONAL PSYCHOLOGY

As we have seen, applied psychologists benefited from the Second World War as much as they did from the First. 'Human engineering', the design of equipment to suit human capacity and adaptability, has grown into a discipline on its own. However, psychologists have not neglected the problem of fitting the man to the job. It has been realized how slipshod and amateur many training methods are. Much research into the basic factors involved in training young people for skilled work has begun – often for the first time in the history of a specific industry. D. H. Holding's *Principles of Training* (1965) gives a good account of this kind of research. These two fields cover much that is new in occupational psychology.

Much occupational psychology is development along the lines laid down in earlier times. Vocational guidance, selection, methods and organization of work, working environment, the improvement of tests – all these long-established topics have continued to receive the attention of those engaged in research. What is different are the improved techniques, and the fact that research is organized on more massive lines. In the U.S.A. new kinds of work have been stimulated by the American 'probings' of outer space, and by the American system of 'early warning' against possible nuclear attacks. In both these fields research into human adaptability to complex equipment and stressful environment has given occupational psychologists a new outlet for their expertise.

This sketch of some of the newer developments in psychology in the decade after the Second World War is far from comprehensive. It may serve, however, to emphasize that there have been no dramatic changes. Improvements in techniques of research, more elaborate apparatus, more sophisticated experiments and a switch of interest to more precisely defined problems – all this may have occurred: but the scope and aims of psychology remain much the same as they were at the start of the war.

CHAPTER TWENTY-FIVE

The Achievements and Limitations of Psychology

I N looking back over the century and a half during which psychology has come into existence, are there any generalizations which a historian might hazard?

Have any specific methods, techniques or skills been discovered which seem to have provided the means for an advance in the science? Fechner's psychophysical methods, Helmholtz's adaptation of experiments in physiology to answer psychological questions, Freud's free-association methods for eliciting 'unconscious' activities? It would seem that the methods and techniques whereby psychologists observe, describe and analyse their data are still very imperfect. In psychology, as in other disciplines, progress is slow but sure, a matter of trial and error, of refining and improving equipment and experimental design and standardized tests until what one uses is a little better than what was available a decade or so earlier. The move away from rationalistic thinking towards observation and experiment was clearly a sound one. Psychologists, in the technical sense, are just beginning to be able to regard themselves as scientists – but their technical equipment is still fairly elementary.

Can we say that there was any psychologist whose theories or general conceptions have been more fruitful than those of others? Were Pavlov and Watson more productive of working ideas than Freud and Jung? Does factor analysis, the gift of Spearman and Thurstone, provide superior insights to those of the clinical psychologists or personality theorists?

It is doubtful if any thinker can claim to have provided psychology with a fundamental set of concepts. Every theory or systematic formulation has its defects and limitations as well as its insights. Psychology seems to have moved in terms of a kind of dialectic: whenever a theory or method has been formulated and used, a contrary view has arisen to correct its errors and bring the thinking of psychologists back towards caution and uncertainty. In its day every 'school' has provided stimulation and guidance, only to dissolve into the past as an 'old' way of thinking – yet having modified the general outlook in some important respect. The Behaviourists, for example, broke the exclusive reliance on 'introspection of consciousness' as the task of psychology and opened up new problems and possiblities. Before them, the Functionalists persuaded psychologists that action, the 'motor' side of the organism, and adaptation to environment, were as important as the sensory-perceptual aspect of the mind.

However, it might be argued that psychology has produced at least three or four great men of supreme importance in the development of a sane psychology.

Francis Galton realized that the definition and measurement of individual differences was a fundamental objective for psychology. The construction and application of tests to isolate and measure individual differences, with the possibility of subjecting the data of such tests to statistical description and analysis, were his inventions. Psychologists have achieved much from the development of Galton's conceptions. He also insisted that psychologists should discover correlations between overt, determinable variables, without getting involved either in the definition of 'intervening variables' or 'hypothetical constructs', or with theories based on a 'model organism'. This approach has proved a practical one, capable of widespread exploitation.

William James also realized that providing a workable description of behaviour was more essential than attempting to model psychology on physiological or physical science. James's contribution was to realize that psychology as an empirical science is bound to meet difficulties and become problematic in a way in which other sciences need not. Any method, technique, theory or hypothesis must be rigorously scrutinized and criticized before being accepted. Only by being shown to be often erroneous, ambiguous or absurd can psychological thinking move forward. Laboratories and clinics may be essential, but it is no bad thing to have an armchair in which to think about the assumptions and methods in terms of which the empirical work proceeds.

James also emphasized the importance of studying the individual personality as a dynamic, changing, complex entity. He saw that methods other than those derived from experimental physiology would be necessary if individual psychology were to develop. He suggested that clinical medicine might provide a starting-point, and he began by introducing data from psychopathology into general psychology. Finally, James demonstrated that it is possible to synthesize and systematize the results of empirical research without constructing a controversial 'theory'. He stuck to a plain, inductive procedure in his systematic psychology. Unfortunately, very few theorists in psychology have followed his example.

It is difficult to decide between Freud and Jung for a third example. Freud, exploiting insights of Janet and Breuer, was the pioneer in emphasizing unconscious, subliminal processes and the primitive character of many human impulses. However, Jung was quick to see the limitations and possible errors in Freud's psychology, and his deviation gave the psycho-analytic movement the controversial character which was necessary for its development. Jung's claim to be one of the great psychologists might shock some strict empiricists; however his claim would seem to be a strong one. His was a highly intuitive, imaginative and creative mind – and psychology has had only too few such intelligences. Jung emphasized the possibility that an adult personality may grow and mature, may change in positive directions, at a time when most psychologists were over-deterministic in their view of human nature. He made the distinction between extraversion and introversion which psychometric researches seem to have confirmed as a basic 'dimension'. His concept of 'integration' has seemed to many to have implications which are confirmed by accumulated clinical data – and, indeed, many of his clinical observations would seem capable of, at least, guiding psychopathological research of the contemporary 'objective-methods' kind towards interesting problems. His enormous erudition (as typified by his opening-up of folklore, mythology and comparative religion as sources for psychological problems and hypotheses) was a characteristic which at least one or two psychologists might have in every generation. The historian, in his Olympian mood, might therefore reconcile the former friends and include Freud and Jung on the list of psychological father-figures.

There have been many able scientists and many ingenious theorists who have their place in any history of psychology. Any choice of great men is bound to be controversial. Galton, James, Freud and Jung do seem to have the marks of genius and to have contributed something crucial to the development of our understanding of what psychology is about.

Many leading psychologists have had a conception of psychology as *the* science of human, and animal, behaviour. All other approaches to human nature were regarded as either imperfect or reducible to psychological theories. Freud, Watson, Hull, Skinner, together with many contemporary 'personality' theorists, regard psychology as being ultimately able to provide a comprehensive account of anything and everything a man or animal does. All possible questions concerning behaviour can be answered, in the long run, only by a scientific psychology. There are many today who would question this view. Since the war some psychologists have come to take a more humble and restricted view of their discipline. There is a limited range of questions to which the several branches of psychology may supply the answers. But there are other groups of questions about behaviour which can only be answered in terms of the techniques of other 'behaviour sciences' such as sociology, anthropology, social economics. Moreover there are some questions about behaviour which are outside the scope of empirical *sciences*, but to which objective and rational answers can be provided as the result of research in history, politics or jurisprudence. Psychologists have no monopoly in the business of describing and explaining behaviour. They merely answer certain kinds of question about behaviour in terms of their own limited varieties of theory and technique.

This view is now increasingly common among psychologists. There has been a reaction against theory-construction and 'big questions'. Many psychologists, having mastered their technical skills, are content to specialize in dealing with comparatively restricted problems without worrying about broader implications or general theories. It is generally thought that psychology is not a coherent and tidy discipline, but a vast and rambling collection of bits and pieces. If it is a 'family' of different methods, techniques and problems, then the family is one which exhibits striking individual differences. The older view that a comprehensive, systematic science of behaviour might evolve has not been abandoned. There are still prominent psychologists, such as Skinner and K. W. Spence, who believe that it must be the goal of psychology. However, this is not so dominant a view as it was thirty years earlier.

Looking back, one might be tempted to be pessimistic over the development of psychology. The results of research are often tentative or open to question. There have been false starts; grand-scale systems have flourished which are now extinct; precise but futile experiments have often appeared in the journals and monographs; there has been muddled thinking which has drifted off into metaphysics or amateur sociology. Yet there has also been slow but definite progress. It cannot be denied that there are several problems which belong to a group of disciplines which may be categorized as 'Psychology', and are not strictly physiological, sociological or philosophical problems. Techniques have been developed which are relatively successful in dealing with these problems. At least some psychological experiments and some psychometric tests and some analytical thinking has provided us with knowledge which we did not have before. Other psychological research has merely confirmed what, in a sense, many people knew already but could not show to be the case objectively. Again, many practical problems have been clarified and even solved by applied psychologists. The story is very far from one of failure or disappointed hopes. It is one of modest but positive progress which justifies the enterprise of the pioneers of the nineteenth century.

Most psychologists would admit that they have not yet mastered their fundamental problems. In all branches of the subject it is probably the case that the big attacks have yet to be launched. This is as true for the history of psychology, a neglected branch of the subject, as for any other. Only when much more work has been done in studying the past efforts of psychologists will we fully appreciate the value of those efforts and the true character of what William James called the 'snares' of psychology.

Bibliography

General

HISTORIES

BORING, E. G., *A History of Experimental Psychology*, 1950. *Sensation and Perception in the History of Experimental Psychology*, 1942.

BRETT, G. S., *A History of Psychology* (3 vols.), 1921.

FLUGEL, J. C., *A Hundred Years of Psychology, 1833–1933*, Part V (1933–63) revised by D. J. West, 1964.

HEARNSHAW, L. S., *A Short History of British Psychology, 1840–1940*, 1964.

MURPHY, G., *An Historical Introduction to Modern Psychology*, 1949.

ROBACK, A. A., *A History of American Psychology*, 1964.

EXTRACTS

DENNIS, W., *Readings in the History of Psychology*, 1948.

HERRNSTEIN, R. J., and BORING, E. G., *A Source Book in the History of Psychology*, 1965.

RAND, B., *Classical Psychologists*, 1912.

SHIPLEY, T., *Classics in Psychology*, 1961.

John Wiley are publishing a series edited by Mandler and Kessen called 'Perspectives in Psychology'. Each volume covers a particular field and consists of extracts from books and articles illustrating the historical development of psychological research in that field. The volumes that have appeared so far are:

Thinking: From Association to Gestalt (J. M. and G. Mandler)
Perception (William Dember)
The Child (William Kessen)
Mathematics and Psychology (G. A. Miller)

C. Murchison's four-volumed *A History of Psychology in*

Autobiography (1930–47) presents psychologists writing about their work and their intellectual development.

Since January 1965, *The Journal for the History of the Behavioural Sciences* (ed. R. L. Watson, published by Psychology Press, Brandon, Vermont, U.S.A.) has appeared quarterly (January, April, July, October). Articles on the history of psychology form the main contents, and there are book reviews of recent works on the history of psychology.

Psychology in the Making, ed. L. Postman (1962), contains articles tracing the history of work on specific psychological problems. The journal *Psychological Bulletin* publishes review articles which examine the development of research into specific problems in recent psychology. The issues for earlier years throw light on history.

Chapter 1: *The Beginnings of Psychology within Philosophy*

HALL, G. S., *Founders of Modern Psychology*, 1912.

RIBOT, T., *La psychologie anglaise contemporaine*, 1870: tr. *English Psychology Today*, 1874 (for Brown, James Mill, J. S. Mill and Bain).

La psychologie allemande contemporaine, 1879; tr. J. M. Baldwin, *German Psychology Today*, 1886 (for Herbart and Lotze).

SORLEY, W. R., *A History of British Philosophy to 1900*, 1920.

BROWN

BROWN, THOMAS, *Lectures on the Philosophy of the Human Mind*, 1820.

WELSH, D., *Accounts of the Life and Writings of Thomas Brown*, 1825.

JAMES MILL

MILL, JAMES, *The Analysis of the Phenomena of the Human Mind*, 1829.

BAIN, A., *James Mill*, 1881.

BIBLIOGRAPHY

J. S. MILL

MILL, J. S., *Logic*, 1836.

BAIN

BAIN, ALEXANDER, *The Senses and the Intellect*, 1855.
The Emotions and the Will, 1859.

HERBART

HERBART, J. F., *Lehrbuch zur Psychologie*, 1816; tr. M. K.
Smith, *A Textbook in Psychology*, 1891.
SHIPLEY, T., *Classics in Psychology*, 1961, pp. 22–50
(excerpts).

LOTZE

LOTZE, HERMANN, *Medizinische Psychologie*, 1851.
Grundzüge der Psychologie, 1881; tr. G. T. Ladd and C. L.
Herrick, *Outlines of Psychology*, 1885.

Chapter 2: *The Beginnings of Psychology with in Physiology*

BELL, C., *The Idea of a New Anatomy of the Brain*, 1811.
The Nervous System of the Human Body, 1830.
FERRIER, D., *The Functions of the Brain*, 1876.
FLOURENS, P., *Expériences sur le système nerveux*, 1825
(excerpts in Dennis, pp. 129–39).
FOSTER, M., *Lectures on the History of Physiology*, 1901.
HALL, M., *Memoires on the Nervous System*, 1837.
HELMHOLTZ, H., excerpts in Dennis, p. 197.
HOCHBERG, J. E., 'Nativism versus Empiricism', in L. Post-
man, *Psychology in the Making*, 1962.
KRECH, D., 'Cortical Localisation of Function', in L. Postman,
Psychology in the Making, 1962.
MÜLLER, J., *Handbuch der Physiologie des Menschen* (2 vols.),
1834–40; tr. W. Bayly, *Elements of Physiology*, 1837–42.
NORDENSKIÖLD, E., *History of Biology*, 1928.

BIBLIOGRAPHY

SOURY, J., *Système nerveux central*, 1899.
WEBER, E. H., excerpts in Dennis, pp. 194–6.
  De tactu, 1834.
  Der Tastinn und das Gemeingefühl, 1846.
YOUNG, T., *Miscellaneous Works*, 1855.

Chapter 3 : *The Emergence of Experimental Psychology*

FECHNER

FECHNER, G., *Elemente der Psychophysik*, 1860; tr. H. Adler, *Elements of Psychophysics*, 1966.

HELMHOLTZ

HELMHOLTZ, H., *Die Lehre von den Tonempfindungen*, 1863; tr. A. J. Ellis, *On the Sensations of Tone*, 1875.
  Handbuch der physiologischen Optik (3 vols.), 1856–66; tr. J. P. C. Southall, *Handbook of Physiological Optics*, 1924–5.
KOENIGSBERGER, L., *Hermann von Helmholtz* (3 vols.), 1902–3 (in German).
MCKENDRICK, J. G., *Hermann von Helmholtz*, 1899.

WUNDT

WUNDT, W., *Vorlesungen über der Menschen- und Tierseele*, 1863; tr. J. E. Creighton and E. B. Titchener, 1894.
  Grundzüge der physiologischen Psychologie, 1874; tr. E. B. Titchener, *Principles of Physiological Psychology*, 1904.
  Einführung in die Psychologie, 1911; tr. R. Pintner, *An Introduction to Psychology*, 1912.

E. B. Titchener in *Experimental Psychology* (1905) discusses the work of German experimental psychologists in detail. E. G. Boring's *History of Experimental Psychology* is also excellent on German psychology.

Chapter 4: *Psychology in Germany 1880–1914*

G. E. Müller is discussed by D. Katz in *Psychological Bulletin* (1935) and by O. Krohn in the *American Journal of Psychology* (1893). C. Stumpf gives an account of his work in C. Murchison's *History of Psychology in Autobiography*, Vol. 1, 1930, pp. 389–441. H. Ebbinghaus's *Über das Gedächtnis* has been translated into English by Ruger and Byssenius 1913 (Dover Books paperback edition 1964). A full account of the Würzburg school is given in G. Humphrey's *Thinking* (1951), Chapters 2, 3 and 4.

J. M. and G. Mandler's *Thinking: From Association to Gestalt* (1964) has extracts from Watt (1905), Ach (1905), Marbe (1901) and Külpe (1912).

E. B. Titchener has references to the work of German experimental psychologists in his *Experimental Psychology* (1905).

Chapter 5: *The Evolutionary Doctrine*

FOTHERGILL, P. G., *Historical Aspects of Organic Evolution*, 1952.
SMITH, J. M., *Evolution*, 1958.

DARWIN

DARWIN, CHARLES, *The Origin of Species by Natural Selection*, 1859.
   The Expression of the Emotions in Man and Animals, 1872.
BARNETT, S. A., *A Century of Darwin*, 1958.
DARLINGTON, C. D., *Darwin's Place in History*, 1959.

SPENCER

SPENCER, HERBERT, *Principles of Psychology*, 1855.

GALTON

GALTON, FRANCIS, *Hereditary Genius*, 1869.
   Inquiries into Human Faculty and Its Development, 1883.

BIBLIOGRAPHY

BURT, CYRIL, 'Francis Galton and His Contributions to Psychology', *British Journal of Statistical Psychology*, 15, 1962.

PEARSON, K., *Life, Letters and Labours of Francis Galton* (4 vols.), 1914–30.

PEEL, E. A., 'The Permanent Contribution of Francis Galton', *British Journal of Educational Psychology*, 1953.

SPALDING, ROMANES, MORGAN AND HOBHOUSE

HALDANE, J. B. S., 'Introducing Douglas Spalding', *British Journal of Animal Behaviour*, 1954.

ROMANES, G. J., *Animal Intelligence*, 1882.
Mental Evolution in Animals, 1883.
Mental Evolution in Man, 1888.
Life and Letters, 1896.

MORGAN, C. LLOYD, *Animal Intelligence*, 1890.
Introduction to Comparative Psychology, 1894.
Habit and Instinct, 1896.
Emergent Evolution, 1923.

MURCHISON, C., *History of Psychology in Autobiography*, 1932, Vol. 2, pp. 237–64 (for Lloyd Morgan).

HOBHOUSE, L. T., *Mind in Evolution*, 1901.
Development and Purpose, 1913.

HOBSON, J. A., and GINSBERG, M., *L. T. Hobhouse: His Life and Work*, 1930.

Chapter 6: *Psychology in the U.S.A. 1880–1914*

JAMES

JAMES, W., *The Principles of Psychology*, 1890.

HEIDBREDER, E., *Seven Psychologies*, 1933 (pp. 152–200 for William James).

PERRY, R. B., *The Thought and Character of William James*, 1933.

The Psychological Review, 1943 (for centenary articles on James by Allport, Dewey, Delabarre and Thorndike).

BIBLIOGRAPHY

HALL

HALL, G. S., *Life and Confessions of a Psychologist*, 1923.
Adolescence: Its Psychology (2 vols.), 1904.
BURNHAM, W. H., 'G. S. Hall', *Psychological Review*, 1925.
STARBUCK, E. D., 'G. S. Hall as a Psychologist', *Psychological Review*, 1925.

BALDWIN

BALDWIN, J. M., *Mental Development in the Child and the Race*, 1895.
MURCHISON, C., *History of Psychology in Autobiography*, Vol. 1, 1930, pp. 1–30.

CATTELL

CATTELL, J. M., *J. M. Cattell, Man of Science* (2 vols.), 1942.

LADD

LADD, G. T., *Elements of Physiological Psychology*, 1887.
ARMSTRONG, A. C., 'G. T. Ladd', *Philosophical Review*, 1921.
TITCHENER, E. B., 'G. T. Ladd', *American Journal of Psychology*, 1921.

SCRIPTURE

SCRIPTURE, E. W., *Studies from the Yale Psychological Laboratory*, 1892–1902.
The New Psychology, 1898.
MURCHISON, C., *History of Psychology in Autobiography*, Vol. 3, 1936, pp. 231–61.

ANGELL

ANGELL, J. R., 'The Relations of Structural and Functional Psychology', *Philosophical Review*, 1903.
'The Province of Functional Psychology', *Psychological Review*, 1907.
Psychology, 1904.

BIBLIOGRAPHY

MURCHISON, C., *History of Psychology in Autobiography*, Vol. 3, 1936, pp. 1–38.

HUNTER, W. S., 'J. R. Angell', *American Journal of Psychology*, 1949.

TITCHENER

TITCHENER, E. B., *Experimental Psychology* (4 vols.), 1901–5.

Lectures on the Experimental Psychology of the Thought Processes, 1909.

FOSTER, W. S., *Studies in Psychology* (Titchener's commemorative volume), 1917.

HEIDBREDER, E., *Seven Psychologies*, 1933, pp. 113–51.

WOODWORTH, R. S., *Contemporary Schools of Psychology*, 1931 edition, pp. 18–42.

THORNDIKE

THORNDIKE, E. L., *Animal Intelligence*, Psychological Monographs, 1898.

Introduction to the Theory of Mental and Social Measurement, 1904.

Selected Writings from a Connectionist Psychology, 1947.

MURCHISON, C., *History of Psychology in Autobiography*, Vol. 3, 1936, pp. 263–70.

WATSON

WATSON, J. B., 'Psychology as the Behaviorist Views It', *Psychological Review*, 1913.

'The Place of the Conditioned Response in Psychology', *Psychological Review*, 1916.

Psychology from the Standpoint of a Behaviorist, 1919.

MURCHISON, C., *History of Psychology in Autobiography*, Vol. 3, 1936, pp. 271–81.

YERKES

YERKES, R. M., *Psychological Examination in U.S. Army*, 1921.

The Great Apes, 1929.

MURCHISON, C., *History of Psychology in Autobiography*, Vol. 2, 1932, pp. 381–407.

Chapter 7: *The Influence of Physiology 1870–1914*

BROWN, DENNY (ed.), *Selected Writings of Charles Sherrington*, 1939.

GASKELL, W. H., *The Involuntary Nervous System*, 1916.

LANGLEY, J. N., *The Autonomic Nervous System*, 1921.

LUCAS, K., *The Conduction of Nervous Impulses*, 1917.

SCHAFER, E. A., *Textbook of Physiology*, 1900.

SOURY, J., 'Histoire des doctrines de l'histologie du système nerveux central', *Archives de Neurologie*, 3, 1867.

RIESE, W., *History of Neurology*, 1959.

TAYLOR, J. (ed.), *Selected Writings of Hughling Jackson* (2 vols.), 1932.

Chapter 8: *British Psychology 1870–1914*

BARTLETT, F. C., 'Cambridge 1887–1937', *American Journal of Psychology*, 1937.

SULLY

SULLY, JAMES, *Sensation and Intuition*, 1874.
   Illusions, 1881.
   Outlines of Psychology, 1884.
   Studies of Childhood, 1895.
   My Life and Friends, 1918.

WARD

WARD, JAMES, 'Psychology', *Encyclopaedia Britannica*, 1885.
   Psychological Principles, 1918.

BARTLETT, F. C., 'James Ward', *American Journal of Psychology*, 1925.

BIBLIOGRAPHY

STOUT

STOUT, G. F., *Manual of Psychology*, 1898.
    Analytic Psychology, 1896.
MACE, C. A., 'G. F. Stout', *British Journal of Psychology*, 1946.

MCDOUGALL

MCDOUGALL, WILLIAM, *Physiological Psychology*, 1905.
    Introduction to Social Psychology, 1908.
    Psychology, the Study of Behaviour, 1912.
MURCHISON, C., *History of Psychology in Autobiography*,
    Vol. 1, 1930, pp. 191–223.

RIVERS

RIVERS, W. H. R., *Instinct and the Unconscious*, 1920.
    Conflict and Dream, 1921.
    Psychology and Politics, 1923.
BARTLETT, F. C., 'W. H. R. Rivers', *American Journal of
    Psychology*, 1923.

MYERS

MYERS, C. S., *Textbook of Experimental Psychology*, 1909.
MURCHISON, C., *History of Psychology in Autobiography*,
    Vol. 3, 1936, pp. 215–30.
PEAR, T. H., 'C. S. Myers', *British Journal of Psychology*, 1947.

SPEARMAN

SPEARMAN, C. E., 'General Intelligence Objectively Deter-
    mined and Measured'. *American Journal of Psychology*,
    1904.
    'General Ability, Its Existence and Nature', *British Journal
    of Psychology*, 1912.
DODD, S. C., 'The Theory of Factors', *Psychological Review*,
    1927.
FLUGEL, J. C., 'C. E. Spearman', *British Journal of Psychology*,
    1946.

Chapter 9: *French Psychology 1870–1914*

BINET, A., 'Le développement de l'intelligence chez enfants', *L'Année Psychologique*, 1908 (extract in Dennis, pp. 419–24).

BINET, A., and HENRI, V., 'La psychologie individuelle', *L'Année Psychologique*, 1896.

BINET, A., and SIMON, T., 'Méthodes nouvelles pour le diagnostie du niveau intellectuel des anormaux', *L'Année Psychologique* (extract in Dennis, pp. 419–24).

Chapter 10: *Psychopathology from Pinel to Psycho-Analysis*

ACKERKNECHT, E. H., *A Short History of Psychiatry*, 1959.

SCHNECK, J. M., *A History of Psychiatry*, 1960.

ZILBOORG, G., and HENRY, G. W., *A History of Medical Psychology*, 1941.

PINEL

PINEL, P., *Traité médico-philosophique sur l'aliénation mentale ou la manie*, 1801; tr. D. D. Davis, *A Treatise on Insanity*, 1806.

GRIESINGER

GRIESINGER, W., *Die Pathologie und Therapie*, 1845; tr. C. L. Robertson and J. Rutherford, *Pathology and Therapy*, 1862.

KRAEPELIN

KRAEPELIN, E., *Lectures on Clinical Psychiatry*, tr. T. Johnstone, 1904.

BRACELAND, F. J., 'Kraepelin, His System and Its Influence', *American Journal of Psychiatry*, 1957.

BIBLIOGRAPHY

BLEULER

BLEULER, E., *Dementia Praecox*, 1911; tr. Josef Zinkin. *Lehrbuch der Psychiatrie*, 1916; tr. A. A. Brill, *Textbook of Psychiatry*, 1924.

CHARCOT

CHARCOT, J. M., *Leçons sur les maladies du système nerveux* (2 vols.), 1880; tr. E. P. Hurdl, *Clinical Lectures on Diseases of the Nervous System*, 1887.

GUILLAIN, G., *J.-M. Charcot, 1825–93*, 1903; tr. P. Bailey, 1909.

JANET

JANET, PIERRE, *The Major Symptoms of Hysteria*, 1907.

MURCHISON, C., *History of Psychology in Autobiography*, Vol. 1, 1930, pp. 123–33.

FREUD (see also p. 444)

FREUD, S., *Die Traumdeutung*, 1900; tr. A. A. Brill, *The Interpretation of Dreams*, 1913.
'The Origin and Development of Psycho-Analysis', *American Journal of Psychology*, 1910.
Zur Psychopathologie des Alltagslebens, 1904; tr. A. A. Brill, *The Psychopathology of Everyday Life*, 1914.

FREUD, S., and BREUER, J., *Studien über Hysterie*, 1895; tr. A. A. Brill, *Studies on Hysteria*, 1960.

Chapter 12: *Behaviourism 1918–40*

GUTHRIE, E. R., *The Psychology of Learning*, 1935.

HOLT, E. B., *Animal Drive and the Learning Process*, 1931.

HULL, C. L., 'Knowledge and Purpose as Habit Mechanisms', *Psychological Review*, 1930.
'Goal Attraction and Directing Ideas as Habit Phenomena', *Psychological Review*, 1931.
'The Concept of the Habit Family Hierarchy and Maze Learning', *Psychological Review*, 1934.

'Mind, Mechanism and Adaptive Behaviour', *Psychological Review*, 1937.

'The Problem of Stimulus Equivalence in Behavior Theory', *Psychological Review*, 1939.

HUNTER, W. S., 'Psychology and Anthropoponomy', in C. Murchison, *Psychologies of 1925*.

ROBACK, A. A., *Behaviourism and Psychology*, 1923.

SKINNER, B. F., *The Behavior of Organisms*, 1938.

TOLMAN, E. C., *Purposive Behavior in Animals and Men*, 1932.

WEISS, A. P., *A Theoretical Basis of Human Behaviour*, 1925.

WOODWORTH, R. S., *Contemporary Schools of Psychology*, 2nd edn, 1948.

Chapter 13: *Gestalt Psychology*

ELLIS, W. D., *A Source Book of Gestalt Psychology*, 1938.

HARTMAN, G. W., *Gestalt Psychology*, 1935.

HENLE, M., *Documents of Gestalt Psychology*, 1961.

KOFFKA, K., *Principles of Gestalt Psychology*, 1935.

KÖHLER, W., *Gestalt Psychology*, 1940.

Chapter 14: *Psycho-Analysis and Its Derivatives*

FREUD

FREUD, S., *Collected Papers*, tr. under Joan Riviere, 5 vols., 1924–50.

Collected Works (in English), ed. James Strachey, 1953– (in progress).

Vorlesungen zur Einführung in die Psycho-analyse, 1916; tr. Joan Riviere, *Introductory Lectures on Psycho-Analysis*, 1922.

Jenseits des Lustprinzips, 1922; tr. C. J. M. Hubback, *Beyond the Pleasure Principle*, 1922.

Das Ich und das Es, 1922; tr. Joan Riviere, *The Ego and the Id*, 1923.

JONES, ERNEST, *The Life and Work of Sigmund Freud*, 1959–61.

BIBLIOGRAPHY

PUNER, H. W., *Freud, His Life and Mind*, 1947.
SACHS, H., *Freud, Master and Friend*, 1944.

JUNG

JUNG, C. G., *Collected Works* (in English), ed. Herbert Read
    et al., 1953– (in progress).
    Wandlungen und Symbole der Libido, 1912; tr. B. M. Hinkle,
    The Psychology of the Unconscious, 1916.
    Psychologische Typen, 1921; tr. H. G. Baynes, *Psychological
    Types*, 1923.
    Psychologie und Alchemie, 1944; tr. R. F. C. Hull, *Psychology
    and Alchemy*, 1953.
    Einführung in das Wesen der Mythologie, 1949; tr. R. F. C.
    Hull, *Introduction to the Science of Mythology*, 1951.
    Contributions to Analytical Psychology, essays and lectures
    tr. H. G. and C. F. Baynes, 1928.
    Modern Man in Search of a Soul, essays tr. W. S. Dell and
    C. F. Baynes, 1933.
    The Integration of the Personality, tr. S. M. Dell, 1939.
FORDHAM, F., *An Introduction to Jung's Psychology*, 1953.
JACOBI, J., *The Psychology of C. G. Jung*, 1942.

ADLER

ADLER, A., *Praxis und Theorie des Individualpsychologie*,
    1920; *Practice and Theory of Individual Psychology*, 1927.
    Menschenkenntris, 1927; *Understanding Human Nature*,
    1927.
    Der Sinn des Lebens, 1933; *Social Interest: A Challenge to
    Mankind*, 1938.
    Problems of Neurosis, 1929.
    The Pattern of Life, 1930.
ANSBACHER, H. and R., *The Individual Psychology of Alfred
    Adler*, 1955.
BOTTOME, P., *Alfred Adler*, 1947.
WAY, L., *Alfred Adler*, 1956.

*

HORNEY, K., *Collected Works* (2 vols.), 1942.
FROMM, ERICH, *Escape from Freedom*, 1941; published in
    the U.K. as *The Fear of Freedom*, 1942.

Chapter 15: *Dynamic Psychological Theory*

WOODWORTH, R. S., *Dynamic Psychology*, 1918.

MURCHISON, C., *History of Psychology in Autobiography*, Vol. 2, 1930, pp. 359–80 (for Woodworth), Vol. 1, 1930, pp. 191–233 (for McDougall).

SPEARMAN, C. E., 'Life and Work of William McDougall', *Character and Personality*, 1939.

Chapter 16: *Physiological Psychology 1918–40*

ADRIAN, E. D., *The Mechanism of Nervous Action*, 1932. *The Basis of Sensation*, 1928.

CANNON, W. B., *Bodily Changes in Pain, Hunger, Fear and Rage*, 1929.
The Wisdom of the Body, 1932.

COGHILL, G. E., *Anatomy and the Problem of Behaviour*, 1929.

FRANZ, S. I., 'The Functions of the Cerebrum', *Archives of Psychology*, 1907 (see also C. Murchison, *Psychology in Autobiography*, Vol. 2, 1932, pp. 89–113).

FULTON, J. F., *The Physiology of the Nervous System*, 1938.

HEAD, H., *Studies in Neurology*, 1920.

KAPPERS, C. U., *Evolution of the Nervous System*, 1929.

LASHLEY, K. S., *Brain Mechanism and Intelligence*, 1929.

Chapter 17: *Experimental Psychology 1918–40*

PERCEPTION

Many of the original articles are in German in *Zeitschrift Psychologie*, the periodical edited by Gestalt psychologists. However, R. S. Woodworth's textbook *Experimental Psychology* (1938), Chapters 18–26, and M. D. Vernon's *Visual Perception* (1937) report most of the crucial experiments. *The Psychology of Egon Brunswick* (ed. K. Hammond), 1966, is another useful source. D. Katz's *Gestalt Psychology* (1938) and Koffka's *Principles of Gestalt Psychology* (1935) are also sources of the original experimental work.

LEARNING

E. R. Hilgard and D. G. Marquis, in *Conditioning and Learning* (1st edn 1940), report the main topics and experiments and provide a full bibliography. G. Humphrey's *The Nature of Learning* (1933) is a typical book of the period. R. S. Woodworth's textbook *Experimental Psychology* (1938) devotes Chapters 5–8 to learning. I. P. Pavlov's *Conditioned Reflexes* (tr. Anrep, 1927) and *Lectures on Conditioned Reflexes* (tr. Gantt, 1928) were influential books. E. R. Hilgard's *Theories of Learning* (1st edn 1948) gives an account of the various interpretations of the experimental result. In Chapters 8, 9 and 10 of C. E. Osgood's *Method and Theory in Experimental Psychology* (1953) there is an excellent discussion of the controversies. All these books have detailed references to articles in psychological journals.

COGNITIVE FUNCTIONS

R. S. Woodworth's *Experimental Psychology* (1938) discusses memory and thinking in Chapters 23, 24 and 25, and quotes most of the crucial experiments. F. C. Bartlett's *Remembering* (1932) and K. Koffka's *Principles of Gestalt Psychology*, Chapters 12 and 13, discuss the new approach to the study of memory. K. Duncker's *Zur Psychologie des produktiven Denkens* (*On Problem-Solving*) (1935), translated by L. S. Lees in Psychological Monographs, 240, 1945, is a celebrated and typical research into thought processes. Many of the experiments of the 1920s and 1930s, with references to the original articles and monographs, are discussed in more contemporary textbooks of experimental psychology. C. E. Osgood's *Method and Theory in Experimental Psychology* (1953) and S. S. Stevens' *Handbook of Experimental Psychology* (1951) have many references to earlier work.

Chapter 18: *The Development of Tests 1918–40*

ALLPORT, G. W., 'A Test for Ascendance–Submission', *Journal of Abnormal Psychology*, 1928.
ALLPORT, G. W., and ALLPORT, F. H., *The A–S Reaction*

Study: A Scale for Measuring Ascendance–Submission in Personality, 1928.

ALLPORT, G. W., and VERNON, P. E., *Studies in Expressive Movements*, 1932.

BECK, S. J., 'Introduction to the Rorschach Personality Test', *Res. Mon. Amer. Orthopsych.*, 1937.

BROWN, W., STEPHENSON, W., 'A Test Theory of Two Factors', *British Journal of Psychology*, 1933.

BURT, C., 'Correlations between Persons', *British Journal of Psychology*, 1933.

The Factors of the Mind, 1940.

ELLIS, A., 'The Validity of Personality Questionnaires', *Psychological Bulletin*, 1946.

ESTES, S. G., 'Judging Personality from Expressive Behaviour', *Journal of Abnormal Social Psychology*, 1938.

FISHER, R. A., *Statistical Methods for Research Workers*, 1925.

FRANK, L. K., 'Projective Methods for the Study of Personality', *Journal of Psychology*, 1939.

FREYD, M., 'The Graphic Rating Scale', *Journal of Educational Psychology*, 1923.

'Introverts and Extraverts', *Psychological Review*, 1924.

FRYER, D., *The Measurement of Interests*, 1931.

GUILFORD, J. P., *Psychometric Methods*, 1936.

HATHAWAY, S. R., and McKINLEY, J. C., 'A Multiphasic Personality Schedule (Minnesota)', *Journal of Psychology*, 1940.

HEIDBREDER, E., 'Measuring Introversion and Extraversion', *Journal of Abnormal Social Psychology*, 1926.

HERZ. M. R., 'The Rorschach Inkblot Tests', *Psychological Bulletin*, 1933.

'Rorschach: Twenty Years After', *Psychological Bulletin*, 1946.

HULL, C. L., *Aptitude Testing*, 1928.

KRETSCHMER, E., *Physique and Character*, 1925.

MACMEEKEN, A. M., *Intelligence of Scottish School-children*, 1939.

MONS, W., *Principles and Practice of the Rorschach Personality Test*, 1948.

PETERSON, J., *Early Conceptions and Tests of Intelligence*, 1923.

RORSCHACH, H., *Psychodiagnostik* (2 vols.), 1921; tr. P. Lemkau and B. Kronenberg, 1942–7.

SPEARMAN, C. E., *The Abilities of Man*, 1927.
The Nature of Intelligence and the Principles of Cognition, 1923.

STEPHENSON, W., 'The Inverted Factor Technique', *British Journal of Psychology*, 1936.

STRONG, E. K., *Vocational Interest Blank*, 1927.

SYMONDS, P. M., *Diagnosing Personality and Conduct*, 1932.

TERMAN, L. M., *The Measurement of Intelligence*, 1916.

TERMAN, L. M., and MILES, C. C., *Attitude-Interest Analysis Test*, 1933.

TERMAN, L. M., and MERRILL, M. A., *Measuring Intelligence*, 1939.

THOMSON, G. H., *The Factorial Analysis of Human Ability*, 1939.

THORNDIKE, E. L., *The Measurement of Intelligence*, 1925.

THURSTONE, L. L., *The Vectors of the Mind*, 1935.
Primary Mental Abilities, 1938.
A Scale for the Measurement of Social Attitudes, 1930.

TUDDENHAM, R. D., 'The Nature and Measurement of Intelligence', *Psychology in the Making*, ed. L. Postman, 1962.

WOODWORTH, R. S., *Personal Data Sheet*, 1920.

Chapter 19: *The Rise of Industrial Psychology*

BOOKS

DREVER, J., *The Psychology of Industry*, 1921.

FLORENCE, P. S., *Economics of Fatigue and Unrest*, 1924.

GILBRETH, F. B., *Motion Study*, 1911.
The Psychology of Management, 1913.
Fatigue Study, 1916.

HALL, P., and LOCKE, H. W., *Incentives and Contentment*, 1938.

MÜNSTERBERG, H., *Psychology and Industrial Efficiency*, 1913.

MYERS, C. S., *Industrial Psychology in Great Britain*, 1926.

MYERS, C. S., and WELCH, H. C., *Ten Years of Industrial Psychology*, 1932.

BIBLIOGRAPHY

TAYLOR, F. W., *Principles of Scientific Management*, 1911.
VERNON, H. M., *Industrial Fatigue and Efficiency*, 1921.
WILSON, R. M., *The Care of Human Efficiency*, 1921.

ARTICLES

FARMER, E., 'The Interpretation and Plotting of Output Curves', *British Journal of Psychology*, 1923.
McDOUGALL, W., 'A New Way of Measuring Mental Fatigue', *British Journal of Psychology*, 1903.
MAULE, H. G., 'Selection Tests for Sorters', *Journal of Industrial Launderers*, 1936.
ROGER, A., 'Uses of Tests in Vocational Guidance', *Journal of Occupational Psychology*, 1939.
SHAW, A. G., 'The Systematic Training of Workers', *Labour Management*, 1936.
'Motion Study in the Home', *A.E.I. News*, 7, 1939.
TAGG, M., 'The Make-Up of the Engineering Worker', *Journal of Institute of Industrial Psychology*, 1923.
VERNON, H. M., 'Report on the Health of Munition Workers', H.M.S.O., 1918.

The Industrial Health Research Board (Gt Britain) published the results of research in I.H.R.B. papers. The following are worth mentioning as typical projects of the period:

BEDFORD, T., *The Warmth Factor in Comfort at Work*, No. 78, 1936.
BURT, C., *A Study of Vocational Guidance*, No. 33, 1926.
ELTON, P. M., *A Study of Output in Silk Weaving*, No. 17, 1920.
FARMER, E., *Time and Motion Study*, No. 14, 1921.
FARMER, E., and CHAMBERS, E. G., *Individual Differences in Accident Rates*, No. 38, 1936.
KIRK, F. C., and F. J., *Tests for Accident Proneness*, No. 68, 1933.
POLLOCK, K. G., and BARTLETT, F. C., *Two Studies in the Psychological Effects of Noise*, No. 65, 1932.
SMITH, M., *Studies in the Laundry Trade*, No. 22, 1922.
WYATT, S., *Incentives in Repetitive Work*, No. 69, 1934.
WYATT, S., and FRASER, J. A., *Comparative Effects of Variety and Uniformity in Work*, No. 56, 1929.

Handbook of Applied Psychology (ed. D. H. Fryer and E. C. Henry, 1950), gives a more contemporary account of the work of industrial psychologists.

Chapter 20: *Child Psychology between the Wars*

BAYLY, N., 'The Development of Motor Abilities during the First Three Years', *Soc. Res. Child Development. Mon*, 1933.

BÜHLER, C., *From Birth to Maturity*, 1935.

BÜHLER, C., and HETZER, H., *Testing Children's Development*, 1935.

BURT, C., *The Backward Child*, 1937.

DENNIS, W., *Readings in Child Psychology*, 1951.

FISHER, M. S., *Language Patterns in Pre-school Children*, 1934.

GESELL, A., *The First Five Years of Life*, 1941.
The Mental Growth of the Pre-school Child, 1925.
Biographies of Child Development, 1939.

GESELL, A., and THOMSON, H., *Infant Behaviour*, 1934.

GOODENOUGH, F., *Anger in Young Children*, 1931.

GOODENOUGH, F., and ANDERSON, J. E., *Experimental Child Study*, 1931.

HOLLINGWORTH, L. S., *Gifted Children*, 1929.

ISAACS, S., *Intellectual Growth in Young Children*, 1930.

JERSILD, A. T., and HOLMES, F. B., *Children's Fears*, 1935.

KLEIN, M., *The Psycho-Analysis of Children*, 1931.

LEHMAN, H. C., *The Theory of Play*, 1948.

LEWIS, M. M., *Infant Speech*, 1936.

LOWENFIELD, M., *Play in Childhood*, 1935.

MURCHISON, C., *A Handbook of Child Psychology*, 1931.

MURPHY, L. H., *Social Behaviour and Child Personality*, 1937.

PIAGET, J., *Le langage et la pensée chez l'enfant*, 1923; tr. M. Warden, *The Language and Thought of the Child*, 1926.
La représentation du monde chez l'enfant, 1926: tr. J. and A. Tomlinson, *The Child's Conception of the World*, 1929.
Le jugement moral chez l'enfant, 1932; tr. M. Gabain, *The Moral Judgment of the Child*, 1932.

PRESCOTT, D. A., *Emotion and the Educative Process*, 1938.

RUSSELL, B., *On Education*, 1926.

SHIRLEY, M. M., *The First Two Years* (3 vols.), 1931–3.
TERMAN, L. M., *Genetic Studies of Genius*, 1926.

Chapter 21: *Social Psychology 1920–40*

ALLPORT, F. H., *Social Psychology*, 1924.
'Influence of the Group upon Association and Thought',
Journal of Experimental Psychology, 1920.

BALDWIN, J. M., *Social and Ethical Interpretations in Mental
Development*, 1897.

BARTLETT, F. C., *Psychology and Primitive Culture*, 1935.

BENEDICT, R., *Patterns of Culture*, 1935.

BERNARD, L. L., *Introduction to Social Psychology*, 1925.
Instinct: A Study in Social Psychology, 1926.

CONWAY, M., *The Crowd in Peace and War*, 1915.

DEWEY, S., 'The Need of a Social Psychology', *Psychological
Review*, 1917.

DUNLAP, K., *Social Psychology*, 1925.

ELLWOOD, C. A., *A History of Social Philosophy*, 1938.

FREUD, S., *Massenpsychologie und Ich-Analyse*, 1921; tr. J.
Strachey, *Group Psychology and the Analysis of the Ego*,
1922.

GINSBERG, M., *The Psychology of Society*, 1921.

LE BON, G., *La psychologie des foules*, 1893; tr. *The Crowd*,
1896.

MCDOUGALL, W., *The Group Mind*, 1920.

MALINOWSKI, B., *Sex and Repression in Savage Society*,
1927.

MEAD, M., *Coming of Age in Samoa*, 1928.
Growing Up in New Guinea, 1930.

MORENO, J. L., *Who Shall Survive?*, 1934.

MURPHY, G., MURPHY, L., and NEWCOMB, T. M., Ex-
perimental Social Psychology, 1937.

SHERIF, M., *The Psychology of Social Norms*, 1936.

TARDE, G., *Les lois de l'imitation*, 1890.

UNWIN, J. D., *Sex and Culture*, 1934.

WUNDT, W., *Elemente de Völkerpsychologie*, 1912; tr. E. L.
Schaub, *Elements of Folk Psychology*, 1916.

Chapter 22: *The Study of Personality 1930–40*

ALLPORT, G. W., *Personality: A Psychological Interpretation*, 1937.

BISCHOF, L. J., *Interpreting Personality Theories*, 1964.

BROTEMARKLE, R. A., 'Clinical Psychology 1896–1946', *Journal of Consulting Psychology*, 1946.

LEWIN, K., *A Dynamic Theory of Personality*, 1935.

MURRAY, H. A., *Explorations in Personality*, 1938.

  'Basic Concepts for a Theory of Personality', *Journal of Genetic Psychology*, 1936.

  Manual of Thematic Apperception Test, 1943.

C. S. Hall and G. Lindzey, in *Theories of Personality* (1957), discuss the principal theories including those of Allport and Murray. The background to the development of personality study is to be traced from William James through the psycho-analytic theories, also through the development of personality tests and questionnaires. The contributions to the study of the individual from child psychology and social psychology are also important. However, it was probably the psycho-analytic movement which gave the study of the human personality, in terms of its individuality and dynamic characteristics, its most vital stimulation. Previous chapters are relevant to the readings for Chapter 17.

Chapter 24: *A Sketch of Post-War Developments*

There is no historical review of psychological developments since the Second World War, but there are several publications which review current developments and which provide a useful source of information about recent psychology:

The Annual Review of Psychology has appeared since 1950 and surveys in reviews and articles the chief contributions published recently.

Current Trends in Psychology (University of Pittsburg Press) appears every two years and contains articles on selected research projects as well as articles reviewing broad trends.

BIBLIOGRAPHY

Contemporary Psychology, a monthly journal, consists of book reviews on psychology and allied subjects.

Psychological Abstracts lists, and provides a brief synopsis of, every article, monograph and book on psychological topics.

The Foundations of Modern Psychology series (ed. R. S. Lazarus) devotes a volume to each main field (learning, perception, social, testing, etc.).

New Horizons in Psychology (ed. B. Foss), 1966, is a comprehensive review of recent research.

Readings in Psychology (ed. J. Cohen), 1964, is a set of articles on principal contemporary developments.

Psychology: A Study of a Science (ed. S. Koch), 7 vols., 1959–65, is a comprehensive introduction to contemporary psychology.

Journals containing original papers are very numerous. *The Psychological Bulletin* regularly contains review-articles reporting developments in research on a specific problem or topic.

INFORMATION THEORY

ATTNEAVE, F., *Applications of Information Theory to Psychology*, 1959.

BROADBENT, D. E., *Perception and Communication*, 1958.

CHERRY, E. C., *On Human Communication*, 1957.

FEIGENBAUM, E., and FELDMAN, J., *Computers and Thought*, 1963.

PHYSIOLOGICAL PSYCHOLOGY

LOUTTIT, R. T., (ed.), *Research in Physiological Psychology*, 1965.

O'NEILL, D., *Modern Trends in Psychosomatic Medicine*, 1955.

OSSELTON, J. W., and KILOH, C. G., *Clinical Electro-encephalographs*, 1961.

PRIBRAM, K. H., 'Towards a Science of Neurophysiology', *Current Trends*, 1954.

'A Review of Theory in Physiological Psychology', *Annual Review of Psychology*, 1960.

RINKEL, M., *Chemical Concepts of Psychosis*, 1958.

UHR, L., and MILLER, J. G., *Drugs and Behaviour*, 1960.

BIBLIOGRAPHY

WALSH, E. G., *Physiology of the Nervous System*, 1957.
WOOLLEY, D. W., *Biochemical Bases of Psychoses*, 1962.

ANIMAL BEHAVIOUR

CATHY, J. P., *An Introduction to the Behaviour of Invertebrates*, 1958.
FISHER, E., 'Chemical Stimulation of the Brain', *Scientific American*, 1964.
HARLOW, H. F., 'Learning Set and Error Factor Theory', in Koch, Vol. 2 (pp. 492–537).
HARLOW, H. F., 'Love in Infant Monkeys', *Scientific American*, 1959.
SLUCKIN, W., *Imprinting and Early Learning*, 1964.
THORPE, W. H., *Learning and Instinct in Animals*, 1956.
TINBERGEN, N., *A Study of Instinct*, 1951.

EXPERIMENTAL PSYCHOLOGY

HUMPHREY, G. (ed.), *Psychology through Experiment*, 1963.
KOCH, S., *Psychology: A Study of a Science*, 1959–65, Vols. 1 and 2.
STEVENS, S. S., *A Handbook of Experimental Psychology*, 1951 (an excellent guide to the knowledge available in the early 1950s).

PERCEPTION

VERNON, M. D., *A Further Study of Visual Perception*, 1957.
The Psychology of Perception, 1962.

LEARNING

BUGELSKI, B. R., *The Psychology of Learning*, 1956 (a good recent text book).
BUSH, R. R., and MOSTELLER, F., *Stochastic Models for Learning*, 1955.
DEUTSCH, J. A., *The Structural Basis of Behavior*, 1960 (this book and the preceding one give accounts of new statistical and cybernetic types of theory).

BIBLIOGRAPHY

HEBB, D. O., *The Organization of Behaviour*, 1949 (an important book).

KOCH, S., Vol. 2, contains a comprehensive discussion of all the newer developments.

COGNITION

BRUNER, J. S., *A Study of Thinking*, 1956.

Colorado Symposium of 1955, and *Contemporary Approaches to Cognition*, 1957 (these two books set a new trend).

NEWELL, A., and SIMON, H. A., 'The Simulation of Human Thought', *Science*, No. 134, 1961 (an account of computer models for thinking). See also *Current Trends in Psychology*, 1961, pp. 152–79.

HUMAN ENGINEERING

BRAY, C. W., *Psychology and Military Efficiency*, 1948.

FITTS, P. M., *Psychological Research on Equipment Design*, 1947.

MCFARLAND, R. A., *Human Factors in Air-Transport Design*, 1946.

CLINICAL PSYCHOLOGY

LEVINE, S., *Experimental Foundations of Clinical Psychology*, 1961.

KELLY, E. L., 'Clinical Psychology in the Post-War Decade', *Current Trends in Psychology*, 1961.

WATSON, R. I., 'A Brief History of Clinical Psychology', *Psychological Bulletin*, 1953.

PERSONALITY

CATTELL, R. B., *Description and Measurement of Personality*, 1946.

Personality: A Systematic, Theoretical and Factual Study, 1950.

EYSENCK, H. J., *Dimensions of Personality*, 1947.

The Scientific Study of Personality, 1952.

The Structure of Human Personality, 1953.

BIBLIOGRAPHY

KELLY, G., *The Psychology of Personal Constructs*, 1955.
ROGERS, C. R., *Counselling and Psychotherapy*, 1942.
  Client-Oriented Therapy, 1951.
SULLIVAN, H. S., *The Interpersonal Theory of Psychiatry*,
    1953.

Also relevant for 'new trends':

MURPHY, G., *Personality: A Biosocial Approach*, 1947.
MASLOW, A. H., *Motivation and Personality*, 1954.
  Toward a Psychology of Being, 1962.

SOCIAL PSYCHOLOGY

HOMANS, G. C., *The Human Group*, 1951.
KAPLAN, B., *Studying Personality Cross-Culturally*, 1961.
SPROTT, W. J. H., *Human Groups*, 1958.

OCCUPATIONAL PSYCHOLOGY

FRYER, D. H., and HENRY, E. R. (eds.), *Handbook of
    Applied Psychology* (2 vols.), 1950.

The best way for the layman to discover what are the most
recent developments in psychology is to attend a class organized by the adult education, or extra-mural studies, department
of a local university or, in England, a course sponsored by the
Workers' Educational Association.

M

Index

Ability, 104–6; inherited, 107–8
Abraham, K., 251
Abreaction, 213, 250
Accident proneness, 353–4
Ach, N., 86
Adler, A., 216, 252, 264–6, 381
Adrian, E. D., 170–71, 279
Aggression, 253, 265
Allport, F. H., 372, 373–4
Allport, G. W., 269, 331, 335, 378, 382–5
American Journal of Psychology, 135
American Psychological Association, 135
Angell, J. R., 149–50, 154
Anima, animus, 261
Anthropology, 374–5
Anthropometric laboratory, 109–10
Anxiety, 253, 266–7
Apparent movement, 281–2
Applied psychology, 424–5
Association laws, 22–3
Associationism, 20, 175
Asylums, 194–6
Attitudes, 383; assessment of, 336–8
Aufgabe, 86

Bain, Alexander, 27–30, 35
Baldwin, J. M., 140–42, 299
Bartlett, F. C., 316–18, 356
Bates, R. F., 422
Behaviourism, 156–67, 225–42
Bell, Charles, 37–9, 44–6
Bernheim, H. M., 206
Bertillon, A., 111
Binet, A., 190–93

Binet–Simon scale, 190–93
Binocular vision, 44–5
Bleuler, E., 203–4
Blodgett, H. C., 307
Bon, G. le, 371
Boring, E. G., 45, 65–6, 115
Brain, 40–43, 401–3; cells of, 42; damage to, 281; localization of, 40, 43; recovery of function of, 41
Brentano, F., 82, 83–4
Breuer, J., 212
Broca, P., 42–3
Brown, T., 21–3
Bruner, J. S., 410–11
Brunswick, E., 294–5
Bucy, P. C., 284–5
Bühler, C., 360–61
Bühler, K., 86
Burt, C., 114–15, 172, 192, 328–9, 340

Cambridge University, 181–6
Cannon, W. B., 283–4
Carr, H. A., 155–6
Catharsis, 207
Cattell, J. M., 77, 110, 137–40
Cattell, R. B., 416–17
Charcot, J. M., 205
Child psychology, 135–6, 358–69
Chronocyclograph, 352
Clinics, 365–6, 413–15
Coghill, G. E., 282–3
Collective unconscious, 259
Colour vision, 63, 80
Comparative psychology, 116–24
Complexes, 258–9
Concept formation, 323

459